BAD BET

BAD BET

THE INSIDE STORY
OF THE GLAMOUR, GLITZ,
AND DANGER
OF AMERICA'S
GAMBLING INDUSTRY

TIMOTHY L. O'BRIEN

TIMES BUSINESS

RANDOM HOUSE

Library of Congress Cataloging-in-Publication Data
O'Brien, Timothy L.
Bad bet: the inside story of the glamour, glitz, and danger of America's
gambling industry / Timothy L. O'Brien.—1st ed.
p.   cm.
Includes bibliographical references and index.
ISBN 0-8129-2807-5
1. Gambling.   2. Compulsive gambling.   I. Title.
HV6710.027   1998
362.2'5—dc21   98-4935

Random House website address: www.randomhouse.com

Printed in the United States of America on acid-free paper
24689753
First Edition
Book design by Oksana Kushnir

For my extraordinary parents,
Barbara Bowers O'Brien (1927–1993)
and Arthur R. O'Brien,
who always knew exactly how
to play a full house

The point here is this—one turn of the wheel and everything can be different. . . . And everybody will not turn away from me as they do now. . . . What am I now? Zero. What may I be tomorrow? Tomorrow I may rise from the dead and begin to live again.

—Fyodor Dostoyevsky, *The Gambler*

ACKNOWLEDGMENTS

Most of this book was completed while I was working for *The Wall Street Journal.* I would never have been approached to do this book had I not had the good fortune to be a reporter for the *Journal,* and I am grateful to the paper for providing me with this opportunity.

Scores of people helped me complete this book, but without the support and help of my wife, Rebecca Bergstrom O'Brien, it never would have been written. She suffered the long hours and loneliness that a project like this entails and still was willing to give me encouragement, advice, and back rubs. Rebecca also transcribed several interviews and managed to explain to our children, Greta and Jeffrey, why Daddy kept locking himself in his office on nights and weekends. I missed the three of you, too.

Brent Bowers, my friend and colleague at *The New York Times,* read almost every chapter of this book with the same grace and attentiveness that he is famous for at the *Times.* No writer could ask for a better editor. Karl Weber, my editor at Times Books, came up with the idea for this book, guided the project through rough waters, and also provided invaluable editing suggestions. John Mahaney of Times Books also helped get the book into print. William Eadington, a professor at the University of Nevada in Reno and the country's leading authority on gambling, was unstinting in his intellectual curiosity and generosity. Howard Schwartz opened the vaults at the Gambler's Book Club in Las Vegas, the single best resource for anyone investigating the gambling world.

Nearly two hundred people allowed me to interview them for this book and I thank everyone who is quoted in these pages. My thanks to those in the gambling industry who subjected themselves to interviews even though they were uncertain what direction the book would take. More than a dozen law enforcement officials spoke to me off-the-record and I thank all of them for their time and patience. Evan Peters is a pseudonym for the compulsive gambler who had the courage to bare his soul to me.

The following people also were particularly helpful: Tony Allevato, Ron Anderson, Jim Asiano, Allen Barra, Bill Bastone, Ralph Berry, Owen Blicksilver, Ned Bonnie, Valerie Braun, Chris Brienza, Jim Burke, Bill

Carter, Eddie Coleman, Walter Cronkite, Anthony Curtis, Gino Donatelli, Frank Donze, Tom Duffy, Paul Dworin, Lisa Einhorn, Alan Feldman, Brian Fleming, Kristina Ford, Steve Forte, Tom Gallagher, Eugene Genovese, Marc Grossman, Henry Gluck, Bob and Elissa Hambrecht, Phil and Adda Hedges, Dan Heneghen, R. D. Hubbard, Kevin Hynes, George Ignatin, Dale Jarr, Eddie Jordan, Ned Kerwin, Stu Kirshenbaum, Mike Klemens, Tom and Brooke Loughlin, Jack Leone, Ed Looney, Bruce MacDonald, Jerry Markham, Mark McAuliffe, Dick McGowan, Jim Milne, Jim Murren, Victor Niederhoffer, Bob O'Brien, Dave Palermo, Bob Peyton, Ken Ramirez, Dennis Redmond, John Rohs, Nelson Rose, Roxy Roxborough, John Schacter, Christie Schlacter, Arnie Snyder, Parry Thomas, Louis Toscano, Bruce Turner, and Larry and Cappy Warner.

CONTENTS

INTRODUCTION:
GOING FOR BROKE

AT ALMOST ANY MINUTE of any hour of any day in some corner of the country, a gambler, lit from within by a desire to strike it rich, drops a quarter through a narrow slit into a squat 200-pound slot machine.

The quarter, a copper wafer sandwiched by thin layers of nickel and weighing less than six grams, falls a couple of inches inside the machine into a small metal detector called a comparitor. To ensure that the coin isn't a counterfeit, the comparitor instantly scans it for weight and content against another quarter permanently lodged in the machine. From there, the quarter continues its brief descent past several optical sensors that measure the coin's motion, searching in milliseconds for any odd movements that might indicate a cheater is tampering with the machine. Finally, ushered with approval through the comparitor, the quarter plunges downward, breaking a thin beam of light emitted by yet another scanner and producing an electronic pulse that prepares the machine for action. The quarter, its mission complete, ends its journey in a large hopper in the bottom of the machine, joining as many as 999 other coins that have preceded it.

Our player then presses a button or pulls the machine's handle, triggering another electronic pulse that tells a computer chip deep inside the machine that the game has begun. Following the chip's command, a computer program randomly generates a number that determines where and when the machine's reels will stop, whether the reel combination is a winner or loser, and, if it's a winner, how big the payout will be. The machines are programmed to pay out small amounts frequently, to attract bettors who prefer repeated stroking, or to pay out larger amounts intermittently, to attract bettors who want to feel like they've really cashed in. Our player, like most slot players, will probably lose far more than she ever takes out of the machine. In return, she may experience those few seconds of adrenaline, sexual joy that course through the body whenever the machine, in its benevolence, scoops a bouquet of quarters out of the hopper and plops them into what the gambling industry delicately terms a loud bowl—a steel tray that permits a longer, noisier drop of coins on the payout. A noisy payout is essential, for it firmly reminds the player, and all those around her, that money does, in fact, talk.

Faceless, gleaming, and the bearers of dreams in late-twentieth-century America, slot machines have helped fuel the most massive expansion of gambling in U.S. history. Institutionalized in an unprecedented fashion, an ancient and unruly activity has become one of the most ubiquitous and well-marketed pastimes in America. And the torrent of cash that spews from our pockets and streams through the corporate boardrooms and darker corners of America's gambling establishment has created a commercial juggernaut. In 1976, we bet $17.3 billion legally. In 1996, we bet $586.5 billion. We lost $47.6 billion gambling legally in 1996, about $14 billion more than New York City's public budget and more than twice as much as the Coca-Cola Company's sales in the same year. Judged by dollars spent, gambling is now more popular in America than baseball, the movies, and Disneyland—*combined*.

We bet in casinos and at the racetrack; we bet on football and basketball games, and we bet on state lotteries and the stock market; we bet in our churches and in our synagogues, and we bet in our offices and in our homes. Yet, as entrenched as gambling always has been in American life, its raptures and demons have never been so easily accessible as they are right now. Social taboos and laws that once confined gambling's availability have been cast aside in a national rush to embrace this most dangerous of games. Some communities, most notably the Mississippi Gulf Coast and some Native American reservations, have been rejuvenated by commercial gambling's recent expansion. Still other places, such as New Orleans and Atlantic City, offer stark reminders of how little gambling can deliver when called upon to be an economic savior. But the siren continues to enchant, because commercial gambling's strongest appeal is to the desperate—to small towns and cities beaten into economic submission; to states stripped of federal tax support and angling for ways to plug holes in their budgets; to Native Americans banished to the outer rim of society; to senior citizens hungry for a sense of belonging and stimulation; and to a minority of gamblers so vulnerable that they will do whatever it takes to keep feeding their habits. All are drawn by the hope that the tug of a slot machine's handle or a roll of the dice will transform them.

The large corporations that have taken over casinos from the mobsters and outcasts who once dominated the industry are quick to take exception to this portrait. They insist that they are in the entertainment business. Desperation is not part of their vocabulary. Supported by well-oiled public relations machinery, an armada of political lobbyists, and increasingly friendly legislators, gambling companies contend that most people wager to briefly escape the grind of a workaday world. And this is true. Most gamblers bet within their budgets and treat a weekend in Las Vegas as just another social outing. But there is a little secret lurking behind this truth: the gambling industry's financial well-being depends on a small, hardcore group of regulars, many of whom are compulsive or problem gamblers. Interviews with casino executives and managers indicate that in most markets the bulk of gambling revenue, as much as 80 percent, comes from a small percentage of gamblers, about 20 percent. The precise extent to which the gambling industry's fortunes rely on compulsive or problem gamblers awaits a thorough statistical analysis. Raw data that would make such a study meaningful lie buried in casino companies' marketing departments. Until recently, the industry has been loath to examine its dependence on compulsive and problem gamblers, because a honest discussion of the matter reveals that the most loyal casino patrons aren't, in the argot of gambling's new retailspeak, simply "customers." Many of them are marks. Viewed in this light, compulsive bettors confront the gambling business with the same threats and challenges that nicotine addiction posed for the tobacco industry. And, like their counterparts in the tobacco industry, gambling executives have spent decades dismissing or ignoring the grim realities at the core of their business.

Of course, wagering in America is about much more than the ravaging of compulsive gamblers, because most bettors gamble for more complex reasons than desperation. The sports world, utterly dependent on the interest gambling generates among its fans, attracts some of the most cerebral bettors in the country, those anxious to match wits with oddsmakers and bookies. A similar breed of gambler inhabits the stock market, where the molten core of the American financial system is at once uniquely innovative and a cauldron of potentially destabilizing speculation.

But it is in the throbbing environment of casinos, and in the more mundane workings of state lotteries, that modern gambling's goals are most blatantly on display. Commercial gambling interests are forever ratcheting up the tempo of their offerings, introducing games and products designed to be played quickly, repetitively, and with a minimum of thought. As the gambling industry becomes more skilled at peddling instant gratification, slower, less frenetic forums for betting, such as race-tracks and bingo halls, have been eclipsed. Speed sells. And it can be sold anywhere, for with the advent of on-line wagering, commercial gambling has, quite literally, entered the bedroom.

So appealing is the cozy prospect of home and hearth that resorts such as Las Vegas have tried, though with only limited success, to repackage themselves as family destinations replete with theme parks and other child-friendly attractions. To beckon the kiddies further, casinos have installed video arcades and day-care centers. Visits to casinos often reveal flocks of adolescents hovering on the periphery of these decidedly adult playgrounds. It is only when tragedy strikes—as it did in early 1997, when a seven-year-old girl was raped and murdered in the bathroom of a Nevada casino—that the propriety of reeling children into the orbit of casinos is questioned. Even so, studies suggest that gambling among children and teenagers has matched legalized gambling's growth, with many children exhibiting all the psychological wounds and social warts of compulsives.

Gambling's expansion during the last decade has been greeted with mounting apprehension and criticism. The most potent come from Christian activists, who bear a striking resemblance to the temperance crusaders who have popped up at various junctures in American history. Moral high-mindedness and human desire have a way of butting heads, and there is nothing like a little bit of vice to stir up a good fight in America. But while there are good reasons to be wary of gambling, there are very few reasons to believe that either the impulse or the activity will disappear anytime soon.

We gamble despite the fact that we know the odds are strongly against us.

We gamble despite the fact that it rarely funds passage out of an eroding middle-class existence once heralded as a bulwark of our society.

We gamble despite the fact that the casino industry only sporadically meets its promise of economic deliverance for sagging communities and cash-strapped states.

We gamble despite the fact that gambling occasionally destroys lives.

We gamble because we can't help ourselves.

We love it.

CHAPTER 1

CYBERSPACE:
BORDERLESS BETTING

WANT TO BET?

No need to make an airline reservation, get into your car, or even walk out of your front door. If you're ready to gamble, simply turn on your personal computer, click the mouse a few times, and launch an Internet browser. In minutes, you can be wagering in the privacy of your home courtesy of Centrebet, an on-line sports betting site based in Alice Springs, Australia.

Alice Springs hardly appears to be on the cutting edge of twenty-first-century gambling. It is a tiny hamlet located in Australia's barren outback, directly east of Lake Disappointment and surrounded by arid scrubland and rugged hills. Although Alice Springs shares Las Vegas' desert heritage, has a local population of inveterate gamblers, and even has a small, struggling casino, it bears little resemblance to Nevada's gambling mecca. Most tourists visit Alice Springs to watch camel races and to trek into the wilderness, not to gamble. But computer bettors and Centrebet have made Alice Springs one of the most popular gambling destinations on the Internet.

"We all can't just hop in a jet and fly to Las Vegas," says Ian Loughlin, Centrebet's assistant general manager. "We're just trying to satisfy the gambler's insatiable appetite."

The reason for Centrebet's popularity is simple: it is convenient, anonymous, and open twenty-four hours a day to almost anyone, anywhere in the world, who has a computer. It offers gambling without walls, without taxes, and without guilt.

"I think it's a great innovation that people can sit in the confines of their own home and disseminate information and place a bet without the stigma of walking down to the corner and placing a bet with [a] bookie," says Loughlin, whose company began accepting wagers over the Internet in early 1996.

Centrebet's gambling site is unadorned, with several simple screens that lead the bettor to a series of rules and regulations and a long menu of possible wagers. Centrebet requires users to be at least eighteen years old, and it offers gamblers the opportunity to bet on football, basketball, and baseball games, as well as horse and auto racing, boxing, golf, cricket, soccer, rugby, and tennis.

Centrebet, which operates with the legal blessing of its local government in Australia, says it will handle about $35 million worth of bets in 1997. The company has an older, more traditional bookmaking operation, but on-line betting is the fastest-growing part of its business, already accounting for about half the wagers it handles.

Gamblers can open a Centrebet account with their credit cards, by sending funds via wire transfer, or by depositing cash in certain banks in the United States, Denmark, or Finland. After putting up the money, each gambler receives a membership number and a password. Then—click, click, click—it's off to the races.

Winnings and losses are credited to or debited from gamblers' accounts. When gamblers want to withdraw funds, Centrebet will mail them a check or wire the money into their bank account. Bet on the World Series, bet on a rugby match. It's all so easy.

It's also loaded with potential pitfalls.

In just a few short years, Internet gambling—or "nambling," as aficionados call it—has emerged as one of the hottest on-line services. Observers of Internet commerce suspect that on-line gambling is as popular in the United States as on-line pornography—porno being one of the few profitable ventures on the Internet. While the exact size of the nambling market isn't known, *International Gaming & Wagering Business*, a trade publication, estimates that about $143 million worth of sports bets were placed on-line in the United States in 1996. The magazine expects that figure to leap to about $760 million by 2000.

Although nambling is dwarfed by the multibillion-dollar casino business, it will unleash challenges for families, communities, and regulators that will match or surpass any of those posed by casinos.

Nambling has created frontiers in computer fraud and money laundering that are largely unexplored. The nambling world is already populated by some individuals who have a history of abuses in other businesses. While companies such as Centrebet are considered reputable within the gambling community, at least one of the other major nambling companies, Interactive Gaming and Communications Corporation, has a track record that might concern even the most fearless of gamblers.

Moreover, nambling's immediacy and ubiquity are unique. It offers dangerous temptations to any gambler unable to control his or her urge to splurge, especially when the casino is always open. And nambling's ubiquity means that Mom and Dad might have to worry about the nagging possibility that Junior is in his bedroom gambling away the family's mortgage.

The world that allows gambling to skirt borders, slip beneath doors, and enter our bedrooms isn't found in the Nevada desert, or in the gentle curve of the Mississippi River, nor is it in the liquor store on the corner, or at a racetrack in Kentucky. It is located in the soft glow of computer screens, in an electronic realm known as cyberspace.

A CYBERSPACE ODYSSEY

As the annals of cyberlore thickened in later years, the tall white contraption sitting in a UCLA laboratory on September 2, 1969, would come to be known as Internet Node Number One.

In a curious way, the gadget was a by-product of the anxiety that had gripped America twelve years earlier, when the Soviet Union won the first race for the heavens by launching its Sputnik satellite. A year after Sputnik pierced the nation's collective conscience, the Defense Department set up the Advanced Research Projects Agency to coordinate and fund scientific research nationwide. As ARPA's pool of scientists expanded over the next decade, the agency began developing a communications network to allow researchers in far-flung locations to share mainframe computers, thus saving ARPA the cost of buying an entire fleet of the expensive machines. The UCLA node, about the size of a small closet, represented the culmination of that network-building effort. And it represented the birth of what we now call the Internet, today's fastest-growing, and potentially most powerful, medium for communications, commerce, and entertainment.

With its ability to route information between computers, the UCLA node was designed to be an electronic traffic cop. Its installation that September led, a month later, to the first "conversation" between computers using the Internet. The author of that initial message was a scientist named Leonard Kleinrock. Kleinrock and a team of researchers had been able to tie the computers together using tricks Kleinrock had developed while investigating applications for "packet-switching," a method of breaking data into little electronic bundles that could be shipped along telephone lines and routed to specific locations. That autumn, Kleinrock and a colleague began typing the word "login" into their computer in Los

Angeles. Their "l" and their "o" appeared on a terminal near San Francisco—just before the system crashed. No matter. The revolution was under way.

Once the new network was up and running, other universities and research institutes pursuing defense-related research were invited aboard, beginning the sprawl of what was still a relatively small system. By 1972, electronic mail was flying around various independent networks in the United States. A year later links were established overseas, in Norway and England. But the Internet's growth was still constrained by its specialized use and by the incompatible computer commands used by participants on different networks. After another team of government scientists lead by Vint Cerf designed a universal language, or "protocol," that allowed data to flow more freely among separate networks, use of the Internet exploded. As Cold War security concerns waned, the government broadened access to the Internet. By the early 1990s the Internet was a true "open system," accessible to anyone, anywhere in the world, who had a computer and a modem.

Private, commercial on-line services had been around since the 1980s, growing alongside the Internet, but it wasn't until 1991 that the government allowed businesses to set up shop on the toll-free Internet itself. Within two years, commercial use of the Internet surpassed its use by academics. The government stopped managing the Internet in 1995, basically leaving oversight of the decentralized system to its participants—a formula that was at once collaborative, creative, and chaotic. In the early 1980s there were barely more than 200 nodes, or "host computers," supplying information and services on the Internet. By 1990, there were more than 300,000. By 1996, there were roughly 10 million. Electronic mail, shopping malls, chat rooms, media, and reference libraries proliferated on the Internet. Terms like "information superhighway" entered the language, and the word "cyberspace," coined in a novel by science fiction writer William Gibson, came to denote the borderless electronic universe of the Internet and its other on-line brethren.

Today, while still in its infancy, the Internet is already transforming businesses as diverse as publishing, banking, retailing, and, of course, gambling.

Nambling is dismissed by traditional casino operators as inconsequential. In the short run that may be true, because cyber-casinos are relatively humble affairs. They lack the ambience and speed they'll need to compete with casinos. But for some forms of gambling, especially sports betting, there is good reason to believe that Internet-based betting will eventually dominate the industry.

As the quality and security of cyberspace gambling improves, it will continue to grow—in fits and starts, but inexorably. Eventually, nambling will deliver what bettors crave in the modern gambling era: fast-paced, furious "action" that is as near at hand as a light switch. The gambler searching for the emotional charge that only action can give will be able to get that high anywhere, anytime, just by turning on the computer.

VIRTUAL VEGAS

In nambling's short history, David Herschman, all of twenty-nine years old, qualifies as a seasoned pro. He founded his company, Virtual Vegas, in 1994, first in a small, sparsely furnished suite along the Pacific Ocean in Venice, California. Now Virtual Vegas does business out of a Santa Monica condominium that is, in Herschman's words, "a programming den full of people drinking Diet Cokes."

The location where Virtual Vegas' programmers boot up their computers every day matters very little, however, since Herschman's casino can be visited from anywhere in the world. Just type the casino's address (http://www.virtualvegas.com) into an Internet browser on a personal computer. A few seconds later, red dice are rolling across the screen. After signing in, you'll enter a cartoonish, "three-dimensional," electronic cityscape that includes a casino, a shopping mall, a chat lounge, a bank, and a travel office. Enter the Virtual Vegas casino and you have a choice of games that include blackjack, craps, and slots.

"I believe this is going to be a huge, huge market. There's a certain psychology to being on-line," says Herschman from beneath his mop of curly blond hair. "The Net's first draw has always been as a place to have fun. People aren't going to go to the Reebok page or the Pepsi page. They're going to come to our page. Gambling on the Net is attractive because you can do it anonymously and in your home."

Herschman briefly ran an import-export business selling Asian textiles after being graduated with a philosophy degree from the University of California at Berkeley. He entertained the idea of also teaching philosophy while running that business, but changed career paths when the on-line industry captured his attention. Herschman says he considered other types of on-line ventures, but chose gambling because he thought it had the potential for the biggest payoff. A student of Buddhism and Hinduism, Herschman says he sees no conflicts between his spiritual and commercial pursuits.

"Those philosophies are about living for the moment and embracing change. That's what the Internet is about, too, and I don't want to be some monk on a hill. I want to do things on the Internet that make the most money, and I think that's gambling."

At one time, Herschman could boast that Virtual Vegas was part of an interactive cable television experiment conducted in Florida by media giant Time Warner, Incorporated. But he lost his blue-chip partner when it pulled the plug on its entire interactive effort in Florida; now he has a partnership with a smaller company, At Home Network. Herschman says Virtual Vegas attracts about 100,000 people per month but will have only about $250,000 in revenue for 1997. Herschman's failure to strike gold on the Internet isn't simply the result of trying to build a business in a nascent industry that is still largely unformed and untested: Herschman runs a casino where gamblers and the house don't exchange any cash.

The classic legal definition of gambling is any activity that involves three things: consideration (i.e., a cash bet), chance, and a prize. Virtual Vegas doesn't strictly qualify. A whirl through Virtual Vegas' gambling den is free, and winners get prizes awarded by some of the site's sponsors. The reason everything is gratis in Virtual Vegas is because any real wagering would violate federal laws that forbid bookies to transmit bets or gambling information across state borders using "wires," such as telephone lines. Only the horse-racing industry is explicitly exempt from that law. That's why only a very few nambling operators have casinos based entirely in the United States.

Herschman is content to wait until the regulatory picture becomes clearer in the United States, confident that Virtual Vegas can become the McDonald's of gambling when and if the rules change. But many other nambling impresarios have set sail for the Caribbean, where the air is warmer and the regulations much more forgiving.

There are currently about thirty Internet sites offering live gambling, according to Sue Schneider, executive director of the Interactive Gaming Council, a Silver Springs, Maryland, trade group. Schneider says that most of the demographic and financial information for the industry is still sketchy, although early visitors to the gambling sites are expected to be upper-income, technologically proficient men in their twenties and thirties—the same people who typically like to surf the Internet looking for other fun and games.

Certain types of nambling are expected to be far more lucrative businesses than others. Because lotteries tend to draw lower-income, impulse bettors who usually aren't computer savvy, Schneider doesn't expect such sites as Interlotto, an international lottery based in Liechtenstein, to be an early hit. Nor does the sagging horse-racing business, with demographics that teeter on the grave, hold much early promise on the Internet.

Sports betting, however, has all the earmarks of being a killer application. "Killer app" is the moniker bestowed on any computer task that enthralls millions of users and produces a financial gusher for the entrepreneur smart enough or lucky enough to introduce it first or most attractively. Sports betting is likely to become a killer app on the Internet because it is a favorite activity among the computer-literate young men who like to surf through cyberspace. And any future growth in on-line sports betting will come at the expense of the illegal bookmaking industry in the United States; the prospect of raking in even a small part of that lucre is what propels nambling companies offshore, primarily toward the Caribbean.

Some of the more prominent sports betting sites, such as Austria's Intertops and Australia's Centrebet, don't need to worry about relocating to the Caribbean. Their home countries already permit them to dial for dollars on the Internet. Others have taken wagering to the skies. Foreign airlines, including British Airways and Swissair, have tested in-flight gambling systems. Singapore Airlines and Austria's Lauda Air are readying similar systems for their planes, though all of the systems would have to be shut off over U.S. airspace to comply with Federal Aviation Administration rules against in-flight gambling.

For U.S. nambling companies that can't set up shop at home or take their business to the air, offshore havens hold the same attraction as they do for banks, investment funds, and other institutions that traffic in cash and prefer to be left alone. As long as companies pony up local taxes and fees, the tiny islands of the Caribbean are content to let visitors conduct business as they see fit, regardless of the sources or uses of the money that flows through the enterprises. Free of the yoke of federal regulation, nambling companies have installed their computers in such hot spots as Antigua, which boasts an undersea fiber-optic link directly to the United States, allowing for crisp, speedy Internet transmissions to gamblers.

Antigua's open-door policy has lured World Wide Web Casinos there. World Wide has corporate offices in Santa Ana, California, but its Internet computer server is housed in Antigua. The reason for this is made clear in a brief statement World Wide has posted on its Internet site: "The Internet is a global communications technology not bound by the laws or control of any one government. Internet casinos are only bound by the laws of their host country. Placing bets cannot be illegal because, despite their origination, bets will technically be placed on the computers at our off-shore land-based casino site that is legally licensed and taxed by the host government." Thus, World Wide argues, it is free to beam its casino straight into gamblers' homes in the United States via the Internet, regardless of U.S. gambling laws.

The privacy and security of all Internet transactions are still not foolproof, thanks to the ingenuity and schemes of computer hackers and other codebreakers, but many nambling companies are offering wagerers all the conveniences of their local bank. World Wide is developing an "on-line debit card" that will allow winnings and losses to be added to or deducted from the card electronically whenever one of its bettors wagers. If a gambler wants to cash in, World Wide says it will deposit winnings "at any ATM . . . anywhere in the world."

Another high-profile nambling operation that has taken a shine to the Caribbean is Interactive Gaming and Communications Corporation, with corporate headquarters in Blue Bell, Pennsylvania, and an Internet server in Grenada. Interactive Gaming has an on-line sports betting unit, Sports International, and an on-line casino division, Global Casinos. Interactive claims that on May 11, 1996, it became the first company to accept a sports bet on the Internet.

Interactive's stock is publicly traded, so it's one of the few nambling companies that openly reports its finances. Interactive says it handled $58 million in bets in 1996 and lost $695,920 on revenue of $2.9 million that same year. Its stock, which trades in the speculative over-the-counter market, has been a real gamble, never rising above $3 a share after the company went public for 56.25 cents a share in early 1996. By late 1997, the stock was trading for about 39 cents a share.

Like its land-based cousins in Las Vegas, Interactive allows gamblers to open an account and bet on almost any sporting event. Unlike those operators, Interactive warns its gamblers that their accounts may not weather any downturns in the company's business. In its annual report, Interactive notes that accounts may not be "readily available to the bettor in case of an emergency or change of plans." Interactive also says that its customers had credit balances of about $1 million in 1996 and cautions that there "is no assurance that the Company will develop the liquidity to repay customers, if required, without other financing."

And Interactive has already had its share of run-ins with law enforcement officials. The FBI executed a search warrant at the company's Pennsylvania headquarters in early 1997, alleging that an illegal gambling business was being conducted there. However, no federal charges had been filed against Interactive by July 1997, and in press releases the company maintains that it hasn't broken any laws. In June 1997, a Missouri grand jury indicted Interactive for illegally promoting gambling, alleging that the company had violated a court order forbidding it to take bets from Missouri residents. Michael Simone, a former banker who personally owns about 50 percent of Interactive's stock and is the company's chairman and chief executive, described the indictment as "bogus" and asserted that it represented a test case for "freedom of speech and commerce" on the Internet.

But gamblers and investors may want to take note of Interactive's pedigree before buying its shares or placing any bets with the company. Interactive began life in 1986 as a video delivery company, Entertainment Tonight Video Express Limited, which ceased operations a year later. The company was dormant until 1994, when it acquired Sports International. It began doing business as Interactive Gaming in 1996. A key figure behind Interactive is Louis M. Mayo, a partner with Simone in Caribbean Communications Limited, a consulting concern that owns about 7 percent of Interactive's stock. Mayo has a history of federal securities-laws violations dating back to at least 1967, and he is currently a defendant in a civil wire-fraud and money-laundering suit brought by the U.S. Attorney's office in Philadelphia. He has loaned about $4 million to Interactive. A woman described in court papers as his girlfriend and a former clothing designer, Rina Moscariello, owns almost 30 percent of Interactive's stock and until very recently was the company's vice president. Moscariello founded Sports International with Simone.

Whatever the character of nambling companies, their very presence has created a growing regulatory nightmare for U.S. law enforcement officials. The scope and sprawl of the Internet currently make consistent policing almost impossible, and cyberspace's inhabitants are by nature an antiregulatory lot. Furthermore, the legal basis for enforcing gambling laws on the Internet is murky, since the Interstate Wire Act, which forbids the transmission of gambling information across state lines, was passed in 1961 when the on-line world didn't exist.

In 1997, Senator Jon Kyl, an Arizona Republican, introduced legislation seeking to make nambling illegal and the National Association of State Attorneys General has also urged the federal government to make nambling a crime. But the Justice Department has expressed a lack of interest in deploying the extensive and expensive resources needed to be nambling's top cop. That has thrown the ball back at the states, and some, particularly Minnesota, Missouri, California, and Wisconsin, have pledged to take an aggressive stance against nambling companies.

"The great concern is that everybody who has access to the Internet will have a video gambling machine sitting in front of them," says Wisconsin Attorney General James Doyle. "By all measures, these kinds of machines are the most addictive and the least social."

Not so fast, say nambling's advocates. They argue that states, such as Wisconsin, that are already heavily involved in the lottery business are hypocrites for bemoaning the proliferation and dangers of nambling.

"My personal view is that yes, it is hypocritical," responds Doyle. "I'm an opponent of the lottery and I don't like the state of Wisconsin going out and advertising the lottery to promote the business of gambling. I think it's wrong."

Yet even taking into consideration these conflicting points of view, there is no question that nambling has the potential to be a much more pervasive presence in people's lives than any form of gambling that has preceded it. Meanwhile, nambling companies are hard at work improving the quality of their sites, adding sound and improved animation to persuade gamblers to visit more frequently and wager for longer stretches. The companies recognize, as casinos did long before them, that a pleasant environment is the surest path to a bettor's wallet.

Although betting in cyberspace represents the beginning of the end of gambling as a social event rooted in the habits and temperaments of different communities, nambling companies still have much to learn from the generations of schemers, rogues, fast-talkers, and corporate planners who have made modern gambling such a force to be reckoned with in America.

All the anticipation and hand-wringing that have accompanied nambling's rise are far out of proportion to the amount of action it currently generates. Gambling's big daddy is still the casino business, which accounted for about 85 percent of all the legal gambling dollars wagered in the United States in 1996. And the starting block for modern gambling's sprint across the country is, of course, Las Vegas.

The Poker Player—I

David "Chip" Reese, forty-six years old, is the best poker player in the world. Other players, such as his close friend and poker legend Doyle Brunson, are better at individual poker games such as Hold 'Em. But ask for an all-around poker virtuoso, and Reese's name is the first on people's lips.

Reese occasionally plays in tournaments, such as the World Series of Poker, which he has never won. But tournament poker players are a different breed from "live-action" players like Reese. Tournament players compete with a prescribed bankroll over a short period of time and, because they can't dig back into their wallet to stay in the game, they depend more on the luck of the draw than live-action players do. Most tournament players would be "broken" by Reese, as at least one World Series winner has been, if they sat down at the same table with him for a few days.

The night Reese dropped out of the 1996 World Series at Binion's in Las Vegas, he won $280,000 playing at a small table just a few dozen feet away from the tournament tables. It isn't uncommon for $2 million or $3 million in cash and chips to be piled atop a table where Reese is playing, and numerous multimillionaires and Wall Street financiers have walked away from a game with him licking their wounds. Cherubic, warm, and as friendly as a small-town mayor, Reese is transformed into a formidable, no-nonsense predator when he plays poker.

Reese's prowess has made him something unusual, almost isolated, in the poker world: a wealthy man with diverse business interests. As one friend of his, a Los Angeles bookie known as Big Al, says: "For every Chip Reese there are a million poker players who are total losers."

You better learn to plug up all your leaks or you'll be broke. I mean, if you have one crack in your chain, you know, in your cement, it'll get exploited. Because in order to survive in this town, you just got to have 'em all plastered up. . . . When people have to make tough decisions, when they really show their frailties, is when they're uncomfortable and they're on unsure ground.

Well, when a guy comes into a poker game and he's playing with the best players in the world, he's on unsure ground. Now the longer you play, you get a little more relaxed, you get a little more tired, you become one of the boys, because it's a very social situation playing cards. You talk about everything in the world, you joke, you laugh, you get comfortable. Now what happens is when these tough choices come up and these tough situations, you see a guy at his core. In other words, if a guy's trying to bluff me, or if a guy doesn't have a good hand and I feel it, I know it. I see him negotiating in his own way in an area where he's not strong.

You get to see the real insides of a guy, things people try to hide, a lot of hidden anger that they might be holding inside. They'll let it loose because they're frustrated, 'cause they just got beaten, but they had the best hand three times in a row. And they slam the cards and they throw it at the dealer, because they're angry. And then you might see somebody else that handles adversity with a lot of grace and a lot of poise. And so you get to really see both sides. You really do get to see the person when you're gambling with them. A lot of times if I'm sort of watching some-body that, say, has a good reputation as a tough gambler, I really don't like to watch 'em when they're winning. I like to see 'em when everything is going wrong, I like to see how they handle themselves then.

♦ ♣ ♥ ♠

I may not win today, I may not win tomorrow, but I know at the end of the month or the end of two months, I know what I'm gonna win. I know what I'm gonna win, just like the casino knows what they're gonna win. So it's not exciting to me, it's work. And that's a little de-generate. . . . I actually started playing poker when I was in kinder-garten. I always hung out with older kids . . . and they played all this poker—well, we didn't play for money, we played for baseball cards, and baseball cards were a huge thing back then.

Our next-door neighbor was a kid named Sherman. . . . And one day—my mom told me this story years later—one day he knocked on my front door and he said, "Mrs. Reese, I have to talk to you." And she said, "What is it, Sherman?" And he said, "Well, it's about Chip. I think you should know that he's been gambling with all the kids."

She said, "Well, that's good, Sherman, [but] he doesn't have any money." And he said, "Well, no, we play for baseball cards."

And she said, "Well, that's good, Sherman, this is a valuable lesson to him: you teach him not to gamble, you know, you go ahead and take all his baseball cards. And that'll be a lesson to him." I was, like, five years old.

And he said, "Well, really, Mrs. Reese, that's not why we're here. He just beat us all and he has all our baseball cards. We'd like to get them back." . . . That was my first gambling story.

Then we started playing for money. I remember this. My parents were having a big party. I think I was about eight years old. And on our street in the summertime at night there was this guy called the dough-nut man, like the Popsicle man, he was in his truck, and he rang all these bells and lights would go off and everything and all the kids would go out and get a doughnut or something at night. Kids don't have money when they're eight years old. . . . I brought about ten kids into the house. And we had just dozens of doughnuts. My mom said, "Where'd you get all these doughnuts?" I said, "I bought 'em for all the kids, with my poker winnings."

You know, I busted them out of all their pennies and all their nickels, and I spent all the money—really, that's kind of my M.O., I've always been a spender. I've never really stopped spending since I was a kid.

In high school I would play poker. We usually had dates on Saturday nights, and then after we would usually go over to a guy's house and play poker all night. . . . My dad didn't gamble that much, but my grandfather . . . he belonged to a club called the Bicycle Club, in Dayton, [Ohio,] where they played gin rummy and stuff. And when I was little, he taught me how to play gin. And I always just took a fancy to gambling. I hung around him, and he liked to play. . . . And I mean I just always liked it ever since I was little. And I always had a flair for it.

♦ ♣ ♥ ♠

I was just, like, groomed to be an attorney. I won speech contests, starred in a lot of the school plays, and stuff like that. I was an excellent public speaker. And when I went to Dartmouth, I really didn't even think about anything else. I thought I was just going to be an attorney. And when I went to Dartmouth, my grades weren't great. I did a lot of things—I got hurt playing football . . . so I only played my freshman year, and then I joined the debate team. Then I flew all over the country debating for Dartmouth.

Let me tell you how I first started playing cards at Dartmouth. I had no money. When I went to school, my dad was in tough times. Almost I couldn't go, because we couldn't afford it. . . . I got my books for my freshman year and everything, and you know, my meals were paid for and all that stuff, and dad would send me $8 a week.

I heard about this poker game, it was at Brown Hall, one of the dormitories. So I went, and it was a $50 buy-in. . . . So I saved, I got that $8, and I saved it for five weeks. And I got $40. Then I went. A friend of mine loaned me $10. . . . I was willing to do anything. So I got in that game. And I never looked back. . . . I was floating in money. And spending it on all my friends, that's kind of what I did. Easy come, easy go.

And then when I got out of Dartmouth, I didn't really want to go to [law] school right away. I wanted to get some money. I got offered a job in Ohio. This was in 1973, as a manufacturer's rep, selling electrical controls. . . . I took this job, it was $15,000 a year, which was pretty good in 1973. . . . After about eight months of it I just hated it, you know? So I decided I might as well go to [law] school.

I was gonna drive out to California and [see] about going to Stanford. . . . So, I drove and I decided to go to Las Vegas, 'cause I had a friend that I grew up with [whose] parents had been transferred to Las Vegas and he'd moved with them out there. I just wanted to see him and I just wanted to see Las Vegas.

I had about $200 when I got to Vegas, and the first night my friend met me at Caesars Palace. He was working as a trainee for a manager for Thrifty Drug Stores. And he just got paid, and he met me at Caesars Palace. We didn't even go to his house. We went to Caesars Palace, I had $200 in cash, I had a credit card, somehow I got like $300 off my credit card. I went completely broke, the first night at Caesars Palace. I didn't have twenty-five cents.

So now we go back to his house, . . . not depressed, just sick. I was flat broke, out in the middle of nowhere. I knew his parents, I grew up with him my whole life, I mean I can stay at his house as long as I want to . . . And I was on the outs with my dad, 'cause of gambling, I mean, he really hated me gambling. . . . I hung out with this kid for a couple weeks, three weeks maybe. He would come home with his paycheck every week and we'd go blow it. Never played poker, went and played blackjack and shot craps. Went out with the girls. I was hanging out at his house. I'd lay by the pool in the day, while he was working, and then we'd go out when he'd get home.

♦ ♣ ♥ ♠

So now, this was really brutal, his dad gets transferred [to Phoenix]. . . . We start playing these games on Thursday, and I'm closing one or two deals a week in real estate, and I'm winning about $1,000 every Thursday playing poker. . . . My routine became, come into the office on Monday, get my leads, close one deal, and then on Thursday I'd play in the poker game. Friday, I'd drive to Vegas. And I'd go to Vegas for the whole weekend . . . and I'd usually lose in Vegas. I didn't play poker, I came here and I played blackjack and just partied around and never really won up here. But I'd go back to my niche and grind it out.

[Then, I was in Las Vegas with my friend Danny Robison] and had about $800. I'd lost money betting on football . . . and I was just gonna turn around and come home. We were over at the Sahara Hotel with some girls, and we happened to notice that [the casino] had a $10/$20 seven-card-stud game. I hadn't played any poker in a year almost. There were two games. And Danny was a very good seven-card-stud player too. Better than I was then. We were close, but he was better than me. So we decided to split it up, each take $400 and we'd each get in a game. We'll take our last shot with this money playing poker.

So we get in the games, we win like $1,000 between us, so we got $1,800. So now we decide, we're just gonna go back to our room, we're gonna sleep, we're gonna see if we can win playing poker. We played poker for about a week and we won about $6,000 or $7,000 playing poker. We just raked these games. We were the best players by far in these games. We were way ahead.

We had a style which eventually everybody adopted in the world. We didn't know we were that good. We had an aggressive style of play. That kind of revolutionized limit poker in this town. . . . It was really a style that we kind of grew up with in Dayton. They play really good poker in southern Ohio, and we were the best players there.

♦ ♣ ♥ ♠

Then Danny went up to the Dunes, and played some guy heads up. Lowball. Got cheated. And we lost all the money. And we borrowed a couple thousand dollars, went back down to the Sahara and started over again. You know, we ran it up again. Now we started playing bigger, we ran it up, ran it up. That was the big movement. My bankroll went from about $30,000 to about $300,000. From then on, I, we, got broke a couple of times.

Johnny Moss had a game at the Flamingo. And I was just sitting in the ten and twenty room. Doyle and everybody hung out in there, and they started a $400/$800 hi-lo split game. I was looking over there, that's your dream, to see all those black chips. And so I kept watching and watching. They wouldn't let me get near the table. I could sit in this game and watch in my seat. And I could see the hands and I could tell these guys couldn't play.

That's when I got up and I went and called Danny. He was asleep. I told him I knew I could win this game. . . . I had a one, two, three, four, six, which nobody could possibly beat. The worst I was gonna get was half the pot . . . and when I caught the last card, I caught a five of hearts. Which made me a perfect low—one, two, three, four, five. And a straight flush . . . I went and made about three hundred somethin' thousand. Never happened to me since. Played millions of hands. That's almost like it's fateful, you know?

Well, it makes you wonder. Like you look up in the sky and say, "Why am I here?" Who would ever dream? I went to Dartmouth and here I am sitting in the Flamingo Hotel [and] I just made a straight flush.

I never planned things out. It just flowed. It just happened. I loved it, I've always loved it. I just never quit enjoying it.

CHAPTER 2

LAS VEGAS:
LET THE GAMES BEGIN

IT IS A NEON-FUELED, libidinous oasis drawn up out of the dust, and on a brisk desert evening in the fall of 1987, an intimate group of 18,000 people gathered in a basketball stadium there to fete Benny Binion on his eighty-third birthday. Guests were treated to several hundred thousand dollars' worth of free beer, free food, and free music performed by Willie Nelson and others, just for stopping by to toast one of Las Vegas' most formidable patriarchs. For thirty-six years, Benny, a former bootlegger and a convicted murderer, had presided over a smoky downtown casino—named, of course, Binion's—that had grown famous among serious gamblers both for its relatively generous odds and as the site of the annual World Series of Poker. Binion's lobby also proudly displayed a large glass horseshoe stuffed with one million dollars in cash. In a town where success had always been measured by such things as the ability to use a million dollars as a mere prop, the time had come to pay Benny Binion homage.

Many of Nevada's most influential figures were in attendance, and two large chairs had been placed near a stage at center court, with Binion happily ensconced in one of them. Seated next to him was Moe Dalitz, a former owner of the Desert Inn and Stardust casinos on Las Vegas' famous Strip and for years the chief puppeteer behind Nevada's political and business scenes. Variously described as the caretaker "of underworld investments in Las Vegas" and "one of the architects of the skimming process," Dalitz had gotten his professional start five decades earlier, running the Cleveland branch office of Charlie "Lucky" Luciano and Meyer Lansky's nascent Mafia.

Seated near Binion and Dalitz was Steve Wynn, a maverick casino operator planning a new casino that, when it opened two years later as the Mirage, would transform the face of modern Las Vegas. For Binion and Dalitz, their best days in Las Vegas had already come and gone. For Wynn, they lay just around the corner. And among the three of them, waves of the city's history and fortunes had risen, receded, and risen again.

Binion was among a group of tough, shrewd family owners who had settled downtown Las Vegas with no-nonsense, whiskey-driven casinos. Well away from the downtown area, the barren Strip had been retooled after World War II by Dalitz and other Mob financiers as a glitzy resort destination where golf, fine dining, and first-rate nightclub acts were on the same menu as hookers and gambling. Wynn, in turn, would eventually lead the transformation of the Strip's casinos into extravagantly themed playlands where gambling was rechristened "gaming" and packaged as a benign form of recreation, a momentary escape supposedly as innocent and as scrumptious as a candy cane.

For its part, Las Vegas, once a barely tolerated haven for that quick fix of social deviance, became a model for the factory town of the twenty-first century.

GAMBLING COMES TO THE DESERT

Las Vegas. The Meadows.

The city was in a region familiar to Native Americans, but it began life in the early nineteenth century as a watering hole in the Mojave Desert visited by Spanish traders en route to Los Angeles. It was later surveyed by the explorer John Frémont, briefly settled and abandoned by Mormons at mid-century, gave shelter to miners still later on, and then was largely forgotten until the railroad resurrected it in the first few years of this century.

As businesses in New York, Chicago, and Salt Lake City demanded better access to a growing Los Angeles, Las Vegas, always a satellite of its southern California neighbor, proved to be the most convenient whistle-stop for a railroad connecting those cities. By 1905, Las Vegas had a train station, speakeasies, brothels, and little else. The construction of the Hoover Dam, beginning in 1931, brought money, jobs, and more people to Las Vegas. But that massive public works project was merely a prologue to changes that would be set in motion by a quieter event that also occurred that year. In 1931, the state of Nevada legalized gambling.

Gambling had thrived informally and illegally in Nevada, as it had in many other parts of the country, prior to 1931. Luxurious casinos had been erected in New Orleans in 1827 and in Washington, D.C., in 1832.

Pendleton's casino in Washington had hosted congressmen and, rumor had it, President James Buchanan, until it shut its doors in 1858. Richard Canfield operated deluxe casinos in New York City and Saratoga Springs, New York from 1890 to 1905, and in 1898 the Beach Club casino opened in Palm Beach, Florida. But during this entire time, the country regularly struggled with the morality of gambling, finding in it a vice that ran counter to popular and often religious conceptions of productivity and useful labor.

Antigambling fervor tended to heat up during periods of great social or economic change. As historian Ann Fabian has pointed out, the condemnation of gambling that surfaced toward the end of the last century emerged as industrialization and urbanization were imposing a new social order on a formerly agrarian nation: "For those whose interests lay in building an economy based on ordered gain, gambling became increasingly dangerous . . . the temptation to gamble had to be eliminated not only because the workers might be tempted to steal but because gambling gains offered an attractive alternative to the small hourly, daily, or weekly wage. To abolish gambling would thus help legitimate wage labors." In other words, punching the clock, and punching it on time, had become so important to the vast industrial forces blossoming at the turn of the century that gambling was now considered more than a distraction. It stood in the way of economic progress.

"The gambling propensity is another subsidiary trait of the barbarian temperament," opined economist Thorstein Veblen in 1899. "But in any case it is to be taken as an archaic trait, inherited from a more or less remote past, more or less incompatible with the requirements of the modern industrial process, and more or less of a hindrance to the fullest efficiency of the collective economic life of the present."

Alas, feisty little Nevada would have none of this.

The state had banned gambling from 1864 to 1869 and again from 1911 to 1931, but most residents flouted the law. During the latter period, Nevadans were so distraught by the clampdown that the law was amended in 1915 to exempt card games and slot machines—which left few other gambling activities to prohibit. Besides, a certain free-and-easy style had long marked the state's affairs. Prostitution was a licensed profession there, and during economic hard times in the 1920s Nevada had cultivated a thriving market in quickie divorces for residents from nearby California.

But the sheer severity of the Depression, which caused the state to teeter perilously on the brink of bankruptcy, led Nevada to embrace casino gambling with singular gusto. The mining business was soft, Hoover Dam workers were easy marks, and local legislators wanted a piece of the black-market lucre illegal gambling was generating. Thus was consummated the first marriage between public policy and casino gambling, a troubled, often sordid, alliance that has inspired other unlikely unions since.

Yet no one in Las Vegas in the 1930s dreamed that the local economy would one day be dominated by gambling. Indeed, a *small* number of casinos was crucial, *Las Vegas Review-Journal* publisher A. E. Cahlan stressed in 1939, for Las Vegas to stay "a somewhat 'nice' play center" rather than a "gaudy" and "rowdy little community like Tijuana."

The gambling genie, however, was already out of the bottle. And newspaper publishers, politicians, and law enforcement officials would have little leverage in determining how fast gambling grew in Las Vegas, or who controlled it. Some of the most corrupt entrepreneurs in the country—a crop of wheeler-dealers who would give whole new meanings to the terms "gaudy" and "rowdy"—had set their sights on the place.

BUGSY'S VISION

After legalization, the first swank casino to adorn Las Vegas was Tony Cornero's Meadows Club, which opened in 1931 just outside city limits. The Meadows Club offered a selection of "table games" that would become standard fare in Las Vegas—craps, poker, roulette, blackjack— and one game, faro, that was disappearing.

Faro was the most popular card game in the country for most of the nineteenth and early twentieth centuries. Its name derived from the French word *pharaon:* the cards originally used in France had drawings of Egyptian pharaohs on them. Faro was introduced into the United States by French émigrés who settled in New Orleans, and became the preferred game of nineteenth-century riverboat gamblers. Faro is simple to play. Cards are dealt face-up from a fifty-two-card deck kept in a small box and controlled by the dealer, or "bank." After a shuffle, the first card showing through the top of the faro box is a dead card, and no bets are made on it. The next card is the player's card, and the following card belongs to the dealer, with all the remaining cards alternating in the same way. The higher of the two cards in play wins. Up to ten people sitting around a felt-covered faro table can wager on either the bank's or the player's cards.

The odds in faro, except when splits occur, are even. That is, perhaps, what doomed it as a popular casino game once Las Vegas began commercializing gambling sixty-five years ago. Any casino needs an "edge" to make money consistently. To achieve that edge, the house doesn't pay off winning bets according to the true odds; otherwise, over time it and the gambler would end up virtually even. By making payoffs lower than what they should be (by paying, for example, $7 for a winning bet that normal odds would value at $10) the house creates its edge. The house's advantage, or "percentage," on table games and slot machines varies widely. But even a small edge will guarantee that over time a casino will take more money from gamblers than it gives them. At even odds, faro could never pay the rent unless dealers were cheating. That was frequently the case in the 1800s, but cheating became trickier to pull off in the twentieth century.

In any event, the Meadows Club was not Tony Cornero's first foray into gambling. He had operated clubs in Los Angeles and casino barges off the California coast, and he was among several southern California casino operators who relocated to Las Vegas after Los Angeles cracked down on casinos there throughout the 1930s. The squeeze on illegal operators in California and in other states such as Texas, where Benny Binion had thrived, made Las Vegas a refuge for these veterans.

Other casinos were opened downtown and then two large casinos, El Rancho Vegas and Last Frontier, opened in 1941 and 1942 far away on Highway 91. Their success convinced gangster Benjamin "Bugsy" Siegel that Las Vegas was ready for him. Siegel arrived in Las Vegas with a showman's vision of the city's future and hoards of Mob cash.

Not every casino operator who came to Las Vegas in the 1930s and 1940s was a mobster. But modern Las Vegas could never have been erected without the vast sums of money organized crime eventually poured into it. No bank or other conventional lender would touch the city at the time, and few legitimate businesspeople had experience running casinos. The bankroll that organized crime brought to Las Vegas had been fattened by trade in everything from prostitution to the numbers racket, but the single largest source of Mob wealth at the time was bootlegging. When Prohibition was repealed in 1933, the fat profit margins that had accompanied bootlegging shrank dramatically. In search of a new market to tap, the country's preeminent rumrunners landed in Las Vegas.

If the Mob brought to Las Vegas a keen insight into human desire and frailty, and the money to exploit them, in the ensuing years it also brought a carnivalesque group of violent, ham-handed thugs who freely used murder and intimidation to protect their sales turf.

There to lead the way was Bugsy.

Originally, Siegel had been sent to Los Angeles from New York by Lucky Luciano, founding father of the Mafia, to secure a stake in a wire service that transmitted horse-racing results and to convince bookies to dump a competing wire. The search for patrons for his wire service took Bugsy to Las Vegas. In 1945, Siegel, Meyer Lansky, and several other mobsters bought the El Cortez, a run-of-the-mill casino in downtown Las Vegas, for $614,000. They sold it for $780,000 seven months later. The proceeds were earmarked for a far grander project, to be located on Highway 91 near the Last Frontier and the El Rancho Vegas, which Siegel had unsuccessfully tried to muscle in on. To get more money for his new project, Siegel persuaded his colleagues in New York that Las Vegas was a boomtown and with enough money the Mob could own it. On both counts, he was right.

When Siegel opened his new casino, the Flamingo, in 1946, it was a radical departure. Its predecessors were gambling joints, nothing more. The Flamingo offered seventy-seven lushly decorated rooms, a golf course, squash and handball courts, a shooting range, a gym, horseback riding, elegant shops, *and* a casino. Siegel's own suite reputedly had bulletproof glass and a secret passageway to the casino's basement, where a getaway car remained on call around the clock.

The Flamingo offered gamblers the illusion of sophistication. In Europe, casino gambling had almost always been restricted by class. Upperclass bettors, who could demonstrate financial wherewithal and were considered more capable of self-restraint than the less affluent, were granted membership in the private gambling clubs. Middle-class and lower-class European gamblers were not. In the United States, gambling was limited by jurisdiction, not by class. The Flamingo merely provided gamblers with the trappings of class and flew in glamorous stars from nearby Hollywood to help sustain the mirage.

But Bugsy soon had more than high rollers on his mind. He understood that if he offered gamblers a full-blown destination rather than just a seat at a blackjack table, the masses would come. After its initial and unsuccessful flirtation with elegance, the Flamingo went after smaller bettors by advertising its low room rates, cheap buffets, promotional events such as raffles, and other lowbrow marketing techniques that all casinos later used. Bugsy also added gassy, gloriously tacky signage to Las Vegas's bag of tricks, adorning the Flamingo's exterior with bubbles of pink neon.

Siegel never lived to enjoy the fruits of his labor. The construction costs of the Flamingo tripled to $6 million; Luciano and others suspected Siegel of stealing money, and when business was slow after the casino opened, Bugsy was murdered. Some claimed he was killed not for stealing from his partners but for repeatedly beating up his girlfriend, Virginia Hill, a darling and confidante of the Chicago Mob. Whatever the reason for Siegel's death, it left to others in organized crime the task of developing the lonely stretch of Highway 91 around the Flamingo into the string of glittering resorts collectively known as the Strip.

MOE DALITZ AND THE ART OF THE SKIM

"There were mountains and palm trees. And people dressed. It was like going out to a cocktail party under a gorgeous sky," recalls Gillian Kabat, a dancer who performed in a lavish floor show at Las Vegas' Stardust casino during the 1960s. "There was lots of candlelight and chandeliers. I never got tired of thinking how glamorous and comfortable it was."

Kabat also remembers singers Louis Prima and Keely Smith performing in the Stardust's lounge; actress Betty Grable, who lived in town, answering her own door to sign an autograph; and Frank Sinatra, Dean Martin, and Sammy Davis, Jr., performing nightly at the Sands casino (a chunk of which Sinatra and Martin owned), as they escorted all comers through the glamorous, absolutely fabulous, outré Las Vegas of the Rat Pack era.

Like an enormous child's top spinning wildly in the desert, its rotation fueled by Angelenos arriving in their cars, tourists winging in on jets, and a nationwide eruption in consumer spending that generated oceans of crisp, green dollars, Las Vegas had become a colorful, unpredictable blur. The town was intimate, chummy, and viciously corrupt.

Between Bugsy's murder in 1947 and John Kennedy's occasional visits to party with Sinatra in the early 1960s, nine major casinos had been built on the Strip. Las Vegas' population had tripled to about 64,000. The city's arrival in the buyer's market of post–World War II America ensured that gambling would no longer be just an underground attraction reached by slipping silently down a dark alley. It would become a consumer product marketed and hyped like milk, laundry detergent, or automobiles.

And the pitch was everything. The opening of one casino was timed to coincide with an atomic blast at testing grounds outside the city. At another, acrobats posed perilously on a chair or a cane atop a neon marquee. At a third, visitors could get stumbling drunk sipping martinis inside a glass observation chamber in the bottom of a swimming pool. All these ploys were used in Las Vegas because the city's public relations specialists, like their cousins in Hollywood, knew that stars, stunts, and lunacy snared oodles of free publicity. As two visiting writers put it in 1955: "These innovations are expensive at first but exceedingly profitable in the long run. The ex-champions lure big gambling sports fans to Las Vegas. Live telecasts make names like Riviera, Sands, Thunderbird,

Flamingo household words from Wytopitlock, Maine, to Rough and Ready, California. And social directors keep the little women and the kiddies happy while daddy loses his sports shirt at the craps table."

Craps tables—indeed, table games generally—were where all the casino action resided at this time. Slots, the potent little moneymakers that now dominate the floors of most casinos, were a backwater thirty and forty years ago. In the richly gendered world of casino gambling, the slots were there simply to keep wives distracted while their husbands stalked big game at the tables.

Today, craps is disappearing from casinos just as quickly as faro did earlier this century. But it was the premier table game of its time. Craps, like faro, was popularized in nineteenth-century New Orleans by the entrepreneurs and con men who first tapped into the fast money that came with commercialized gambling. Originally played by African Americans, it derived from the British dice game of hazard, in which losing rolls were known as crabs. In the 1940s, craps was embraced by casinos because it ideally suited the tastes of the World War II veterans visiting Las Vegas during those explosive years. Many of them had learned how to play the complex dice game on blankets aboard troopships.

The craps table, with its rounded corners and its green felt emblazoned with arcane, flirtatious messages ("Come"; "Don't Come"; "Pass"; "Don't Pass") is perhaps the most elaborate gambling show a casino puts on. Four people are needed to run the table, with two dealers managing action at each end, a "stickman," who moves the dice around the table with a curved wooden rod, and a "boxman," who oversees the action and settles bets.

The dice are passed around the table to each of as many as twelve "shooters." A shooter rolling a 7 or an 11 is an instant winner. A 2, 3, or 12 is an instant loser, or "craps." Any other number rolled becomes the shooter's "point"; the shooter keeps rolling until the point is hit again. When a 7 is rolled after the shooter's point is established, he or she loses and the dice change hands. But the real intricacy of the game is in the betting, not the shooting. About twenty-four different bets can be made on any roll of the dice, either for or against the shooter, or on particular configurations of the dice.

Yet for today's gamblers, used to the instant gratification of slots, craps simply takes too much time to learn. Craps also intimidates uninitiated gamblers who are hesitant to display their ignorance in a casino environment, where savvy posturing is just as much a part of the elixir as is the remote possibility of winning.

Craps, like baccarat and roulette, requires no skill on the gambler's part. Because of the slight advantage the house enjoys, craps will prove to be a loser for anyone who plays it long enough. In the argot of serious gamblers, it is a "negative expectation" game. But, of course, Las Vegas exists to make negative expectations disappear. And it was through the lounge acts starring Sinatra, the floor shows featuring topless dancers, and the endless offers of free drinks and lazy afternoons by the pool that Las Vegas convinced its mostly male patrons in the 1950s and 1960s to forget about their losses from the night before. Casinos were even willing to lose money themselves on all the cheap food, beverages, lodging, and entertainment that enticed gamblers into the clubs, because those losses were more than offset by the huge profits gleaned at the gambling tables.

Although the promotion of Las Vegas casinos was deliriously innovative in the post–World War II years, management was hopelessly corrupt. During this heyday of Mob influence in the city, all the major Strip casinos were either controlled by or beholden to organized-crime families from New York, Chicago, Detroit, and Kansas City, as well as elsewhere.

The Desert Inn, for example, which opened in 1950, was nominally run by the avuncular Wilbur Clark. It earned a well-deserved reputation as one of Las Vegas' most elegant establishments catering to high rollers, or heavy bettors. But when Clark, who began building the Desert Inn in 1947, ran out of money in 1949, he sold 74 percent of his interest in the project to Morris "Moe" Dalitz. Clark became just a front man. The Desert Inn was a Mob joint.

Before coming to Las Vegas, Dalitz had cut his teeth bootlegging and operating illegal gambling joints for organized-crime associates in the Midwest. He was also a close associate of Jimmy Hoffa, the Mob-linked head of the International Brotherhood of Teamsters labor union. Dalitz's involvement in the Desert Inn meant that from day one that casino was in hock to the Mob. Although it was Clark who carried out many of the ceremonial duties and put a public face on the Desert Inn's operations, it was Dalitz who called the shots. He hired all the casino bosses, and he decided how the resort's funds were used. Over time, Dalitz became one of Las Vegas' most active corporate citizens, helping to build Sunrise Hospital (with Mob-tainted loans from the Teamsters' Central States Pension Fund), the Stardust casino (with Teamsters funds), a later expansion of the Desert Inn (with Teamsters funds), and the La Costa resort, outside San Diego (with Teamsters funds).

Dalitz was considered a shrewd casino manager, who kept things humming in a company town bent on profits and largely closed to blacks and other minorities. But to validly assess the capabilities of the management at any casino of this era is difficult because everyone in Las Vegas was skimming money from the casinos' coffers.

While a *Wall Street Journal* writer estimated in 1955 that a "well-run casino in a strip hotel" would earn about $5 million to $6 million a year (or about $19 million to $22 million in today's dollars) it is impossible to know how profitable any casino actually was, because organized crime figures and those fronting for them spent those years fine-tuning the art of the skim.

In its simplest form, skimming meant taking cash from the counting room after the casino's daily win had been carted in from the cashier's "cage." Before all that loot was recorded in a ledger book, skimmers would stuff some into a pocket, a bag, or a suitcase and spirit it away. The money trail then could be disguised so that the Internal Revenue Service or unwary business partners didn't know the cash ever existed.

A slightly more refined method of skimming involved "markers," big lines of credit granted to high rollers and other gamblers. If a high roller left town with an unpaid marker, the casinos would write it off as bad debt when they reported their taxes. But later they would track down the gambler, collect the marker, and bring home the cash. The bad debt remained on the company's books, while proceeds from the marker were distributed around the executive offices.

Perhaps the only other business that juggles as much cash in one place at one time as a casino is a bank. And Las Vegas casinos in Dalitz's day essentially became banks for many Mob enterprises, funding everything from resort developments and loan-sharking to political corruption and narcotics smuggling. Dalitz was described in a 1978 FBI memo as "the individual who oversees the operations of the LCN [La Cosa Nostra] families in Las Vegas . . . [He] makes certain that there is no cheating with regard to the skim money taken out of the casinos and further, that there is no fighting among families for the control of various casinos."

Although the Justice Department and the U.S. Senate launched high-profile investigations aimed in part at weeding out the influence of organized crime in Las Vegas during the 1950s and early 1960s, it would take another two decades for the Mob to be run out of town. At the federal level, FBI director J. Edgar Hoover presented the biggest roadblock to active prosecution of the Mob. Hoover was an avid gambler who reportedly relied on Mafia honcho Frank Costello to place his bets. The Mob also may have been aware of other Hoover secrets that went unpublicized during his lifetime. Perhaps as a result, Hoover publicly displayed doubts about the existence of organized crime, and through most of his career he kept the FBI on the sidelines as the Mob became entrenched in Las Vegas. Even if Hoover had been supportive, any federal agency would have required extensive cooperation from local law enforcement and regulatory agents to build a strong case against organized crime in Las Vegas. That wasn't going to happen in Moe Dalitz's Nevada.

Indeed, the state didn't even have a regulatory body to oversee the casinos until 1955. In that year, bad publicity surrounding the revelation that Mob boss Meyer Lansky was connected to the financing of the Thunderbird casino forced Nevada's hand. The state subsequently shut down the Thunderbird and established a three-member Gaming Control Board to investigate applicants for casino licenses and enforce gambling regulations. Four years later, as federal scrutiny and public concern continued to mount, the state passed the Gaming Control Act, which established a five-member Gaming Commission to oversee the Control Board.

Still, for the next twenty years, the Gaming Commission was little more than a rubber stamp. At best, it encouraged occasional bouts of musical chairs at some casinos, with a new front man stepping in to represent the same Mob interests. At worst, it succumbed to bullying from those it was charged with regulating. For example, in 1965, a Desert Inn co-owner and Cleveland mobster named Ruby Kolod was accused of using cash scooped from the Desert Inn's cage to invest in a questionable oil deal with another mobster. The Gaming Commission, pushed by then governor Grant Sawyer, entered Kolod's name in the infamous "Black Book," a list of individuals forbidden to own or associate with any Nevada casino.

It was an unusually tough stance for the Gaming Commission, and it didn't last: Dalitz began pressuring the commission. Just two weeks after Kolod's name went into the Black Book it was removed. Dalitz, Kolod, and others then brought their weight to bear in the next gubernatorial campaign, donating hundreds of thousands of dollars to Sawyer's challenger, Paul Laxalt. Laxalt won, and during his occupancy of the governor's mansion no new names were added to the Black Book's ranks. For good measure, Laxalt named Dalitz a "special assistant to the governor." A spokesman for Laxalt said the former governor was "never asked for the time of day by Dalitz."

Some point to the much-ballyhooed arrival of multimillionaire Howard Hughes in Nevada in 1966 as the moment when the transition from Mob rule to blue-chip credibility in Las Vegas occurred. However, that is largely a myth. Organized crime hung on as tenaciously as ever, and Dalitz and others reaped a windfall from the frantic buying spree that Hughes, whose mind was already deteriorating, embarked upon when he landed in Las Vegas.

Hughes had been looking around for new stakes to claim in 1966 after the government forced him to sell his holdings in Trans World Airlines for $546 million. Ample cash in hand, he moved to Nevada and proceeded to buy six Las Vegas casinos during the next four years. The first was the Desert Inn, for which he paid $13.2 million in 1967. But for that price, all Hughes garnered was the right to operate the casino until 2022. Ownership of the Desert Inn's land and buildings was retained by Moe Dalitz, who then stayed on as a "management consultant" to the casino.

Dalitz generously agreed to forgo a salary for his managerial services. But the Desert Inn's once-robust profits suddenly almost disappeared once Hughes took over. The same thing occurred at another Hughes acquisition, the Sands. Together, the two resorts' combined profits for all of 1967 and 1968 were only $5 million—far less than what the Sands alone used to ring up in just one year. In all, Hughes' Nevada operations began bleeding between $3.2 million and $14 million a year during his sojourn there.

If Nevada regulators and others wanted to credit Hughes with cleaning up the town, Dalitz and other members of his Las Vegas clique saw Hughes' arrival for what it was: an opportunity to take an unbelievably wealthy mark to the cleaners. Hughes would ultimately invest more than $150 million in Nevada, overpay for many properties, and lose millions of blatantly skimmed dollars from casinos he owned. Not until the late 1970s, when the highly publicized skimming of the Stardust casino by organized-crime figures burst into view, did the Mob's stranglehold on Las Vegas casinos begin to weaken. As late as 1979, federal law enforcement officials believed that as many as six major Las Vegas casinos still had organized-crime ties.

But the Mob's grip on Las Vegas had grown weak a decade earlier. By the late 1960s, many of the Mob joints were stale and the excitement that gripped the town when the Rat Pack was in residence had lost some of its charge. During such creative slumps, Las Vegas has always had a history of reinventing itself. This time it would be a most unlikely whirlwind who would stir things up. He came from outside Las Vegas, and his name was Jay Sarno.

GAMBLING IN FANTASYLAND

Detailed replicas of such statuary as the *Venus de Milo* and Michelangelo's *David*, life-size fiberglass centurions guarding the entrance, eighteen fountains spraying thirty-five-foot columns of water, and a huge elliptical driveway marked the spot where the modern casino era began thirty years ago.

The original name of the resort located on a dusty corner of Flamingo Road and the Strip was the Desert Palace. But when it re-opened in 1966, it was called Caesars Palace. And the high rollers who eventually thronged to the tables there, and helped make it the most internationally recognized name in the casino business, affectionately shortened the name to Caesars.

Caesars was five years in the making, every detail in the planning process thoroughly pored over by a roly-poly, Barnumesque, forty-nine-year-old hotel operator named Jay Sarno. Sarno, who stood five feet seven inches tall and weighed 260 pounds, was an obsessive and unlucky gambler, a front man for the Mob, and a dreamer whose outlandish appetite found its home in Las Vegas.

Prior to Sarno's arrival in Las Vegas, the town was dotted with twinkling, uninspired resorts, all of them largely indistinguishable from one another. When Caesars opened, it did more than merely set a new standard in kitsch. Caesars paved the way for Las Vegas to become America's adult fantasyland, a place where a country's obsession with riches intersected with its inhabitants' desires to find themselves anywhere other than where they were. Caesars was the first casino to anesthetize gamblers in a bath of flamboyant, baroque unreality. Now American casinos were distinct from their staid European counterparts not only in terms of the class of people they catered to, but also in terms of the absurd thump-thumping, lights-in-your-eyes, *oh-my-God* quality of the experiences they offered.

Caesars was the Roman empire as only Las Vegas could envision it. The resort's lavish restaurant was called the Bacchanal Room. Its coffee shop was the called the Noshorium. Its 800-seat showroom was the Circus Maximus. The lounge was Nero's Nook. The casino was Caesars Forum. On opening night, Caesars updated the town's blustery history of public relations. Crooner Andy Williams headlined a production called "Rome Swings" and Caesars invited 1,800 guests, many of them celebrities and politicians, to attend the festivities. It spent $1 million to serve up two tons of filet mignon, 300 pounds of crabmeat, and 50,000 glasses of champagne. Noting "Roman Empire Reborn in L[as] V[egas]," the city's *Review-Journal* informed its readers on the eve of the opening that the food and drink laid out for the guests amounted to "ten billion calories."

Caesars, the first new casino in town since the Stardust was completed in 1958, was lavishly distinct from all of its brethren on the Strip. Most of the other Strip resorts started out as low-slung affairs, little more than oversized cinder-block motels wrapped like horseshoes around a swimming pool and adjacent to a golf course. When tourist traffic heated up later, many of them added a small hotel tower to the property.

If any of these owners had thought about creating an over-the-top *theme* for their resorts—which they hadn't—they might have blanched at including Roman slaves trotting around a restaurant offering massages. Caesars wasn't just a resort. It was a daily event, it was all pure Sarno, and gamblers loved it.

Caesars sprawled across thirty-four acres and was capped by a fourteen-story hotel with 680 rooms, its design inspired by Sarno's own wonderfully absurd brand of hoo-ha. "Over the years that I have been creating hotels, I've discovered that the oval is a magic shape . . . conducive to relaxation," Sarno remarked. "If you examine Caesars' casino, you will find that it is oval-shaped. I even incorporated the oval design into the dice tables, which affects the dice angle geometry. Because the casino is shaped in an oval, people tend to relax and play longer."

Of course, casinos have always induced gamblers to play longer—and thus increase their likelihood of losing—by eliminating bothersome windows or clocks that might tell bettors how much time has passed. But Sarno's loopy schmaltz added to Caesars' allure. Caesars' lobby was speckled with gold leaf, lined with Brazilian rosewood, and featured a sixty-six-foot serpentine sofa covered in red suede and framed in white marble. The registration desk was gold tile topped with pearl-blue granite. Caesars' casino had one of the world's largest crystal ceiling fixtures.

Such touches contributed to construction costs of about $19 million, a figure Sarno's publicity machine inflated to $25 million. Very little of the money came out of Sarno's own pocket. Most of it came from the Teamsters pension fund, Las Vegas' ubiquitous piggy bank. Sarno's Cabana Motel chain had been a beneficiary of Teamster funds long before Sarno took Las Vegas by storm. In 1958, his Atlanta motel received $1.8 million from the Teamsters, and in 1959 his Dallas motel got $3.6 million. The land underneath Caesars had been leased from investor Kirk Kerkorian, and between 1965 and 1972 the Teamsters pumped $20.4 million into the resort. Federal Bureau of Investigation memos said that Sarno was emperor of Caesars in name only and that the true owners were midwestern and New England organized-crime families.

On Caesars' opening day in 1966, the *Las Vegas Review-Journal* reported that Jimmy Hoffa was in attendance to monitor the $10 million the union had already invested in construction loans. What did the union leader think of the Caesars investment? "They're in good shape financially here," Hoffa answered. "We've got twenty-year money in here."

Not that any of this mattered a bit to Sarno. He had been given the money and told to have fun with it. Caesars was the offspring of an idea man who loved gambling but didn't know the first thing about actually running a casino. In this respect, Sarno wasn't alone. Although the Las Vegas casinos were cash cows, they were often comically mismanaged during this period. According to one individual familiar with the management of the Sahara casino in 1965, the resort didn't know how much revenue it took in during the first sixty days of that year, never kept a profit-and-loss statement, and had no idea which table games its customers preferred. The money poured in anyway.

Caesars gave the gambling world more than great theater. It later added some important new twists to how gambling was marketed. It courted conventioneers, went after foreign high rollers ("whales"), and in the 1970s started the Las Vegas tradition of booking major boxing matches and televising them. Casinos weren't permitted to advertise gambling nationally, but the Caesars name stuck with all the boxing fans who tuned in to watch the fights on TV. When they thought of Las Vegas, they thought of Caesars. And the fights also could be used as a promotional device to corral high rollers who might have gone to the Desert Inn or some other casino.

Table games still dominated the casino floor during Caesars' glory days. "The pit was the game and the clients were all white males," says Vince Eade, who worked in Las Vegas casinos before becoming director of the University of Nevada–Las Vegas' International Gaming Institute. "Management used to make decisions based on superstition or luck. They wouldn't hire left-handed or red-haired dealers because [managers] believed they were unlucky."

Every casino manager was worried that someone else might try to skim the gambling winnings before they could skim them for themselves, so the casino was a cauldron of suspicion. To see a dealer or pit boss chatting with customers or other employees on the casino floor immediately raised concern among managers that a skim might be in the works. "The dealers were told to dummy up and deal. If you interact with customers, you're fired," Eade says.

If Caesars marked the beginning of Las Vegas' ascendance as an adult fantasyland, it was also one of the last major casinos built there with only male gamblers in mind. From its plush red carpeting to its Dionysian tumult, Caesars represented the apex of virile, muscular Las Vegas. In the years ahead, Las Vegas would discover that women had an equally strong attraction to gambling, and the new casinos built to draw them in would be entirely different from Caesars.

CIRCUS CIRCUS—GRINDING THE LOW ROLLERS

In a town that had grown short on new ideas, Sarno came up with his second outlandish one in 1968, a year before he and his partners sold their Caesars holdings for $60 million. He called his new playpen Circus Circus. Although Sarno originally aimed Circus Circus at the same high rollers he had entertained at Caesars, in other hands it would later become the first casino that avoided high rollers and courted the great unwashed masses of American gambling: middle-class and lower-class families.

Disgusted by the high prices he had to pay big-name entertainers to appear at Caesars, Sarno hit upon the idea of hiring cut-rate circus acts instead. From this bit of whimsy emerged Circus Circus, a pink and white, tent-shaped big top on the Strip. A merry-go-round spun at the entrance to the resort. Inside, a trapeze act performed above the casino floor, and a diver periodically plunged sixty feet into an enormous, water-soaked sponge. Gamblers could descend to the first floor from the second by sliding down a fire pole. Clowns on stilts hawked tickets. All-you-can-eat buffets cost 97 cents.

Among the seventeen carnival games offered by Circus Circus was a traditional baseball toss. But if a gambler hit the target with the baseball, the prize wasn't "a teddy bear or a photo of you and the missus in your Sunday best, however. [It was] an eye-popping 10 seconds of a naked girl bouncing out of a spring-loaded bed and gyrating wildly to rock-and-roll music . . . sort of a combination of Sodom and Gomorrah and Disneyland."

Like Caesars, Circus Circus was an attempt to graft casino gambling onto an out-of-this-world experience. But this time, Sarno missed his mark.

The high rollers hated Circus Circus. They didn't like the sideshow distractions, such as the live elephant that had been trained to roll dice at the craps table but in its wanderings occasionally pooped on the casino floor. From the start, Circus Circus lost reams of money, and by 1974 it was losing $300,000 a month.

Although Sarno was as inept a manager as ever, it is impossible to tell now how much of Circus Circus' losses were due to folly and how much were due to fraud. Even though Circus Circus was apparently hemorrhaging money, the Teamsters pension fund kept pumping fresh resources into it. In 1971, the fund purchased the land underneath Circus Circus for $2.6 million, leased it back to the resort, and then loaned the casino $15.5 million. In 1972 and 1974, respectively, the Teamsters invested another $2.6 million and $7.6 million in Circus Circus.

Records at the Nevada Gaming Commission and the Securities & Exchange Commission reveal who some of Circus Circus' other owners were. Allen Dorfman, a Chicago attorney who represented the Teamsters, had been given an option in 1968 to buy 6.8 percent of Circus Circus' stock. (Dorfman was later murdered in an alleged Mob hit.) Carl Wesley Thomas, one of the most innovative skimmers in Las Vegas history, was also a stockholder. According to one individual familiar with Circus Circus' corporate history, the resort's jewelry store was owned by Tony Spilotro, an enforcer for the Chicago Mob.

Thomas, put on the witness stand in 1985 during a federal trial of mobsters accused of participating in the Stardust skim, testified that Dorfman ordered him to oversee a skimming of Circus Circus' profits. "He [Dorfman] told me there were obligations to fulfill and he wanted my help in fulfilling them," Thomas said. "It was my understanding that a fee had to be paid for the loans, and I was to do the skimming [to pay the fee]."

Meanwhile, Sarno was flailing. Between 1969 and 1974, he had lost almost $4 million gambling in Las Vegas casinos, had been charged with bribing an IRS agent, and had to explain to the SEC the sudden discovery at Caesars of over $1 million in $100 bills that hadn't been recorded in the casino's books.

Only eight rambunctious years had passed since Sarno first set foot in Las Vegas, but his casino days were already nearing an end. After a failed attempt to start another casino in the early 1970s, Sarno left the business. In 1974, he sold his interest in Circus Circus to Bill Bennett and Bill Pennington, two gutsy men who unexpectedly discovered that casino gambling could seduce an audience other than high rollers. In their hands, gambling became a favorite pastime of Joe and Jane Six-pack—the low rollers.

"They decided you didn't need high rollers; you could reach the mass market with good food and cheap rooms. The kids could come too," says Diana Bennett, Bill Bennett's daughter. "It just wasn't what Las Vegas was all about [at that time] and I don't think anyone thought it could be successful. . . . It was still thought of as a Frank Sinatra business."

Indeed, Bennett and Pennington themselves still thought of casino gambling as a Frank Sinatra business when they bought Circus Circus. The casino was carrying a huge amount of bad debt from Mexican high rollers, but the pair believed they could still pursue gamblers like that, if they maintained credit policies tougher than Sarno's.

But after getting rid of the burlesque shows and moving some of the carnival acts away from the casino floor, Bennett and Pennington stumbled on something they hadn't expected. Southern California families began flocking to Circus Circus. Maybe the high rollers were annoyed by circus acts, but low rollers loved them because their children loved them. The partners had only enough financing in place to keep the casino open for about four months, so they began doing everything they could to appeal to those families.

Bennett literally took an ax to the casino's baccarat tables, favorites of the high rollers, and replaced them with blackjack tables offering low minimum bets and floors crowded with cheap slot machines. Bennett and Pennington no longer considered casinos a Frank Sinatra business. In fact, they didn't even think of their trade as gambling. The partners approached the casino as just another retail business and they took to calling Circus Circus a "store." They added another 400 hotel rooms and priced them so the store would always be fully occupied with shoppers.

Both men were perfectly suited to this moment.

Bennett had gained his retail experience running a chain of extremely successful furniture stores. He subsequently lost a fortune investing in another business and declared personal bankruptcy in 1965. Out of desperation, he took a casino job—and found he had a knack for the business. An adept manager in an industry populated by buffoons, he moved quickly through a series of high-profile positions. Pennington, also a savvy manager, owned a slot and keno machine business when he met Bennett. The pair became partners in 1971 by investing in an electronic gambling machine company called Western Equities. They sold Western Equities in 1977; renamed International Game Technology, the company went on to become the largest slot machine manufacturer in the country.

By the time the partners reached Circus Circus in 1974, they had the skills to make their casino a place that could be brightly lit, resolutely lowbrow, cheaply operated, unintimidating to the uninitiated, and honestly run. These moves might have had Bugsy spinning in his grave, but Circus Circus became immensely profitable.

Judged only by the standard of making an enterprise hum, Bennett and Pennington had nailed it down. A decade after they bought Circus Circus, their company owned five casinos that threw off $274 million a year in revenue and boasted profit margins of 12 percent. In the mid-1980s, when almost every other Las Vegas casino, including Caesars, was in a slump, Circus Circus claimed it had as many as 20,000 people a day passing through its doors, none of whom were given free luxury suites or fat lines of credit for gambling. To handle the overflow from its hotel, Circus Circus operated a fifty-one-acre plaza where visitors could park their recreational vehicles for $10 a night. Every day the lot was packed with more than 400 RVs parked door-to-door.

If anybody in the early 1980s wanted a peek at the future of American gambling, this was it. By grinding down low rollers, Bennett and Pennington had built what is still one of the most consistently profitable companies in the casino business. For years, "grind joints" was the industry term for cheap, often tawdry roadside casinos that offered low-stakes play with horrible odds. Slowly, but surely, patrons of these clubs were ground down, perhaps losing only $5 or $10. They never lost the tens of thousands, or occasionally hundreds of thousands, a high roller might drop in a sitting. But statistically, the low rollers were a more reliable gold mine. For one thing, they rarely, if ever, won big sums, while high rollers sometimes stung a casino for a huge amount of money (although most inevitably would lose it again later on). So anyone managing a high-roller business had to contend with the volatility, and the consequent unpredictability of earnings, that came with that territory. For another thing, the universe of high rollers was a small one. Low rollers were everywhere.

Circus Circus was nothing more than a grand, family-friendly grind joint that could process low rollers through its casino in numbers that small, roadside grind joints only dreamed about. In proving that low rollers were the most lucrative chunk of the casino business, Circus Circus set in motion a gradual eclipse of the high-roller business on the Strip.

Caesars' lesson—build a unique, out-of-this-world resort and, if it's run well, people will be pounding on your door—wouldn't be forgotten. But Caesars' high concept for high rollers would be applied in a variety of different settings, all built on the steady flow of low-roller business that Circus Circus first exploited. Table games would increasingly be shunted to the sides of the casino floor to make room for slot machines. And slot machines, performing like the effective little cash registers they were, reeled in low rollers in such vast numbers that Las Vegas built some of the most mammoth facilities in the world to accommodate them. In turn, gamblers crowded the slot machines like so many patients in a hospital ward, tethered for hours to their intravenous feeders.

THE SLOTS TAKE OVER

"Slot machines aren't intimidating [to gamblers] because they're a bit mindless," observes Bud Russell, the recently retired chief executive of slot machine giant International Game Technology. "From a business standpoint, the ideal casino is a slot house."

Charles Fey, a thirty-seven-year-old German immigrant and mechanic, invented the modern three-wheel slot machine in a San Francisco machine shop in 1899. Other, simpler versions of gambling machines already existed, but Fey perfected the technology. He named his creation the Liberty Bell. Unlike its predecessors, which required an attendant to open the machine and pay off any jackpots, the Liberty Bell paid out immediately into a small dish in the base of the machine. Fast payouts made the machine a hit in local taverns, where about 3,000 slot machines were already operating prior to the advent of the Liberty Bell.

Fey's Liberty Bells accepted nickels and had a maximum payoff of $1. He made only a hundred of them, and he tried to guard them by leasing them to bars. "He was a manufacturer but he didn't want to sell his machines to other people because they were so lucrative to operate and you couldn't patent them," says Fey's grandson, Marshall Fey. "Then a company in Chicago just stole one of the machines out of a bar in San Francisco and started making copies."

Even with poachers stealing his devices, Fey went on to make a smorgasbord of other slot machines until he was eighty-two. "The games he built were all mechanical until the electronic age changed the machine," Marshall Fey adds.

The electronic age did more than change the machine, however. It changed the whole makeup of modern casino gambling. In the 1950s and 1960s, about 75 percent of a casino's win came from table games and 25 percent from slot machines. Those figures are almost inverted in Nevada now, with 62 percent or $4.4 billion in 1995, of the state's casino win coming from slot machines. Casino executives say some nominally high-roller resorts, such as Caesars, already derive about two-thirds of their revenue from slot machines, and the pressure to make room for more slot machines will only continue to grow. The idea that brawny old Caesars could generate more than 65 percent of its revenue from slots was unthinkable in the 1960s. There were 90,612 slot machines in Nevada's casinos in 1985. Ten years later there were 160,083. As other states have legalized gambling, slot machines (which include video poker and blackjack machines) have grown to be Nevada's largest export product.

Slots were banned in most states, including California, starting in 1909. Over the next few decades, politicians would stage periodic raids on illegal slot arcades, taking sledgehammers to the machines, but such grandstanding did little to slow the proliferation of the devices. Illegal manufacturers still abound, particularly in Arizona and Tennessee; some of them are the most vicious operators in the gambling business, relying on brute force and intimidation to sell their wares. Many have organized-crime ties, and law enforcement officials say jukebox and vending machine companies have historically been fronts for illegal slot machine distributors.

Nevada, of course, provided a refuge for slot manufacturers when it legalized gambling in 1931. Slot machine technology evolved slowly from the days of Charles Fey, changing slightly in the mid-1960s when Bally Manufacturing introduced electronic circuitry that allowed bettors to deposit more than one coin at a time and so play for larger jackpots. Circus Circus began demonstrating the might of slot machines in the mid-1970s and by the late 1970s, when play on $1 slots surpassed 25-cent machines in profitability, other Nevada casinos started paying attention. In 1983, slot revenue surpassed table game revenue for the first time in Nevada.

Then came the computer microchip, allowing for more combinations of winning numbers, video poker machines, and "linked progressive" jackpots. Linked progressives, introduced by International Game Technology, link jackpots at the company's "Megabucks" machines in casinos all over the state. Just as in a lottery, Megabucks jackpots keep growing larger until someone wins. And just as in a lottery, the chances of winning stink.

Anyone dumping a quarter into a linked progressive slot machine is going to lose about $10 of every $100 they bet, because the machines typically retain about 10 percent of the money dumped into them. On other slot machines, the house edge can be as high as 20 percent or as low as 3 percent. By comparison, roulette, itself a bad bet, has a house edge of 5.3 percent, the most oppressive edge of any classic table game but hardly a match for the edge the house can gain with a slot machine.

Despite these horrendous odds, slots still draw gamblers—particularly the middle-aged and senior citizens—like magnets. Las Vegas likes to market itself as a destination for thirty-somethings and their kids, but the city's Convention and Visitors Authority says that the median age of its gamblers is forty-six years old; 44 percent of the visitors are fifty or older, and 18 percent are sixty-five or older. A visitor to the Strip sees far more gray-haired fanny-packers than the town's advertising would suggest. As Glenn Schaeffer, president of Circus Circus says, Las Vegas' clientele "skews old."

The Imperial Palace runs one of the most cavernous casinos on the Strip, an uninspired vault that is usually teeming with senior citizens. On a recent afternoon there, a group of seniors in baseball caps and polyester were gathered around a bank of slot machines to play in the casino's daily slot contest, Wild Times.

No question, they were having fun. "Come on Emmy, red, white, and, blue. Red, white, and, blue," they cheered loudly, invoking the color combinations that would allow Emmy to tame those Wild Times. Yet farther back in the casino, rows of elderly gamblers sat listlessly in front of the slots, repeatedly tugging at the handles, barely acknowledging payoffs, blankly dumping quarter after quarter into the machines.

Ralph Engelstad owns the Imperial Palace, and the casino's success has turned the former construction man into a multimillionaire. A big draw at his establishment is an automobile museum that houses one of Adolf Hitler's staff cars, a gleaming reminder that Engelstad was fined $1.1 million by Nevada casino regulators in 1989 for using his casino to throw birthday parties honoring Hitler. Engelstad had ordered bumper stickers emblazoned with the motto "Hitler Was Right," and served a cake decorated with a red-and-black swastika. His collection of Nazi memorabilia included a life-sized portrait of Hitler, inscribed "To Ralphie from Adolf," as well as a portrait of Engelstad in a Nazi uniform, inscribed "To Adolf from Ralphie."

Engelstad apologized profusely at the time he was fined, saying he was just trying to liven his parties up a bit. "I've always tried to give them a theme to make them more fun," he said. "It's clear that my historical interests were channeled in a direction of very poor taste."

Engelstad and his competitors have benefited from advances in slot technology that allow them to track players electronically, telling the house such things as how much a bettor has wagered and the size of the last bet. Dollar-bill acceptors have increased the volume of play, and casinos are looking forward to the day when more patrons are comfortable sticking a plastic debit card into the machines, allowing for even faster wagering. In the quest to get cash into gamblers' hands more quickly, automated teller machines that players use to draw on their bank accounts and credit cards have become commonplace in casinos. To do its part in helping to stoke gambling fever, tax preparation giant H&R Block briefly set up shop in four Nevada casinos a few years ago and offered gamblers tax-refund "anticipation loans" that could keep them on the merry path of wagering even if their cash ran out.

Casinos also have begun marketing to slot players in a way that used to be reserved for high rollers. This includes slot clubs, which offer membership cards and casino "comps" such as free food and drink for joining. When members insert their cards into the slot machines, a computer readout tells the casino data such as which machine the bettor likes to play, what her name is, how much money she usually wagers, her birthday, names of family members, and a favorite drink or cocktail.

Casinos say such tools allow them to serve gamblers better by allowing the casino to offer all the perks that tell a slot player that this isn't just a place to gamble, it's a place where they're loved. But, just as frequent-flyer programs promote loyalty to an airline, the slot clubs also encourage a gambler to remain faithful to a particular casino. Casinos have also been known to ventilate their gambling halls with various scents to see if the exotic aromas encourage more betting. They also experiment regularly with different colors of glass on slot machines, to see which colors entice the most bettors.

Perhaps today's most prototypical Las Vegas casino is Palace Station. Located not on the famous Strip, but off a nearby highway, it approximates Bud Russell's vision of the "ideal casino." Palace Station's casino is 84,000 square feet filled with thousands of slot machines. It is a favorite of local players, who prefer to avoid the touristy Strip, and these gamblers helped drive parent company Station Casinos' total revenue to $293 million in fiscal 1995, up from $169.5 million a year earlier.

Yet in its resolute devotion to extracting cash, there is a morose hollowness to Palace Station. It houses a large bingo room inhabited by the most senior of senior citizens, a cadre of milky-skinned gnomes dutifully filling in their cards. Palace Station's casino also has banks of video poker machines, which many local gamblers prefer to slot machines because there's a very small house edge in video poker if the machines are played correctly. In some cases, good video poker players actually have an edge over the house. For most, though, the machines are losers.

Frances Fox, a fifty-eight-year-old room clerk at the Luxor, used to visit Palace Station about three times a week to play video poker for a couple of hours, wagering (and usually losing) about $40 each time. "I only play video poker because you can pretend like you're thinking," she said. Her children urged her to stop gambling because she occasionally bounced checks, something that never happened in Illinois, where she lived before moving to Las Vegas in 1990.

"Once you win, you're stuck because you think you're gonna win again. And if you lose, you want to make it up."

Fox, who once thought she'd never ease off of the video poker machines, slowed the pace down in 1997 because of a "bill problem" and "two new grandchildren" who occupied more of her time.

"I'm a reformed woman. Gambling is not my bad thing anymore. It only took me six years to kick the habit."

"THERE ARE NO SUCKERS IN A CASINO"

Steve Wynn, the impresario of Mirage Resorts and the most influential figure in the modern casino business, brooks no ridicule of his slot machine "customers." Poster boy for the gambling industry at a time when its march across the country has ignited a bitter public debate about its social and economic impact, Wynn grows progressively more animated when discussing gambling's merits.

"I tell you that there are no suckers in a casino. . . . It implies ignorance, and more importantly it implies that there's a predator involved, which has to be me," he says. "All you've got to do is find one customer at the Mirage who can't tell you what the house percentage is against him, find one person there who's there to make a living, who thinks that they can win in the casino as a matter of fact as opposed to being pure luck. . . . These people are here for diversion."

True, the majority of Las Vegas' gamblers are there for diversion. But it's also true that casinos draw substantial portions of their revenue from heavy bettors who patronize slots and low-stake table games with a devotion that goes beyond mere diversion. Conventional wisdom has it that compulsive gamblers—those hooked on gambling just as other people are hooked on nicotine, heroin, or alcohol—make up about 5 percent of the adult population, or about 10 million people, with about 1 percent of the compulsive population being active gamblers at any given time. A Harvard Medical School study released at the end of 1997 indicated that in the United States and Canada about 1.14 percent of the adult population and 5.77 percent of youths were active compulsive gamblers. The same study found that 1.6 percent of adults and 3.88 percent of youths had been compulsive gamblers at some point in their lives. Problem gamblers—those who regularly wager beyond their means but aren't addicted—make up a larger portion of gamblers. The Harvard study found that 2.8 percent of adults and 14.82 percent of adolescents were active problem gamblers, while 3.85 percent of adults and 9.45 percent of youths were problem gamblers at some point in their lives. Moreover, the study found that gambling disorders have been increasing in the United States and Canada over the last two decades.

Both compulsive and problem gamblers contribute significantly to the gambling industry's revenue. How significantly? It's hard to measure precisely.

Jeffrey Lowenhar, marketing director at the Hilton, says that about 30 percent of casino revenue in Las Vegas comes from just 10 percent to 20 percent of the gamblers. The Mirage and a few other casinos that cater to high rollers snag an even larger percentage of their revenue from an even smaller, and far wealthier, group. Lowenhar says 95 percent of the Hilton's revenue comes from just 2 percent of its gamblers. But casinos like the Mirage and the Hilton are statistical anomalies. Most casinos don't have the facilities or resources to go after the narrow and lucrative high-roller market. Another obstacle to clearly analyzing gambling habits is that the only gamblers who can be observed in large numbers are those who have been captured by the casinos' marketing databases. There are many gamblers who haven't signed up for the casinos' gratuities and thus cannot be reliably tracked. Furthermore, the major Strip casinos in Las Vegas now draw half their revenue from noncasino activities such as rooms, shows, and food.

The composition of casino revenue is clearer in markets that don't enjoy Las Vegas' resort trappings. In Atlantic City and the newer riverboat markets that depend on gamblers who make day trips, executives say a mere 20 percent of the gamblers deliver a whopping 80 percent of the revenue. This is a crucial ratio, which often gets lost when gambling is looked at as just another benign form of popular recreation. For within that vital segment of heavy bettors whose losses drive the casinos' revenue are a large number of compulsive and problem gamblers.

Frank Fahrenkopf, head of the American Gaming Association, an industry trade group, disputes the idea that compulsive and problem gamblers prop up casino revenue. Casinos "don't target compulsives. They are targeting repeat customers. This is a very competitive business," says Fahrenkopf. "People can't continue gambling if they are compulsives. They eventually lose all of their money."

Compulsives, of course, have found myriad ways, including theft, to raise gambling funds once their cash runs out. And there is good reason to believe that compulsive and problem gambling is a bigger revenue source than the industry cares to acknowledge.

"My concern is that this is not a minor issue on the revenue side," says William Eadington, an economics professor at the University of Nevada at Reno and a leading authority on gambling. "I think if you restrain people who are compulsive or problem gamblers it would have a very significant impact on the revenue" of casinos.

Although the vast majority of people who gamble do it for fun, compulsive gambling represents an ethical dilemma for the casino industry. Since large chunks of casino revenue are built on the losses of a relatively small portion of gamblers, and since problem or compulsive gamblers are likely to make up a sizable portion of the heavy losers, there is a serious question about the extent to which casinos thrive on the addictions of such gamblers—profiting, in essence, from a crippling human weakness.

Nonetheless, Wynn scoffs at the notion that gambling encourages people to blindly throw their money away. "Are we suggesting that our love affair with consumerism in America is all based upon real products filling a real need? Or is something else going on—people giving themselves something that they want, that they don't need, but they want?

The idea that you can dictate how people should dispose of their income is ridiculous. And to suggest that betting on a football game or the outcome of a turn of a card is inherently immoral is preposterous."

THE RISE AND RISE OF STEVE WYNN

Volatile, vindictive, charismatic, and smart as a whip, the fifty-four-year-old Wynn is responsible for helping to revive Las Vegas at a time when many had written it off as a dead market. He understands every facet of the gambling business and is considered by analysts and peers to be the finest casino operator in the country. He has entered and exited gambling markets with perfect timing, and he has introduced a level of sophistication into the design and operation of gambling resorts that has yet to be matched.

Gambling is now perceived as a more gentrified pastime than ever before, and the quality of the properties Wynn has developed has played a large role in shaping that perception. Wynn is master of a Las Vegas that now boasts twelve of the world's thirteen largest hotels, greets 28 million visitors annually, and on any given month in 1995 hosted gamblers losing $333 million to $430 million in its casinos.

Wynn says he got hooked on Las Vegas as a ten-year-old boy taking business trips there with his father, an East Coast bingo parlor operator who was a compulsive gambler. After his father died in 1963, Wynn took over the family's bingo operation in Maryland. Bored, he departed for Las Vegas three years later.

Wynn entered the casino business in 1967, when he bought 3 percent of the Frontier casino for $45,000 and became its slots manager. The Frontier was controlled by Detroit mobsters at the time, although Wynn says he got his stake in the casino through a banker named John MacArthur. But Wynn's mentor, Parry Thomas, says Wynn got his spot in the Frontier through the efforts of an individual named Maurice Friedman. Friedman was a ubiquitous Las Vegas operator who was named as a front man for the mob in a federal complaint filed in Michigan. A spokesman for Wynn says Thomas wasn't "recollecting that detail properly" and that "Friedman had nothing to do with the Frontier." Three months after Wynn invested in the Frontier it was seized by regulators because of its organized-crime ties and sold to Howard Hughes. Wynn was never charged with any wrongdoing in the incident.

Parry Thomas, then the most powerful banker in Las Vegas, represented Hughes. Thomas controlled Valley Bank, one of the earliest lenders to the casino industry, and from that perch he became a king-maker in Nevada. One of the keys to Valley Bank's growth was its role as a conduit for Teamster loans, a fact that Thomas never disguised, although it earned him the title of "hoodlum banker" during Las Vegas' early years.

"I've got to see that this community stays healthy," Thomas once said. "I'll take dollars from the devil himself if it's legal—and I don't mean anything disparaging toward the Teamsters by that."

Thomas' ties to Las Vegas insiders ensured that over the years Valley Bank's fortunes grew. In 1992, Thomas sold the bank to San Francisco behemoth BankAmerica Corporation in a $460 million stock swap, making him one of BankAmerica's largest shareholders. Through it all, Thomas was orchestrating young Steve Wynn's ascent in Las Vegas.

The pair met during the Frontier debacle, after which Thomas helped Wynn take control of a liquor distributor. Eventually, Thomas also helped Wynn gain control of the Golden Nugget, a sagging downtown casino that Wynn had begun buying shares of in 1969.

Flexing his ample political muscles, Thomas had helped push through a state law in 1969 allowing publicly traded companies to own Nevada casinos without having to submit to background checks on investors who held less than 5 percent of the company's shares. That same year, Continental Connector, a publicly traded company presided over by none other than Parry Thomas, agreed to take over the Golden Nugget.

Continental had a checkered history. It already owned the Dunes casino and had several Mob associates among its executives and investors. One of these was Morris Shenker, an attorney who represented Jimmy Hoffa; Shenker owned about 40 percent of Continental's stock. Continental had repeatedly come under SEC and IRS scrutiny regarding questionable uses of cash from the Dunes cage and other evidence of skimming. Because of such abuses, the company's shares were eventually delisted from the American Stock Exchange.

Shortly after Continental agreed to buy the Nugget, the SEC blocked the deal, citing Continental for issuing "false and misleading financial information" about its revenue and earnings. A few weeks later, in early 1970, Golden Nugget called off the Continental merger.

But Wynn continued buying Golden Nugget stock, becoming one of the casino's largest shareholders. Wynn says that he made his original purchase without knowing of Continental Connector's plans, and he continued accumulating shares after Continental's deal fell apart. He says he was not fronting for the Continental group or Thomas when he made his later stock purchases, although Thomas was instrumental in getting Wynn a seat on the Nugget's board of directors in 1973.

Prior to Wynn's arrival, the Nugget was poorly run. Wynn, who says he discovered that many at the Nugget were stealing money from the casino, told fellow board members that he would sue the company for mismanagement unless changes were made. In 1973, at the tender age of thirty-one, Wynn took control of the entire operation.

Over the next several years, spending lavishly, he transformed the Golden Nugget into the only elegant casino in the downtown area. Then, just when some thought he had dangerously overextended his finances revamping the Nugget, Wynn set his sights on the new East Coast mecca of Atlantic City. In 1980, with financing from a then relatively obscure Drexel Burnham Lambert junk-bond guru named Michael Milken, he opened a Golden Nugget casino there, on the site of a former motel he had bought two years earlier for $8.5 million. The Atlantic City property was a hit; in 1987, Bally Manufacturing, facing takeover pressure, bought it for a whopping $140 million in cash and stock and the transfer of a $299 million mortgage.

Wynn now says the $439 million package Bally paid him was about $100 million more than he believed the Atlantic City Nugget was worth. He also says he was ready to leave Atlantic City because he was having trouble expanding there and the market had begun to stall. His timing was excellent: he left Atlantic City just before the casino business there went into a tailspin. And he returned to Las Vegas when that town was still stumbling from a gambling recession and struggling with the perception that it couldn't grow anymore with Atlantic City gambling now in the picture. Two years later Wynn would open the Mirage, his signature casino.

Wynn's rise has not been entirely untrammeled. In several instances, organized-crime figures have been uncomfortably close to his organization.

In 1983, New Jersey regulators criticized the Atlantic City Nugget for extending credit to Nicky Scarfo, head of Philadelphia's Scarfo-Bruno crime family, even when the Nugget knew that Scarfo was gambling under an alias to avoid detection. The Atlantic City Nugget's second-largest shareholder, Edward Doumani, was forced to sell his 5.2 percent stake in the casino in 1984 because he, as casino regulators described it, "repeatedly and consistently associated himself with organized crime figures and other unsavory or notorious persons." Regulators also said Doumani had helped Joey Cusumano, an associate of Chicago and New York mobsters, get a job as a baccarat dealer at the Las Vegas Nugget. And Mel Harris, marketing chief of the Atlantic City Nugget, was forced to resign in 1986 after it was revealed that in 1984 he had met twice with Genovese crime family chieftain Anthony "Fat Tony" Salerno.

Wynn, thumping his fist on his desk, says he has never had personal contact with mobsters in his entire career. "I have never met or had any contact with a hoodlum, personal contact, in my life, either directly, through intermediaries, over the telephone, by carrier pigeon, by semaphore signals, in any way," he says. "To the extent that Joe Schmo, who was not on the excluded list, played craps at the Golden Nugget and I was there with Frank Sinatra and they came to a high-roller party, I may have been in the same room. But I, Steve Wynn, have never met or had anything to do with a hoodlum."

Wynn's assertion is vouched for by casino regulators in Nevada and New Jersey, who, after lengthy investigations, say they have never found any evidence suggesting that Wynn is a Mob associate. Las Vegas as a whole is now considered largely free of Mob control, although regulators say there is still a presence in the junket business and among some casino suppliers.

"I think it's premature to pronounce the Mob dead [in Las Vegas], but it's certainly no longer at the core and probably only exists at the periphery," says Bill Bible, chairman of Nevada's Gaming Commission. "We now concentrate a lot of our work on financial issues such as capitalization and managerial experience."

Through government approval and the spread of gambling nationwide, Las Vegas' reputation has been sanitized to such a degree that large, publicly traded corporations such as ITT and Hilton are proud to have a piece of the action. Las Vegas, its boosters now claim, is not just a gambling resort. It's an entertainment center, and casinos say people come for the food, the shows, the shopping, the happy feeling of it all.

Before the Mirage opened, in 1989, few operators besides Steve Wynn foresaw this turnaround. The downturn in Las Vegas during the 1980s had been so severe that in 1986 the *Las Vegas Review-Journal* cited a state study revealing that thirty of the state's ninety-five casinos were losing money. During this slump, Wynn began planning the 3,000-room Mirage, a $565 million project on eighty-five acres next to Caesars that he financed in part with his windfall from the sale of the Atlantic City Nugget. The Mirage would be the biggest resort ever built on the Strip, and the first new casino there in fifteen years. Critics quickly labeled it too big to survive.

Indeed, the financials were daunting. The parent company, Golden Nugget (later renamed Mirage Resorts), floated $540 million in junk bonds through Milken's network to build the Mirage. Prior to the casino's opening, the parent company's debt had climbed to $900 million, or 88 percent of its capital base, and the Mirage needed to pull in revenue of $1 million a day just to break even. Caesars was the only resort in town that had approached that number.

But the resort's construction and finances were meticulously planned. Wynn's team got hold of the financials for Caesars, the MGM Grand, and the Las Vegas Hilton, and then analyzed the performance of those properties. They also analyzed hotel occupancy patterns in two 2,800-room hotels. Las Vegas hotels have astoundingly high occupancy rates, regularly topping 90 percent—the industry average is about 65 percent—but that is achieved by maintaining rock-bottom prices. Wynn projected full occupancy for the Mirage, but he planned on charging premium prices for its rooms—unheard-of in Las Vegas.

Construction costs at the twenty-nine-story resort ultimately ballooned to $620 million. But the money bought something that hadn't been seen on the Strip before. The Mirage was not designed to appeal to hardcore, male gamblers, as Caesars had been, although it embraced Caesars' penchant for over-the-top fantasy. Nor was it designed only to target low rollers, as Circus Circus had been, although it had a healthy respect for the less well-heeled. The Mirage was designed to appeal to men and women who wanted to go on vacation, and who didn't necessarily consider themselves gamblers.

Wynn's design team had looked at five-star hotels all over the world and decided to model the Mirage on tropical resorts they had visited on Maui. Before construction began, Wynn's architects built miniature scale models of the resort and examined them through periscopes, taking photographs so they could determine what visitors' perspectives would be as they wandered around. The Mirage's colors were bright pastels, unlike the dark red and black of Caesars' interior. The casino wasn't visible from the entrance, as it was at most other gambling resorts, but was preceded by a "living lobby," a massive atrium filled with tropical plants and trees. A 20,000-gallon aquarium, home to several sharks, was installed behind the registration desk. A dolphin tank was near the pool, white tigers roamed behind a glass wall near the lobby, and a forty-foot volcano erupted every fifteen minutes in front of the resort. All the rooms and attractions were designed with the tropical theme in mind so the Mirage would always be, in the words of its creators, "in costume."

And tourists came in droves.

THE MIRAGE AND THE NEW VEGAS

The Mirage arrived at the right time. Public attitudes toward gambling had softened. Widespread participation in state lotteries had undercut the popular perception of gambling as a vice; the number of retirees with extra money to spend was growing; and baby boomers were allotting a bigger portion of their budget to entertainment than had previous generations. Wynn understood that the way to attract those boomer dollars was to cloak gambling in the happy robes of entertainment rather than in the smoky, illicit garb of an overblown gin joint.

In 1990, after its first full year of operation, the Mirage had raked in $409 million in revenue, or about $1.12 million a day. The resort's cash flow, which measures a company's earnings before interest, depreciation, and taxes are deducted, soared to $201 million in 1991, a record for an individual casino. By 1995, the Mirage had revenue of $790 million, or $2.16 million a day, and cash flow of $229 million.

Those figures weren't generated just by gambling. The Mirage also housed five restaurants, a health spa and beauty salon, an upscale shopping arcade, and a huge showroom. Almost half of the Mirage's revenue now comes from noncasino sources, such as food, lodging, and entertainment, all areas other casinos once considered money losers that merely helped funnel traffic toward the casino. The Mirage upped the ante, demonstrating that people would pay top dollar for lodging and entertainment in Las Vegas if those goodies were presented in an attractive package.

The money that poured into the Mirage allowed it to quickly begin retiring its massive debt and to finance expansion with its own funds or through cheap lines of bank credit. And the success of the Mirage and of Circus Circus' Excalibur, a mammoth Camelot knockoff that opened a little later than the Mirage, inspired a subsequent burst of local construction. This second wave of building resulted in the pyramid-shaped Luxor, Wynn's own Treasure Island, and the 5,000-room MGM Grand, a vast, impersonal, emerald-green warehouse that proved a nightmare to operate.

Buoyed by the glowing publicity Las Vegas subsequently received, the casinos began to aim their marketing toward children in order to coax their parents to the country's newest family resort. This effort ultimately faltered when it became apparent that all the lures built for kids, from roller coasters to theme parks, weren't paying off. But Las Vegas was back, brought to you now in cheery, gentle tones by showmen such as Steve Wynn. Not that some of Las Vegas' other draws ever departed, even as the casinos began hitting the family-friendly high notes. Every day in the middle of the Strip, display racks and handbills advertise such lures as "Totally Nude Adult Entertainment Lesbian Shows" (for the man "who keeps his boots on") and phone numbers of women like "Michelle," who is "18, fresh out of school, and ready to make you drooool."

Yet the new Las Vegas is the one tourists see. For residents, the city has always been a little different. The entertainment and recreation industries are components of the service economy being heralded as a replacement for America's old industrial network. A preview of one way that transition is shaping up is on display in Las Vegas.

Hundreds of thousands of new jobs have been created in Las Vegas since the end of World War II. The city's population surged to 1.6 million in 1996, up from 465,000 in 1980. Comfortable, tidy residential areas have sprung up around Las Vegas, but the fastest-growing city in the United States also has to contend with its own unique set of problems. Although retirees have been a key component of the city's population growth, many of those who have recently relocated there—about 70 percent, according to some studies—are people who have fled the economic downturn that beset California during the 1980s and early 1990s. Desperate for a job and with little money in their pockets, they don't tend to stay very long. The annual turnover rate in most casinos, where managers say the yearly wage for most jobs is $15,000 to $18,000, is a lofty 48 percent. Pawnshops in Las Vegas are open twenty-four hours a day; if you're really desperate for cash, the shops will even take your car.

Municipal planning in Las Vegas, except for airport expansions, has always been scattershot. The schools are overcrowded and the dropout rate is high, traffic is congested, and alarms are regularly sounded about the quantity and quality of the city's water supply. An arid desert is hardly the most hospitable location for people, golf courses, or elaborate fountains, and there are concerns that boomtown Las Vegas will test the limit of its water supply early in the next century. Abnormally high rates of juvenile delinquency have plagued the city since the 1960s, and local police say Las Vegas is home to some one hundred street gangs, 4,000 members strong. Well-organized gangs from Los Angeles, drawn to the loot floating around the casinos, have arrived in town and the rate of violent crime—homicide, rape, and the like—is soaring.

Moreover, according to a study conducted in 1995 by the U.S. Centers for Disease Control and Prevention, Nevada boasts the highest suicide rate in the country. The state is currently studying whether this remarkable statistic is due to reporting differences compared with other states, or to other factors such as financial hardship caused by gambling losses. Another 1997 study, which showed higher personal bankruptcy rates in locations with more than one gambling facility, noted that Nevada's personal bankruptcy rate was 50 percent higher than that in the rest of the nation.

Compulsive gambling by Las Vegas residents, which dealers and waiters say they see all the time in local casinos, is largely ignored by the casino owners. While one local health care official estimates that 12 percent of the city's population has a compulsive-gambling problem, no entirely reliable statistics on compulsive gambling in Nevada are available. This is because, until very recently, neither the state nor the casinos have ever bothered to study the problem. To do so would have meant acknowledging its extent—and in Nevada, gambling capital of the country, that's a no-no.

Despite its social problems, Las Vegas continues to grow. Although land sells for $1 million to $2 million an acre on the Strip, another extraordinary wave of building has begun, led by Mirage, Circus Circus, and others. More than 10,000 hotel rooms will be added to the city's stockpile over the next few years, pushing the total past 100,000 and igniting renewed concerns that casino companies are overbuilding. Some casino companies will stumble or fail. But barring the legalization of casino gambling in California, whose population is still Nevada's lifeblood, gambling in Las Vegas will continue to thrive.

♦ ♣ ♥ ♠

In a sign of how sanitized Las Vegas' image has become since Moe Dalitz ran things, Mirage Resorts was anointed by *Fortune* magazine in 1997 as the second most admired company in the United States, after Coca-Cola. Possessed of a finer aptitude for reading consumer demand than it once had, Las Vegas has turned the mall at Caesars Palace into, per square foot, the highest-grossing shopping center in the world.

The Mirage and its competitors peddle the illusion that a trip to Las Vegas is primarily about spectacle; if visitors happen to want to gamble, the casinos are waiting. But attempts by well-run Las Vegas companies to build dazzling family attractions have fallen flat, because casinos are not merely secondary elements of Las Vegas' appeal. Nor will they ever be. Casinos remain the heartbeat, the raison d'être, for everything that has grown in Nevada's sand. That won't change, even for the Mirage. Commonly perceived as a high roller's paradise, the Mirage relies heavily on the slot crowd—just like every other operator.

"There's a lot of wealthy people in this world, and the Mirage knows how to cater to them," says Steve Eisenberg, a casino analyst with the investment firm Oppenheimer & Company. "But it's the fanny-packers, Mr. and Mrs. Middle America, that is the audience the casinos are after. Even Steve Wynn." Since the day the Mirage opened its doors, two-thirds of its gambling revenue has come from slot machines, with only a third coming from table games.

To be sure, the dominance of slot machines hasn't meant that high rollers are no longer important in Las Vegas. Baccarat has emerged as the most lucrative niche in Las Vegas' high-roller market, though only a few casinos in town, including the Mirage, Caesars, Hilton, the MGM Grand, and the Desert Inn, have the wherewithal to compete for the players. The game, derived from one introduced to France from Italy in the middle of the fifteenth century, has always drawn wealthy players from "hot" economies. In the 1970s, the baccarat enthusiasts were the scions of oil money from the Middle East or Mexico; in the 1980s they were Japanese industrialists. Now players from the Pacific Rim, particularly Taiwan, Singapore, Malaysia, Hong Kong, and Indonesia, dominate the baccarat tables.

Baccarat players enjoy the most exceptional comps extended to Las Vegas' gamblers, including free jet service, limousines, deluxe lodging, private chefs, and other forms of pampering. Demand for these big spenders is so strong that some casinos have taken to offering them 15 percent discounts on their markers—money they still owe the casino— in exchange for their continued patronage. Baccarat pits are usually roped off and come with a private dining room and bathroom. Top-flight baccarat players will sometimes play for $250,000 per hand, and the potential gain to casinos from these players is huge. Hilton spent $40 million building three lavish villas for the exclusive use of its biggest baccarat players and their retinues. The villas were opened in early 1995, and Hilton says the $40 million expenditure was paid off six months later from the casino's baccarat winnings.

Such stakes, and the flaunting of great wealth, have surrounded baccarat with an air of glamour. It is, after all, the casino game preferred by James Bond. But the card game is as simple and as brainless as slots. It is dealt by one player out of an eight-deck "shoe," with two two-card hands being dealt. The gambler holding the shoe is the "bank" and the other gambler is the "player." All gamblers at the table, as many as fifteen, bet against the casino as to which hand, the bank or the player, will come closest to adding up to nine. The value of tens and face cards is zero. If two cards equal more than 9, then 10 is subtracted from the total, so, for example, a 7 and an 8 equal 5. There's nothing more to it than that.

In baccarat, the casino has a tiny edge on both the bank's hands and the players', and a lofty 14 percent edge on ties. It also pads its cut of the action by charging a 5 percent commission on winning bank wagers. But casinos can be badly burned by a lucky baccarat player, specifically one who makes big bets, wins, and then leaves the table quickly. Casino executives say that Australian media kingpin Kerry Packer won more than $25 million playing baccarat at the MGM Grand between 1993 and 1995. ITT, trying to draw more baccarat action to the Desert Inn, expanded its credit lines and raised its table limits in 1995. The strategy was successful that year, but in 1996 the casino got burned, according to individuals familiar with the Desert Inn's baccarat pit. Gamblers like Packer, known for short, high-stakes bursts of play, can wreak havoc on a casino's earnings. For that reason, negotiations with a baccarat player about the size of bets and the length of play are usually, though not always, undertaken before a casino welcomes him through the door. And for that reason, boring but dependable slot machines are the bread and butter of the casino business and will continue to nourish its growth. No casino makes it on high-roller business alone anymore, not even the Mirage.

Wynn knows this, of course. His singular contribution to gambling isn't the creation of a casino that targets low rollers or a casino that targets high rollers. It's the creation of casinos that seduce both groups and suck them in off the street by offering incomparable spectacle. Wrap a casino in a fantasy, put in those slots, and open the doors. As Wynn himself says, the Mirage, at its core, is simply a "better mousetrap" than its predecessors on the Strip. And that state-of-the-art mousetrap is run by the gambling business's consummate showman, luring tourists who might have been reluctant to visit a casino only a generation before.

The Mirage's casino measures 95,500 square feet and has 2,250 slots, 118 table games, and a high-tech bookmaking operation for horse racing and sports betting. It is large, yet is designed to feel intimate. There are no big, empty spaces to look across, and much of what the eye rests upon is pleasing. But the layout is also disorienting. The tropical atrium leads visitors into the center of the resort; they leave the atrium not knowing where they are, although they wind up standing in the middle of the casino. The casino is the center of the entire resort, and everything else—shops, restaurants, and moving walkways—feeds into that center. As is in most casinos, visitors who want to get to phones, elevators, bathrooms, shows, or popular restaurants will first have to pass long banks of slot machines and table games. The configuration of the casino floor is driven by the popularity of each game, so slot machines determine the placement of everything else in the Mirage. Nickel slots, favorites of the elderly and very low-budget bettors, are stuck out of sight because gamblers who want them will always seek them out. More profitable machines, like $5 and $25 slots, are stuck right in the middle of heavy foot traffic at the Mirage.

To watch hordes of visitors wander through the Mirage is to understand how Las Vegas has learned to feed casino gambling to the masses. The Mirage may not look like a gambling joint, but cards and slots are what keep its coffers full.

"Gaming didn't become a big business until it came to Las Vegas, where it became a large, democratic entertainment experience," says Wynn. "I believe that what's been going on here, and what took gaming into the big-business category is when it started to really be the party. And that couldn't happen in a small private room in the back of a London club."

True. It could only happen in America.

Las Vegas, a city draped with apparent riches but troubled at its core, has convinced other towns across the country that casino gambling can make miracles happen. But for many reasons—its isolation, its history, its kitschy splendor—Las Vegas is inimitable. Communities that have welcomed commercial gambling for economic revival have had uneven results, but all have learned that the wagering business amounts to much more than racy diversion. They have learned what it means to hold a tiger by the tail.

The Veteran—I

Pauline Brogan is a member of that heavily populated and special class of gamblers who keep casinos in the black. She's a senior citizen and, most important, she's a regular customer. Brogan has gambled on and off for all her adult life. But now, at the age of seventy-seven, the Edison, New Jersey, resident has made gambling the centerpiece of her social calendar. She visits Atlantic City at least twice a month and is rewarded with free meals, charming gifts, and a casino hostess who treats her like an old, important friend.

Brogan says she keeps her gambling in check by paying attention to her budget and stopping if she feels she's lost too much money. Gambling hasn't caused any great tragedies in her life. It is just something she enjoys doing, something that adds spice to her twilight years. Unlike most of her friends, Brogan prefers roulette to slot machines. Roulette, she says, reminds her of church bingo.

♦ ♣ ♥ ♠

My biggest win is $1,600. I have two daughters and two granddaughters, and I play their birthdays. And I just had a great-grandson, so I've been playing his birthday number, 22, and I won all my money last time on 22. I win on 13, 17, 3, and 21.

I might borrow before I'm broke. If I'm losing, I might borrow $100 before I'm broke. . . . See, I never start with $100. I start with $40 or $50. . . . I don't start doubling up unless I start winning. If my $50's

gone, then I move to another table so I don't have a chance to lose
$100. And a lot of times, not all the time, but most of the time that you
change to another table it makes a big difference. Of course it does,
'cause each dealer spins different numbers. It's the metal of the wheel or
whatever. But I never start with $100. I always start with $40 or $50
and if that doesn't do anything I change tables. But I think it's easy to
lose a lot of money when you start with $100.

When you go there [to the casino] you forget your aches and pains.
I had a heart attack, I had angioplasty, I had open-heart surgery, I had
a severed artery, and I almost bled to death. And I thought that was the
end of my life, that I would never do anything, or enjoy anything. I find
that in Atlantic City I feel like I'm eighteen years old . . . I don't think
about anything that happened to me, the cardiac arrest—that was the
scariest thing of all, to know that you died and you came back. But at
home, a lot of times, like last winter, we had a period of January, February, March, that you couldn't get out of the house with the ice and the
snow and all. Every time I'd get a twinge or something I thought, "Oh-
oh, what's the matter?" When I go to Atlantic City I can walk.

Right now, I can't walk. I have cramps in my legs. Thank God, when
I go to Atlantic City I've never had a pain or an ache or a headache or
anything. So my doctor always tells me it's therapy. Unfortunately it
doesn't come off your insurance. But he said it's one of the most effective
means of therapy. And there are some rehabs that actually have gambling devices in the rehabs for that one purpose.

When you walk through those doors it's a luxury feeling that you
don't have unless you go to the Hyatt to a wedding. It gives you the
same feeling if you went to the Hyatt to an elaborate wedding. You
would have that feeling of being somebody special. Just the luxury of it.
It's a glamorous atmosphere. It's something that you don't live with
every day.

The only other time I had that feeling actually was when I was in the
Navy. Because, wherever you went you had the feeling of being special. . . . You'd go to pay your check and the waiter or waitress would tell
you that somebody already paid your check. And that's the feeling you
get down in Atlantic City, that you're somebody special. You forget the
ordinary, that you have dishes to wash or clothes to wash or a kitchen
floor to scrub. Since most of us don't have live-in maids or anything. You
feel special.

♦ ♣ ♥ ♠

Harrah's had not only soda, but they had apple juice and grapefruit
juice in little bottles. I always remember the first bingo I went to, I think

it was the Castle. As many cans of soda as you could [drink], you could go up and get two or three cans of soda. We were going out, this couple had, each had a canvas bag. They were going out the door, they filled the canvas bags with soda, and he had a coat and sweater on, and he had soda in his pockets. And you know, I said to my friend, how could they do that and not even feel embarrassed? . . . I hate that. I mean if you can afford to go to a casino, you can afford a case of soda. Right?

That's why I don't like "senior citizen," the words "senior citizen." It means that you're looking for something for nothing. . . . I use all of my comps. I feel that the casino, whether I win or lose, they owe me something for being a guest there. I'm a guest in their hotel. And if I get any kind of a comp, or money back . . . I use 'em all. I feel they owe me that.

It's an escape. Well, I go because I like to gamble, because if I just wanted to get away for the day, I'd just go down to the shore.

I stay up all night. I don't go to bed. . . . First of all, one of the big things other than gambling that I love is watching people. You meet all kinds of people, all types. You see people that are dressed weird, dressed beautifully, dressed sloppy. You see people that are very cultured, and you can always tell people with class. That's why I like Harrah's. Harrah's, most of the people there have class. I mean, it's not like the Boardwalk casinos. That's one of the things that makes you feel special at Harrah's.

And at night, that's when you see the interesting people, I mean the people that are sort of like you. They're up and they're walking around, and they go in for a cup of coffee. I very seldom talk to people, but every now and then somebody strikes my fancy. Oh, I don't like to talk, when I'm playing.

I go to bingo to play bingo. I hate to sit near anyone who [talks]. . . . If I feel I want a social evening I'll invite somebody to my house and say, "Let's have coffee and talk." When I go to bingo, I want to play bingo. I don't want to miss any numbers. I enjoy waiting for that next number to come up. And when I play roulette, it's the same thing. You know, I'm playing roulette, and I don't want my attention [diverted] because I like to enjoy the game.

The same number can come up at bingo three or four times. I've seen numbers come up on the wheel four times in a row. But you can't guarantee a number at all. It's actually the luck of the wheel. . . . I've played slot machines that have hit like crazy and I get back the next morning and you don't get nothing.

At Harrah's, I play the old mechanical machines, and there are only about ten left. . . . There are no old quarter slots, and no more half-dollar slots. There are just a few of the old dollar ones. Because they hit.

I hate the computerized. I always make sure that I spend $40 on the progressive [slot machine]. I always figure if you're meant to hit it, you'll hit it on the first $20, or the first $30, and if you spend more than $40 on it then forget it.

♦ ♣ ♥ ♠

A lot of people say, "I hate Atlantic City." I love it. I'd go every day if I could.

I'm not a day person. I'm a night person. And I love playing. I never go to bingo during the day. As much as I love bingo, bingo is not my thing during the day. Atlantic City is not my thing during the day.

Gambling in the old days was a social thing. They had bridge clubs. It was social. They played for money, it wasn't for any exorbitant amount. The men played differently. The men played for blood, but not women in those days. I keep thinking about my mother. She wasn't a gambler, she really didn't even like cards. But because of my dad, and most of the people he played with were business associates, they decided that they'd like to have Saturday nights with their wives and they all loved to play cards.

And she would never play cards during the week like we do. You know, "Come on over for a game of cards." Gambling for women has sort of been elevated. Almost all women gamble today. Well, I think it changed with the casinos and the lottery. Two things sort of meshed to-gether. Even when the lottery first started, women didn't gamble like they do now. I mean, some of these people really spend a lot of money on lottery tickets. The woman you play cards with spends $48 on lottery tickets alone. She's a widow and she's eighty-six years old.

In the 1930s and 1940s, very few women gambled. . . . I don't even remember a lot of women going to the track in those days. I had a neighbor who was a regular at the track. And he was a big gambler. I don't know whether it was unladylike, it was just something that ladies didn't think of doing.

Today we're all senior citizens, and we are sort of getting to the end of things. . . . Young people don't feel like going. . . . I have a twenty-one-year-old granddaughter, and she kept on saying, "Nana, when I turn twenty-one will you take me to Atlantic City?" Just so she can see what it looks like, 'cause she's never been down there. And I said, "Mandy, you wouldn't like Atlantic City, unless we went on a Saturday night." Because you see nothing but old people. You think the whole world is made up of old people. You don't see any pretty shapely young girls walking around, during the week. Maybe one out of three hun-

dred. . . . There's no good-looking young fellows. . . . They're all old. They're walking with canes and crutches and wheelchairs, and tripods.

In fact, I get really annoyed. I almost got tripped with a tripod about three times, because they think they own the place. But the thing is, the young people today are not gamblers. I mean this is another world for them, because they have too many interesting things to do. . . . Atlantic City is not their thing except for the show and dinner. . . . Show me a senior, two seniors, that'll get all dressed up on a Saturday night and go to Broadway to a show. I don't know of anybody.

CHAPTER 3

ATLANTIC CITY:
RESORT OF BROKEN PROMISES

HANDS, FINGERS AND HANDS, hands, fingers and hands, hands, fingers and hands.

They can move around a card table as nimbly as those of a concert pianist, as precisely as the talons of a falcon. They carefully flip cards, allowing the eyes to see and the mind to calculate, determining the stakes in one of the gambling world's most ruthless, closely fought contests: the daily confrontation between a casino, its blackjack dealers, and professional card counters.

Card counters are players who secure an edge by tracking the value of cards dealt and remaining in a blackjack deck. They often work in teams and, with paramilitary precision, have been mounting assaults against casinos for years. And casinos, deploying sophisticated ceiling cameras capable of minutely scrutinizing the action at any table in the house, have responded in a variety of ways. Sometimes dealers are instructed to shuffle the decks so frequently that card counting is next to impossible. Sometimes card counters are dragged into back rooms and viciously beaten.

Each side enters the fray in deadly seriousness, because the outcome determines who is in charge, who wins, who keeps the cash. It is a battle waged between those who have the money and those who haven't, between companies that have mastered the art of separating gamblers from their dollars and individuals bent on outwitting large, seemingly invulnerable institutions on their own turf. It is the age-old struggle between the bank and those who want to break the bank.

But card counting represents that rare occasion in legalized gambling when the edge sometimes falls to the bettor rather than to the house. If top-notch card counters play their cards right and have a bankroll large enough to absorb a string of sizable losses, they can take a casino for hundreds of thousands of dollars in a single sitting. Card counters like Tom Hyland, considered by his colleagues to be one of the best blackjack players in the world, are known to work with as many as thirty-five or forty team members, playing off $1 million to $2 million bankrolls. Hyland's presence in a casino can send shivers down the spines of managers anxiously guarding their vaults. Atlantic City's Claridge Casino Hotel, for one, has compiled a thick dossier on Hyland and various members of his team in an effort to track their activities.

"Aliases and deception are all part of the mystic [sic] that has kept the Hyland Team one step ahead of [casinos]," the dossier states. Replete with photographs of Hyland and his cohorts, as well as descriptions of some of their techniques, the dossier is just one more piece of artillery in the card-counting wars.

"When I started out, I had always believed that casinos were glamorous and they want you to win because it's good advertising. But now I think these guys would just as soon pick people up by their ankles and shake nickels and dimes out of their pockets if they could get away with it," says the thirty-nine-year-old Hyland. "Their best policy would be to deal and stop using countermeasures, because they slow down the game. Casinos lose money when they try to stop us."

Perhaps it was inevitable that such duels would be staged in Atlantic City, a gambling town that from the get-go has been a monument to grift. More than a century ago, long before gambling became its only reason for being, Atlantic City was invented by entrepreneurs seeking to create a breezy seaside outpost for residents of nearby Philadelphia. In short order, Atlantic City also became an outdoor shopping mall, an amusement park, and a lowbrow cabaret. A launching pad for the modern preoccupation with conspicuous consumption, it was a place that "sold its wares cash-on-delivery, and the pocketbook was its only coat of arms."

And if gambling in America has evolved into the country's purest form of conspicuous consumption—because gambling's medium is money—then perhaps it was also inevitable that Atlantic City would eventually draw the likes of Donald Trump, an uncomplicated hustler whose brief heyday pumped a new level of comic vulgarity into the country's obsession with a fast buck.

THE HOT SLOT SPOT

On sultry summer days, New Jersey thoroughfares are jammed with snaking lines of traffic heading for the state's sunny beaches. Roaring southward amid the cars making this trek are armadas of buses packed with mostly elderly and middle-aged passengers who have a cooler, darker destination in mind: one of the biggest slot farms in the country, Atlantic City.

The buses will exit the Garden State Parkway, wind onto the Atlantic City Expressway, and make a beeline for a town that really isn't the "city" it has claimed to be for all these years. Smaller in size than New York's Central Park and home to only 38,000 people, Atlantic City is a little community that has only seemed bigger because the designs on it have always been larger than life.

Cruising along the Atlantic City Expressway, the buses will pass billboards promoting the best casino for winning a "Lotta Loot," the best place to indulge in "Quartermania," and the site of the "Hot Slot Spot." Passing beneath a large billboard touting Atlantic City as "America's Favorite Playground," the buses will lurch past blocks of abandoned, decrepit housing, rubble-strewn lots, and shabby stores. In short order, the buses will arrive at a wall of casinos that face the Atlantic Ocean with their concrete backs to the town.

Atlantic City has festered like an open wound in New Jersey's side for decades, a dreary testimonial to unfulfilled economic promises. New Jersey legalized casino gambling in Atlantic City in 1976 as a "unique tool of urban redevelopment," heralding gambling as a cash cow that would reverse Atlantic City's long decline and usher in an era of renewed prosperity. But, for the most part, Atlantic City has become nothing more than a large neighborhood craps game with a little more glitz and glitter thrown in, its street corners haunted by a vaudevillian past.

A small group of white people settled in the area in 1790, on territory that for centuries had been home to the Absegami Indians and after them a tribe named the Lenni-Lenape. By the middle of the nineteenth century, Absecon Island, on which Atlantic City would be built, was a steady draw for visitors seeking a break from the hot summer weather that smothered bustling nearby cities like Philadelphia.

In the early 1850s, Jonathan Pitney, a local doctor, convinced Richard Osborne, a Philadelphia engineer, to join him in an effort to link Absecon Island by rail to Camden, New Jersey, and then build a spa that would entice nearby Philadelphians to make the trip. The site was still unnamed, but "Bath" and "Surfing" were leading contenders for that honor. In December 1853, with the Camden and Atlantic Railroad near completion, Osborne outlined a town plan before the railroad's board:

"I unrolled a great and well-finished map of the . . . bathing place, [and] they saw in large letters of gold, stretching over the waves, the words, ATLANTIC CITY," Osborne later remembered. "This title was greeted with enthusiasm by the board. The name was unanimously adopted and that day 'Atlantic City' came into existence on paper."

In early 1854, Atlantic City was incorporated. The town was laid out in a simple grid with its streets named after states and its avenues named after bodies of water, a map that would later provide the names of properties for the board game Monopoly. The two-and-a-half-hour train ride from Camden to the beach was an immediate success, attracting throngs of shop clerks and others from Philadelphia's lower middle class. Atlantic City's virtues were first promoted as medicinal, and visitors were encouraged to believe that a pleasant stay at the beach and regular soakings in hot baths would cure whatever ailed them.

By 1860, Atlantic City had only 687 residents, but could house as many as 4,000 tourists a day. Simple wood-frame hotels and bathhouses dotted the town, though streets and sidewalks were usually choked by mounds of white sand. To conquer the sand, Atlantic City began building the famous Boardwalk.

The first boardwalk in Atlantic City was built in 1870. Its thick wooden planks made strolling the beach more attractive to city dwellers eager to keep their shoes clean and their socks dry. Subsequent versions of the Boardwalk were built after the first few were washed away by storms, destroyed in freak accidents, or simply splintered beneath the clattering feet of tourists. In 1896, the Boardwalk was expanded a fifth and final time. Four miles long and forty feet wide, it ran in front of a series of ostentatious oceanfront hotels and provided access to dozens of shops, arcades, fortune-tellers' booths, beer gardens, and the world's first Ferris wheel.

Single men and women soon became some of Atlantic City's greatest fans. They came in search of the well-publicized, seductive breezes blowing through the weekend retreat. While the romantic possibilities in Victorian-era New Jersey were relatively sedate by later Atlantic City standards, the town still permitted visitors a respite from some of the more stringent moral sensibilities of the time: you could show a little skin at the beach.

As the town grew, so did its platoon of con artists and snake-oil salesmen ready to fleece the unwary. And as visitors continued to flow in, the madcap, often freakish roar of Atlantic City grew progressively louder. Atlantic City attractions came to include bouts between midget boxers, a giant typewriter, premature babies displayed in incubators, eating contests, Siamese twins, horses diving sixty feet off a platform into the ocean, and electrified corporate billboards that lighted the night sky ("Shave Yourself—Gillette Safety Razor"). Scores of vaudeville acts played in Atlantic City as well. The Ziegfeld Follies debuted there before moving to Broadway. In one theater, W. C. Fields juggled. Out on the Boardwalk, Harry Houdini escaped.

All of this—the shows, the surf, the sensations—was grist for a nonstop publicity mill that made Atlantic City one of the East Coast's most popular resorts. Its appeal and the unique, frequently unsavory nature of its attractions kept other seashore towns in the region from trying to compete on the same scale.

Between 1870 and 1940, Atlantic City's ripest years, the town's permanent population grew from 1,043 to 64,094. Although the Atlantic City of yesteryear has often been portrayed as a stomping ground of the well-heeled, in reality most of its visitors for most of its history were common folk. "A remarkable myth about the city took shape in the late 1960s. It held that Atlantic City was once a showcase of elegance, a playground of the cream of society, which lost its upper-class clientele and turned into a commercialized proletarian bazaar," writes historian Charles Funnell. "As a result, [this myth maintains,] commercialization displaced refinement, and the vulgar crowd squeezed out the gentry."

All this was a pleasant fantasy. Wealthy visitors did frequent the finer hotels, but overall the town's activities, architecture, and character reflected the tastes of an emerging mass market. Appropriately, once the Miss America Pageant got under way in Atlantic City in 1921, the town tapped painter Norman Rockwell, sentimental fantasist of America's middle class, to judge two of the contests in the 1920s. Atlantic City percolated because it swept up the extra wages earned by the growing industrial middle class while providing a momentary summertime hiatus from the monotony of increasingly routinized workplaces. And it had a nice beach.

Atlantic City also thrived because it was able to tap a large black workforce for low-paying service jobs in its hotels, restaurants, and showrooms. By 1910, blacks made up 25 percent of the town's population, a far larger proportion than that of other Northeastern cities at the time. Not that the presence and contribution of blacks was ever fully embraced by the region's white majordomos.

"What are we going to do with our colored people?" *The Philadelphia Inquirer* complained in 1893. "Atlantic City has never before seemed so overrun with the dark-skinned race as this season, probably because the smaller proportion of visitors makes their number more prominent. At any rate, both the boardwalk and Atlantic Avenue fairly swarm with them during bathing hours, like the fruit in a huckleberry pudding. This has gone so far that it is offending the sensitive feelings of many visitors, especially those from the South."

If better-paying jobs, political power, and white schools were closed to blacks, in every other sense Atlantic City was always an open town. Gambling, prostitution, and bootlegging thrived. The three vices floated together, as they had in so many other cities across the country, orbiting the Boardwalk's dizzying entertainment complex.

At the turn of the century, Atlantic City flouted New Jersey laws that forbade liquor sales on Sundays. Brothels proliferated despite occasional attempts to clean up what town fathers dutifully called a "family resort." And illegal gambling joints ranged from the backs of cigar stores, with five-cent limits, up to the more regal Dutchy's and Levy's clubs, where $5 and $10 bets were accepted. Later, Skinny D'Amato's 500 Club and Charlie Schwartz's Bath and Turf Club both featured illegal gambling. Future Philadelphia Mob boss Nicky Scarfo got his first job tending bar at the 500 Club, and both gambling joints flourished until the Kefauver Committee swept through town in 1951.

During Prohibition, inlets surrounding Atlantic City were principal East Coast hideaways for bootleggers running rum in speedboats. So important was the location that Al Capone, Lucky Luciano, and other mobsters convened in Atlantic City in 1929. Photographed strolling proudly next to Capone during the summit was Enoch "Nucky" Johnson, political boss of Atlantic County from 1914 until he went to prison in 1941.

As head of Atlantic County's Republican machine and the party's treasurer, Nucky controlled commissioners, judges, cops, and the purse strings. Kickbacks from bootleggers, gambling joints, and prostitution rings lined Nucky's pockets, greased the wheels of one of the most corrupt political machines in the country, and made sure law enforcement wouldn't get in the way of Atlantic City's rollicking style.

"No public road or building could be let without first seeing that Nucky was taken care of. Not a horse-race betting room, brothel, gambling casino, numbers banker, or petty racketeer could operate without cutting in the boss. In magnitude these rackets, daily shaking down tens of thousands of citizens and visitors to the famous seashore resort, compared favorably with those of Al Capone in his prime," journalist Jack Alexander wrote in 1942. "In Atlantic City, if a New York or Chicago racketeer set up a casino or bordello, the local lads merely complained to the police vice squad, which drove the interlopers out of town."

After Nucky was convicted of tax evasion, his mantle passed to Frank "Hap" Farley, a Republican who inherited Johnson's party posts and picked up the added plum of a state senate seat. At his peak, Farley reigned as one of New Jersey's political power brokers, with the muscle to engineer the construction of the Atlantic City Expressway and the Garden State Parkway. And Hap orchestrated all this from his Atlantic City office on New York Avenue and a Friday night table at Orsatti's Restaurant. Farley's regime carried on Nucky's traditions, siphoning money from the Boardwalk and the backrooms while Atlantic City tingled.

Then the music stopped. Or, more accurately, it petered out.

Atlantic City never fell. It was abandoned in pieces as tourists grew tired of the old vaudevillian riff and as air travel made it cheaper and easier to spend a holiday in more exotic surroundings. Outside developers might have revived some of the tourist trade, but local hoteliers chased them off by threatening to cut them out of the convention business. The chamber of commerce responded by encouraging local weathermen to describe cloudy days in the decaying resort as "partly sunny."

After 1940, Atlantic City's population began to shrink. In 1950, there were 61,657 residents; by 1970, only 47,859. As whites, local retailers, and big employers such as the Atlantic City Electric Company fled the town, low-income blacks relocated there from the South. In just ten years, between 1960 and 1970, the proportion of the local population that was black rose from 18 percent to 43 percent. By early 1977, Atlantic City boasted an unemployment rate of 23 percent.

Yet even as the air was sucked out of the town, and as racial tensions boiled in the 1960s and 1970s, Atlantic City politicos still took their cut of governmental and licensing fees, known locally as "ice money." An economy built on a hustle had engendered a political environment built on a hustle, and nothing was in place to halt Atlantic City's slide. It languished as a barnacle-bitten remnant that creaked awake only a few months a year.

Then, in search of a destiny, Atlantic City got casinos.

When New Jersey legalized gambling in Atlantic City in 1976, it gave the nod to an activity that had already helped define the town for many decades. But in contrast to the casino palaces of today, it was informal, backroom gambling that had once sprouted there. And at the turn of the century, gambling coexisted with scores of other vibrant businesses. It wasn't the only game in town. But by 1976, all of that had changed.

"It was like the scene in *2001: A Space Odyssey* where the cavemen are standing around looking at the monolith and not knowing what to do with it," recalls Atlantic City's current mayor, Jim Whelan. "That's what casinos were like in Atlantic City—nobody here was prepared for the economic forces that were unleashed."

One company, however, was prepared: Resorts International.

THE CASINOS STAKE THEIR CLAIMS

At first blush, Resorts International would have seemed the most unlikely vessel to be chosen for the honor of ferrying legal gambling into Atlantic City in the late 1970s.

New Jersey's governor, Brendan Byrne, and other law enforcement officials had rattled their sabers in the wake of legalization, warning of dire consequences should organized crime or any other disreputable elements try to lay claim to this most disreputable of cities. And over the next two decades, New Jersey regulators for the most part did an admirable job of keeping the Mob from exercising direct control over any Atlantic City casino. This was in stark contrast to the lame efforts of Las Vegas regulators prior to the late 1970s and early 1980s.

But despite all that, Resorts, a company rife with seedy associations, Mob ties, and suspect business practices, marched right into Atlantic City. State regulators began cracking their whip only after Resorts was licensed.

Resorts International, Incorporated, began life in 1958 as the Mary Carter Paint Company, changing its name in 1968 once its go-go casino operations had eclipsed the slower-moving paint business.

Although Resorts was publicly traded, the company remained firmly in the control of its chairman, Jim Crosby, whose family owned 60 percent of the voting stock. Crosby's dominance was so complete that he could tap Resorts' treasury, and shareholders' funds, to speculate wildly on securities beginning in the late 1970s. In 1984, Crosby's losing trades in options and bonds cost Resorts more than $23 million, leading one Wall Street wag to suggest renaming the company "James Crosby Trading."

Crosby's taste for risk, and for operating on the edge, led Resorts into the casino business. The company secured its first casino license in 1965 in the Bahamas with the help of its well-wired local attorney, Stafford Sands—who also happened to be the Bahamian minister of finance and tourism. Sands was forced from office two years later over alleged improprieties in his relationships with other gambling interests.

In 1967, Resorts appointed Eddie Cellini head of its casino on Paradise Island. Cellini's brother, Dino, was an associate of Mob boss Meyer Lansky, and Eddie had worked in other casinos tied to Lansky. Meyer, always on the lookout for new gambling markets after Fidel Castro kicked him out of Cuba, had worked hard to bring the Bahamas into the fold. By the early 1960s, Lansky had a casino up and running there, paving the way for Resorts' later entry.

According to a 1978 report from New Jersey's Division of Gaming Enforcement, the investigative arm of the state agency regulating casinos, Resorts had lined up more than $20 million in financing for its Paradise Island casino "through persons or organizations of unsuitable character and nature." That list included financiers with criminal records and others with links to the ubiquitous Lansky.

All this was known to New Jersey regulators before Resorts received its permanent Atlantic City license in 1978. Yet it became the anointed one, the first company permitted to operate a casino in the state.

In retrospect, perhaps that shouldn't have been a surprise, because Resorts had been pushing for legalization in Atlantic City since 1970. Later, the company hired influential local lawyers and also funded the lobbying efforts that ensured the legalization of gambling in 1976. In short, Resorts had helped build the door it walked through.

Attempts to legalize gambling in 1974 had been spurned by New Jersey residents, who were opposed to statewide gambling, wary of organized crime, and uncomfortable with proposals for state-owned casinos. When the wheel turned again in 1976, gambling's supporters were ready.

The 1976 casino referendum, pitched as a way to save a deteriorating community, proposed privately owned casinos and limited legalization to Atlantic City. Moreover, a fat portion of casino revenue was earmarked for a fund that would subsidize a variety of services for the state's senior citizens, a voting bloc needed if legalized gambling was to become a reality. Gambling's promoters were getting their foot in the door by portraying themselves as the gallant rescuers of society's most vulnerable people, a ploy that would be adopted later by other industry proponents.

A well-oiled lobbying and public relations machine, the Committee to Rebuild Atlantic City, was put in place by the referendum's backers. Of the $1 million budget CRAC had at its disposal, $200,000 came from Resorts, the biggest contributor to the effort. In addition to its CRAC contributions, Resorts spent another $100,000 for its own lobbying campaign.

Resorts also locked up the services of Marvin Perskie, a lawyer whose nephew, Steven Perskie, had sponsored the gambling legislation in the state assembly, and of Pat McGahn, a lawyer whose brother, Joseph McGahn, served in the state senate. Long before the referendum was put before the public for a vote, Marvin Perskie had tipped off Resorts that his nephew was going to introduce gambling legislation. That bit of advice sent Resorts on a frantic land-buying spree in Atlantic City, which would ultimately make it the largest private property owner in town and a huge force in the city's future development.

"Look, it's no big honor to have a gambling city," Atlantic City mayor Joseph Lazarow said before the referendum. "But it's the only way we know to save the town and get the hotels we need."

New Jersey's Casino Control Act passed easily in 1976, a symphony of political backscratching and acquiescence to lobbying dollars that one writer called "a lesson in civics the likes of which none of the reporters covering it had ever received in high school."

The part of the referendum dealing with taxes had been carefully guided by casino interests. State programs for senior citizens were to be funded by an 8 percent tax on casinos' gross revenue. The tax designated for urban redevelopment in Atlantic City, however, was limited to 2 percent of gross revenue and only kicked in *after* companies had earned enough money to pay off their initial investments. How redevelopment funds were to be administered was only sketchily defined. That lack of clarity later led to bureaucratic infighting over who got the redevelopment funds and how they were spent; the consequent political mismanagement in Atlantic City stalled redevelopment initiatives for more than eight years.

Once the referendum passed, Resorts began opening its corporate files to state investigators. But before they completed their screening, Governor Byrne amended the gambling act to allow for temporary casino licenses. Resorts got one in March 1978.

When the Division of Gaming Enforcement (DGE) recommended later in the year that Resorts be denied a permanent license, its recommendation was ignored by the Casino Control Commission, the state's licensing body, whose members were political appointees. The CCC's first chief, Joseph Lordi, had been appointed by his close friend Governor Byrne, even though Byrne was in receipt of a state report outlining Lordi's past connections to organized-crime figures.

Similar circumstances surrounded a relicensing of Resorts in 1985, when the DGE threatened to revoke Resorts' license after it learned that fees paid to the company's attorneys wound up in bank accounts belonging to Bahamian prime minister Lynden Pindling. The CCC overruled the DGE in that instance as well.

For its part, Resorts said in 1978 that it didn't know that some of its past employees or associates had Mob ties until those facts surfaced in the media. Resorts said other questionable activities were the work of rogue employees, operating independently of company management. After a lengthy hearing, Resorts was granted Atlantic City's first permanent casino license in 1979.

By that time, the company had been operating alone in Atlantic City for almost a year and had demonstrated an awesome ability to make money. More than anything, the wads of cash Resorts was processing, and the jobs it created, made it an Atlantic City darling that only the most daring of politicians would have tried to kick out of town.

Crowds stood several bodies deep when Resorts opened its doors in 1978 in the old Chalfonte–Haddon Hall hotel, once owned by Quakers who forbade liquor in their establishment. Some 300,000 people poured into Atlantic City on opening weekend, and so thick was the crush to enter Resorts that stories circulated about gamblers opting to pee in their pants rather than give up their seats at the betting tables inside.

At a press conference shortly after Resorts opened, Jim Crosby drew skeptical looks from reporters when he projected that his Atlantic City casino would have revenue of $100 million in its first year. Yet in just its first seven months of operation, the casino had revenue of $134 million, well above the $45 million it cost Resorts to convert the Chalfonte. At the end of the year, Resorts had raked in $225 million in Atlantic City.

The game was afoot.

Proposals for new casinos were submitted by thirty-six companies between 1978 and 1979. By the end of 1979, Caesars World, Incorporated, and Bally Manufacturing Corporation had opened casinos. A year later, eight others were under construction in Atlantic City.

"I think we have committed ourselves to keeping this as a wholesome family resort," Mayor Lazarow deadpanned when Resorts opened. "From this day on, I think we will see a city of growth and prosperity."

If Atlantic City never morphed into a cozy family resort, prosperity did reign eventually. The question was, to whose benefit?

EASY MONEY

Resorts' financial success in Atlantic City and the increasing commercialization of gambling suddenly made the industry palatable to lenders other than the Teamsters Union. Insurance giant Aetna Life & Casualty made its first casino loan in Atlantic City, ponying up $60 million to Caesars World in 1979. In the late 1970s, Continental Illinois National Bank backed Bally, and Morgan Guaranty Trust led a bank syndicate arranging a $135 million facility for the Del E. Webb Corporation.

Much of this money came at a premium, carrying interest rates between 11 percent and 12 percent at a time when commercial loans typically carried interest rates of about 9 percent. But casinos were so profitable that the terms weren't considered onerous; the overconfidence those profits bred among Atlantic City casino operators would come to haunt them several years later.

Nonetheless, gambling's arrival in Atlantic City was a watershed for casino operators, an event that marked the beginning of their formal acceptance into the American business establishment. Las Vegas wasn't the only major casino market in the country anymore. Just seven years after Resorts opened, Atlantic City was drawing 27 million tourists a year, twice as many as Las Vegas.

In 1980, Bally, Caesars, and Resorts were each winning an average of $500,000 *per day* from gamblers. The three casinos created 11,000 new jobs; Atlantic City's real-estate tax base had doubled. By 1984, the new boomtown had eleven casinos with 40,535 full-time employees. Total revenue at the eleven casinos was almost $2 billion, higher than Las Vegas' take, and the casinos were contributing more than $300 million a year in taxes to the state.

On the other hand, rapes and robberies rose 33 percent in the first year after Resorts opened, and the crime rate has remained higher than it was in the pre-casino era. Increased rent and property taxes drove many of Atlantic City's retirees and low- and middle-income residents out of town amid a boom in real estate speculation that saw total assessed property values shoot up from $317 million to $2.2 billion between 1976 and 1985. Small stores and restaurants closed their doors, unable to compete with the casinos. Hundreds of thousands of local teenagers were also drawn to the gaming tables. More than 173,000 teenagers were denied entry to Atlantic City casinos in 1986; another 34,000 were hauled off the casino floor, where their presence was illegal. And on tracts of pricey but undeveloped land, row upon row of dilapidated housing continued to rot.

But Atlantic City sat squarely in the middle of the country's most densely populated region, and the bad sights and bad smells didn't keep people away. Because the town had only a tiny airport, its visitors came in cars and buses, mostly in buses. Those buses got crowded. In 1978, only 743,000 passengers came to Atlantic City by bus. In 1985, 12.6 million bus riders came to gamble.

None of these bus riders were high rollers. They all played slot machines, and few of them stayed in town for more than several hours. The patina of high-roller action was in place, particularly at Caesars and the Sands, but the table games were just window dressing in most Atlantic City casinos. Slots were the lifeblood of the place, as they would be in every new location that adopted casino gambling after Atlantic City. Unlike Las Vegas, which drew tourists from across the country, the new gambling markets would be supported by low-stakes day-trippers who came, who saw, and who lost.

In a sense, gamblers in the new locations wouldn't be *tourists* as much as *visitors*, because there was nothing to *tour* in the newly fat locales pumped up by gambling. There were just the casinos. Certainly Atlantic City hasn't recovered any of the entertainment and full-fledged resort elements that characterized it earlier in the century, although by the late 1990s the town was taking its first serious strides toward doing that.

Atlantic City's appeal was to all those who wanted to gamble quickly and wanted a long shot at becoming rich. For the elderly, Atlantic City's bread-and-butter clientele, it became a place to chase the years away.

"You're all alone, and the children are all grown and away. Or maybe you lost your husband. How much time can you spend cleaning your house?" says Helen Piccola, a seventy-five-year-old resident of Edison, New Jersey, who is a regular visitor to Atlantic City. "When you go to Atlantic City it's like a magnet because it clears your mind of everything. It makes you feel like you're seventeen again and in a different world. . . . Your blood boils when you get to Atlantic City. We just get out of the car and your blood boils. It's better than having a man."

Because the city didn't need to be beautiful or diverse to attract an elderly slot crowd whose blood was boiling, it remained largely as it was: tattered. Very few people wanted to stay for the weekend or even a night. And all the casinos built in Atlantic City so far have been monotonous, largely indistinguishable barns. Yet until the mid-1980s, most well-marketed Atlantic City casinos had no trouble making money.

All that money created some ticklish regulatory problems.

Chastened by criticism of how easily Resorts slipped through New Jersey's screening process, state regulators clamped down on subsequent applicants. Before getting its license, Bally had to sever its relationship with its chairman William O'Donnell because of allegations that he had Mob ties. Caesars had to drop its chairman, Clifford Perlman, and his brother, Stuart, for the same reason.

New York and Philadelphia organized-crime families staged a bloody battle as they jockeyed to try to get a piece of the action in Atlantic City. But besides compromising one mayor, Michael Matthews, and infiltrating the union that represented hotel and restaurant workers, organized crime was largely held at bay by local law enforcement officials and the FBI.

Other, quieter problems erupted inside the casinos, revolving around the thorny issue of credit. Casinos grant big lines of credit to high rollers and repeat customers, many of whom are problem or compulsive gamblers, in an effort to keep the heavy bettors playing at their tables. Besides encouraging loyalty, the logic behind bestowing juicy markers on a gambler is that it usually convinces him or her to play longer and consequently lose more money.

Of course, if you give enough people free money, some of them are never going to pay it back. So a well-run casino will monitor its credit balances closely to keep a lid on losses from deadbeat gamblers. For their part, regulators cast a wary eye on large bad-debt figures, which may indicate there's some skimming afoot.

And by the early 1980s, Atlantic City casinos had stretched the concept of "credit" to the breaking point, inviting scrutiny from regulators. According to a state investigation in 1983, Atlantic City's casinos were engaging in "irresponsible and callous credit decisions" that were "luring many patrons—including gambling addicts—into personal degradation and financial self-destruction." Moreover, the investigation found that "criminal elements, including organized crime members and associates, enjoyed an access to the gaming tables that casino executives themselves encouraged by the fawning disbursement of easy credit and lavish complimentary services."

For gamblers like Samuel Rosenblum, a wealthy Philadelphia businessman who rang up $1.3 million in credit at three casinos in two years, the casinos simply wrote off $873,000 and settled with him for the remaining $427,000. Rosenblum's deficits were less painful than they might have been for his hosts because tax law allowed casinos to write off amounts totaling as much as 4 percent of their revenue to offset such debts. This neat tax trick also permitted casinos to lower the amount of money they had to kick in to the social programs designed to benefit from the legalization of gambling.

For gamblers like Joseph Pedula, a Mob hit man, the casinos offered "customer deposit privileges" that allowed him to tuck away $540,000 at Resorts alone. Nominally, the money could be drawn down, like a line of credit, for gambling. In reality, law enforcement officials suspected that Pedula's funds were being laundered. State investigators said that easy credit financed loan-sharking and narcotics trafficking by the Mob, and allowed casino profits to be skimmed.

Today, regulators say Atlantic City's casinos have much tighter credit controls than in the mid-1980s, but similar problems still crop up. In 1993, Caesars was fined $477,000 for failing to collect a $718,000 marker from Leon Mishkin, a Venezuelan high roller. Caesars was also ordered to ante up about $60,000 to cover taxes it would have had to pay had it collected Mishkin's debts.

Yet even though Atlantic City's casinos pamper favored patrons like Mishkin with easy credit, they have always tried to leave one group of gamblers out in the cold: professional card counters.

THE WAR AGAINST THE CARD COUNTERS

Card counters have stalked casinos since 1962. In that year, mathematician Ed Thorp's book, *Beat the Dealer,* appeared. Based on research of winning blackjack combinations that Thorp had churned through a computer, *Beat the Dealer* provided a roadmap of "basic strategy" that players could navigate to try to beat the house.

Beat the house? Yep.

While almost every other bet in a casino is a loser over time, blackjack, played correctly and with a bankroll large enough to absorb a string of losses, is the one game in which an astute player can eventually come out on top. Like most card games played in the United States, it has European roots but a murky lineage. Several European countries assert parentage, with gambling historian John Scarne deciding in favor of Italy because of blackjack's similarity to baccarat and another Italian card game called seven and a half. Blackjack's rules are straightforward: A bettor plays against the dealer, and whoever comes closest to 21, without going over, wins. Picture cards are worth 10, aces are worth 1 or 11, and number cards are counted at their face value. A player loses automatically if he or she "busts," goes over 21. If both player and dealer tie then it is a "push" and, depending on house rules, no money is exchanged or the dealer wins.

Like the slots, blackjack was once a little-noted outpost in casinos, a game spurned by serious bettors. It was introduced into American casinos early in this century and got a boost when Las Vegas made it standard fare after legalizing gambling there in 1931. Routinely referred to as 21, the game became known as blackjack when casinos started paying bonuses to bettors who hit 21 with an ace matched to the jack of clubs or the jack of spades.

But blackjack took a long time to catch on. A visit to any Las Vegas casino in the late 1950s would have revealed dozens of craps tables, with the number of blackjack tables a very distant second. Then along came *Beat the Dealer* in 1962. The book's wild popularity meant blackjack was no longer an also-ran. Within just a few years, it was the most heavily played table game in casinos. Everybody wanted to play it, because *Beat the Dealer* outlined "A Winning Strategy for the Game of Twenty One."

The book said that any time a deck was rich in high cards such as 10s, picture cards, and aces, the bettor had an edge over the dealer. Players could track, or "count," cards by assigning −1 to high cards and +1 to low cards. As the count turned positive, it meant more high cards were left in the deck. Thus, players saved their biggest bets for those moments when the count had reached a large positive number. Counting was then buttressed by "basic strategy," which outlined strict rules for when players should "take a hit," "stand," "split" pairs of cards, or double their bet, depending on their hand and whatever cards the dealer was showing.

Other mathematicians, notably Peter Griffin, have since refined the theories and techniques Thorp introduced, but the fundamentals remain the same. And in the stampede to play blackjack that followed *Beat the Dealer*'s arrival, casinos had to begin devising ways to keep card counters at bay. In the early 1960s, Las Vegas casinos forbade the splitting of aces, but had to reverse themselves when action at the blackjack tables subsequently came to a halt.

In later years casinos introduced other tactics to deter counters, including frequent shuffling and card shoes filled with as many as eight decks. But frequent shuffling meant that fewer hands were played at the tables, thus reducing the amount of revenue the casino could pull in at a blackjack table. Besides, the best card counters proved adept at "shuffle tracking," a sophisticated way of determining where 10s, picture cards, and aces were located in newly shuffled decks. As the years wore on, card counters became increasingly sophisticated and many began using microcomputers and other concealed devices to aid their efforts.

Casinos raised the stakes further, inserting card "mechanics" as dealers to cheat players and sometimes resorting to physical intimidation. In 1985, two card counters at Binion's in Las Vegas were brutally beaten by three casino employees and then told that they would be killed and dumped in the desert. A security guard at Binion's told authorities investigating that incident that about a hundred gamblers had been roughed up at Binion's between 1974 and the early 1980s. The two counters beaten in 1985 sued Binion's, and the case was later settled out of court.

Casinos have also come to rely heavily on the services of Griffin Investigations, a Las Vegas detective agency (unconnected to mathematician Peter Griffin) that disseminates a "face book" with photos of known card counters and also provides casinos with investigators who follow suspected teams of counters as they play. A widely used product in casino surveillance rooms, the B.J. Tracker, is a computer with a database of more than two dozen known card-counting techniques. If a player is suspected of card counting, a surveillance camera examines the cards he is playing. That information is fed into the Tracker, which then identifies what counting method the player is using.

Although many card counters rely on their wits to beat casinos at blackjack, and judges in a number of lawsuits over the years have ruled that counting isn't cheating, many casinos still claim a right to eject counters. In Nevada, it is now legal for a casino to ask anyone it suspects of card counting to leave. In Atlantic City, where no such law exists, surveillance teams frantically try to track counters and instruct dealers to shuffle frequently if counters are at their tables. Of course, card counters aren't angels. To help them track cards, many use concealed electronic devices strapped to their bodies or hidden in a shoe. Others rely on more mundane methods, such as trying to peek at a dealer's hole card.

The war between casinos and counters has created a cadre of gamblers who approach blackjack with steely intensity. They play the game methodically, never deviating from basic strategy, and they try their best to remain incognito. They are disciplined and they are relentless. They are people like Tom Hyland.

Hyland began playing blackjack in Atlantic City after dropping out of college in 1979. He played low-limit, $2 tables at Resorts and slowly began building up his bankroll. After six months, he and a friend had each turned $1,000 into $4,000. Then they pooled their money with $8,000 from two other players. Six months later, the foursome of card counters had turned their $16,000 into $100,000.

From that point on, Hyland began assembling the biggest and most well-managed counting teams casinos have ever faced. At first, most teams were four to five players strong; then Hyland demonstrated the ability to keep more than three dozen players working together effectively. He recruited people who trusted one another, and he enforced that trust with voluntary polygraph tests anytime a counter lost a large sum of money.

Hyland and his team have worn wigs and false mustaches to foil casinos, but he is now so well known in Atlantic City that disguises don't work. Hyland believes that Griffin Investigations long ago added his picture to their face book, and he is party to a class-action lawsuit filed against Atlantic City casinos charging them with illegal restraint of trade.

Hyland says he has been threatened at gunpoint by management at a Caribbean casino and says he has been beaten with a walkie-talkie in a Las Vegas casino. On a recent visit to Trump Plaza in Atlantic City, Hyland played only a few minutes before a manager lowered the betting limits at the table. Lowering betting limits softens any loss the casino might experience when confronted with a skilled player. Although New Jersey once required casinos to give gamblers thirty minutes' notice before changing limits, the law has since been changed. Asked by an observer why he was changing the betting limits, Ernie Trasatti, a Trump Plaza shift manager, replied: "We're the casino, we can do what we want."

Despite these roadblocks, Hyland says he is still able to make a good living counting cards. On any given night, he can win or lose $20,000.

On some nights, he's won or lost $100,000. On average, he expects to make about $100 to $200 per hour counting cards.

Hyland, however, represents the elite of card counters. For all the worry casinos have about them, few counters have the wherewithal to assemble large teams. Solo operators, often succumbing to stress and odd hours, usually don't enjoy long careers. Many counters have to endure numbing losing streaks, which will crush them if their bankrolls aren't big enough. Average counters, exploiting a meager 1 percent advantage over the house, earn only about $30,000 to $60,000 per year, according to Anthony Curtis, a former card counter who now publishes gambling newsletters and books in Las Vegas. For the smaller group of counters who travel around the world and pursue the game relentlessly, counting brings in as much as $250,000 a year. That kind of money, and the thrill of beating casinos at their own game, keep counters coming despite the hardships of their trade.

Battling counters head-to-head are the casino's dealers. Among the ranks of casino employees, a certain glamour attaches itself to dealers. But for most dealers, the job ends up being neither glamorous nor very well-paying. Even when they are dealing to average players, dealers know someone is not going to be pleased with their performance.

"The [card] players are the front line and the line in back of you is the pit bosses," says Al, a dealer at Atlantic City's TropWorld casino, who asked not to be further identified. "If the players start winning, then you get pressure from behind you—a tap on the foot: 'Did you shuffle the deck right?' If the house starts winning, then you get pressure in front of you— guys jumping up and screaming in your face, sometimes threatening you. There's an unbelievable amount of stress for dealers. Every night."

To cope with the stress, many dealers end up abusing drugs or drinking heavily. Some become compulsive gamblers, while others, tempted by the money sliding across the green felt, become participants in schemes to defraud the casino.

Although veteran dealers at Las Vegas' biggest casinos can make between $65,000 and $100,000 a year, dealers at most other casinos there make much less. In Atlantic City, dealers are paid about $4 an hour and, as in Las Vegas, rely on tips for the bulk of their income. Atlantic City's dealers say that with tips the typical dealer there earns between $12 and $17 an hour, or about $25,000 to $35,000 a year.

Although Atlantic City's dealers have periodically fought to unionize, they've never been successful. As the saying goes, if you want to make money in a casino you have to own one. And it was this logic that ultimately landed Atlantic City in the tender clutches of Donald Trump.

"A HELL OF AN OWNERSHIP"

When Donald Trump opened his first casino in Atlantic City in 1984, the town's business patterns were firmly in place. Early on, casino operators may have thought that high rollers would flock to Atlantic City, and politicians who pushed for legalization may have had visions of Monte Carlo dancing in their heads, but the reality was quite otherwise. Atlantic City's was a market built on low-stakes slot players who cruised in on buses, and by the mid-1980s most casinos had fallen into a perennial routine of trying to outbid one another for these gamblers' allegiance.

To corral legions of bus customers, casinos offered slot players incentives that included a free roll of quarters, a lunch voucher, and a coupon that could be redeemed for cash at a later date. The struggles for the souls of slot players continue today, and they frequently rip into the bottom line of Atlantic City casinos. While many casinos there boast of the huge revenues they glean from slot play, noting how favorably it compares to Las Vegas, the cost of generating those revenues often strips away their profits.

Although the typical Atlantic City gambler loses about $35 playing the slots, it can cost the casinos almost that much to bring him or her there in the first place: $10 to $15 in free quarters, a $5 to $10 lunch voucher, and a $5 cash rebate. On top of that, casinos pay bus companies a small commission for each rider hauled into Atlantic City. In the third quarter of 1996, profits at all of Atlantic City's casinos fell 32 percent, to $77 million, from $113 million in the same period a year earlier. The reason profits tanked: casinos spent $163 million from June through September on freebies meant to coax gamblers into the city.

Casino operators had also originally expected to draw players from a 300-mile radius around Atlantic City. This would have included most of the largest northeastern and mid-Atlantic cities. But the actual market proved to have a 125-mile radius and to draw mainly on Philadelphians and New Yorkers popping in for the weekend. In Atlantic City today, about 60 percent of the money won by casinos each year is lost by gamblers between midnight on Friday and six P.M. on Sunday.

New casino towns that sprang up in other parts of the country after Atlantic City would prove the same point: such places draw the bulk of their visitors from nearby, and developing a resort requires much more effort than merely opening the doors of a casino.

Wedded to their low-stakes gamblers, Atlantic City's casinos did little to try to make their facilities anything more than assembly lines for processing quarters. Many hotel rooms were empty, and the airport languished. Casino companies such as Resorts, which had large holdings of undeveloped land throughout the area, simply sat on their assets and fended off accusations that they were more interested in real estate speculation than in Atlantic City's future.

The monotony of the casinos was also reinforced by regulatory restrictions. If Atlantic City regulators did an exemplary job of keeping organized crime from controlling the casinos, they often went overboard in their efforts to regulate other parts of the casino business. This made it hard for casino executives to pursue even the mildest innovations or marketing strategies that might have helped them make their properties more distinctive.

In 1989, one casino had to ask for regulatory approval to throw a Halloween party for high rollers. After almost a dozen bureaucrats reviewed the request, a three-page memo was sent to the casino detailing ways to improve benchmarks for judging the costumes of party-goers.

Many regulations have been loosened since then. "When we started going here the only other jurisdiction was Las Vegas, which had a horrible reputation. So we put a very strict regulatory structure in place," says the current Casino Control Commission chairman, Brad Smith. "Over the years we've discovered that as time goes on, after starting tough, we can ease up on things."

To be sure, by the mid-1980s everybody in Atlantic City, from politicians to casino operators, seemed to need someone to keep an eye on them. Until Jim Whelan was elected in 1990, every mayor in the postcasino era had either legal or leadership troubles. Millions of dollars that the casinos had contributed to the city were misappropriated or squandered through bureaucratic haggling brought on by the vagueness of the original casino legislation. By 1984, almost $100 million earmarked for economic development in Atlantic City hadn't been spent because no one trusted the local government. That year, the state established the Casino Reinvestment Development Authority to oversee how development dollars were spent. The new agency was to be funded by a 1.25 percent tax on casino revenue. Overnight and with the stroke of a pen, the amount of money to be contributed to Atlantic City by its casinos had dropped almost 40 percent from the original 2 percent figure promised when gambling was legalized. In due time, the state even began letting casinos advise the CRDA on how the money was to be spent. Eventually, more of the CRDA's money would be used to build hotel rooms for the casinos than low-income housing for Atlantic City's residents.

Even with their economic development burden lightened in the mid-1980s, casinos still managed to come up with novel interpretations of what constituted community reinvestment. Caesars, for example, requested a $625,000 development credit for a two-story stone statue of the Roman emperor Caesar Augustus that it had erected in front of its casino.

Yet, despite the political corruption, the regulatory burdens, and the financial limitations of their clientele, most casinos in Atlantic City were making scads of money by the mid-1980s. In 1985, the casinos pulled in $2.13 billion in combined revenue, producing an overall profit of $103.5 million. The accepted wisdom was that Atlantic City was going to eclipse Las Vegas as the country's top gambling market. And into town marched Donald Trump.

Trump's face today is soggier and more weary than that of the young, blond huckster who started taking New York by storm in the late 1970s. And his business record and personal life have been subjected to the kind of brutal scrutiny he managed to avoid when he first ventured into Atlantic City. The man remains unbowed, however. Seated in his Trump Tower office in Manhattan in 1996, Trump sputters like a downed power line.

"The thing people don't know about me is . . . Donald Trump is in two businesses. I'm not in one. You take a Wynn, a Circus Circus, they're in one business. I'm in two businesses. I'm probably the biggest in real estate in New York and it's a big business. . . . I own most of my stuff. I own one hundred percent of Trump Tower. My buildings I own, for the most part. . . . I have this huge company that's real estate. I also have this huge company that's gambling. So I have two huge companies."

Nick Ribis, head of Trump's Atlantic City casinos, nods in agreement, chiming in with a smile that the fifty-year-old Trump is "the biggest conglomerate in the world."

The window behind Trump's desk offers a view up Fifth Avenue to the Plaza Hotel, a jewel Trump owned momentarily before the skein of assets he assembled in the 1980s began to unravel. Although he also once enjoyed unfettered control of three Atlantic City casinos, those properties began sinking beneath a mountain of debt and barely survived a restructuring imposed by creditors to mend Trump's erring ways.

Undeterred, Trump now insists that he is "back." Flashing a bespoke truculence, he went out of his way in a *New York Times Magazine* column he wrote to sneer at former employees who, during his organization's crisis years, "broke quickly, like the weak puppies they were." Wind him up to discuss the reality of his business fortunes and Trump's enthusiasm is unstoppable. He lets it be known that firmly, finally, he will always be with us. Ours.

Trump notes that he will own half of his casino business once the entire operation is taken public, and he relishes the heft he says this will give him in comparison to his arch-rival in the industry, Steve Wynn: "That's a hell of an ownership, because Wynn owns seven percent of Mirage and I'll own fifty percent [of my casino company]. And the thing is, my company's larger. See, my gambling company is larger. Probably the largest gambling company in the United States . . . bigger than Mirage, that's bigger than Caesars by far, that's bigger than all of them. . . . And yet with them it's a full-time deal, with me it's not. So, you know, it's pretty impressive stuff."

Neither the biggest real estate developer in New York, nor the biggest casino operator in the country, nor a self-made millionaire, Trump thrives by ignoring the truth or offering various shades of it. Mirage Resorts, in which Wynn holds 16 percent of the shares if all of his options are exercised, had a stock market capitalization that by late 1996 was twenty times as large as that of Trump's casinos. In terms of the value placed on all U.S. gambling companies by the stock market, Trump's company wasn't even in the top ten.

"It's very important for [Trump] to say these things, but you'd have to ask a doctor about why he does that," says Wynn with a sigh.

Breathless to the point of seeming oblivious, Trump now inhabits a shadow left behind by the spotlight that once enveloped him. He briefly embodied a decade's fascination with accumulation and became a media invention of such outsized proportions that few at the time bothered to notice that his business "empire" eventually had nothing to support it but hype. Absent the imprimatur of his father, who founded the family's real estate business, and the willing suspension of disbelief by several of the country's largest banks, Trump would have remained just another eager loudmouth. But he *did* have his father's support, he *did* have the banks' money, and in a short, dizzying burst of transactions, he *did* make quite a splash. As Trump's biographer Wayne Barrett notes, Trump arrived in Atlantic City fresh from a flurry of celebrated Manhattan real estate deals that had enthralled the media and made him a "colossal new force, a phenomenon whose day had come."

Before all that, Trump served a long apprenticeship with his father, Fred, a politically connected developer. After World War II, Fred amassed a collection of middle-income housing projects in Brooklyn and Queens, which by the late 1960s had earned the family a fortune once estimated at about $40 million. The exact value of the Trump family's private holdings has always been difficult to pinpoint, in no small part because Donald has regularly floated unsubstantiated proclamations of his wealth. Trump joined the family business in 1968 and used it as a launching pad in 1974 to enter the high-stakes, cutthroat world of Manhattan real estate development. His first successful project, in a partnership with the

Hyatt Corporation, was the renovation of a sagging Midtown hotel into what became the Grand Hyatt.

Although Donald drew the accolades for the Grand Hyatt Hotel when it opened in 1980, the entire project bore Fred Trump's stamp. Fred had spent decades cultivating local politicians, and New York's political honchos later saw to it that the Grand Hyatt got a forty-year tax abatement from the city. This, the first abatement ever granted in New York to a commercial property, was worth at least $100 million. Moreover, nobody would extend Donald financing for the project on his own. Lenders ultimately demanded Hyatt's guarantee before a $70 million construction loan was approved. And while Trump frequently pitches his construction projects as always coming in on time and under budget, he acknowledges that the Grand Hyatt cost at least $30 million more than originally projected.

From the Grand Hyatt, Trump went on to build Trump Tower. It was a black glass and pink marble monolith embossed, in two-foot-high brass letters, with its builder's name—all delivered to the good people of New York in 1983 on the back of another ten-year, $26 million tax abatement. Public sustenance aside, the construction and financing of the building involved astute maneuvering on Trump's part and was an unqualified success for the young builder. Garish, pricey—a true reflection of its times—Trump Tower sealed its creator's fame.

Celebrities rushed to buy Trump Tower apartments, and the retail atrium became a tourist attraction. In short order, a $201 million investment had generated a profit of at least $75 million. An added bonus was annual earnings of $17 million produced by the building's commercial and retail space; Trump shared this money with his lender, the Equitable Life Assurance Society.

Trump Tower was such a hit that lenders and investors, envying Equitable, lined up at Trump's door, ready to take him at his word even when his words were blather. Trump was already at the pinnacle of his career and Atlantic City, swimming in cash, beckoned.

Trump had begun assembling a casino site in Atlantic City in 1980, when Resorts' success there had become apparent. Trump originally leased several parcels from a number of companies, including one controlled by an organized crime associate, Kenny Shapiro, and Daniel Sullivan, a Teamsters Union operative with a shadowy past.

Forced by casino regulators to sever his ties with Sullivan and Shapiro, Trump bought them out for $8 million in 1983. It was the toughest action regulators ever took against Trump in Atlantic City. Anxious to have a marquee name in town, regulators ignored such curiosities as Trump's long-standing relationship with infamous Mob consigliere Roy Cohn. As time went on, and Trump became the town's dominant force, the desire of local regulators to monitor his business practices waned further.

Trump received his casino license in 1982, but while light construction had begun on his site, he still lacked the financing to complete the $220 million project. Then Trump struck a deal with Holiday Inns, Incorporated, owner of Harrah's casinos, that left the corporate giant reimbursing Trump for tens of millions he had already invested—some of which had been lent to him by his ever-present father. In return, Holiday Inns got a 50 percent stake in the casino and agreed to cover the remaining costs.

The casino, which opened in 1984, originally shared the partners' names. But after a series of bitter legal disputes, Trump later bought out Holiday Inns for $73 million and renamed the casino Trump Plaza. At first he needed to do very little to make money there: the casino was located at the base of the Atlantic City Expressway and simply sucked up the buses as they pulled into town.

Only a year after Trump Plaza opened, Trump pounced on another opportunity. Regulators denied the Hilton Hotels Corporation a license because of the company's past dealings with alleged Mob attorney Sidney Korshak. The irony of Hilton being suspect because of Korshak while Trump was seen as unsullied in spite of Cohn became even greater when Trump snapped up Hilton's nearly completed casino. For $320 million, Trump got a dormant property Hilton was desperate to unload as it tried to fend off a hostile takeover bid launched by Steve Wynn. To finance the purchase, Trump borrowed $280 million from Manufacturers Hanover. Trump guaranteed the loan personally—something he publicly stated he never did in his business dealings.

The casino, renamed Trump's Castle, was quickly recapitalized so Trump could get most of his cash out of the company. Two weeks after he bought the Castle, he issued $352 million in mortgage bonds that kept him in control but left the company saddled with a load of debt that required $41 million in annual interest payments just to keep the casino from sinking. With two casinos in hand, and no experience in the gambling business, Trump started preying on other operators in Atlantic City.

"I don't think Donald has the patience, or the interest, or the attention span, to be a hands-on operator," says Al Glagow, a streetwise casino consultant who has worked closely with Trump in Atlantic City. "He's just a deal maker. He blows in and then he moves on to the next deal." And while Trump's peculiarly American celebrity imparted enough gravitas so that he was queried by the media for opinions on nuclear weapons policy and taken seriously in his short-lived aspirations to the White House, his business practices became increasingly reckless.

Little of this was apparent just after the Castle purchase. Trump's influence in Atlantic City grew, and he began throwing his weight around in big and small ways. Road improvements he had promised the city during his licensing hearings were long delayed. To meet city beautification ordinances, Trump tried to have Trump Plaza's parking garage—a blank white slab emblazoned with his name—declared a work of art.

Trump also launched apparent takeover bids for his former partner, Holiday Inns, and another competitor, Bally's. Whether these were serious efforts or instances of that form of corporate extortion dubbed greenmail, they were part of a speculative frenzy that put once financially healthy operators on a steady diet of junk bonds, swamping Atlantic City in debt. Junk bonds, whose trashy name is bestowed on them by rating agencies convinced that owning the high-yield securities is so risky that they deserve a very bad grade, became fashionable in the 1980s as financier Michael Milken's currency of choice.

Milken, who later went to prison for securities fraud, neither invented junk bonds nor was the only one peddling them. But he was the biggest, wiliest player in the junk market. His firm, Drexel Burnham Lambert, used the instruments to help fund risky propositions in new industries such as cable television and cellular telephones, offered them to corporate raiders launching takeovers of more mature companies and also packed junk into the portfolios of savings and loans that later went belly-up. For the casino industry, Milken was the new sugar daddy, the purse that replaced the former largesse of the Teamsters' pension fund. In some cases, such as the funding of Steve Wynn's casinos, Milken's junk financed growth. But mostly, junk sold by Drexel and other brokerage firms left Atlantic City casinos, as well as companies in many other industries, dangerously larded with unproductive debt.

Atlantic City casinos increasingly used junk bonds for pricey takeovers, defensive maneuvers, and refinancings instead of using them to enhance or expand their properties. By the late 1980s, as the Northeast began sinking into a recession, Atlantic City, once a cash geyser, started to stall. Competition for gamblers grew fierce, and profit margins at the casinos began to shrink, at the same time as their debt payments began to skyrocket.

In 1983, Atlantic City's nine casinos together had a cash flow of $275.4 million. By 1990, twelve casinos that year jointly lost, before taxes, $267.2 million. Amid the carnage, Trump was going shopping.

In 1987, Trump acquired control of Resorts, whose patriarch, Jack

Davis, had died a year earlier. Resorts, which had more than $600 million in junk bonds on its books and was withering, had been trying to complete a massive new casino called the Taj Mahal when Davis died. With the acquisition of Resorts, Trump had control of three casinos, and would have a fourth if the Taj was completed. He also became Atlantic City's largest private landholder, controlling lots on which a new high school was to be built and others that were supposed to be topped, but never were, with new low-income and middle-income housing.

Although regulations at the time didn't permit one person or firm to own more than three casinos, regulators allowed Trump to complete the Resorts acquisition on condition that he shutter Resorts once the Taj opened. After a series of disputes with Resorts' remaining shareholders over a lowball offer Trump made for their shares and a fat management contract he awarded himself, entertainer Merv Griffin made a counteroffer in 1988 to buy the entire company. Trump and Griffin jabbed and bluffed their way to a deal that ended disastrously for both men and for the investors who backed them. Griffin got Resorts, Trump got the Taj, and both businesses soured.

Griffin financed his purchase of Resorts in late 1988 with $325 million of Milken's junk bonds. Less than a year later, Griffin and Resorts stopped making interest payments on almost $1 billion in junk debt, and the company soon sought bankruptcy protection from its creditors. By the time the Taj opened in early 1990, at a price tag of $1 billion, it was already apparent that only a miracle could make the casino generate the $1.3 million a day it needed just to break even. Atlantic City was in a slump, Trump had little interest in or knowledge of casino management, and his three casinos were notoriously uncooperative with one another. A little more than a year after it opened, the Taj was bankrupt.

Despite his mounting debt, Trump had purchased New York's Plaza Hotel in 1988 for $405 million—in borrowed money. In 1989 he picked up an aging fleet of jets from Eastern Airlines (quickly renaming them the Trump Shuttle) for $365 million—in borrowed money. Moreover, as reported by *The Wall Street Journal*'s Neil Barsky, Trump had personally guaranteed $500 million of some $2 billion in loans that banks such as Citicorp, Chase Manhattan, and Bankers Trust had so willingly dumped on him.

All of Trump's holdings were encumbered by $3.2 billion of debt, with junk bonds sold by Merrill Lynch and Bear Stearns for the casinos making up about a third of that. Even though Trump Plaza and Trump's Castle were carrying $683 million in debt, Trump managed to charge the Castle $5 million one year for the use of his yacht. In 1996, Trump said his personal guarantees on loans amounted to a staggering $1 billion.

Although the casinos were foundering, New Jersey regulators gave Trump the slack he needed to keep his head above water. With a third of the city's gambling market under his control, it proved to be difficult for them to do otherwise. For instance, when Trump came close to missing a mortgage payment on the Castle in 1990, casino regulators allowed Fred Trump to purchase $3 million in gambling chips to get Donald over the hump, even though the maneuver flouted state regulations.

Ultimately, Trump's casinos would all seek bankruptcy protection; other executives would be installed by the banks to manage his properties; and Trump would forfeit many of his showier holdings outside of Atlantic City. The Plaza Hotel, half of which Trump had already turned over to the banks, was sold in 1995 for $325 million—$80 million less than Trump paid for it. The Trump Shuttle was taken over by the banks. His biggest real estate holding in Manhattan, the West Side Yards, went into default and was taken over by an investor group that kept Trump on as a minority partner and property manager. After working so furiously to promote his name, Trump is now left with nothing else. He is valued in business circles only as a front man, as a human marquee.

Trump narrowly avoided personal bankruptcy in early 1995, after banks extended a deadline for paying back at least $115 million of the debt he had guaranteed. Trump's casinos still carried hundreds of millions of dollars of debt, but the operations had begun to show a profit as the Atlantic City market rebounded. And the willingness of investors to gamble on Trump's name allowed him to create a publicly traded holding company for his casinos in 1995 and to foist $795 million of the Taj's debt on his new shareholders. Just a few months later Trump palmed off more of his liabilities on his shareholders when he sold the Castle to the public company for $490 million ($165 million in stock and cash, and the assumption of another $325 million in debt that Trump had racked up). The price was about $100 million more than some analysts thought the Castle was worth. But even those analysts were too optimistic. When the public company later tried to sell a controlling stake in the Castle to an outside investor, the transaction valued the property at about $314 million, or about $176 million less than Trump was paid for it.

Financial columnist Allan Sloan observed that the transaction (which eventually fell through) was further evidence that "shareholders and bondholders have to be total fools to ever think that Donald Trump will put their interests ahead of his own." Trump's maneuvers helped the public company's stock plummet 66 percent in 1996, to $12 from its high of $35.50 that year. By mid-1997, the stock had sunk even further, selling well below the $14 each share had fetched when first traded, almost two years earlier. In the summer of 1997, Trump changed the Castle's name to the Marina and then announced his intentions to sell one of his casinos to help reduce almost $2 billion in debt that the public company was pinned under.

Still, emboldened by the fact that his holdings have stopped hemorrhaging red ink, Trump has come around to a novel interpretation of why he fell so far so fast in Atlantic City and New York: banks and investors wouldn't lend him *more* money. "The cash flow dried up because . . . when it came time to refinance, there was no financing around. This is the thing, I always assumed that whenever it was time to refinance [you could]," Trump asserts. "I mean, I had bonds coming due and you couldn't get ten cents' worth of financing even though you were making a lot of money because the banks were out of business."

Sure that his touch is back, Trump is active in Atlantic City again. He recently opened a fourth casino, the World's Fair, in a hotel he bought years ago. The World's Fair is a tawdry slot hall festooned with cheap murals depicting scenes from Atlantic City's past; among the murals is a monumental portrait of Trump, beaming down on the rows of senior citizens lined up at the slot machines below. With such decorative flourishes, Trump is convinced that, at long last, Atlantic City is poised to become a premier resort.

"It's got something Las Vegas and almost no other place has. The Atlantic Ocean," Trump points out. "That's something you can't buy. In Las Vegas, if you turn on the sprinkler you have to pay a fine. I mean we have the entire Atlantic Ocean in Atlantic City."

PROMISES, PROMISES

How fully Trump's casinos can rebound from their recent flameout is still an open question, in part because other, much larger operators are now pursuing the Atlantic City market with much more diligence than Trump has ever mustered. Hilton Hotels and ITT, engaged in a brutal takeover battle, still plan to dig into their deep corporate pockets to gussy up their existing properties, and Mirage Resorts and Circus Circus have announced plans to enter Atlantic City. Mirage Resorts' return has been widely heralded as the surest sign that, at long last, casinos may transform Atlantic City into a desirable place to visit and live.

Along with these hopes for yet another rebirth comes a new generation of casino executives bearing a fresh brand of casino-speak. "We can now transport the entertainment mega-resort to Atlantic City in the new environment there," says Circus Circus president Glenn Schaeffer. "It will extend the marketing beyond the drive distance and transform

Atlantic City into a destination resort. . . . We'll transform those plain old boxes into the more fluid architecture of the megastore."

In their zeal to attract new business, New Jersey regulators have also become more accommodating to casinos, allowing such former no-nos as twenty-four-hour gambling and a larger percentage of slot machines on casino floors. Gripped by antiregulatory fervor, the regulators also have signed off on some questionable practices that clearly target the most vulnerable gamblers. The state now permits cash machines to be placed adjacent to the gambling tables, so bettors can get more money without having to go through the inconvenience of actually leaving their seats. The ATMs present a temptation that only the most disciplined of gamblers will avoid. Compulsive gamblers commonly use credit cards to gamble, and a 1997 study found that Atlantic County, the only county in New Jersey where casino gambling is legal, had a personal bankruptcy rate 71 percent higher than the rest of the state.

Atlantic City's loosened regulatory regime gave all of the city's gamblers, compulsive or not, more opportunities to lose their money and helped spur a record-breaking cash flow of $724 million at the casinos in 1995, up from $304 million in 1990. But even in this more favorable regulatory environment, Atlantic City's casinos sometimes still manage to steer themselves into corners. By 1996, cash flow for all the casinos was shrinking by more than 10 percent per quarter as the casinos' inability to wean themselves from the ruinous bus wars started to devour their profits once again.

In addition to the extra money the casinos are sucking in, the city's boosters point to other changes. More visitors are coming to Atlantic City in cars, and the old airport is finally being renovated. Occupancy rates are now on a par with Las Vegas', propelling the construction of thousands of new hotel rooms. And the city has $70 million budgeted for public works improvements and a general face-lift over the next nine years. Atlantic City is also—finally—beginning to reap some visible rewards from the casinos' presence: a new minor league baseball stadium; a new $268 million convention center; and blocks of affordable housing that went up in the 1990s.

But twenty years into its waltz with gambling, Atlantic City is still a dour, troubled town.

To be sure, the city would have continued to erode even if the casinos had never come. And many of its social and economic problems predated their arrival. Some of the economic benefits from the casinos, primarily jobs, aren't as apparent in tiny, black-dominated Atlantic City as they are in the surrounding, largely white towns. But many of the extraordinary claims originally made for the advent of casinos—an Atlantic

City renaissance, a renewed entrepreneurial base, jobs for thousands of unemployed black residents—still haven't fully materialized, twenty years after the casino referendum was passed. Whereas casinos on the Las Vegas Strip get about 40 percent of their revenue from nongambling activities, only 10 percent of Atlantic City casino revenue comes from such sources. Atlantic City has no movie theaters and only recently got a supermarket, conveniences common to noncasino towns but anathema to casino operators, who want all food and entertainment to be safely locked behind their doors.

Decades of resentment hang over Atlantic City. The development of the site for Mirage Resorts' proposed casino, which will slice through a black residential neighborhood, has fueled an outcry among some residents that New Jersey and local government favor casinos over Atlantic City's inhabitants. For residents who hung on in Atlantic City despite the casinos' encroachment, property taxes increased 64 percent between 1989 and 1995.

Perhaps the most visible testimony to the limits of what casinos can accomplish is Atlantic City High School. The building is an impressive, sprawling facility built for $80 million, most of which came from taxes levied on casinos. But in spite of all of the money poured into the high school, old problems persist. The high school's students are racially divided, dropout rates are high, and test scores have been so poor that the school is being specially monitored by the state.

Jobs in the new service industries require employees with particular skills—promptness, an ability to manage routines, and the courage and tenacity to subsist on low wages chief among them. For teenagers attending Atlantic City High School, any motivation to achieve may be stunted by their scanty job prospects. Although casinos employ 40,000 people in Atlantic City—2,000 more than the population of the town—the town's unemployment rate is more than 15 percent, about two and a half times the average unemployment rate in the rest of New Jersey. The fact of the matter is that Atlantic City's residents have remained impoverished during the casinos' twenty-year trek through their town.

"There has been some good and some neglect, and I think it's because the people writing casino legislation didn't take into account how much of an impact the casinos would have on Atlantic City," says William "Speedy" Marsh, district coordinator for a local community group. "Just look at this place. It's decimated. . . . There's a skills shortage here. People don't have a work ethic or a desire to work. We need job training programs, not a minor league baseball stadium."

On the drive out of Atlantic City, past odd assortments of rubble, over potholes, and across deeply pitted roads, billboards begin to dominate the expressway again. One billboard features a picture of a bearded rabbi admonishing gamblers that "The time of your redemption has arrived."

Preachers of all stripes have wandered America's cities and countryside for three centuries, warning the wayward to get their lives in order and to stop gambling. But a country enamored of vice yet unwilling to embrace it has never found a comfortable nook in which to house its most primal desires, choosing instead to adopt a peculiar moral schizophrenia. So it is that gambling, like all the vices, has always struck a deeply moral chord in America, the depths of which became clearer as riverboat casinos began plying the inland waters of some of the most conservative, God-fearing regions in the country.

The Compulsive—I

Evan Peters is a thirty-nine-year-old compulsive gambler who is now a prisoner in a federal penitentiary. A former police officer and a gifted athlete, he succumbed to a craps habit that caused a divorce, ended his law enforcement career, estranged him from almost all the people close to him, sent him on two tours through the federal prison system, and left him with a despondency that borders on the suicidal. Peters is brutally candid about his gambling troubles and blames no one but himself for his ills. ("He always blames himself after the fact, but never before the gambling becomes a real problem," says his girlfriend, Patty.) Yet, despite his remarkable candor and his recognition that his gambling habit has left him broke, alone, and afraid, Peters remains constantly vulnerable to the belief that he still might score one "big win" that could turn his life around.

Compulsive gambling was officially recognized as a mental disease by the American Psychiatric Association in 1980, although its terrors have been known to philosophers and writers through the ages. There is no clear consensus on what, precisely, a compulsive gambler is. The American Psychiatric Association defines a compulsive gambler as someone who is unable to resist the urge to bet and consequently disrupts his or her family, personal, or professional lives. Gamblers Anonymous says compulsive gamblers share three central characteristics: the inability and unwillingness to accept reality; emotional insecurity; and immaturity. Recent medical studies indicate that there may be a biological side to compulsive gambling, similar to the unique chemical reactions liquor triggers in alcoholics. Many compulsive gamblers have other dependencies, such as alcoholism or drug addiction, but in Peters' case that isn't true. He never smoke, drank, sniffed, or injected. He just couldn't keep his hands off the dice and cards.

♦ ♣ ♥ ♠

On holidays, we'd always go to my grandfather's, like on Christmas or New Year's. And when I was young—seven, eight, nine—we used to go to Brooklyn. They used to have the card game. And my grandfather used to always sit at the head of the table.

They would all sit, ten to twelve people at the table. I remember watching those games and seeing the thrill when they'd win. They used to let us go under the table and used to have the dollars, the fives, the tens, and the quarters. They used to rake the quarters in, and they used to drop some on purpose. We'd scurry under the table and we'd get the coins and stuff. And I remember having loads of quarters.

Then we'd go to another table. Like four or five of us, we grandkids, and we would play. Not knowing what we were playing, just doling the cards out and putting money in. Pretending.

Then we moved from Astoria to Flushing. And I met a group of friends and stuff, and we always gambled. I always remember gambling not only for the baseball cards . . . we always used to play Monopoly. We always used to have a good poker game going. Anywhere from thirteen to seventeen [years old]. We really had some poker games going. You could win some money there.

And we just loved to gamble. We never drank, never smoked, never did any kind of drugs, never. We always were into sports and we were outstanding in sports.

When it came to sports I was always the captain or let somebody else be captain. I was always the first one picked. Always. If I go out, I don't care what level I play or who I play against, not that I'm trying to brag, but I'll probably be the best player on the team, on both sides of the team. . . . I just was always good. In baseball especially. Football, anything close to me I would catch.

My dad never came [to watch my games]. Once in a while he did, and I remember when he did come it was special. So everybody says it has something to do with my dad and all this stuff. And I'm thinking, and I'm saying, you know, how do we know? You know, I never went to therapy, never talked to anybody about it, but, uh, I know I love my dad. And he died very young.

When I was sixteen I wanted to leave, I wanted to run away from home badly. . . . I just wasn't comfortable. I used to sneak out at night. Out of the house. I would just walk around. I used to take a knife for protection. I would just walk around. I liked to be out.

The more I think about things, I think everything kind of hinged on my dad. He set certain things off into me. . . . My dad used to hit us here . . . welt marks . . . I used to hate his guts. I used to hate his fucking guts.

And I remember back then, going with a couple of friends, and we used to do burglaries. For money . . . I was stealing to get money so I could go gambling. When I was sixteen. Oh yeah, I had the gambling bug. . . . I would say I was thirteen when I had either daily, or at least three to four times a week, a good poker game.

You could win, you could win $100, $150, which was a lot back when you were fourteen, fifteen. And so that's where it really started. Didn't know anything about the game, never played anything but poker when I was younger—all kinds of poker. That was our excitement. Never really accumulated anything. If I needed money, I would gamble. . . . Why work?

♦ ♣ ♥ ♠

[After high school I joined] the Marines and was stationed in Washington at Eighth and I [Streets]. I met this good friend of mine, Ryan Kloster. . . . We got along real good, and he really got me into gambling. Big time . . . He had a car and we used to drive back to New York every weekend. That's when I first started going to these after-hours places, gambling. I think they were in Brooklyn. Used to go into a restaurant, used to go upstairs and used to have the whole second floor full of card tables. . . . It was the late seventies, 1977, something like that.

Later on, I used to go to Sixty-first Street down First Avenue, like between Sixty-first and Sixtieth. And we'd go in this club that was definitely Mob run. You had to knock on the door—big metal door, and they'd open. Literally, like the movies. And they had given [Ryan] a pass. He'd been there before. And he could bring people, and then you'd go in and that would be like a regular casino. . . . It was just like Atlantic City was and I'd never went to Atlantic City yet.

And I remember that craps. Craps really had me. . . . I learned how to play craps. I liked the action. . . . When I go and I play craps, I—not that I yell—I say, "Come on guys, let's go," you know, "Come on"—I kind of get into it a little bit. I don't really, I would never yell. . . . Every-

body else would yell, and I was nice and calm. Win or lose, that's always how I was. If I lost all my money I would be pissed, but I wouldn't give them the benefit of knowing.

I always tried to put this big act on, that if I had $10,000 or $20,000 or $30,000, and I lost that, that really meant nothing to me. And I wanted to put that image out.

I won $69,000 at the Sands one day with this guy Johnny Savino who won $131,000, and we were yelling, and that was the only time I was yelling like, "Come on, one more." . . . I mean, this kid was betting $5,000, $6,000 on the 5 and 9, $6,000 on the 6 and 8. Every time, he got hit, I mean he was getting big money. I mean, he won $131,000 in about forty minutes. . . . And I remember taking the racks all big orange and white chips, only the big chips. I would only take $9,900 every day to avoid the tax, avoid the slip for the IRS.

When Atlantic City opened up, we stayed the night and we waited for Atlantic City to open up and we were right in there, boy, the first. . . . And I had no idea what to do. Played a little slots. . . . And I remember really being intimidated. . . . Now, coupled with the Brooklyn action now I got Atlantic City, and I was really learning, I was really learning.

To this day I never have wanted casino credit. I never borrowed from shylocks. I used to lend money, but I never used to borrow. No, it was basically, when I was a cop, I used to lend money. To other cops, like a side business.

When I got released from [the Marine base] I went to Okinawa. . . . In our own club, in the base, they had a slot machine. . . . Boy, I used to play that machine for hours and hours. And after a while, like I would lose $100 to $200. But I remember, if I played it long enough it would always hit. If I stayed from a certain hour to a certain hour it would always hit.

I remember getting off one machine to go get some more quarters, guy goes in, puts two quarters in, wins the jackpot; all the money that I was putting in 'cause I was just waiting for it to hit. I almost died, I almost died.

[After I left Okinawa] I went to Florida and played baseball for a year. Used to go to the races down there. Well, they had the greyhounds, a couple of guys down there liked the greyhounds, but I liked the jai alai.

So I went back [to New York] and got married. I was twenty-one. I got engaged, I had my dress blues, got married in '79. . . . I started working for my father. And I remember a time that we went to Atlantic City, and I had like $1,200 on me and my dad didn't carry that kind of money. He really wasn't that big on the credit cards, and I sat down [to gamble], and I remember how heartbroken they were when we were *going home. I said I lost $1,000, $1,200, and he was really heartbroken. I could just see it. The atmosphere, you could cut it with a knife. He really was disappointed. Again, more disappointed in me.*

And my mom, I think my mom was always a gambler, definitely. I've gone a hundred times with my mother to Atlantic City. . . . She loves it. She's addicted to it. . . . Then I got married, I started working for my dad and my dad and I got real close, maybe till he died, which would be fifteen years ago, and I haven't been back to his grave once. He's buried right near Louis Armstrong.

I always wanted to be a police officer, and [one day] I got my chance. My brother's father-in-law was a police lieutenant in Newark, and I got on the list. . . . I made a lot of good arrests. I got awards. . . . And I was gambling all through my time on the force.

I was on the force seven years. I was two and a half years on housing. Two years later, I made detective. I made around $40,000 with overtime, which was pretty good. I was making more than that doing home improvement on two buildings. . . . I would buy, refinance, improve, sell. Make money. I learned quickly. I wasn't no landlord, but when I collected rent, people gave me tens and twenties. Boy, it was a lot of cash.

I didn't have many relationships with women in general. . . . I met this one girl, Cathy. I was with her six years. I really loved her. [My wife] Lisa knew. She was pregnant with [our son] Evan, and she almost committed suicide.

Meanwhile, the gambling was big at this point. Making a lot of money. When I really started gambling, which probably was '85 . . . the big money, $50,000, $60,000 . . . the home improvement [added to] my check [gave me] $1,500 a week. Well, I used to find a game. There was a game in Newark, while I was patrolling, I used to go upstairs and that was a heavy game. . . . But I was here in uniform, full uniform, and I was saying, "What am I doing?" But this is how much gambling, here in full uniform, I got my gun on me, and it wasn't really out of control yet.

Now in this time I met Johnny Savino . . . and the guy always had money—big, big boy, about six three, 300, 400 pounds. Big. And we became good friends, just became good friends. . . . We used to go down to Atlantic City all the time. That's when I really got really into craps, 'cause that's all he played. Craps. And we played at the Sands. That's where he got all his comps and markers.

I remember going home and I had all this money on me. And I remember, like, flashing it in front of my brother. . . . He gambled in Atlantic City once in a while. But if he loses $400 or $500 that would be a *lot. And the guy makes a six-figure income, but if he lost $500 he would stop there. And he thinks I'm trying to show it off or whatever. God knows, like in two or three days, three to four days, I probably lost it all.*

♦ ♣ ♥ ♠

When you get a bad beat, you're playing ten to fifteen hands in an hour. You're throwing your money in, and cards aren't really good cards, so you "tilt"—you'll spend all your money right away. Let's say you have a $10,000 bankroll and you say, "I'm only going to lose two thousand at any time." You get to that $2,000 point, you don't get any action. "Well, I'm gonna play a thousand," and then another thousand, and now you're starting to tilt.

In the end, the money management issue is the most important. That's, if you have good money management, you can overcome any bad loss or good win. If you have good money management. Which I never really had. I did for a while. But you just lose it, you just can't help yourself sometime.

I'll always remember winning. I always remember winning. And when I lost, I can't ever remember when I lost.

Always craps . . . I used to love it. I always won in craps, and then I hit that big win in the Sands and that was it, now I really started playing. . . . I remember going back and I remember on the crap table I brang down $10,000. And I would play $100 pass line, $200 in the back, and I must've lost fifteen to twenty passes in a row. I went through the $10,000 like, oh, man, I was sitting down and I was sick.

I remember going home. I said, "I can't believe this." Not only did I not get any action, but the way I lost all the money, I mean, there's no way. How could it be so bad? How could the dice be so cold?

Once in a while I'd have a big win. And then I had a lot of money for additional action. Depending on what I would play. But it became where I needed to have the money or at least to win just so I could keep playing. And that became the most important thing.

I don't know where that ever hit me. But that's where it became where it wasn't so much that I'd won or lost, but how long could I stay in the action. . . . I was so selfish. I knew I wanted to get laid, and I wanted to gamble.

CHAPTER 4

NEW ORLEANS:
MISCHIEF IN THE BIG EASY

A CHILD OF MAMMOTH GLACIERS that furrowed through the upper regions of North America eons ago, the Mississippi River begins unwinding in Minnesota as it slowly slices down the center of the United States.

It carries 500 million tons of sediment each year to the Gulf of Mexico as it traverses territory near southern Illinois that was once covered by a prehistoric bay. The rich, silty deposits borne by the river's currents filled in this bay over thousands of years, creating vast acres of prime farmland. Over the slow trickle of geologic time, the Mississippi eventually extended its mouth hundreds of miles south of Illinois, leisurely licking its way around what is now New Orleans and creating a delta more than 10,000 square miles in size before expiring in the Gulf.

Meandering in lazy swirls for 2,348 miles and with a drainage area that covers about 40 percent of the country, the "Father of Waters" passes lands that have witnessed the rise and fall of ancient Native American civilizations; expeditions by Spanish and French explorers; the traffic of steamboats and barges; the long, brutal shadow of slavery and the cotton trade; industrial furnaces and manufacturing plants that have produced aluminum and assembled agricultural machinery; and the recent explosion of casino gambling.

The Mississippi's southern reaches are the muddiest, the deepest, and those most weighted with the languid mysteries and sordid miseries of Southern history. Several important cities sprang up along this stretch, but none was more linked to the economic forces and sodden passion of the river's southern tail than New Orleans.

Together, the Mississippi River and New Orleans spawned one of America's oldest gambling cultures. Gambling thrived in a region that romanticized individual daring and whose economy depended in large part on the risky, unpredictable hurly-burly of river trade. Nonetheless, gambling also existed uncomfortably in a region that came to be known as the Bible Belt, thanks to the stern outlook of the strain of Christianity that called it home.

Gambling in the South would wax and wane during the eighteenth and nineteenth centuries, its fortunes floating on the mercurial moral tides of passing decades. That pattern would be seen again in the late twentieth century, as riverboat gambling became so widespread that paddle-wheel shipyards began constructing new vessels at a rate last seen during the Civil War. But although the exterior of some of the new riverboats might be recognized by Huck Finn, their interiors, packed with blinking, ringing slot machines, are high-tech emporiums whose sights and sounds would be more familiar to Luke Skywalker.

As this new generation of riverboats ignited an anxious public debate about the direction of the country's values and economy, and as the gambling industry seduced cash-hungry local and state governments, New Orleans tried to reclaim its old position as a gambling capital. In its quest for a piece of the action, the city would slip into a quagmire that engulfed one of the casino industry's most capable companies, exposed the continued presence of organized crime in some parts of the gambling business, and fed the appetite for corruption that has long been a hallmark of Louisiana politics.

And while New Orleans stumbled from miscue to miscue, its neighbors in Mississippi quietly and effectively created the third-largest casino market in the country.

A SPECULATOR'S PARADISE

New Orleans was founded on the whims of a gambler. John Law, a Scottish gambler and financier, had worked his way into the confidence of France's royal court by offering to establish a French central bank in 1716. Two years later, Law used the bank's resources to start the Compagnie d'Occident, popularly known as the Mississippi Company, which founded New Orleans in the hope that French settlers could harvest treasures from the North American interior. Although the Mississippi Company's stock collapsed after a spectacular, speculative run-up, New Orleans survived. As grain, lumber, and animal pelts were floated downriver to New Orleans, the city became a nexus for trade between North America, the Caribbean, and Europe. A bawdy, cosmopolitan port town where slaves were auctioned, yellow fever hung in the air, and political intrigues were hatched, New Orleans later changed hands between the

French and the Spanish before Napoleon ultimately ceded it to the United States as part of the Louisiana Purchase.

Only 17,000 people lived in New Orleans in 1810, but by then the city already had more gambling halls than New York, Boston, Philadelphia, and Baltimore combined. Two years later, Nicholas Roosevelt, a relative of two future presidents, piloted the first steamboat to visit New Orleans. The advent of the paddle wheeler meant faster travel and more efficient shipping on the Mississippi and marked the beginning of a riverboat era that enriched the Crescent City.

Shortly after steamboats began plying the Mississippi, entrepreneurs seeking wealth like that wrung from tobacco production in the Southeast trooped into the lower Mississippi Valley and set up sprawling, fantastically lucrative cotton plantations. As slavery and cotton production expanded in the area, beginning in 1820, New Orleans also became a receptacle for the commerce, culture, inequities, and raucousness of the antebellum South.

The French and Spanish who built New Orleans enjoyed games of chance without any of the moral compunctions of their Puritan and Anglican neighbors who settled the northeastern United States. Dice and card games flowed freely into the Crescent City, gaining devotees among whites, freed blacks, and slaves. Even when Louisiana outlawed gambling in 1812, New Orleans received a special dispensation that allowed its residents to continue rolling the dice.

The lower Mississippi during this period was a speculator's paradise; fortunes were quickly made and lost in rapid-fire land deals, commodity trades, and currency manipulation. Along the banks of the Mississippi, in Memphis, Vicksburg, and Natchez, tough enclaves of flatboat workers and river travelers sprang up. Here the vices, especially gambling, were freely and frenetically practiced. New Orleans had a similar district, known as the Swamp, where whorehouses, saloons, and dangerous, crooked gambling dens proliferated.

Later, during the heyday of plantation culture, with its penchant for more aristocratic trappings, New Orleans erected more elegant lounges where gentlemen could gamble. Ultimately, fourteen such gambling establishments were sprinkled around New Orleans, the first being John Davis' Théâtre d'Orléans club—which masqueraded as an opera house— at the corner of Bourbon and Orleans Streets. The clubs operated around the clock, were lavishly appointed, for the most part honestly run, and featured fine food and wine. But when yet another speculative economic bubble in the lower Mississippi burst in 1837, the ensuing depression ruined most of these clubs.

Less ornate gambling joints rose up again about a decade later, and by the 1850s New Orleans also had more horse racing than any other city in the country. As a crossroads for itinerant merchants, international trade, and unabashed hedonism, New Orleans blissfully and persistently thumbed its nose at the moral conventions of the time. In other cities, however, gamblers toed a very thin line and their welcome sometimes ended abruptly and violently.

In Vicksburg, Mississippi, in 1835, five men were hanged and one tarred and feathered for being part of a professional gambling clique that, according to contemporary accounts, was linked to abolitionist groups and plots to spur slave revolts. Whether or not the murdered gamblers took part in abolitionist activities, they were clearly thought of as a threat to Mississippi's rigid social hierarchy—a hierarchy deemed necessary in a state where whites were heavily outnumbered by slaves. Gambling, offering a milieu in which classes and races sometimes mixed publicly, was an easy target for those worried about broader threats to the social order.

Like many of the frontier states, Mississippi was settled by Christian fundamentalists, primarily Baptists, whose religious practices were simple, democratic, anti-"Papist," and looked to the Bible for strict guidance on matters of spirituality and personal behavior. This view didn't accept debauchery in any form, and if Louisianans were content to have a "modern Sodom" like New Orleans in their midst, most Mississippians were not.

Vicksburg contained some fifty gambling dens of all shapes and sizes, and one resident complained in 1835 that the town was being overrun by gamblers. "Our streets everywhere resounded with the echoes of their drunken and obscene mirth, and no citizen was secure from their villainy."

So it was in July of that year that the city gave all professional gamblers twenty-four hours to leave town. When the deadline had passed, armed citizens and local militiamen marched from gambling den to gambling den, hauling roulette wheels and faro tables into the street and burning them. When five gamblers took up arms to defend their club and shot a member of the crowd breaking down their door, they were overtaken and lynched. Their bodies were left dangling for a day and then dumped into a ditch.

Gamblers got the message. Up and down the lower Mississippi, owners of gambling halls fled many of the river towns and sought sanctuary in New Orleans. Even as these gamblers took to the river in flight, another type of gambler appeared on the scene, one who floated from town to town, never planting roots. His lifestyle nonetheless earned him a mythic place in American culture: the riverboat gambler.

By early 1834, 230 steamboats and 4,000 flatboats were registered to cruise the Mississippi. While East Coast steamboats had deep hulls and were usually opulent, those that plied the Mississippi were shallow hulled and cheaply built. Several types of steamboats cruised the Mississippi: "packets," which carried passengers and cargo; "showboats," which were floating music halls; "towboats," which shoved cargo barges along; and "ferries," "gunboats," "dredges," and "light tenders."

Packet boats were the most common vessels on the Mississippi and the ones immortalized by Mark Twain and other writers. Usually, only the upper deck of a packet was well appointed; it was reserved for first-class passengers. A "social hall" fitted with a dining room and a bar might stretch the length of the boat, and here most of the gambling took place. Below the upper deck was space given over to much drearier cabins and room for cargo. Freed slaves, known as roustabouts, and immigrants carried out the grueling and dangerous task of loading and unloading cargo. The packets had life spans of about five years, and their fragility made pilots reluctant to race one another. River hazards and faulty construction sent many of the packets to the bottom of the Mississippi. By 1849, there were 600 packets on the river, even though 520 had sunk that same year because of collisions, fires, or exploding boilers.

Because of the immense amount of trade that flowed on the Mississippi in the early nineteenth century, the paddle wheelers became ready places to find travelers flush with cash. Many passengers were either on their way to purchase goods or had just sold them; either way, their pockets were full, and they were ripe for the picking by riverboat gamblers.

In the popular imagination, every riverboat gambler looked, dressed, and acted like Rhett Butler:

Beau Brummell in all his glory was no greater dude than the riverboat sports. They ordered their boots from Paris. The brims of their dark slouch hats had a spectacular swagger and even their high hats had a naughty curve to the brim. Broadcloth coats reached down beyond the knees, trousers were undertaker black or soft gray, with the trend to loud checkered pants beginning only with the Civil War. Up to that time the gamblers, like the plantation gentry, favored low-necked, loose collared white shirts, the cuffs edged with ruffles. On ties flashed magnificent stickpins. Vests were showily adorned with hand-painted designs or sporting scenes and beautified with pearl or stickpin buttons. The really elegant gambler wore an expensive, immense watch of gold, jewel-bedecked, on a gold chain, and bedizened his fingers with diamond and ruby rings [writes gambling historian Henry Chafetz]. To many an ordinary, law-abiding citizen the [riverboat] gambler represented reckless-ness and quick fortune, a flashy mockery of their drab, workaday lives.

At the height of the steamboat era, 800 riverboat gamblers worked the Mississippi, according to one estimate. In the lore that came to sur-round them, and in stark contrast to the dubious reputations of gam-bling hall owners, riverboat gamblers were popularly thought of as chivalrous, independent, and living by a strict code of honor. They kept small guns in their belts and slender daggers concealed in their boots, al-ways ready to defend themselves. Among the most famous of these men were Jimmy Fitzgerald and Napoleon Bonaparte White, both of New Orleans; an Englishman, Richard Hargraves; and George Devol of Ohio.

"Some men are born rascals, some men have rascality thrust upon them, others achieve it," Devol recalled in his memoirs. "In the flush days of gambling on the Mississippi I used to take everything. If a man did not have the money, I would not refuse diamonds or a stock of goods. On one occasion, when I was going from Memphis to Cairo on the *Belle of Memphis*, a little game was started and I won ten first-class mules."

The reality of riverboat gambling was less glamorous than the leg-end. However much they may have tried to mimic the dress and man-ners of plantation owners who gambled money earned off the backs of their slaves, most riverboat gamblers were card cheats who learned their trade in some of the tougher gambling dens along the Mississippi. And while a few of the fancier steamboats afforded a luxurious setting in which to gamble, the action at most tables was nonstop, rough, drunken, frequently violent, and often crooked. Only a small portion of riverboat gamblers made enough money to dress elegantly, and most worked in teams rather than alone. Many favored simple, sometimes grubby cloth-ing to appear less threatening to potential marks. They played for long, tense hours into the night, often lost their riverboat winnings by gam-bling and whoring at ports of call, and constantly had to be ready to jump ship, rather than draw their guns, if their victims realized they had been cheated. Cole Martin, a riverboat gambler, looked back on his ca-reer in an 1896 memoir:

It's very pretty to read about, but the real thing was not so nice. The black-eyed, black-mustached hero gambler that you read about was anything but a hero. There was no chivalry in his nature, and he was ready for any dark deed that would profit him. Of course I am speaking of the professional gambler, for everyone gambled: If they had not done so the professional's occupation would have been gone. The chivalrous ones were the young Southern planters, reckless, but not mean, who would play the full limit and get fleeced.

A good card handler could deal cards from any part of the deck he chose and, if need be, shave or bend cards so they could be recognized during a poker game. Marked cards, those stamped with minute symbols that indicated their value to a knowledgeable observer, made their first appearance on riverboats in the 1830s. Although the manufacture of marked cards was illegal in Europe, it wasn't in the United States, and riverboat gamblers purchased tainted decks printed to their own specifications. Cards were usually purchased from bartenders in the steamboat's saloon, so riverboat gamblers would typically bribe the bartender to slip a marked deck into a high-stakes game.

If gamblers themselves wanted to slip cards into a game, concealed mechanical devices helped do the trick. Gamblers could shop by catalog from "sporting houses" for little goodies they could wear under a shirt or vest and load with aces and face cards. One New York sporting house offered an "arm pressure vest machine" for $15 that it described as follows: "You press against a small lever with the arm (an easy pressure of three-quarters of an inch throws out the cards [in] back of a few others held in your left hand), and you can reach over to your checks or do anything else with the right hand. . . . The motions are all natural, and do not cause suspicion."

Although the extent to which riverboat gamblers cheated may not have always been known, it was commonly assumed that they were predatory. And that fact didn't really bother anyone: "Few people doubted that gamblers cheated, but it was widely held that they won money primarily from 'suckers' who did not deserve to have it or could easily afford to lose it," notes historian John Findlay. "Victims were frequently portrayed as members of groups out of social favor—Jews, foreigners, slaveholders, immigrants, or the spoiled sons of wealthy families."

Paddle wheelers didn't operate under any particular legal jurisdiction, so riverboat gamblers enjoyed some breathing room while aboard. The pilots of the packet boats knew that gambling drew more travelers and helped fatten the boat's take on liquor and food, so they also welcomed the presence of riverboat gamblers. Many steamboat pilots considered it good luck to have a gambler aboard.

Perhaps riverboat gamblers were more socially acceptable than owners of land-based gambling dens because people felt less threatened by them. Since they never stayed in one place very long, their presence might have been considered less of a cancer ready to overtake the communities they inhabited. Over time, people also came to believe that riverboat gamblers embodied many of the values of frontier individualism; hence the mythology that eventually surrounded them.

But the riverboat gambler's era faded along with the steamboat. The Civil War halted most commercial traffic on the Mississippi, and after the war the railroad began to supplant the steamboat as the preferred way to travel. On the river, large barges began moving greater tonnage than steamboats could handle.

A fabled 1870 race from New Orleans to St. Louis between two steamboats, the *Robert E. Lee* and the *Natchez*, was the last hurrah of the paddle wheeler. Most had disappeared, along with the gamblers who walked their decks, by the end of the nineteenth century. Boosted by the transcontinental railroad and various gold, silver, and oil rushes, settlement and commerce shifted west, and the economic boom of the lower Mississippi became a distant memory.

The river towns of the region withered in the post–Civil War years. Devastated by war, slow to industrialize, and home to a large, illiterate, and dependent population of former slaves and a smaller population of poorly educated whites, the deep South fell behind the rest of the country. The region remained tied to cotton, and when the crops were ravaged by boll weevils during the first three decades of the twentieth century, the economy rotted further.

Some towns along the upper Mississippi, like Galena, Illinois, which were completely dependent on steamboats also faded. But many others, such as Rock Island, Moline, and East Moline, Illinois, as well as Davenport and Bettendorf, Iowa, built brawny industrial centers that by the early 1970s boasted several hundred major manufacturing companies.

New Orleans' economy, bolstered by its large port, new rice farms, and sugar cane, remained stronger and more diversified than others of the lower Mississippi. But the city never fully recovered from the Civil War, and its economy and politics remained speculative and scandal-ridden as it cycled through booms and busts at the end of the century. Eventually, New Orleans lost its regional dominance to Atlanta, which was better served by railroads.

THE GOLDEN OCTOPUS

New Orleans was occupied by federal troops from 1862 to 1877, and during that time Louisiana, its economy ravaged by falling cotton prices and the lifting of the protective sugar tariff, unleashed a lottery that was the first of its kind.

Lotteries were once illegal under Louisiana's constitution. However, in 1868, the Louisiana Lottery Company, a private corporation, went into business with the approval of state legislators who had been richly bribed to amend the constitution two years earlier. Charles Howard, a fast-talking thirty-six-year-old from the East Coast, ran the company on behalf of a gambling syndicate based in New York. Howard had earned his gambling stripes working on riverboats; he first came to New Orleans to manage the Alabama and then the Kentucky lotteries' operations there (between 1840 and 1860, all states except Alabama, Kentucky, Missouri, and Delaware prohibited lotteries). Howard purchased the goodwill of Louisiana's legislators by lining their pockets with hundreds of thousands of dollars in gold coins. Some grateful politicos also received an added bonus of free stock in Howard's company.

The lottery company was given a twenty-five-year state charter that authorized it to "establish a solvent home institution and ensure fairness" and to "raise funds for education and charitable purposes for the citizens of Louisiana." It was also given a local monopoly on lottery wagering after the state shut down other lotteries and numbers games. The company received tax-exempt status in exchange for $40,000 a year in charitable donations, a small portion of what it eventually raked in each year.

What made the Louisiana lottery unique was that it was everywhere. Lotteries had existed in other states, but, unlike others, Louisiana's lottery was marketed nationwide via mail and through branch offices in New York, Chicago, Kansas City, and most other major cities—a feature that led critics to name it the Serpent. In some years, almost half the mail that passed through the New Orleans post office involved the lottery.

Although more than 90 percent of the lottery's tickets were sold outside Louisiana, it was wildly popular at home. More than a hundred shops in New Orleans, where the lottery company was based, sold lotto tickets for such daily, monthly, and semiannual drawings as the "Grand Golden" and the "Grand Extra." Daily tickets cost between 25 cents and $1 and carried top prizes of $2,500 to $3,000. Monthly tickets cost $20, with a top prize of $300,000, while semiannual tickets cost $40 and could fetch a grand prize of $600,000. The odds of winning were, predictably, atrocious.

"The man who buys a ticket every day at every drawing will have only one chance in 84 years to draw even the $243.35 prize," the *New Orleans Democrat* observed at the time. "Old Methuselah himself had he bucked up against the lottery from his earliest childhood to the day of his death and bought a ticket every day would have found himself winner of $2,678.85 after having spent about $250,000 on the lottery."

By 1890, the Louisiana lottery was taking in $28 million a year (about $487 million in 1996 dollars) with profits of $8 million (or $139 million in 1996 dollars), according to congressional testimony. Although most other lottery companies at the time were permitted by law to keep only 15 percent of all wagers for administrative expenses and profits, Louisiana allowed Howard's company to keep almost 50 percent. Some of the public proceeds of the lottery were put to good use. The first waterworks in New Orleans, for example, were paid for by the lottery, and schools were upgraded with lottery funds. But for the most part Howard used his company's fat purse to buy off politicians, control newspaper coverage of the lottery, and burnish the lottery's public image through occasional good works, such as flood cleanups. Howard's chutzpah established a tradition that later gambling interests would use to even greater effect.

To dispel any doubts that the lottery's drawings were honest, Howard's company trotted out two heroes of the Confederate army, Generals P. G. T. Beauregard and Jubal Early, to "monitor" the events. Both generals, aging and broke, presided over drawings in the company of nuns who watched as blindfolded black boys picked the winning numbers each day at four P.M. in the "Lottery Home" on St. Charles Avenue.

Whether or not the drawings were honest, one reason Howard's company was so profitable was because it kept all unsold tickets, usually about a third of those available. If an unsold ticket won, then the lottery company simply kept the jackpot for itself. As the lotto's profits rolled in, the savings rate of New Orleans residents plummeted. According to one estimate, savings deposits at local banks dropped from $2 million in 1880 to $915,000 in 1890, although it is impossible now to determine how much of this was attributable to betting on the lottery.

Lotto mania led some store clerks and businessmen in New Orleans to steal money to play, while an elaborate system of superstitions began to guide some gamblers' choices. Seeing a drunken man meant one should play 14; seeing a dead woman with gray hair meant picking 49; dreaming about fish called for 13. And "priests were kept so busy blessing tickets brought to them by Catholics that the archbishop was compelled to forbid such practice."

As different factions in New Orleans came out for and against the lottery, and the company continued to sway elections and legislation with juicy bribes, public sentiment nationally turned against the "golden octopus." The federal government effectively eliminated the lottery company's reach and earnings power by cutting off access to the U.S. mails. Louisiana declined to renew the lottery company's charter when it lapsed in 1893. Undeterred, one of the lottery company's principals decamped that year to Honduras and continued operating the lottery from there until 1907.

Even with the lotto gone, gamblers in New Orleans had other options. By 1880, the city had more than eighty gambling halls, all of which were quietly supported by an accommodating and corrupt police force. A "reform" mayor, Joseph Shakespeare, finessed public distaste for the spread of the halls by limiting licensing to sixteen operators, who were required to contribute to local charities.

Over the next several decades, gambling in New Orleans was sometimes legal, sometimes not, depending on how the political and cultural winds blew, but it was always easily available in small joints scattered around the city and state.

In the early decades of the twentieth century it was Huey Long, the state's legendary and larger-than-life governor, who helped gambling interests gain a firm and lasting foothold in Louisiana. Long rose to power in 1928 by deftly tapping into working-class unrest and railing against business interests, specifically companies such as Standard Oil, that had been developing the state's abundant oil and natural gas reserves for almost twenty years. Gambling operators, however, were spared the Kingfish's animus.

In 1934, about a year before he was murdered, Long gave the go-ahead to East Coast Mob boss Frank Costello to set up shop in and around New Orleans. According to recently declassified Federal Bureau of Investigation files, Huey and his brother, Earl, opened the door to the Mob in exchange for multimillion-dollar payoffs. Making quick work out of this golden opportunity, the Mob planted 1,000 slot machines around New Orleans, opened several casinos outside the city, and took over bookmaking operations throughout the state.

The slot machine supplier to Costello's casinos was Lion Manufacturing of Chicago. Lion would later be renamed Bally Manufacturing, issue publicly traded shares, and become a beneficiary of Teamsters pension fund loans.

During the 1940s and 1950s, the swankiest casino serving New Orleans was the Beverly Country Club, just across the Mississippi River in Jefferson Parish. Sporting silk wallpaper, crystal chandeliers, and big-time entertainers such as Carmen Miranda and Jimmy Durante, the Beverly was owned by Costello, Meyer Lansky, and the head of organized crime in New Orleans, Carlos Marcello.

Another nearby casino, the Club Forest, accepted $25,000 bets downstairs and installed machine-gun nests behind the air-conditioning vents upstairs, all of which was choreographed to big-band music conducted by the one and only Guy Lombardo.

Until a reform movement swept the larger casinos away in the 1950s, local politicians and police turned a blind eye to illegal gambling. Cops could look forward to a little extra cash from the casinos stuffed in with their paycheck each month, and slot machines and back-alley casinos stayed in business through the 1970s.

In the meantime, the petrochemical industry had revitalized New Orleans' port and its economy. By the early 1970s, New Orleans was the second-busiest port in the country, after New York, and 72 cents of every dollar of the city's income came from port-related trade. When the Arab oil embargo sent oil prices sky-high, domestic petroleum producers in states like Louisiana struck it rich.

With the oil industry's growth burgeoning in the early 1980s, New Orleans regained its status as the country's largest port, transporting 61 million tons of cargo in 1983 alone. It had the country's only offshore facility for unloading large oil tankers, and the petrochemical industry provided the metropolitan area with 160,000 jobs and a payroll of almost $3 billion.

Then the bottom fell out.

When oil prices went into free fall, so did New Orleans. Oil companies shut down. With little but tourism on which to pin its immediate economic hopes, the Big Easy decided in the early 1990s to reach for the brass ring that already had entranced Atlantic City: legalized gambling.

POVERTY IN TUNICA, BOOM IN BILOXI

New Orleans' foray into legalized gambling followed similar attempts by other Mississippi River towns. As cities that once hosted barges and freighters laden by the world's most potent industrial economy now looked to the mighty Mississippi for a quick fix in the early 1990s, riverboat gambling reappeared for the first time in more than a century.

The earlier gambling boom along the Mississippi had been a by-product of economic growth, but the new explosion was a deliberate response to economic decline. Most new gambling markets are ringed with economic distress, and it was no accident that most of the towns that adopted riverboat gambling were, like Atlantic City, desperate for ways to jump-start their economies.

Casinos make more money per square foot than any other business, and sagging urban and tourist areas see legalized gambling as their short-est route to recovery. Looked at only in terms of job growth and in-creased tax revenue, the casino experiment thus far has worked for some cities. For many, including New Orleans, it hasn't.

The modern riverboat gambling era began on April Fool's Day, 1991. Two small companies, their efforts roundly dismissed as inconse-quential by major casino operators, opened riverboat casinos in Betten-dorf and Davenport, Iowa, that day.

The two Iowa cities, along with neighbors across the river in Illinois, had been ravaged by plant closings and painful layoffs at such giant cor-porations as John Deere, Caterpillar, and International Harvester. The closings left 8 million square feet of industrial floor space vacant in Iowa and tens of thousands of people out of work.

To combat the crisis, Iowa legalized gambling in 1989 after five years of intense lobbying by gambling interests and a county-by-county referendum on the issue. Iowa, a deeply conservative state that had pre-viously kept a tight lock on its liquor cabinets and its morals, allowed the gamblers in but then held its nose, the way one might when letting a mangy pet into the house. Iowa imposed strict guidelines on the gam-bling companies. Operators had to pay a 20 percent state tax on their revenue. Gamblers aboard the riverboats could wager no more than $5 per bet and could lose no more than $200 per visit.

Despite the limits, the boats were a hit, and three others were soon opened in Iowa. Tourism doubled in the region after the riverboats opened, and during the five Iowa riverboats' first year in operation they paid about $13 million in state taxes on revenue of almost $65 million.

If gambling in Iowa occurred in a vacuum, the state might have been able to make limited gambling succeed. But economic development via riverboat casinos became a beggar-thy-neighbor process, with other states along the Mississippi River easing restrictions to make themselves more attractive to operators who could fatten the municipal tills.

Illinois approved riverboat gambling without imposing any betting or loss limits. Iowa's riverboat market subsequently collapsed. Besides having looser regulations, the Illinois boats were also closer to Chicago. Every casino market depends on close proximity to a large metropolitan area to draw gamblers—Las Vegas, for example, has Los Angeles, and At-lantic City has Philadelphia and New York—so fraying, bleak Illinois towns such as Joliet had a leg up on the more remote Iowans.

Barely a year after riverboats began plying Iowa's waters, the *Em-press* riverboat opened in Joliet. The city, which had been abandoned by U.S. Steel in the early 1980s and suffered unemployment rates as high as 25 percent, instantly began raking in almost $1 million a month in taxes.

A year later, with another riverboat afloat, Joliet was getting $1.5 million a month in taxes, 16 percent of its budget, from casinos. The money was used to spruce up the downtown area and rebuild other parts of the city. Just three years after opening, the *Empress* had profits of $203 million. And the casinos brought in new, albeit low-paying, jobs. All was well so long as Chicago, or any city closer to it with more desirable environs than Joliet, didn't legalize gambling. When riverboat casinos later started operating in Indiana, revenue at Joliet's casinos fell sharply.

But Joliet's numbers caused the big gambling corporations to rethink their aversion to the riverboat market. The biggest gambling companies had been hesitant to enter the riverboat markets because they felt the pickings would be slim. Their hesitation ended after several counties in the state of Mississippi also threw open their doors to smaller gambling companies that quickly began hauling in mouthwatering profits.

One of the first riverboats to test the new gambling waters in Mississippi was named, aptly enough, *Splash*. Owned by the proprietors of a Kentucky nightclub, *Splash* was a dingy pink tub that in 1992 docked alongside a tiny northern Mississippi town named Tunica.

Tunica County, of which Tunica is the seat, is sparsely populated and covered with cotton fields so vast that escaping across them must have seemed hopeless to the slaves who toiled there 130 years before *Splash* dropped anchor.

Tunica is racked by such grinding poverty that until recently its poorest residents, all of them African Americans, had no plumbing and dumped their excrement in open ditches that ran beside the tiny shacks they lived in. According to the 1980 census, Tunica was the poorest county in the poorest state in the country. The 1990 census rated it the fourth-poorest county in the country, with an unemployment rate of 13 percent, widespread illiteracy, and per capita income of less than $7,000.

Splash was welcomed to Tunica's docks only after local protests prevented the county from permitting a hazardous-waste incinerator to do business there. Mississippi had set up the broad parameters of the state's gambling law and then empowered its counties to decide for themselves whether to allow wagering. But gambling in Tunica was approved without a vote. Tunica County's board of supervisors simply endorsed casinos on their own after a cursory public hearing. In October 1992, *Splash* chugged into town.

Splash had Tunica to itself; no other boats would open in Tunica for another eleven months. At once, its casino was crammed with 1,400 people; hundreds more waited in line outside. For the large throngs of blue-collar workers heading to the slots and tables, *Splash* offered to cash paychecks on the spot.

Splash's owners, Rick and Ron Schilling, had no experience in the gambling business, and a month after the casino opened it was temporarily shut down for regulatory violations that resulted in a $100,000 fine. A year later, *Splash* was fined another $250,000 for "bookkeeping" problems.

"These guys were real mom-and-pop operators," recalls a former Mississippi regulator. "Everybody thought, 'Getting in Mississippi is easy because if *Splash* could get licensed I can get licensed.'"

But Mississippi soon began to tighten its licensing procedures. When George Hardie, the founder of a notorious California card club called the Bicycle Club, tried to open a casino in Tunica, he was rejected because of questionable financing.

The Schillings, who have gone on to bid on riverboat contracts elsewhere in the country, ultimately invested about $23 million in what became a two-barge operation in Tunica. The casino's revenue in its first year shot past the most wildly optimistic estimates to reach $150 million. As soon as it became apparent how much money the casino was earning, *Splash* ceased being the only game in town.

Because *Splash* employed 1,300 people, while the town of Tunica only had 1,175 residents, unemployment dropped dramatically, and continued to drop when three other casinos arrived. Then, in a heartbeat, those casinos closed, as several bigger players including Circus Circus and the Promus Companies' Harrah's unit opened facilities in the northern part of the county, closer to the much bigger pool of potential gamblers in Memphis.

Splash later went out of business, in part because it was a dump but also because of a loophole in Mississippi's gambling law that its competitors exploited. Since the law said the casinos merely had to be surrounded by water, some operators, such as Harrah's, just dug moats around their casinos that were fed by canals leading to the river. This allowed companies in Tunica to build away from the river and closer to Memphis.

Today, Tunica County's ten casinos, rising incongruously from flat, fertile cotton fields, together generate about $740 million in annual revenue. With Grand Casino opening the third-largest casino in the country there in 1996, the take is expected to climb higher in 1997—unless Grand, which will have to transport hotel guests by shuttle to its mammoth casino, turns out to be an expensive flop. Increased competition in Tunica, as in all casino markets after the first companies arrive, has squeezed the profit margins of many operators.

Yet even with the onslaught of casino development, it is still a challenge for some gamblers in this part of the country to come out of the closet. "These people are Bible Belt and don't like people in their church knowing they're gambling, so they don't like giving their name to people in a casino," says Randy Roberts, general manager of Circus Circus' Tunica casino. "They're all worried their minister will get mad at them if he finds out they've been gambling."

Casinos were destined to have an especially dramatic impact on Tunica County because, like Las Vegas, very little was there before casinos arrived. Although the county has a better telecommunications system and better roads because of the casinos' presence, it also has to contend with sharply higher crime rates (including the murder of a couple in a casino elevator and an investigation of money laundering), traffic jams, and increased compulsive gambling, which typically plague casino markets.

Moreover, the best-paying casino jobs have gone to people from outside Tunica. For the local population, unused to the rhythms and responsibilities of formal work, casinos have been a welcome opportunity but a challenge that overwhelms many of them. Like their counterparts in Atlantic City, Tunica's poor remain stuck in a cycle of joblessness and poverty that won't be cured overnight by any type of business. The county's unemployment rate, which can swing wildly because the population is so small, fell to 8.7 percent in 1993 before rising back to 12.9 percent in 1995.

The town of Tunica remains a slow-moving backwater, largely because all of the county's casinos are now located far north of it. Caught in the shell game of riverboat casino development, the county is hostage to the possibility that its neighbor to the north, De Soto County, will legalize gambling and cut off Tunica's access to Memphis.

"I think there would be a mad rush to De Soto County if gambling was approved there because it's closer to our main feeder market," says Joe Hasson, general manager of Harrah's Mardi Gras casino in Tunica. But Hasson is quick to point out that few operators consider it likely that nearby jurisdictions will legalize gambling.

Yet Belz Enterprises, a Memphis concern that is a partner with Harrah's in Tunica, has been pushing aggressively for legalization in De Soto County. Should that occur, Tunica's gamblers—black and white, little old ladies and tank-topped good ol' boys flaunting ponytails and tattoos—will leave and probably never return.

Still, Mississippi, by allowing an unlimited number of gambling licenses, all types of betting, and lower taxes, has also turned its southern coast into a casino market that has sucked in gambling companies from all over the country.

Casinos began doing business along Mississippi's Gulf Coast in 1992, two months before *Splash* opened. Biloxi, one of the principal

Gulf cities and Confederate president Jefferson Davis' last home, had been an open town long before the state legalized gambling in 1990.

Considered "sin city" by Baptists in the rest of the state, Biloxi for most of this century was a fishing town and a resort frequented by visitors from New Orleans and Mobile. Rumrunners had used it as a stopping point for smuggling illegal liquor during Prohibition and for decades thereafter when Mississippi remained a dry state. Tourists sunned on segregated beaches, munched shrimp, and watched such comedians as Andy Griffith and Jim Nabors perform at Gus Stevens Restaurant and Lounge in the 1950s. Gus' place served black-market liquor and housed slot machines all over the club, including in the kitchen.

Like other places—for instance, Hot Springs, Arkansas, and Covington, Kentucky—where local officials had allowed illegal gambling to flourish, Biloxi offered an assortment of slots, craps, and high-stakes poker games in bars along the town's waterfront during the 1950s and 1960s. More glamorous gambling spots could be found in such Biloxi casinos as the Fiesta, Mr. Lucky's, and the Raven. Local officials openly admitted that gambling was Biloxi's biggest business in the 1950s and the mayor and police chief made no bones about the fact that they accepted bribes from local casino owners. So prevalent was gambling in Biloxi that by the early 1960s military officials at nearby Keesler Air Force Base barred its personnel from sixty-two businesses in Biloxi that offered slots, blackjack, or craps.

By the mid-1960s, most of Biloxi's casinos had disappeared. The casinos' decline began when the state, though it had long winked at illicit gambling in Biloxi, forbade liquor sales in casinos even though it already had overturned long-standing laws forbidding the sale of alcohol elsewhere in the state. The rest of Biloxi went into a tailspin after Hurricane Camille tore apart the area in 1969 and improved highways made it easier for Gulf Coast tourists to bypass it in favor of Florida's more attractive beaches.

When political scandals swamped other development efforts aimed at reviving the faded resort in the late 1980s, voters in Biloxi's county narrowly approved gambling in 1992. One of the first casinos to arrive was the *Isle of Capri*, built from a pair of riverboats so downscale that competitors dubbed them the Pile of Debris. More to the point, the two riverboats were originally known as the *Diamond Lady* and the *Emerald Lady* and had done business first in Bettendorf and Fort Madison, Iowa, respectively.

The riverboats were owned by a scrap-metal dealer named Charlie Goldstein who had left Iowa's tight regulations behind for the freer-flowing waters of Mississippi. The boats' arrival in Biloxi offered an example of how quick riverboat-gambling companies were to abandon one town if another location seemed to be more accommodating. In the wake of the *Emerald Lady*'s departure, Fort Madison residents lost 600 jobs, and the town was stuck with the debt payments on a new, $2.6 million dock.

Fort Madison unsuccessfully sued the *Isle of Capri*'s parent company, saying the gambling concern had taken advantage of the town. The company says its move was unavoidable. "There was an awful lot of bitterness from municipalities in Iowa, and who can blame them? But if we don't make the right business decision, we don't survive," says *Isle of Capri*'s general manager, Tim Hinkley. "We had very limited capital and we closed the boats down in Iowa on July 5 and opened here [in Biloxi] on August 1. We had no idea what we would encounter, we just thought it had to be better than Iowa."

Chastened, Iowa subsequently removed all betting limits on its riverboats. The move, which guaranteed bigger losses for bettors and higher profits for operators, persuaded the *Isle of Capri* to open a new casino in the state and caused Iowa's casino market to rebound.

The looser rules also helped cause the number of Iowans who reported a "gambling problem" to triple to 5.4 percent of the population in 1995 from 1.7 percent in 1989, according to a study by sociologist Rachel Volberg. For the year ending June 30, 1996, 884 Iowans with gambling problems sought help from state agencies—up 57 percent from a year earlier, according to Iowa's Department of Public Health. Hot lines set up by the state to aid problem gamblers logged 14,000 calls in the same period, up from 3,700 the year before.

Iowa also eased up on cruising requirements for its riverboats. In this turnaround, riverboats that were once pitched to Iowans as less threatening because they would be cruising the Mississippi River settled into a largely stationary condition that the industry dubbed "permanent dockside."

Today, nowhere is the concept of "permanent dockside" more apparent than in Biloxi. None of the eight casinos now in Biloxi are true riverboats. Since state gambling law demanded that the casinos be water-based, Biloxi responded with huge barges that, when linked together, housed casinos the size of football fields. All of them are basically indistinguishable from land-based buildings.

Although a major hurricane could rip Biloxi apart again, the city is in the midst of a building boom that is bringing Mirage Resorts to town and is spawning the construction of several high-rise hotels.

Both the new construction and the barges' arrival were set in motion by the results posted by Biloxi's first three casinos. Just five months after opening in 1992, they hauled in more than $75 million in revenue. The numbers ignited a Wall Street feeding frenzy for small casino stocks—many of which later tanked—and led to a stampede of big casino companies bound for the Gulf Coast.

Tourism in Biloxi has skyrocketed, with more than 6 million visitors in 1995, and the local airport is expanding its jet service. Revenue projections call for the casino market to top $1 billion in the next few years, most of it derived from slot machines. Even though job turnover rates are high at the casinos, about 35 percent, many local residents say the economic benefits and jobs have tempered their original aversion to casinos.

On a more disturbing note, day care centers have sprung up at Biloxi's casinos to assist gamblers who tote their kiddies with them. While making it easier for children to be brought closer to the action hasn't yet caused any problems in Biloxi, it has done so elsewhere: in 1997, seven-year-old Sherrice Iverson was raped and murdered in a bathroom at the Primadonna Casino in Primm, Nevada, after she wandered away from a video arcade between three A.M. and five A.M. while her father was gambling.

Thick traffic jams are now a daily event in Biloxi. The sewage system is strained, and there is a growing number of homeless people. Local restaurants have been squeezed, unable to compete with the rock-bottom food prices casinos offer to lure gamblers inside. Crimes such as bank robberies and muggings, (the latter, in Biloxi, usually take place in casino parking lots) have also jumped considerably.

Competition among the town's casinos is fierce—particularly on weekends, which produce 60 percent to 70 percent of their revenue. A few of the casinos have flirted with bankruptcy or disappeared. But Biloxi has helped make Mississippi the third-biggest casino market in the country. Casino revenue statewide was $1.7 billion in 1995, compared with $7.3 billion in Nevada and $3.3 billion in New Jersey.

"It's a high, high degree of entertainment here. There aren't people blowing their paychecks here," says Bob Peyton, who has worked in every major casino market in the country and is now general manager of the Lady Luck casino in Biloxi. "Lake Tahoe was the same way, people didn't blow paychecks there either. But you saw [paychecks being lost] in Vegas and Atlantic City. Over time, as Biloxi generates a national draw, you may see more of those problems."

But local fears that more people would squander their paychecks and lose their souls as riverboat casinos spread across America's heartland and into the Bible Belt have ignited a backlash against gambling that is still playing out.

CASINO CASH AND THE BACKLASH

At the forefront of casino opposition are religious leaders. While defining their critique in modern economic terms, they draw on a uniquely American tradition of moral antipathy toward gambling that first found its clearest expression some 300 years ago in the voice of the Puritan clergyman Cotton Mather.

Mather condemned gambling as an "appearance of evil . . . forbidden in the word of God." Mather's moral certitude continues to inform the viewpoints of many of gambling's modern critics. Through the years, gambling has usually been bundled with tobacco, alcohol, sex, and drugs to form a family of vices condemned by moralists as a pox upon the land—even as many Americans have exuberantly tiptoed out their back doors to partake of these forbidden fruits.

The most vocal and best organized of gambling's current opponents are members of the National Coalition Against Legalized Gambling, a grassroots organization based in Galena, Illinois, and headed by the Reverend Tom Grey, a Methodist minister.

"These guys should have stayed in Vegas, but they came out from under their rock and tried to say this garbage was family entertainment," Grey says. "Now they've unleashed a ton of opposition."

"Casinos come in here and tell me they're going to bring gambling into my community and ninety-five percent of the members of my church are going to have fun, but five percent are going to lose everything they have," he continues. "Well, that's five out of every one hundred members of my flock. We're to love our neighbor, not fleece our neighbor."

Acknowledging that he is an heir to the moral traditions of his faith, but recognizing that because of changing values in America he can't "win the battle" against casinos "on the basis of morality," Grey assails the industry on economic grounds: "The guys running the companies pay themselves a lot of money and leave a lot of damage behind."

Well, yes and no. In some significant instances, casinos have had a positive impact on the communities where they've operated. Casinos are not always economic leeches, but neither are they just the merry entertainment enterprises their owners would have people believe. And in the great debate emerging over casino-led economic renewal, critics and backers alike have spouted fantasies to win support for their arguments.

William Eadington, the University of Nevada at Reno economist, is fond of citing examples of dubious number-crunching. Some of gambling's critics, Eadington notes, have latched on to figures from a nonexistent organization called the American Insurance Institute, which claims that 40 percent of white-collar crime is caused by gambling. The figure has been widely circulated in the media and in academic studies, even though the "institute" doesn't exist and there is no empirical basis for the statistic. Conversely, Eadington points out that in 1992 executives from Hilton, Caesars, and Circus Circus made wildly optimistic predictions—based on reports from consultants hired by the casinos—about job growth in Chicago that would be spurred by a proposed $2 billion casino there. The casinos predicted upwards of 40,000 new jobs, a figure Eadington says was as much as four times larger than the number that would actually have been created.

Most economists agree that true job creation and economic growth take place only in a casino market that, like Las Vegas, can draw gamblers from outside the community. In smaller, local markets, the money wagered just replaces money that would be spent on other goods and services. Mississippi's Gulf Coast, southeastern Connecticut, and, perhaps, Atlantic City have the potential to become resorts, but most other locales will end up shuffling their money around rather than expanding their economies.

Nor can state budgets rely on much of a boost from casinos. While casino taxes in sparsely populated Nevada accounted for 39.5 percent of the state budget in 1995, casinos contributed only 1.9 percent of the state budget in New Jersey that year. Mississippi casinos chipped in a healthy 4.5 percent of the state budget in 1995, and that percentage may grow. But taxes from Illinois casinos amounted to well less than 1 percent of the state budget in 1995. Casinos will typically add meaningfully to the budget pie only in small, poor states.

The social costs of gambling, what economists like to call externalities, are hard to quantify. But every casino market has had to deal with rising crime, strained infrastructure, increased personal bankruptcies, and the loss of tax revenue from other businesses, such as restaurants and state lotteries, that can't compete with casinos.

Moreover, the shrinking of America's middle class that has accompanied the growth of service industries like casinos may not bode well for the country's future economic health. Yes, casinos have brought jobs, but they are relatively low-paying service jobs rather than much better-paying manufacturing jobs. If this world of lower wages and unstable employment helps to create a thin upper tier of haves and multitudes of hardly-haves, with a scanty middle class in between, then serious social problems may be on the horizon.

Commercial gambling's growth along the Mississippi over the last decade has far too often been a race to the bottom, with each struggling town trying to grab a piece of the action before its neighbor does. As local legal barriers fall before the mighty engine and inflated promises of the gambling industry, towns with few resources are making uninformed decisons about a business that will permanently change the texture of their communities.

"We still have a lot to learn about the positive and negative impacts from gaming," Eadington says. "Economic benefits [of casinos] can be bid away by competitors, or ineffective enabling legislation, or just by a bad location or poor execution. And compulsive gambling remains a very real problem."

Of course, allowing commercial gambling to lay claim to the hopes of battered communities should be considered from more angles than those permitted by the narrow mantra of jobs-budgets-and-taxes. Commercial gambling is not just another business. It depends upon and profits from the ineffable longing people have to change their lives in an instant, as if they were rubbing a magic lantern. Amid all the competing data and studies introduced by casino gambling's critics and proponents is the fact that gambling can be an enormously destructive force in many communities and in many lives.

Casino executives claim they aren't oblivious to the dangers of compulsive gambling, especially because their own employees are the most at risk. The few studies done of casino employees show that as many as 15 percent of them, or 55,000 workers, have a compulsive-gambling problem. Within the general public, a far larger number of people struggle with compulsive gambling. The most sensitive and thoughtful casino executives seem to be sincerely troubled by the severity of the problem.

"I worry about compulsive gamblers but I don't know what to do about it," says Jim Parry, former president of TropWorld casino in Atlantic City. "They don't come into the casino wearing scarlet letters."

But, of course, casinos don't just wait for serious gamblers to stroll through the doors. They tug them in with free rooms, free food, free drink, and free entertainment—all of which casinos deduct from their taxes as a business expense. They also offer lots of credit to heavy gamblers and will even fetch them at their homes in a limousine if necessary. Moreover, while casinos are constantly on the prowl for card counters, their vigilance suddenly wanes when a stumbling-drunk gambler is emptying his wallet at the tables.

Heavy gamblers aren't the only ones coddled by the casinos' gravy train of perks. Casinos have also laid claim to politicians of all parties and at all levels around the nation. Every major industry hires lobbyists and greases politicians with campaign contributions to promote its business interests, but in recent years gambling companies have become unusually active participants in this time-honored tradition.

Between 1991 and 1996, when the casino boom was in full swing, gambling companies lobbed $4.5 million into national political campaigns, according to the Center for Public Integrity, a Washington, D.C., watchdog group. That level of spending makes the gambling industry a political force at the federal level on a par with the National Rifle Association and the United Automobile Workers.

In 1994, when President Clinton considered a 4 percent federal "sin tax" on gambling revenue to help fund welfare reform, the casino industry successfully scrambled to kill the proposal. In the wake of that action, casinos founded a full-time trade group in Washington, the American Gaming Association, and installed former Republican National Committee chairman Frank Fahrenkopf as its president.

While Republicans, particularly former senator Robert Dole, have since received most of the casinos' largesse, tidy piles of money have gone to Democrats as well, including President Clinton. Steve Wynn alone helped raise and contribute hundreds of thousands of dollars to Dole, although Clinton's rise in the polls forced Wynn to increase his bet on the Democrats as well.

At the state level, the stakes have been still higher, because states have more authority to regulate gambling than the federal government does. The gambling industry dished out more than $100 million in political donations and lobbying fees to sway state legislators between 1992 and 1996, according to an investigation by *Mother Jones* magazine. Gambling interests spent more than $16 million in Florida in 1994 in a failed attempt to legalize gambling there. In Missouri, gambling companies spent $11.5 million that same year to successfully lobby for the legalization of slot machines in casinos. Missouri House Speaker Bob Griffin, a Democrat, resigned in 1996 amid an investigation of allegations that he sought favors for casinos he represented as a lawyer while still holding office.

Other states also joined the fun. To help secure a casino license, the Nevada casino company Primadonna Resorts offered $20 million to two Illinois political consultants connected to bigwigs in that state's Republican-led legislature. Primadonna didn't get the license, and the money wasn't paid, but the consultants were quite happy to tell the *Chicago Tribune* that Primadonna's offer wasn't the highest they'd received.

Former Illinois governor James Thompson, who signed the bill legalizing casinos there, now represents casino interests as a lawyer. Among his clients is Argosy Gaming. William Cellini, an influential Republican fund-raiser and Thompson confidant, is one of Argosy's largest shareholders. Argosy, which has been subpoenaed by a grand jury as part of an investigation into casino licensing practices in Indiana, received an exclusive license in 1991 from the Illinois Gaming Board to operate a riverboat casino in Alton, Illinois. The gaming board's members had been appointed by Thompson, and after Argosy was licensed one of them went to work for a company in which Cellini was a major investor. Argosy went public in 1993, and Cellini has since snared at least $7.8 million selling his stock. By mid-1996, Cellini's remaining stake was worth about $10 million.

All this political and financial maneuvering was merely a warm-up, however, for what would occur when casinos returned to the great honeypot of American gambling: New Orleans.

HANDS IN THE TILL

In 1986, Louisiana governor Edwin Edwards, himself a high-stakes craps player who traveled with cronies to Monte Carlo (on his 1993 tax return he would report gambling winnings of $308,000), stood before voters in a local civic club and presented a cure for his state's rumpled economy.

Edwards urged the audience to pressure state legislators to approve a lottery for the first time in almost a century, and to demand the legalization of casino gambling. Mangling some lines from Shakespeare, Edwards warned antigambling forces that he would rally voters behind him: "I'll go to what Marc Antony said when he released the avenging crowd on the assassins of Julius Caesar: 'Mischief, thou art afoot. Work thou now what trouble thy will.' "

Mischief began to work its will in Louisiana seven years later, when riverboat casinos started cruising around New Orleans. In the intervening years, Edwards had left office after being acquitted of federal racketeering charges, only to return in 1992 after defeating former Ku Klux Klan leader David Duke in an election marked by bumper stickers reading, "Vote for the Crook: It's Important!"

Gambling's legalization in Louisiana was in keeping with the ribald, mercenary customs of the state's business and political life. The long, sordid history of gambling in Louisiana had eventually produced a state constitution expressly forbidding its legalization. No problem: Louisiana legislators just dropped the "bl" in "gambling," and in 1991 they voted instead to legalize "gaming."

Then the money rushed in. By 1994, state Senate president Sammy Nunez was traipsing around the Senate chamber handing legislators

$2,500 checks that had been signed by a local casino operator and Edwards benefactor named Louie Roussel. All this was perfectly legal in Louisiana. Yet the subsequent public outcry over the event offended Nunez because, as he later pointed out, most of the checks weren't doled out on the Senate floor. Most, the Democrat said, were handed over in his apartment or office.

But it was Edwin Edwards himself who set the standard for how Louisiana politicians should deal with casinos. He resumed the governorship just in time to oversee the awarding of fifteen riverboat casino licenses, sparking a series of events that the New Orleans Times-Picayune would describe as a "travesty" proving the state to be "a place where public officials too often wink and chuckle at ethical and legal violations."

In a lengthy investigation, the Times-Picayune found that no objective criteria were used in determining which companies got licensed. Of the forty-three companies that applied, those chosen all had close ties to Edwards. The governor himself apparently never made any money directly on these deals. But his friends and relatives, as well as friends and business partners of fellow Democrats, all profited handsomely. Edwards' four children set up companies to supply the casinos, and listed their business line as the telephone in the governor's mansion.

And when Louisiana decided to legalize video poker, organized crime stepped up to the plate.

Video poker, considered by experts to be one of the most addictive forms of gambling, was approved for state truck stops in 1991. That year, Bally Gaming, a machine manufacturer controlled by its former parent, casino giant Bally Entertainment, decided to supply video poker machines to the truck stops. Bally chose a company called Worldwide Gaming to be its distributor and put up millions of dollars to fund it.

The FBI knew Worldwide well. Wiretaps revealed that the company was controlled by associates of the Marcello, Gambino, and Genovese crime families and was to be their vehicle for infiltrating the video poker industry. According to a 1991 FBI debriefing of Mob informant Al D'Arco, the Marcello family had "a large number of police and political contacts in Louisiana as high up as the Governor's office." And according to a confidential report by New Jersey casino investigators, Bally chose Worldwide after Governor Edwards indicated at a 1992 "political gathering" attended by executives from both companies that if Worldwide "was involved, [Bally] would be one of the first companies licensed in Louisiana."

This wasn't Bally's only flirtation with organized crime. Bally had first rolled into New Orleans with Mafia kingpin Frank Costello in the 1940s, when the company was known as Lion Manufacturing. Foreshadowing later practices, it worked with a local, Mob-owned distribution firm named Runyon Sales. Chicagoan William O'Donnell, a Lion executive who had started out in the company's purchasing and sales departments in the 1940s, used Runyon shareholders' financial backing to buy Lion in 1962, three years after its founder died. In 1968, O'Donnell changed Lion's name to Bally.

In 1971, Bally, its Louisiana distributor, and a member of the Marcello family were indicted in New Orleans on federal racketeering and illegal gambling charges. Bally was eventually cleared, although its distributor was found guilty. But Bally later resumed doing business with the distributor, a move that New Jersey investigators described in a confidential report as the "appearance if not the fact of organized crime affiliations" and that helped prevent O'Donnell from procuring a casino license in Atlantic City in 1980.

When federal prosecutors indicted Worldwide for racketeering in 1994, they painted Bally Gaming, no longer controlled by Bally Entertainment, as a victim—this, despite court documents showing that Bally continued its relationship with Worldwide even after learning about some of its Mob ties. Prosecutors in Louisiana were criticized for propping up Bally in order to have the victim they needed to make a case against Worldwide, a criticism the prosecutors dispute. Louisiana went ahead and licensed Bally Gaming to sell slots in the state. By 1996, all twenty-four people indicted in the Worldwide case, none of them with Bally, had been found guilty.

The video poker debacle reached full bloom when federal wiretaps unveiled in 1995 suggested that several Louisiana legislators had accepted bribes from truck-stop owners who wanted to make sure video poker wasn't outlawed. By the summer of 1997, however, only two lawmakers had gone to trial, there were no convictions yet, and federal prosecutors were being criticized for releasing the wiretaps before charges were filed.

But the nadir of Louisiana's return to big-time gambling came with Edwards' successful push in 1992 to make New Orleans the site of the world's largest land-based casino. The company that accepted the challenge, Harrah's Entertainment, Incorporated, one of the biggest and most carefully managed casino companies in the country, ended up with a disaster on its hands.

HARRAH'S ROLLS SNAKE EYES

Harrah's, founded by William Harrah in Reno in 1946, introduced most of the modern management practices later adopted by other casinos. It was the first to use daily profit-and-loss statements, the first to take an "eye in the sky" approach to floor surveillance, and the first to use busing as a mass-marketing technique. (At one time, Harrah's was the nation's second-heaviest user of buses, after the U.S. military.) Many chief executives at other casino companies had earned their stripes working for Harrah's, and they considered themselves the industry's elite. Harrah's remained free of organized-crime control and in 1971 was the first casino company approved for a major stock exchange listing. For decades, the company enjoyed double-digit earnings growth.

In 1980, Holiday Inns, a lodging company that opened its management meetings with prayer, built chapels next to some of its motels, and had taken its name from an old Bing Crosby movie, bought Harrah's for $300 million. Harrah's headquarters were relocated to Memphis, Tennessee, where Holiday Inns was based and where all forms of gambling, including bingo, were outlawed.

Holiday Inns, recognizing that one casino in a major market could make more money than all its motels combined, quickly expanded Harrah's operations from Reno and Lake Tahoe to Las Vegas and Atlantic City. Casinos soon dominated the company, which changed its corporate name to Harrah's. It built a brand identity by offering modest, cookie-cutter casinos to middle-class gamblers who wanted predictability and good service. For a time, the formula worked magically, and Harrah's continued to have consistently profitable casinos.

Still trying to diversify geographically, Harrah's was one of the first big companies to move into the riverboat market and Indian gambling. But, to its detriment, it also ignored the trend toward themed casino resorts that Mirage Resorts and Circus Circus had so effectively exploited. And then Harrah's went after New Orleans.

The contest to win the coveted casino site involved the inevitable stroking of Edwards, and every bidder retained individuals with close ties to the Ragin' Cajun. Developer Chris Hemmeter and a partner, for example, flew Edwards and Sammy Nunez to resorts in Hawaii and Colorado. Though Hemmeter, who had the lease on the casino site, lost the bid, he wound up as a minority partner with Harrah's after it was selected for the project.

The targets were huge. The proposed casino, called Harrah's Jazz, would feature 200,000 square feet of gambling space and cost $425 million to complete. It would employ 4,000 people, draw 5.6 million visitors a year, and have annual revenue of $600 million. Harrah's believed that when Jazz was completed the company would have the biggest draw in one of the biggest tourist towns in the country.

But all of Harrah's projections proved dismally wrong. When a casino opened temporarily in early 1995 while the main casino was still being built, the magnitude of that error became apparent. The smaller casino had revenue of only $13.1 million a month, far below the forecast of $33 million a month. Revenue projections for the main casino were scaled back from $600 million to $400 million even as the project's cost, inflated by haggling with the city and state, nearly doubled to $823 million.

As it turned out, visitors to New Orleans wanted to listen to real jazz and dine in the French Quarter, not gamble in a part of town many felt was unsafe. In an urban setting with true alternatives for tourists, gambling wasn't a sure bet. Most of the gamblers at Harrah's Jazz were locals who didn't bet very much, and the casino became one of the biggest flops in the industry's history.

"We still think that, had the casino opened on the original schedule, it would be the biggest, most profitable casino in the country. The Mississippi Gulf Coast never would have gotten started had our casino been built," says Ralph Berry, a Harrah's spokesman. "We also think that what happened at the temporary casino shouldn't be confused with the permanent casino. The temporary casino was in a bad part of town, and the permanent casino was in a very different place. We never should have opened the temporary casino in the first place."

Just before Thanksgiving in 1995, with the main casino unfinished and the temporary casino open for only six months. Harrah's sought bankruptcy protection for Jazz. Two of New Orleans' riverboat casinos soon followed the same path. And Edwin Edwards, who in his salad days had ponied up a suitcase full of cash to pay off a $500,000 marker owed to Caesars Palace, declined to seek reelection in 1995. His successor, Mike Foster, who campaigned as an opponent of gambling, ultimately softened his stance against the industry.

"The economic growth and diversification that were supposed to follow legalized gaming into Louisiana have not surfaced," Standard & Poor's observed in the wake of the New Orleans fiasco. "The demand for gaming . . . was zealously overestimated."

Still, the national demand for gambling was strong enough that, by 1997, it was legal in some form in every state except Utah and Hawaii. The end of an economic recession and public unease with the industry's growth slowed gambling's spread across the country. But six states now had riverboat casinos; Florida offered "cruises to nowhere" on ships that sailed into international waters for the day so passengers could gamble; several states had full-blown land-based casinos; the lottery was everywhere, and dozens of Indian tribes had discovered that casinos could reverse centuries of hardship.

The Poker Player—II

*There was a point [at which] my dad and I kind of made our peace. . . .
My dad still thought that I was in Arizona selling real estate. I used to
write letters, send them from Phoenix. I just couldn't tell my dad what I
was doing.*

*Then I played in a little poker tournament, and I won it. And I got
written up in* Sports Illustrated. *. . . I forget when it was, '74 maybe. It
was an article about young players, the new breed of poker player. And
the article was about the dichotomy between the old-time Texans and
the new educated guys that were coming up. And Bobby [Baldwin] and
I were in the article as the young guys. They had Doyle [Brunson],
Johnny Moss, and those guys as the old-timers.*

*Somebody came in my dad's office and showed him the magazine.
So that's when I told him the truth. My dad's pretty stubborn. He's kind
of an old—he just really was against me gambling. And then I brought
my mom and dad [to Las Vegas] and they went to the casinos, they saw
how nice the people were. That's when I finally kind of made peace with
my dad.*

*I went through a stage where I was a little bit bored with what I was
doing. You reflect and you think, "Well, I'm not really doing anything for
anybody." . . . So I called my dad up and I said, "You know, I'm just not
really enthralled with what I'm doing right now." And I was actually
thinking about going back to law school.*

*My dad said, "Are you crazy?" He says, "My friends, all of us, are so
envious of what you're doing." He said, "I didn't think it years ago," but
he said, "What greater thrill is there in life than doing what you love? It's
not even a job to you. You've loved it since you were a little kid. It's your
passion. You just loved it."*

◆ ♣ ♥ ♠

*Then I got to the point, say, in my middle or early thirties, I'd had
about ten years of the good life . . . I'd look around I'd see the old-time
gamblers that had done it all their lives. And they'd gone through the
entire roller coaster. They'd gotten a hold of big money, they were sixty
or seventy years old, broke, sitting in the casino doing the exact same
things they did when they were twenty years old. And they would always tell me, like even the successful ones, when I was in my early
twenties, they'd say, "You know, you need to get out of this business.
Don't do this your whole life, you're gonna be a lonely man." And I'd*

say, "I'm not gonna do this my whole life." And they'd say, "Well, you think you are, but you're not." And I'd say, "Not me." . . . But this is me. And this is gonna be me whether I have money or don't have money.

I've invested money, and I can quit playing cards now. I can quit if I wanted to, but it's not my nature. Leopards do not change their spots. In gambling, that's like one of the rules of the jungle when you're trying to read a man or a man's habits. He may try and decoy you for a little while, but if you've got something about his nature, he can't change it. It'll come back out. You read off those kinds of things.

How does a kamikaze pilot who's been trained all his life to be a kamikaze pilot turn around when he's ten miles from his destination, and say, "I'm not gonna do this"?

I'm a much more sexual animal after I've lost than after I've won. It's really an interesting phenomenon. When I make the giant win, the giant score, it's almost like the euphoria that you felt or the high, it's almost like you've already reached your climax. It really works that way. And—who knows?—we're sexually driven, maybe it's all interrelated. Maybe that's what's so compulsive about gambling. Maybe it's sexual. I don't even know the answer to that.

That's one thing that's pretty neat about [Las Vegas]. You feel it being here, don't you? It's very primal. You really let your hair down, let yourself go, and nobody cares, and it's almost expected.

It's really, it's terrible to say it, but I can't believe I was in the poker room. I mean, it seemed so natural at the time. Ten years ago, fifteen years ago, to be right in the thick of it was fun. And now it's really work for me to be down there. The mentality of everybody there is so much different than mine. Maybe it's because they're trying to do what I already did, but also my priorities have changed. It's not that they've changed. I've changed. Away from, just away from it all. Now my life with my family is my priority. And the gambling's just a means to an end to me now.

I can't say I don't like it. The one thing I do know, I'm still a pretty sick little puppy, because I still need to live on the edge. . . . The edge of the cliff. In order for it to make my juices flow, I have to have disaster lingering out there.

♦ ♣ ♥ ♠

I should do things much more conservatively in my gambling. I probably bet more than I should bet on sports. It's like when I play poker I want to play, where if I get beat up, I want to get beat up.

I mean, I can see it in people. People take so much punishment. They have to enjoy it. I mean, they couldn't take it if they didn't enjoy it. There's people who can't take a punch, that don't do it. They just can't take that kind of punishment. But there are people that can take tremendous amounts of punishment.

Doyle [Brunson] has a tremendous threshold for pain. . . . He is one of the greats. He's sixty-three years old and he's still competing with everybody. Believe me, you lose some of your fine edge. Most guys sixty-three can't play at the top anymore. I don't know how to describe it. It's like being an athlete. There's an intangible, it's like an athlete may lose a little speed and strength, but a poker player loses the fine edge of alertness. There's a certain alertness that you need to have.

I find that I don't really have the alertness if I just don't play for a long time. . . . Once I play for about a week, I'm right back. I'm, like, tuned in, and if I go play, my wife will tell you, if I go play in a poker tournament, and play in it, go there every day, it's almost like we have to rebound when I come home. 'Cause I'm a different person. I'm more aloof.

And you come home, and your family expects everything to be just like it was. But it's like you're drained, physically, mentally drained. It's like being—I can only describe it from what I've heard—it's like being an air traffic controller. Where you go into this long session, like tense, zoom. Then you come out of there. It's like somebody's trying to destroy you. The enemy's there, and if you make a wrong move, you're destroyed. You're in that situation for two or three weeks, or a month, every day. Sleeping in a hotel, getting up, going into the arena. And then, all of a sudden, you're coming back into normal lifestyle. It's not easy. It takes a week sometimes to really chill out.

♦ ♣ ♥ ♠

[Three-time World Series of Poker champion] Stuey [Ungar] wears these glasses because they cover his nose. His nose literally looked like the Elephant Man. His nose fell apart with cocaine. And he had plastic surgery and they couldn't repair it. It still looks bad. He's had one or two surgeries.

He came from the Lower East Side of Manhattan. Grew up with Mob guys. He always had a combat mentality. Stuey had at one time a good heart. He wasn't that bad of a guy. But he really isn't a good guy anymore. . . . And I used to be pretty close to him. We were together all the time playing, competing against each other, and he had a very quick mind. And we really communicated well because we had the same sense of humor on things. . . . But he never had any goals in life.

You have to be goal oriented. . . . You have to want to do something with what you win. The tool is money. Now, it's an interesting thing: to be a great player you have to have disregard for the money. To where you can play the game while you're at the green felt jungle. Play the game without even thinking about it as money. But guys that . . . are not goal oriented just play until they lose it. They just play to play. They keep playing. And eventually, they'll lose.

MASHANTUCKET:
THE RAINMAKER

BENEATH A GLASS SKYLIGHT in the largest casino in the Western Hemisphere, a 4,700-pound urethane statue of a Pequot Indian called the Rainmaker arches his back and aims a laser-tipped arrow at a distant horizon. Every hour, amid recorded chants, lightning claps, rumbling thunder, and wolf howls generated by a Moog synthesizer and orchestrated by a computer, the $2 million display tells the story of an epic drought and how brave Pequot warriors went to a mountaintop to ask their gods for water.

Every hour the gods answer. After a bright green laser beam shoots from the Rainmaker's arrow, the imaginary skies part and a misty nimbus of rain falls to glisten on the plasticine warrior's scalloped muscles. And every hour, at the tables and slot machines that line the casino's floor, tens of thousands of gamblers lose some $93,000 in a flood of money that has enriched a small Native American tribe on a lushly wooded reservation in a once-quiet corner of Connecticut.

This newfound fountain of wealth is off an interstate highway just north of New York. It is Foxwoods Resort Casino, owned and operated since 1992 by the Mashantucket Pequot Indians.

Taking advantage of the legal autonomy Indian tribes enjoy, the Pequots have built a breathtakingly lucrative casino franchise in a state where casinos are otherwise outlawed. Nationally, revenue from Native American gambling climbed from just $121 million in 1988 to $5.3 billion in 1996—about 11 percent of all the money lost legally by gamblers in 1996—and Foxwoods has become a beacon for other tribes hoping to cash in their chips.

Although most Native American cultural and spiritual traditions historically rejected individual ownership of property, let alone the cutthroat nature of today's free markets, casinos are now welcomed by many tribes as an economic equalizer that has begun to make up for more than 300 years of defeat and deprivation at the hands of white America.

"We attempted to empower ourselves economically through means that were closer to our hearts and who we were than gambling was," says Michael Thomas, a member of the Pequot tribal council. "But none of those things worked out. Gambling has given us a way to take care of seven generations of Pequots that will follow us. We wanted to make sure that the types of things that happened to our people in the past could never happen again."

Located on the Mashantucket reservation near the small town of Ledyard, Foxwoods is believed to be more profitable than any other casino in the country, and possibly the world. Because it is privately owned, the casino's finances aren't precisely known. But the casino has agreed to remit 25 percent of its monthly slot revenue to the state of Connecticut. In fiscal 1995, Foxwoods gave the state $142 million, which means its slot haul for the year was $568 million. Slots provide about 70 percent of the average casino's revenue, with table games making up the balance. So the casino pulled in approximately $811 million for the Pequots in 1995. That figure doesn't include what the resort earned on food and drink, bingo, entertainment, and hotel rooms, which would have helped pump up Foxwoods' gross revenue toward the $1 billion mark—all tax free.

The funds guarantee that the Pequots, members of a tribe that had almost vanished twenty years ago, have access to free health care and job training, low-cost housing, free education, college scholarships, and well-paying jobs. On top of their salaries from casino-related jobs, each adult in the 450-member tribe receives a five-figure or six-figure annual bonus, while children have money tucked away in trust funds.

But gambling as a long-term solution for most of America's Indians is questionable. Foxwoods' prosperity derives from the fact that for five years it was the only casino in New England. Its monopoly ended in 1996 with the opening of another Native American casino nearby, a joint venture of the Mohegan tribe and Sol Kerzner, a South African casino operator. Should Rhode Island's Indians or the state of New York legalize gambling—both of which are real possibilities—Foxwoods' turf would be threatened further. And for all the wealth the Pequots have earned, most Indians in the rest of the country remain desperately poor and far too isolated geographically to be rescued by casinos. Yet the tribes that have cashed in on casinos still view gambling as an indispensable, and delicate, lifeline.

"We live in fear that casinos will be just a fad or will be taken away from us," says Tim Giago, a Lakota Sioux who is editor and publisher of *Indian Country Today*, a newspaper based in Rapid City, South Dakota. "Tribes are sitting on casinos right now that could be wiped away with the stroke of a pen if Congress turns against us. How can we plan fifty years ahead if we don't know what's going to happen tomorrow?"

"BLOTTED OUT FROM UNDER HEAVEN"

When Richard "Skip" Hayward, a relentless twenty-six-year-old pipe fitter and a Pequot, returned to his tribe's southeastern Connecticut reservation in 1974, his grandmother had already been dead a year. Elizabeth George Plouffe had been one of only two Pequots still residing on the 204-acre reservation. Recognizing the danger that the Pequots might disappear forever, her grandson anxiously began rounding up dispersed tribe members to help bolster the Pequots' claim to their land and their vanishing heritage. Hayward began mapping out a plan that ultimately led to casino gambling and the rebirth of a people Herman Melville had said more than a century earlier (in *Moby-Dick*) were "as extinct as the ancient Medes."

The doomed whaling ship in *Moby-Dick* was named after the Pequots, an apt metaphor for the injustices and genocide that had accompanied the settling of New England by Europeans. The Indian tribes that had populated the northeastern United States prior to the Europeans' arrival became the first Native Americans to lose their land, their history, their freedom, and their dignity in a pattern that would mark the entire westward settlement of the country by whites.

Pequots—the name means Fox People—had hunted and fished along Long Island Sound for hundreds of years before Dutch and English traders arrived in the 1600s. The Pequots controlled the flow of wampum—polished shells that served as money in all transactions between Indians and Europeans—so anyone wishing to do business in the region had to deal with them. But unlike the French and Dutch, who generally ventured to North America for trade rather than conquest, the English came with colonization in mind, and were correctly perceived by Native Americans as a greater threat to their way of life.

For a time, the Pequots peacefully traded furs with the colonists until, according to a sketchy history blurred by the biases of two increasingly antagonistic cultures, a series of misunderstandings and killings on both sides led to war. In 1637, English soldiers, aided by Mohegan and Narragansett Indians, slaughtered 300 to 700 Pequots in a surprise attack near Mystic, Connecticut. Some one hundred survivors fled into nearby swamps, but they were captured and sold as slaves to other Indian tribes or to Caribbean planters. Any other Indians in the region who claimed to be Pequots were threatened with beheading.

At one time, the Pequots had numbered about 13,000 and were one of the most powerful tribes in New England. But smallpox, introduced to the New World by Europeans, had reduced the tribe to about 3,000 people by 1637. After the massacre, some 1,000 Pequots remained. Although the Puritans were themselves refugees from religious persecution, they felt little compunction about taking land from Indians, whom they considered unfit to inhabit it. A one-sided "treaty" signed in Hartford in 1638 declared the Pequot nation dead—or, as a Puritan historian of the time had it, "blotted out from under heaven."

Yet hundreds of Pequots remained in the area. Over time the tribe split into a western faction, the Mashantuckets, and an eastern faction, the Pawcatucks. Even after the massacre, the Mashantuckets continued to assist colonists who inhabited a settlement called Pequot Plantation, near present-day New London. The goodwill thus created led the Connecticut Colony to grant the Mashantucket Pequots 500 acres of land in 1651. In 1666, the Mashantuckets were given 2,000 acres in an area that encompasses their modern reservation.

Despite the official grants, the colonists had little respect for the Pequots' right to the land. Moreover, Indian tribes typically had no idea of English property law and believed that land was held communally, not owned individually, and thus could never be conveyed or sold to anyone. Until the eighteenth century, the Indians had no written language, and their inability to read English further undermined their capacity to fully understand or carefully negotiate land treaties, a fact the colonists exploited. To top things off, hard liquor flowed freely before and after treaty negotiations, a ploy used by the colonists to wring concessions from their drunken counterparts. With the colonists' superior military force as the ultimate factor, land treaties often meant very little.

After the Revolutionary War, in order to protect Native Americans' interests, George Washington made sure that the federal government, not the states, retained the exclusive right to negotiate land treaties with Indian tribes. The Constitution expressly gave Congress the power to regulate commerce with Native Americans, and the Indian Trade and Nonintercourse Act of 1790 made it illegal for land to be taken or bought from tribes without congressional approval. But many states continued to do as they pleased, emboldened by a federal government that was loath to challenge them and thereby risk threatening the new nation's tenuous union.

So the Pequots' land was gradually pared away, first to 1,600 acres and then to 989. Some was sold by the Pequots to raise money, but much was simply taken away. The reservation was slashed further in 1856, when Connecticut auctioned off 785 acres of the site without consulting the Pequots. The state put $8,000 in proceeds from the sale into a trust for the tribe.

As the size of the reservation shrank, so did the number of people inhabiting it. With few ways to make a living on the 204 acres that remained, most Pequots left and started marrying into other ethnic groups. Those who chose to stay relied on basket-weaving, selling firewood, and the meager interest from a small trust fund as sources of income. The number of Pequots on the reservation dwindled first to the hundreds, then down to the teens. Finally, there were almost none.

The few Pequots left on the reservation in the early 1970s lived in dilapidated housing and kept to themselves. Then Connecticut proposed to convert the reservation into a state park once Elizabeth Plouffe died, reasoning that with her death the tribe would be extinct. Plouffe had told her grandson never to give up what little land the tribe still had. Hayward decided to act.

Like many Pequots, Hayward lived off the reservation, working for the Electric Boat shipyard in nearby Groton. He quit his job and implored other Pequots to do the same and return to the reservation before it slipped through the tribe's fingers. His pleas met with surprising success. By 1975, Hayward was tribal chairman, governing fifty-five people living on the reservation—no small feat, given that generations of crossed bloodlines had complicated the task of locating true Pequots. All those welcomed back to the reservation had to prove that they were related to a Pequot listed on the tribe's 1900 or 1910 census and descended no more than four generations from a full-blooded Pequot. Almost every Pequot living on the reservation today is descended from one of nine sisters listed in those turn-of-the-century censuses. Children of those sisters married widely and eventually created a rainbow of Pequots, some looking distinctly African-American, others more fair-skinned. Some tribal elders opposed intermarriage, and the variety of bloodlines that resulted created racial rifts within the tribe that have yet to mend.

Nonetheless, once Hayward and the reunited tribe had reclaimed the reservation they set themselves two goals: improved housing, and self-sufficiency through economic development.

During the 1970s and early 1980s, the Pequots, prodded by Hayward, undertook a variety of economic development projects. They had lukewarm results. Backed by government loans, the Pequots started a logging business and a maple syrup business; they even tried raising pigs. All fared poorly. The most spectacular failure was a hydroponic vegetable business that aimed to grow lettuce in a year-round greenhouse for sale to restaurants and gourmet shops. The lettuce project, though propped up by a $90,000 federal loan, wilted.

Meanwhile, the Pequots had also been campaigning for federal recognition as a tribe, which would make them eligible for larger housing and social service subsidies. In 1983, Connecticut's congressional delegation quietly pushed through an act recognizing the tribe in exchange for the Pequots' dropping a seven-year-old lawsuit against the state seeking the return of 800 acres of former reservation land. The Pequots also got $900,000 for dropping the lawsuit, giving Hayward the opportunity to come up with yet another business proposition. This time, he chose bingo.

THE NEW BUFFALO

Gambling has a long history in Native American culture. While enormous differences in language, lifestyle, and outlook exist among the hundreds of Indian tribes in the United States, gambling is a common thread. The Yakima Indians were heavy bettors who gambled regularly, while the Mohave wagered only on special occasions. Other tribes, including the Mandan, Huron, Yurok, and Pawnee, had members who gambled until they lost all their possessions. For centuries, most Indians have participated in "hand games" or "stick games," competitive gatherings that were first used to settle spats among members of a tribe.

Indians still play hand games and the rules are simple. Two players or teams face each other; one player is given both a marked and an unmarked bone or stick. Opponents try to guess which of the player's hands holds the unmarked stick. Sometimes the contest is between two large teams, and the sticks are passed among several players on a team while their supporters sing and dance to distract their opponents.

Different tribes play other variations on hand games. The Pequots, for one, play the "snake game." In this game, played during the winter, a stick is stripped of its bark and a V-shaped trough is dug into the ground. The winner is the player who can drive the stick most deeply into the trough, with people betting on the outcome. Betting on a victor is a vital part of the hubbub surrounding hand games, and the wagering can be big. In the past, horses and blankets were at stake. Later, Indians bet money, like everyone else.

These games of chance serve a larger purpose for Native Americans

than mere play. The singing and dancing that accompany them are rituals intended to preserve a cultural heritage and to build a sense of tribal
unity. These simple games are also a far cry from the commercial gambling enterprises Native Americans are now building. Hand games bear
as much resemblance to Foxwoods as a friendly Saturday night bridge
game does to a Las Vegas poker tournament. Thus, many Indian tribes
underwent wrenching debates in the early 1980s about whether bingo
was a culturally appropriate commercial enterprise. The bingo option
had been made possible by several legal challenges that affirmed Native
Americans' long-standing status as sovereign nations with the right to
regulate and conduct life on their reservations as they saw fit, subject to
oversight from the federal government. That included the right to legal
gambling.

The first significant lawsuit involving Native American gambling
was mounted by Florida's Seminole Indians. Florida had a $100 limit on
bingo pots in 1979, when the Seminoles opened a high-stakes bingo hall
that offered prizes as high as $10,000 or more. When the Broward
County sheriff's office and Florida's state attorney general tried to shut
down the bingo operation, the Seminoles sued the sheriff's office in federal court. The court ruled in favor of the Seminoles, noting that Florida
had no regulatory power to limit Indian bingo.

This paved the way for other tribes to offer high-stakes bingo, and in
1983 Hayward, who had visited the Seminoles' bingo palace, floated the
idea of a bingo hall to his fellow Pequots. Many tribe members were Baptists and Jehovah's Witnesses, two Christian denominations that frown on
gambling. An anxious moral debate ensued that split the tribe in two.
Bingo was voted down. But Hayward kept pressing the issue. He won over
enough Pequots so that two years later bingo was narrowly approved.

At first, money was a problem. When construction of the bingo hall
began in 1985, the Pequots put $675,000 into the project, but Hayward
was gunning for a $4 million club. The Pequots' initial investment was
enough to erect a steel shell, but the tribe was still far short of what Hayward felt it needed to attract a large clientele.

A local builder named Charles Klewin agreed to complete the bingo
hall while the Pequots went searching for the other $2.3 million they
needed. Hayward spent months in Washington and secured a 90 percent
federal loan guarantee, but he still lacked a lender. Banks are often reluctant to lend to Indians because the most valuable asset most tribes
have is their land, which the federal government holds in a perpetual
trust for them. That makes it impossible to take land from Indians anymore, regardless of the circumstances, but it also makes it impossible for
most tribes to use the land as collateral for large commercial loans.

After enduring dozens of rejections from banks, Hayward finally lined up a loan from UBAF Arab-American Bank, which had experience lending to other tribes. The bank also committed to financing a 46,000-square-foot bingo hall and lent the Pequots $3.9 million to complete it. Because the Pequots had no experience running a bingo hall, they hired Penobscot Indians from Maine to manage the operation and train them.

The bingo hall opened in 1986, offering games that cost from $25 to $350 to enter. It started raking in money right away, grossing about $6 million in its first year. By the early 1990s the club had annual revenue of $20 million and earnings of $4 million a year. Those riches allowed the Pequots to pay back the Arab-American loan in eighteen months and to buy out the Penobscots' management contract early. In 1990, the Pequots felt they were ready to build a casino.

As with bingo, the way had been paved by lawsuits. No sooner had some states gotten used to Indian bingo than tribes started chasing a far larger prize: casino gambling. The prospect of casinos on reservations put state governments and traditional gambling companies in a lather, and both parties did everything they could to stop Indian gambling's advance.

When the tiny Cabazon band of Mission Indians opened a card room in a small trailer on their Palm Springs, California, reservation in 1980, local law enforcement officials took notice. The door to the card room was padlocked by the police four times before the Cabazons successfully sued the state in federal court in 1985 to keep the trailer open. The state appealed the decision all the way to the U.S. Supreme Court, and it was widely anticipated that the Court would shoot down the Cabazons. But the Supreme Court had a surprise in store. In its 1987 decision in the Cabazon case, it noted that California already had legalized card rooms in other locations and also permitted a state-run lottery, horse racing, and bingo. The Court reasoned that because California had legalized gambling elsewhere, the state couldn't prohibit or regulate similar forms of gambling on reservations there.

As it turned out, California regulators had good reason to be concerned about the Cabazons' card room. In 1991, *San Francisco Chronicle* reporter Jonathan Littman revealed that it was financed and managed in 1980 by organized-crime figures Tommy Marson and Rocco Zangari. In 1981 the Cabazons' vice chairman, Alfred Alvarez, was murdered shortly after alleging that cash was being skimmed from the tribe's gambling enterprises. The Cabazons have repeatedly said that they were unknowing victims in these incidents.

But the 1987 Supreme Court ruling said that even if California had a legitimate interest in keeping criminal elements out of Indian gambling, such concerns still didn't permit the state to forbid Indian gambling entirely. The Court had resoundingly reaffirmed Native American sovereignty: the only entities that could authorize or regulate any activity, including gambling, on reservations were the Indian tribes themselves. States, the high court said, had to get out of the Indians' way.

The ruling set big casino companies on a tear for Washington, scrambling to get legislators to pass a regulatory act that would temper the Supreme Court decision and throw a roadblock in front of tribal gambling. The result, strongly supported by states and the gambling industry and opposed by Native Americans, was the Indian Gaming Regulatory Act of 1988. It required federally recognized tribes and states to negotiate "compacts" outlining what kind of gambling ventures tribes could pursue, and thus gave states a bigger role in the process than they might otherwise have had. If states refused to come to the bargaining table or sign off on a compact, however, tribes could sue them in federal court.

But the lawsuits that followed served only to briefly delay a gambling boom on barren reservations, which had once been so inhospitable to economic activity. Gambling was, Indians observed, the "new buffalo."

Between 1988 and 1996, about 110 of the nation's 554 federally recognized tribes opened 230 gambling operations, more than half of which are full-fledged casinos. Indian gambling's massive and sudden expansion across the country paralleled the growth of riverboat gambling. Wisconsin and Minnesota have the heaviest concentration of Indian casinos, and many tribes there have done very well. The money has funded new infrastructure and schools, better health care, trust funds, and, in some cases, tribal investment accounts. But no tribe has become as formidable a casino operator as the Pequots.

THE PEQUOTS STRIKE GOLD

Flush with confidence and cash from their successful bingo run, in 1990 the Pequots began looking for someone to finance a $55 million casino. Once again, nobody responded. Once again, Skip Hayward kept looking until he found a backer: Malaysia's Lim family, owners of Southeast Asia's largest casino. While the Lims charged high interest on the loan, they did not get any equity in the casino. The final price tag for the original casino was $60 million.

Building began on a 250,000-square-foot complex, to be called Foxwoods, that would include more than 40,000 square feet of gambling space. But before the Pequots could open Foxwoods, the state tried to block them. The Pequots argued that because Connecticut permitted charities to hold "Las Vegas Nights," the tribe could offer a similar menu of blackjack, roulette, poker, and craps in a casino of its own. The state disagreed, and refused to negotiate a gambling compact with the Pequots.

But when the Pequots sued the state in 1991, a federal court ruled that Connecticut's refusal to bargain with the tribe constituted "bad faith" under the Indian Gaming Act and compelled the state to begin negotiations. After the ruling, Connecticut governor Lowell Weicker, who had been part of the congressional delegation that won federal recognition of the Pequots eight years earlier, tried to repeal the state law allowing charities to hold Las Vegas Nights. The move failed, as did an attempt by the Nevada Resort Association, a lobbying arm for that state's gambling companies, to get the federal government to block the casino.

Foxwoods opened in 1992, and a year later the Pequots hammered out an agreement with the state that allowed the tribe to add slot machines to its casino. The Pequots agreed to give the state 25 percent of Foxwoods' monthly slot revenue, or a minimum of $100 million annually, in exchange for a slot monopoly; if casinos were legalized elsewhere in Connecticut, the Pequots would stop forking over the booty.

The Pequots originally intended to keep Foxwoods open only eighteen hours a day. But the casino stayed open around the clock from the moment its doors opened, and the Pequots have never looked back. Sitting right in the middle of 22 million people with no other casinos nearby, Foxwoods became a phenomenal draw. Almost half its gamblers come from Connecticut, a quarter from Massachusetts, 15 percent from Rhode Island, and the remainder from New York and northern New Jersey. They are solidly middle-class, overwhelmingly in love with slot machines, and, because of Foxwoods' regional monopoly, cheap to court. It doesn't require a lot of advertising or comps to get Foxwoods' gamblers in the house, making the casino more profitable than those in Las Vegas or Atlantic City.

By 1996, 45,000 people *per day* were visiting Foxwoods, forcing a huge enlargement of the original facility. It now has 250,000 square feet of gambling space, dwarfing the next largest competitor, Las Vegas' MGM Grand, which has 175,000 square feet devoted to gambling. Foxwoods is a $650 million complex with 4,428 slot machines, 307 table games, and 12,025 employees. The resort also has a modest shopping mall, a high-tech movie theater, two hotels, more than a dozen restaurants, and oversized parking lots that look like concrete tundras. And the Pequots are hard at work adding still more rooms, more gambling space, and more parking. But where the MGM Grand looks and feels cavernous, Foxwoods, while still vast, manages to feel far less overwhelming. Fitted with a stony facade and trimmed in pleasing blue-green hues, Foxwoods offers gamblers a gentle embrace in the style pioneered by Steve Wynn at the Mirage: *Come, come to happy land. Come, come and lose your money.*

Foxwoods has picture windows and verandas that offer a commanding view of the surrounding forest. Its grounds are dotted with first-class Native American sculpture and art. For the most part, Foxwoods is also devoid of the glitzy kitsch that is a hallmark of the casino esthetic. It does have its moments, however. Waitresses in the casino's lounge wear skimpy pink or green "Indian" outfits with matching feathers in their hair, looking like extras from the set of *F Troop*. While other Indians revere feathers as ceremonial marks of honor, the Pequots are comfortable using them as marketing props.

Yet Foxwoods has been such a potent wellspring of cash that the Pequots have been able to spend mightily to help ensure that Native American culture is protected—donating $10 million to the Smithsonian Institution's Museum of the American Indian, for example. On the reservation itself, the Pequots are completing a $130 million museum and research center that will specialize in the histories of the Eastern Woodland tribes.

In the two decades since Hayward brought the tribe back to Mashantucket, the reservation has grown from little more than 200 acres to 5,000 acres, two and a half times as large as the parcel colonists granted the Indians more than three centuries ago. The tribe has built its own fire station and EMS unit on the reservation, as well as a multimillion-dollar community center. The Pequots have also shown good business savvy. Some tribes have hired management companies such as Grand Casinos to run their casinos in exchange for a hefty 30 percent to 40 percent cut of the revenue. In other instances, tribes have been cheated out of millions of dollars by management companies that overcharged for supplies or services or outright stole cash. In 1992, the Pequots wisely set up their own management company and then hired outsiders to show them the ropes—for salaries, not a piece of the profits.

The sudden burst of gambling wealth has also attracted scores of would-be Pequots to the reservation, and the tribe, already made up of members whose bloodlines are often far removed from the original Pequots, has to screen for bogus claimants very carefully. Federal studies estimate that only 60 percent of all the nation's Indians were full-blooded in 1980. That portion is expected to fall to 34 percent by the year 2000 as more Indians intermarry and as the lure of casino riches spurs the first tribal growth in decades. The Pequots, alarmed that intermarriage would further thin the tribe's bloodlines and make current tribe members' children and grandchildren ineligible for membership, changed the standard by which it allows applicants to join the tribe. In 1996, the Pequots quietly dropped a requirement that all members have one-sixteenth Pequot blood and now require candidates merely to prove that they are descendants of a Pequot whose name appeared on the 1900 or 1910 census.

When it comes to their children, more than bloodlines concerns Pequots. Members of the tribe are worried that Pequot children may be spoiled by the tribe's riches, and occasional spats about nepotism and compensation have crept into tribal affairs. Fifty-year-old John Holder, garrulous and energetic, epitomizes as well as any Pequot the extraordinary changes that have washed over the tribe. Holder served as a point man in the Vietnam War, taking the lead position on military forays into the jungle. The nightmares he experienced after returning to the United States have long since faded, but he says the sound of a helicopter and certain smells on walks in the woods still evoke frightening memories of the war. He took a blue-collar job at Electric Boat after coming home from Vietnam and then returned to a hardscrabble existence on the reservation in 1980. Today, he oversees the tribe's many construction projects.

On a recent afternoon, Holder supervised the construction of a new pool at his house, where, without a trace of irony, he proudly displays a framed autographed photo of the movies' famous "Injun" fighter, John Wayne. Holder also owns several cars, including a vintage Corvette, which are lined up like trophies in his small driveway. Still, despite the bounty brought to him by Foxwoods, Holder misses the simplicity of tribal life before the casino was built.

"The first years were a little tough but fun," recalls Holder. "Things are more bureaucratic now and less volunteer oriented. Everyone knows there's money now, and things seem less tightly knit."

"DAMN CASINO"

Although the Pequots have made donations to local causes in the towns surrounding Mashantucket and replaced many of the jobs in the region that disappeared during the 1980s and 1990s as federal defense contracts dried up, there is a high degree of animosity among neighboring whites toward the casino and the Pequots. Some of this is understandable. Traffic jams snarl the roads surrounding Foxwoods, problem and compulsive gamblers have surfaced, and children hover outside the casino late at night while their parents roll the dice. In 1996, a Massachusetts couple was arrested for locking a nine-year-old boy in their car all night while they gambled at Foxwoods. The temperature was about twenty-two degrees when the shivering boy was found in the car early the next morning by another patron, who notified police. The couple didn't return to the car for another seven hours.

Foxwoods has also disrupted the lifestyles of local residents, who are fiercely protective of the rolling hills and tidy stone walls that evoke images from Robert Frost's poetry. When a massage parlor briefly opened in the area, residents were frantic. Now a huge amusement park is likely to be built, drawn by the crowds Foxwoods attracts. In 1996, the Mohegan tribe, which hundreds of years earlier helped the British try to stamp out the Pequots, opened the region's second casino, not far from Foxwoods. While Foxwoods suffered a brief drop in its slot win, it appears the Mohegan casino is more likely to expand the local gambling market than to eat into Foxwoods' business permanently. And the increased casino action has heightened the anxiety felt by people living nearby.

"When we arrived here eleven years ago there were cows across the street and no street lights," says Deeda Brennan, a Ledyard resident. "But our road is good and it goes directly to the casino. We have so many taxis go by now, I can hail one at the foot of my driveway. . . . I never worried about my daughter's safety, but I do now. . . . We used to be able to see the stars at night but it's like when a mall comes with bright lights—you can't see the stars anymore. Damn casino."

As the Pequots have attempted to buy more land and annex it for Mashantucket, thus taking it off the property tax rolls and out of the budgets of surrounding towns, a bitter feud has erupted between locals and the tribe. Some of the anxiety about the Pequots comes from the rapidity with which the tribe has become a major economic and political player in the region. Although the portion of slot revenue it remitted to the state in 1995 represented only 1.5 percent of Connecticut's budget, the tribe is now the single largest contributor to the state treasury.

The Pequots also spin the political money wheel quite handily, kicking in $500,000 to the Democratic National Committee in 1994 and earning Skip Hayward invitations to the Clinton White House. Casino wealth, or at least the prospect of it, has launched other Native American tribes into the world of hardball political lobbying. In 1997, Interior Secretary Bruce Babbitt, overseer of the Bureau of Indian Affairs, was caught in the middle of allegations that hefty political donations from several tribes gave them the leverage needed to convince federal regulators to quash a Wisconsin casino proposal pursued by competing tribes. Babbitt denied any improprieties, although none of the tribes denied using aggressive lobbying to try to steer the political process in their favor.

Beyond the reasonable concerns and anxiety that any casino provokes, however, there is a certain amount of bigotry underlying criticism of the Pequots. Tribal sovereignty never bothered politicians, businesspeople, and residents in most states when Indian reservations were desolate hovels. Now the moccasin is on the other foot. For the first time in centuries, some Indians have more economic muscle than their neighbors and competitors. It is an uncomfortable reality for some of the tribe's critics—especially those gambling moguls whose Atlantic City casinos underperform Foxwoods.

"If you look at some of the Indians on the reservations that you have approved, they don't look like Indians to me," testified Donald Trump before Congress in 1993. For good measure, Roy Cohn's protégé also shared one other grave concern: "Do the few hundred members of the tribe deserve to make all the money they're making? . . . It's obvious that organized crime is rampant on the Indian reservations."

Trump's accusation is exaggerated; according to William Esposito, assistant director of the FBI's criminal investigative division, there has been no broad-based effort by organized crime to infiltrate Indian casinos. That's not to say that mobsters haven't gotten their foot in the door at the reservations now and then. Every new casino market, Indian *and* non-Indian, has drawn old gangsters out of the woodwork.

Indian casinos in Minnesota and Michigan were targeted in the early 1990s by associates of East Coast mobsters, until the schemes were uncovered and some of the principals indicted. (Among them was International Gaming Management, a company that also sold video poker machines in Louisiana and developed casino sites in Mississippi before failing to get a license there.) Other incidents of Mob intrusion into Indian casinos seem small-caliber compared with early Las Vegas. In the late 1980s, for example, small-time Mob associates got a piece of the action at a Mohawk bingo hall in upstate New York before a bloody confrontation led to their ouster. In 1993, a group linked to the Chicago underworld made an abortive effort to take over a tiny Indian bingo hall outside San Diego. Foxwoods also has been stung. A boxing promoter and the casino's entertainment director were forced out by the Pequots in 1994 after background checks uncovered links to the Scarfo crime family of Philadelphia. And during the summer of 1996, alleged members of New England's Patriarca crime family were caught directing a betting scam that involved Foxwoods dealers.

"We do in excess of $3.6 million a day in cash transactions and spend $113 million a year on goods and services, so I'm sure there's somebody trying to take a shot at us," says Foxwoods chief executive Mickey Brown. "I've never had a problem we couldn't handle, but I have had problems that have alarmed me." (Brown, a well-regarded former New Jersey casino regulator who is close to Skip Hayward, was forced out as CEO in the summer of 1997 by a tribal council bridling at Hayward's authority, according to individuals familiar with the matter.)

Money laundering—the effort to disguise a source of dirty money, such as drug sales, by moving cash through banks, brokerage firms, or casinos—may be a larger problem on reservations than organized crime. But it is a potential problem at all casinos, not just those owned by Native Americans.

Casinos are tempting locales for drug dealers hoping to launder their funds. They can walk up to the cage and ask for, say, $12,000 worth of chips. They hand over the cash, get their chips, gamble for a few hours and lose a little bit, and then go back to the cage. They exchange whatever chips they have left, say, $9,800 worth, for cash. Voilà: drug money has been transformed into legitimate "gambling proceeds."

In 1970, the Bank Secrecy Act was passed as a way to foil money launderers. The law requires banks to file reports on cash transactions of $10,000 or more. The reports identify the person transferring the money and help provide a trail that law enforcement officials can follow if necessary.

Casinos weren't originally covered by the Bank Secrecy Act. After it was discovered that drug traffickers were using casinos to launder money, the Treasury Department broadened the law in 1985 to include them. But Nevada casinos got an exemption from the disclosure law after intense lobbying by then-senator Paul Laxalt, a Nevada Republican who had close ties to both the casino industry and the Reagan administration. Atlantic City casinos, lacking a guardian angel with Laxalt's leverage, weren't granted the same privilege.

Nevada operators argued that complying with the Bank Secrecy Act would scare off high rollers who wanted to keep their gambling habits private. The state imposed its own regulation requiring identification of gamblers exchanging $10,000 or more, but it doesn't require disclosure from gamblers cashing in chips worth $10,000 if casino employees attest that the chips were won in the casino and weren't involved in an effort to launder money. Whether casino employees have the ability or the courage to make such a call is an open question; the Treasury Department has complained over the years that Nevada regulators have inconsistently enforced the state law.

The Nevada casino industry remains the biggest cash-based business in the country not subject to federal cash reporting regulations. Indian

casinos were only recently brought under the umbrella of the Bank Secrecy Act. In 1996, the law was expanded to include Indian casinos with
revenue of $1 million or more. Before then, federal authorities had only
limited authority to review cash transactions at reservation casinos.

Larger casinos such as Foxwoods have voluntarily complied with all
federal cash-reporting regulations since they opened, and law enforcement officials say they have no reason to believe that Foxwoods has
major money-laundering problems. But smaller, less rigorously managed
Indian casinos have. In Minnesota in 1996, Darrell "Chip" Wadena, leader
of the White Earth band of Chippewa Indians, was found guilty of federal money-laundering and embezzlement charges in connection with
the tribe's Shooting Star Casino. Wadena, who was also found guilty of
election fraud, had run the Chippewa tribe with an iron fist for nearly
twenty years. His tenure illustrated how many tribal leaders still operate
like nineteenth-century Irish ward heelers, controlling votes, budgets, and
services with ruthless determination.

Corrupt leaders and parasitic outside casino managers have been
able to prey upon some tribes in part because the federal agency chartered to be a trustee for Native Americans was asleep at the switch when
casinos were first introduced to reservations.

The Bureau of Indian Affairs, which recently acknowledged losing
track of $2.4 billion in tribal trust funds over the past two decades, was
completely unprepared to deal with the onrush of Indian gambling. Another agency created specifically to regulate tribal casinos, the National
Indian Gaming Commission, didn't become fully operational until
1992, four years after the Indian Gaming Act was passed. Tribes were
free to go their own way during that time, and some fell on their faces.
Since then, the NIGC's regulatory approach has changed; while some
tribes had complained it was overzealous, the commission's critics now
describe it as too freewheeling.

"Indian gambling grew so quickly, and our resources are stretched
very thin," says Tom Acevedo, a NIGC spokesman. "We have thirty-three
people regulating two hundred thirty gaming operations and a hundred
and ten tribes. We're also considered a secondary regulator to the tribes
themselves. We're here to provide general oversight, not be a primary
regulator. That's the tribes' job."

THE LIMITS OF GAMBLING GOLD

Perhaps the biggest burden casinos have placed on Native Americans is
the public's perception that gambling has enriched every tribe. Legisla-

tors have cited the wealth created by gambling as justification for big cutbacks in federal aid to Indians. Yet the majority of Native Americans still live amid some of the grimmest poverty anywhere in the country.

There are approximately 1.2 million Native Americans in 555 tribes around the country. Almost half the tribes are in Alaska, and most of the 900,000 Indians who live on or near reservations are in such remote locations that gambling will never do for them what it has done for the Pequots.

Most reservations are so desolate they cannot support even simple crops; one of the few outside industries that has been drawn to them is hazardous waste disposal. The unemployment rate on most reservations is about 50 percent, and the average Indian household has an annual income of less than $7,000. The average education level of Native Americans is the sixth grade, and public schools on reservations are overcrowded and badly in need of repair. Infant mortality rates are about four times the national average, and child abuse is a major problem on some reservations. High alcoholism rates continue to plague the Native American population, and homicide and suicide rates are also well above the national average.

By the end of 1996, 184 tribes had gambling. But a 1997 study by the U.S. General Accounting Office indicated that just ten tribes accounted for more than half the money earned in 1995 at 178 of 281 reservation gambling halls reviewed by the federal agency. Some Indians, such as the Navajo, the nation's largest tribe, have rejected casinos on moral grounds. Others, such as the Lakota Sioux, the nation's second-largest tribe, still hold out hope for gambling.

The Lakota, the tribe of Red Cloud, Sitting Bull, and Crazy Horse, and once the mightiest of the Plains Indians, are now wretchedly poor people. Since the middle of the nineteenth century, their lives have been circumscribed by a foreign culture that overwhelmed them and by public policies that stripped the tribes of economic and social vitality.

The nomadic Lakota domesticated the feral horses that had been introduced to the continent by Spaniards. The tribe's mastery of horses allowed them to sweep across the Great Plains and track great herds of buffalo for thousands of miles. They valued family, emphasized individual freedom and spirituality, and governed themselves democratically, but also were brutal conquerors of other tribes. The forces that ultimately overcame the Lakota were set in motion in 1829, when Andrew Jackson became President. Jackson, a former Indian fighter, considered Native Americans barbaric and signed the Indian Removal Act of 1830. It called for relocating Indians from the eastern U.S. to west of the Mississippi River—by force if necessary.

At the time, Jackson's policies were challenged by the Supreme Court. In two decisions, Chief Justice John Marshall ruled that the Indians were sovereign nations with an inalienable right to their lands in the east. Jackson reputedly dismissed the rulings with a quip: "John Marshall has made his decision; now let him enforce it." The Indians lost their land and headed west.

When explorers first arrived on the Great Plains, the Lakota greeted them with open arms. But by the 1850s, white settlers began driving the buffalo away, and relations grew hostile. When the U.S. military tried to secure the Bozeman Trail into Montana for gold prospectors—in violation of an earlier agreement—the Lakota fought back.

Under Red Cloud's leadership, the Lakota defeated the U.S. Army in a series of battles that ended with the Fort Laramie Treaty of 1869. The Army closed down its forts along the Bozeman Trail and ceded the Lakota a huge reservation that spanned the western two-thirds of present-day South Dakota.

But two developments ensured that the Lakota wouldn't be left alone. General William T. Sherman, the hard-fighting Civil War leader, took command of the U.S. Army in 1869. "The more I see of these Indians, the more convinced I am that they all have to be killed or maintained as a species of paupers," Sherman said. Then gold was discovered in South Dakota's Black Hills, in the heart of the Lakota reservation.

The Black Hills were the center of the Lakotas' spiritual world. The people of the tribe believed that their ancestors had fallen from the stars onto the Black Hills and been reborn in canyons deep inside the mountain range. Lakota warriors went there to commune with the Great Spirit. But in 1874, scouts from George Custer's Seventh Cavalry found what Indians called "the yellow metal that makes white men crazy." A gold rush followed, and the Black Hills mining towns of Deadwood and Lead were founded.

Deadwood became a quintessential frontier town as the chance of riches drew prospectors and entrepreneurs to the Black Hills. Inevitably, professional gamblers followed.

Just as the riverboat gamblers rode the economic boom of the lower Mississippi River, so the frontier gamblers, their successors, claimed a place in the speculative boom of the Wild West. The frontier gamblers retained many of the riverboaters' mannerisms and trappings. Deadwood, where Wild Bill Hickok was shot in 1876 holding aces and eights, was populated by marks irresistible to the professionals: miners, railroad workers, and prospectors, all flush with cash. And those marks were relieved of their money with the same skill and subterfuge as were travelers on the Mississippi.

"They were the lily-fingered leisure class of Deadwood—the gamblers who seemed never to toil nor spin, yet always were arrayed in fine linen and broadcloth fresh from the tailor's iron," wrote Estelline Bennett, who arrived in the Black Hills as a five-year-old in 1877. "They appeared on the streets in the early afternoons immaculately and expensively attired, quiet-mannered, and soft-spoken. They strolled up and down Main Street with a magnificent leisure."

As white settlers made their way to Deadwood, following a path carved out by Custer and called Thieves' Road by the Indians, the Lakotas' holy grounds were transformed by the cyclone of American industrialization. A major confrontation was brewing, and it came soon enough.

Financial speculation and the collapse of the Northern Pacific Railroad in 1873 had brought on a national economic crisis that caused business interests and the federal government to increasingly prize the Black Hills' mineral wealth. So, in 1875, the United States ordered the Lakota to sell the mountain range. A few Lakota agreed to the sale, but most refused, and the United States called on the Army to force them out. Several months later, troops, including Custer's elite cavalry, attacked. The Lakota and other tribes wiped out Custer and his soldiers at Montana's Little Big Horn River in 1876. It was the Indians' greatest victory, and their last.

Thereafter, William Sherman oversaw the destruction of the Lakota nation. Seven million acres of the 26-million-acre reservation, including the Black Hills, were taken away from the Lakota in 1877. The tribe was confined to the remaining land. Administrators tried to turn them into farmers, but the tribe couldn't adapt to a sedentary way of life. As they fell into blighted disarray, the Lakota came under the influence of a cult that prophesied a great victory if a ceremony called the Ghost Dance was performed. The ritual, some Lakota believed, would make them impervious to the U.S. Army's bullets.

When the Army tried to arrest Sitting Bull in 1890 for allowing the Ghost Dance, he resisted and was murdered. The ensuing turmoil ended with the Wounded Knee massacre, when at least 153 Lakota, most of them unarmed and many of them women and children, were slaughtered by the Seventh Calvary, Custer's old regiment. The conquest of the Lakota was complete.

Over the next century, unable to attract investment on reservation land, all Native American tribes became dependent on federal subsidies granted by various treaties. They had little hope for a better future and were resigned to living in squalor. Today, about 20,000 Oglala, largest of the Lakota's seven tribes, live on the Pine Ridge reservation in South

Dakota. Pine Ridge, hundreds of miles of light green grass scarred in broad swaths by the lunar beauty of the Badlands, is a forlorn, poverty-stricken place dotted with a few parched towns. Some small businesses have gotten started on Pine Ridge, but they haven't created enough momentum to change things very much. About 90 percent of Pine Ridge's income comes from the federal government, and most of that is spent outside the reservation. Alcoholism, poverty, and suicide prevail.

An armed uprising by Indians near Pine Ridge in the early 1970s called for the return of the Black Hills to the Lakota. That hasn't occurred. But in 1980, the Supreme Court upheld a $122 million award to the tribe as restitution for the historic land grab, declaring that "a more ripe and rank case of dishonorable dealings will never, in all probability, be found in our history." The award, which has since grown to about $400 million, could be used to spur development, but the Lakota have refused to claim it. Instead, they want the Black Hills returned to them with compensation for being deprived of their use. So they wait.

Meanwhile, others have found riches in the Black Hills. The Hearst empire's Homestake Mine, site of the biggest gold lode ever discovered in the United States, still probes the mountains' ample veins. Tiny, declining Deadwood was reborn in 1989 with the legalization of gambling there. And above Deadwood, the actor Kevin Costner, director and star of the epic film about the Lakota, *Dances with Wolves*, is building a lavish casino.

PRAIRIE WIND

On Pine Ridge, hours from Deadwood and everywhere else, the Lakota have opened their own casino. The Prairie Wind Casino is a large, dreary trailer located on the southwestern edge of the reservation. A tall electric sign, rising out of the prairie grass like a sparkler, fronts a gravel drive leading up to the trailer. A phone call to the casino gets this message: "Prairie Wind Casino—no hoopla, just moola!"

There is very little hoopla about Prairie Wind. It has 175 slot machines, four blackjack tables, and one poker table. Most of the gamblers are Lakota with a smattering of senior citizens from Nebraska and Wyoming. There are no windows, an occasional fly buzzes by, and some of the furniture is broken. No liquor is served, but a small snack bar sells sandwiches.

"You'd think people wouldn't come to a smoky, tiny trailer, but they do," says Wayne Barber, a Lakota who manages Prairie Wind. Barber, a former dealer and pit boss in Deadwood, opened Prairie Wind in 1994 with $2.5 million from Bill Bernard, a Deadwood casino operator, and Marlyn Erickson, a Rapid City businessman.

Barber says Prairie Wind has 120 employees, almost all Lakota, who get about $6 per hour and receive no benefits. The casino, he says, has revenue of about $1 million per month and earns $200,000 a month. The Lakota get 70 percent of the profits, with the rest going to Barber's group, which calls itself Turn Key Gaming.

Erickson and Bernard's building loan is being paid off out of Prairie Wind's operating budget, so the Lakota get what's left over. The tribe's Gaming Commission is supposed to be able to audit the casino's books. But Tommy Tibbitts, the commission's chairman, says no audits have been conducted because Pine Ridge's tribal council has yet to authorize an auditing budget.

A permanent casino is planned for the current site, but as of 1996 Turn Key wanted $5.3 million to build a structure originally budgeted at $4 million. The tribe is balking at that price, and there's some talk the existing casino will close. Whether to open a casino was heavily debated by the tribe, but the discussion revolved around jobs, not whether a casino was in keeping with Lakota culture. Prairie Wind has brought some jobs, but hardly enough to make a difference on a reservation where several thousand Lakota are unemployed.

"Everybody saw what happened in Connecticut and Wisconsin and Minnesota and wanted that for here. But we're in the middle of the plains, and it's just not going to be the same for us." says Danelle Not Help Him, director of the Lakota Fund, an economic development group on Pine Ridge. "I think there's plenty of other good businesses we could get into other than casinos if we did them right. But investors are hard to find for the small businesses we need, because they don't get big returns right away. They know they'll get big returns if they invest in a casino, so that's where the money goes."

Whether any more tribes will have the option of opening casinos is now unclear. In a landmark states' rights decision, the Supreme Court ruled in 1996 that tribes can no longer sue states that won't negotiate a casino compact, because to do so violates the states' own constitutional right to sovereign immunity. That leaves tribes with the right to open casinos after negotiating with the state government, but with no remedy if states choose not to negotiate. Indians may try to negotiate directly with the federal government. But more than likely, the Indian Gaming Act will have to be revised so its ambiguities can be resolved. Meanwhile, heated standoffs between Indians and lawmakers continue in several states.

Yet in their rush to restrict the scourge of Indian casinos, most states are apparently content to overlook their own long-standing involvement in the wagering business. For it is state governments that have made one of the most significant contributions to enhancing the social respectability of modern gambling. They have given us the lottery.

The Veteran—II

I'm from a long line of gamblers. My dad was a gambler. I began gambling when I was, like, eighteen.

I never played cards. Dad was a card player. He went to the track. Well, he wouldn't go to the track often, but he played cards. He belonged to the Elks in New Brunswick, and they had men who had their own businesses and they played cards in the afternoon and then Saturday night was the wives' turn.

I was in the Navy during [World War II] and a group of us decided to go to Las Vegas. And, I was stationed in Washington the whole time. Right next door to home. I was a baby. I didn't want to go too far. I was a WAVE. Yeah, I was a wacky WAVE. . . . Vegas was very, very nothing—like, it was mostly desert. . . . Anything was fun then. I mean, you were just glad to be alive, or to be able to get around. . . . We got there on an Army transport plane.

I played bingo at home in New Jersey. My grandmother, she liked to go to bingo, she lived with us when I was eighteen. And bingo was not a really big thing—in fact, it was run by individuals. There were no state laws then, and my father owned a business in Highland Park and that was in the '40s, and I was, like, sixteen I think. And my dad started bingo up with the Highland Park Fire Department. And they were professional money raisers, there were no state laws or state regulations and anybody could run bingo. And they reaped the profits. They ran the bingo and then took maybe 80 percent. And then gave the organization 20 percent.

My grandmother used to like to go to bingo. But she wouldn't go alone, so she used to drag me along with her. I went gladly with her, because I knew she enjoyed it. And then they gave prizes instead of money, you got table lamps. . . . I just went for her. But I remember I won a beautiful wool suit one year.

I went to the track a couple times in Baltimore, I think it was Balti-

more. I don't remember the name of the track. My father gave me the money to bet. He would help me with my gambling. And then after the war I got married and I didn't do any gambling.

Then I came back to Edison and I worked bingo. And I hated it. They usually didn't have enough workers because my daughter went to Catholic school and everybody had to do their share of working. The pastor we had was the type of person who got people to work. And the pastor we had would have so many workers that he'd say, "Pauline, why don't you get a couple of [bingo] boards and play." And I hated it. If I won I'd sit there and hate it every minute. But then I got to like it, so from two boards I went to three, and then to four and five and that's how my gambling went on.

Then, of course, Atlantic City opened, and I went to Resorts the first week it opened.

The format has changed. When it first opened in Resorts, you had to pay $5 for even a glass of Coke. There were no comps, no nothing. Well, you had to wear a jacket, no jeans, no shorts, no bathing attire.

A lot of people were against it. I would say most people were against it, Atlantic City opening. . . . You have to stop and think. When Resorts opened up, we had been to Atlantic City the summer before. We went down to a wedding outside of Atlantic City. And we stayed in Atlantic City at one of the big hotels, I can't remember which one it was. . . . You would not believe what it looked like. All the hotels were closed, most of the big hotels had one floor open, you know, that's it. And maybe their café and dining room, but only one floor open for business.

We stayed in this big—it was one of the biggest hotels down there, it was so musty from being unused. The Boardwalk was all closed. There was nothing on the Boardwalk.

Well, we went to the wedding and we went back to the hotel. We decided we'd walk on the Boardwalk, and we went up and changed our clothes—there were eight of us staying at this hotel, I think. And we came down, the desk clerk called one of the fellows over, and they said, "You goin' out on the Boardwalk?" And they said, "Yes." And [the clerk] said, "We'd advise you not to do that. It's very unsafe, and make sure you stay with your group." And when we got out on the Boardwalk, and it was patrolled by police cars, the police cars went up and down the Boardwalk. And it was very desolate, nothing, maybe on the whole Boardwalk that we coverered maybe six shops were open.

So, then Resorts opened up, and with Resorts they started to spruce up [but] you can't compare it to Las Vegas. . . . I didn't play anything when I first went down, 'cause I didn't like slot machines. I still don't like slots there. Occasionally, yeah. The only place I play slots is at Harrah's, because they have some of the old machines in there.

Now, I used to play blackjack, when I first went down. And I really went for the day out really, more than anything else. . . . But that changed, I think about six years ago. I started playing roulette.

♦ ♣ ♥ ♠

Harrah's is my favorite casino. I was down at Harrah's overnight, and about four days later, in the mail, I got one of their marketing things, you know, you have the comps and coins, the coupon. And I got a room, a discount room, it was $2.85 off the room. Well, I was furious when I read that because I thought, "I mean, $2.85? If I can afford to go overnight, I mean $2.85 is not gonna help me one way or the other."

So I opened my mail and there was this little yellow note and a pencil and I wrote, "Here's your $10 back and you keep the $2.85, you know Harrah's was always my favorite casino, but I thought no more, I'll find another one." Signed my name and mailed it.

So about two weeks later I was in Atlantic City, and I came home. My husband, who hates Atlantic City, he likes me to go. Because he likes me to enjoy myself and do what I like to do. . . . I said, "Anybody call?" And he said, "Yeah, Harrah's called."

And I said, "Come on, Frank, who called?" And he said, "I'm telling you, Harrah's called." And I said, "Will you tell me who called?" He said, "Paul, look." He showed me the pad, He said, "A person by the name of Betsy called you and she's the hostess down there."

And so I called her. So she said, "You know, Pauline . . . if more people would do what you did, you'd have better comps, you'd have better everything down here, because we like to know our regular customers, and we like to cater to them. Any time you want a room in this casino, you just call, here's my number, and you have a free room."

She gave me her number, and since then, this has gone on four years. I can have a room anytime. I never ask for one on weekends, so I don't know. I have gotten—my food account is always a hundred dollars or more, I have a card—they have a club, Harbor Club, and you can go when it's open, from ten to ten. And you can go in there and eat, buffet, and they have television and they have a bar and you take one guest. And there's nothing comes over your casino account, I mean it's all free.

And it worked. I mean, I'm going more and gambling more, so I guess it worked. Unfortunately, it's too easy to get there now. 'Cause I'll call for a room and I'll think, "Well, maybe they'll say no this time." Because I like going, but you know, of course, money.

I gamble about $300, or $400 [each time I go]. . . . I try to stay within my range. Sometimes if I'm with a friend I borrow. . . . I have a theory on gamblers. Most gamblers are superstitious. If I play with borrowed money, I always win. I don't know why, maybe it's all in my mind. Maybe I was gonna win anyway. But it always turns out that if I borrow $100, I get it back threefold.

CHAPTER 6

ALBANY:
DOLLARS AND DREAMS

Everything in Albany, including the state capitol building, an imposing hybrid of Romanesque and Renaissance architecture, succumbs to the long fault line of Nelson Rockefeller's ambition: a graying marble-and-concrete mall known as Empire State Plaza. In any other city, the capitol building would dominate its surroundings. But in Albany it merely anchors one end of a staggering project that the former governor of New York said was inspired by the Dalai Lama's palace in Tibet.

Rockefeller, heir to a baronial fortune commensurate with his appetites, also proudly compared the construction of the plaza to the creation of the great pyramids of Egypt. Indeed, the plaza was pharaonic in scope. From the start of construction, in 1962, until its completion, in 1978, its price tag climbed from $250 million to $2 billion. Parts of the complex have a faintly Tibetan style. Most, however, is resolutely Bauhaus and sterile. Five state office buildings, four of them twenty-three stories tall and one forty-four stories tall, are stuck into the heart of the plaza like mighty granite nails. Incongruously plopped down amid the sharp horizontal and vertical lines created by the plaza's other structures is "the Egg"—an enormous, ovate arts center that from afar could be mistaken for an engorged satellite dish. The entire plaza rests upon a five-story platform that is a quarter of a mile long and an eighth of a mile wide.

To help make way for that gargantuan platform, Rockefeller had about one hundred acres of a neighborhood called the Gut rolled up like an old mattress and hauled away. Thousands of residents, mainly low-income Italians, were unceremoniously shunted aside. The Gut was a scruffy part of town, to be sure, a district of bordellos and poverty, where the gangster Jack "Legs" Diamond was killed in 1931. But more than an old, ethnic neighborhood was replaced by the plaza. An entire approach to governing was also dismantled.

Albany once had been a laboratory for innovative social programs and public spending that guided national public policy for much of the 20th century. During Al Smith and Franklin Roosevelt's tenures as governors from 1918 to 1933 (with a three-year hiatus after Smith was defeated in 1920), Albany's legislature passed such measures as child labor laws, rural electrification, unemployment insurance, and large-scale educational aid that later inspired much of the New Deal. Albany in that era was a city where public policy was inspired by something more than building for the sake of building and spending for the sake of spending. Albany led a state where public policy rested on more equitable financial foundations than fiscal gimmicks like lotteries.

In 1966, as the plaza was being erected and New York's finances were on a course that would eventually bring the state to the edge of bankruptcy, Rockefeller reluctantly acceded to voters' approval of a lottery that legislators claimed would boost funding for public education. By 1996, the Empire State's constituents would be betting $10 million *per day* on the New York Lottery—the largest lottery in the United States and the fifth-largest in the world.

Pick Three, Pick Six, PowerBall, Instant Winner, Lotto: in whatever form they take, modern state lotteries have been with us since the mid-1960s, budget Band-Aids for legislators unable or unwilling to tackle serious problems seriously. Gamblers lost $16.2 billion after betting $42.9 billion on lotteries in thirty-seven states and the District of Columbia in 1996. States paid out about $26.7 billion in prizes and earmarked about $13.8 billion for education, senior citizens' programs, and other causes, with about $2.4 billion covering the lotteries' operating expenses.

But all those billions kept by the states are actually slim pickings given the size of most of their budgets. Lotteries, despite hype that paints them as a boon to state treasuries, only kick in about 3 percent of the total tax revenue in most states. Still, they have an impact far beyond the revenue they generate. Lottery drawings have become familiar television events, as common as game shows and the evening news. Those who actually overcome the stratospheric odds against landing the largest jackpots become instant celebrities the moment they receive the oversized checks dutifully awarded in front of cameras and klieg lights.

More than any other form of modern gambling, lotteries have brought betting out of the closet. Propelled by festive media coverage and sustained by the government's seal of approval, lotteries have helped transform gambling's seedy image. In its most recent incarnation, the lottery is a recreational and harmless lark for most people, a chance to rub up against the visceral thrill of striking it rich. For the poor, however, a lottery ticket is a more complicated affair, one that feeds off their faint hope of escape even while it fits all too snugly into the traditions of their luckless neighborhoods.

And while it is the lottery's big-jackpot games that have drawn the most attention and have generally caused the least harm, a new generation of instant games is now the main engine of growth for many lotteries. This is to be expected. Commercializing gambling in any setting, whether in the public sector or the private, has always led, in the end, to games that target gamblers' need for a quick fix, for the immediate, delicious gratification promised by a slot machine or a scratch-off lottery ticket. As New York's lottery ads once advised, all you need is a dollar and a dream.

"WHAT A RAGE WE HAVE FOR LOTTERIES"

Lotteries, like most forms of gambling, are a timeworn species. The word "lottery" derives from the ancient practice of casting or drawing lots— usually wood sticks, pebbles, or any other counting device—to divide land, as Moses did, or to determine the winner of a contest. Roman centurions at Calvary drew lots for Jesus Christ's garments as he died on a cross above them—forever enshrining exactly who holds the high and the low ground in the perennial debates about the morality of gambling.

Lotteries were also used in China, Japan, and Greece. The emperor Caesar Augustus—offering grand prizes of slaves and a villa—used lotteries to fund the upkeep of Rome. During the Middle Ages, from about 500 A.D. to 1500 A.D., lotteries were used almost like auctions, to sell a variety of goods; this practice slowly spread throughout Europe. A lottery was used to refortify Burgundy in 1420, and Columbus' voyages to the New World were partially financed by lotteries. The first time a lottery offered cash as a prize was in Florence in 1530, and the Florentines began teaching French operators the tricks of the trade about three years later. England's Queen Elizabeth I introduced the first government-chartered lottery in 1566 to finance her colony in Virginia. From then on, European governments regularly used state lotteries to finance special projects. England, for example, used lotteries in 1569 to fund the Cinque Ports, in 1612 to finance the Virginia Company's tobacco venture in Jamestown, and in 1660 to ransom English sailors enslaved on Turkish galleys. Private lotteries, plagued by scams and undoubtedly offering unwanted competition to the crown, were outlawed in England in 1699. Things went along swimmingly for the public lottery until 1826, when an unknown thief took off with all of the loot, resulting in a ban on all lotteries in England that lasted until 1994.

America's lottery experience followed a similar path. Colonists had become acquainted with lotteries not only through their English benefactors but also through the Dutch. In 1665, the Dutch sponsored a lottery to aid New Amsterdam's poor, and lotteries quickly became a familiar part of colonial life. Before the Revolutionary War, there were an average of six lotteries in each of the thirteen colonies. Such elite Ivy League universities as Harvard, Yale, Princeton, and Columbia were built in part through lotteries. Ben Franklin used a lottery to buy cannon to defend Philadelphia at the onset of the Revolutionary War, and George Washington used a lottery to arm and pay his troops. Denmark Vesey, a former slave and black leader, bought his freedom in 1800 with $600 of $1,500 he had won in a lottery. Religious groups of almost every denomination, including Baptist, Presbyterian, Catholic, and Jewish, also benefited from lotteries.

"You could scarcely imagine what a rage we have for lotteries. 8,000 tickets sold in four days in the Marblehead lottery," a Boston minister named Jeremy Belknap wrote to a friend in 1790. "I wonder Secretary [of the Treasury Alexander] Hamilton does not hit upon a lottery. It would be more popular than laying a duty on salt, which, if he does will greatly injure our fisheries."

Lotteries remained popular well into the nineteenth century. As economists Charles Clotfelter and Philip Cook have noted, "[Nineteenth-century] lotteries appear to have been viewed as more akin to charitable contributions for public purposes" than to gambling. Clotfelter and Cook cite a report by a nineteenth-century observer who said that the lottery was "not regarded at all as a kind of gambling; the most reputable citizens were engaged in these lotteries, either as selected managers or as liberal subscribers. It was looked upon as a voluntary tax . . . with a contingent profitable return for such subscribers as held the lucky numbers."

In the eighteenth and nineteenth centuries, most governments had few viable options for raising money. The power to tax was limited and the bond market immature. Some larger cities were able to issue municipal bonds for the first time in the 1820s, and records on the overall level of municipal debt were first kept in 1843. But many communities without taxes or bonds at their disposal to finance public works looked to lotteries to fill the void. The first lottery operators were often local volunteers or members of a group slated to receive some of the lottery's revenue. But as lotteries expanded during the century, they became more complex to administer, and a network of private operators developed to help run them. With the assistance of these operators, by 1832 eight eastern states were using lotteries to raise $66.4 million annually, or $1.04 billion in 1996 dollars—four times the federal budget at the time. Tickets were expensive, which usually limited legal play to wealthier members of society, and drawings were held only once or twice a year.

The network that sprang up to market the lotteries comprised two groups of middlemen: contractors and brokers. Contractors printed and collected tickets, ran the drawings, administered prizes, and handled all the paperwork. Brokers, hired by the contractors, purchased tickets from them and resold them to the public at a higher price. Yates & McIntyre, a New York firm, was one of the biggest operators of the time and ran lotteries in several states.

This system was ripe for fraud and given the large sums of money involved, juicy little scandals ensued. By 1830, the scandals had created widespread opposition to lotteries and by 1840 most northern states had outlawed them. By 1860, lotteries were legal only in Delaware, Kentucky, and Missouri. But the private operators displaced by the crackdown on lotteries weren't left without a home. Many of them refashioned their pitches to become some of the country's largest banks and brokerage firms.

Economic uncertainty and distress, always among the great engines spurring the growth of commercial gambling, led several western and southern states to revive lotteries for about a decade after the Civil War. But fraud surfaced yet again. A Kentucky lottery had built roads, hospitals, and the first church in Frankfort. But in 1878 the state outlawed its lottery, leaving only one other state with a lottery up and running: Louisiana. After the infamous Louisiana Lottery Company was forced out of business in 1893, no legal lottery would operate in the country again until 1964.

But a little bit of law had never gotten in the way of people's desire to gamble. The lottery was no exception.

In 1818, after contractors running the "Medical Science Lottery" in New York were caught with their hands in the till, Albany's legislators ruled that no new lotteries would be licensed in the state after 1820. But those already licensed kept on humming for more than a decade.

"In no place have I seen so many Lottery Offices as in the City of New York. They are numberless in Broadway. Their puffing exceeds all belief," wrote C. D. Arfwedson, a British tourist, in 1833. "Each collector called heaven and earth to witness that he was the luckiest among his worthy colleagues. One of them went so far to affirm, that he paid prizes to a larger amount than would liquidate all the debts of bankrupts in the United States."

More than fraud had led Albany to begin clamping down on lotteries. The cultural milieu of the nineteenth century, especially in the state of New York, was riddled with moral conflicts that still surround gambling today.

New York was the only original colony to have been controlled for an extended period by a European power other than England, and the Dutch influence in the state remained strong for decades after the Revolutionary War. The area around Albany had been settled in 1614 by Dutch merchants who found the location, and the fortress they built there, ideal for controlling fur trade along the Hudson River. Extensive landholdings were granted to families, such as the Van Rensselaers, that settled the area, and they grew wealthy by keeping a portion of the crops produced by renters of their land. When the English vanquished the Dutch in 1664, then chartered Albany as a city in 1686, they kept this semifeudal system in place. It lasted until the 1840s. Upstate New York ended up retaining a much more aristocratic and, even after the Revolutionary War, pro-British mien than many of the other colonies. It also put Albany, which became the state capital in 1797, at odds with such places as New York City, which openly embraced entrepreneurs, the slave trade, and workers from a hodgepodge of countries and various religious backgrounds.

During the early nineteenth century, as New York City embarked on an extraordinary period of economic growth, towns upstate were swept up in the religious fervor and Bible meetings that constituted the social and spiritual phenomenon known as the Second Great Awakening. "I want to see our State evangelized," one devout layman vowed at the time. "Suppose the great State of New York in all its physical, political, moral, commercial and pecuniary resources should come over to the Lord's side. Why it would turn the scale and could convert the world. I shall have no rest until it is done."

While some religious sects born in the Second Great Awakening, such as the Mormons, left New York for the frontier, others stayed behind, determined not to be silenced by cultural conflict. By the middle of the century, evangelical Protestant reformers had become a powerful force in the area around Albany, where the feminist and temperance movements were also born, and they lavished their attention on their favorite den of iniquity: New York City. In 1850, the city had about 6,000 gambling halls, or about one for every eighty-five people living there. The reformers condemned liquor, sex, and gambling, and extolled the virtues of hard work and abstinence. Their numbers included Sylvester Graham (who advocated a meager diet of fruits, vegetables, and "Graham crackers" to control lustful feelings that might lead to "venereal indulgences") and, later in the century, Henry Comstock (who founded the Society for the Suppression of Vice and denounced, among other things, birth control, saloons, and the writings of George Bernard Shaw).

Still, Saratoga Springs, just north of Albany, flourished as a casino and horse-racing town after the Civil War despite its location in the birthplace of temperance. And New York City, far more complex culturally than Saratoga Springs, was not a place where antivice crusaders would easily win their battles. Albany's legislators might shut down lotteries, but a large number of people still wanted to play the game, particularly among the urban poor. The poor were devotees of the underground lottery, a game that had operated alongside the legal lottery since the mid-eighteenth century and was known on the street as "policy."

Ignoring Protestant reformers' messages of thrift and discipline, which did little to ease the uncertainty of their lives, "African-American city dwellers and poor immigrant women . . . bought policy slips and continued to gamble on the possibility that the market economy was no more rational, no more just, than the random numbers of a lottery drawing."

Policy took its name, if not its methods, from mainstream commerce. The tickets, whose numbers were the same as those available for betting on the legal lottery, were likened to an insurance policy. Most lottery tickets in the nineteenth century were expensive, costing about $5 each, or about $75 in 1996 dollars. But for a few cents, the urban poor could buy a policy slip for a price that guaranteed them a corresponding portion of the lottery jackpot if they had the winning number. The poorest neighborhoods had the heaviest concentration of policy shops, which were usually housed in small stores that also sold lottery tickets. Store owners welcomed the action because they received a 12 percent commission on their sales from legitimate lottery operators, who gladly funded the lucrative underground activity.

New York and Chicago, home to large numbers of immigrants and blacks, had the busiest policy shops. While little is known about the gambling habits of African Americans prior to the Civil War, the growth of policy games after the war offers one of the first glimpses. For their betting strategies, many urban black gamblers depended on "dream books." These cheap pamphlets, peddled on the street, offered advice on the best numbers to choose depending on a dream the gambler had the night before. Dream books quantified chaos and woe to the gambler who ignored their mystical advice. Within the black community, and in some poor white neighborhoods, such tracts as *Old Aunt Dinah's Policy Dream Book* and pamphlets written by "Professor Abdullah" and "The Gypsy Witch" were best-sellers. In the pages of these leaflets, dreaming about a white man represented a threat to one's freedom; the dreamer should pick 876 when placing a policy bet. Dreaming about a black man meant success was near and 121 was the number to bet.

But policy made too much money for outsiders to ignore it. White politicians in New York, able to trot out corrupt policemen to protect sales turf or beat up on the competition, often had ultimate control over the black-owned policy shops. As the Gilded Age's freshly minted robber barons threw up their ornate mansions on Fifth Avenue late in the century, and as New York became home to ever larger numbers of blacks and immigrants dreaming of mansions of their own, the policy business expanded. It also began to change.

When New York outlawed its lotteries, depriving the state's policy operators of a steady source of winning numbers, they simply used results from lotteries in other states like Louisiana. But by the turn of the century, legal lotteries had disappeared in every state. So policy operators started drawing their own numbers—and drawing them far more frequently than legal lotteries ever had, sometimes several times a day. Chicago became home to the most elaborate policy operation in the country, with cheap wagers available on several series of numbers with jackpots of varying sizes. In New York, policy was reduced to one game with an easy formula: a three-digit figure, usually determined by the handle (that is, the total amount wagered) at a local racetrack, was selected each day. Whoever picked that number won. This simple version of policy was called the numbers, and it became wildly popular in New York.

Several big cities in the Northeast and Midwest had a vigorous numbers trade during the early twentieth century, but New York had the most action. Although the origins of the business are murky, the first numbers operators may have been West Indians who set up shop in Harlem. And surviving as an operator was a precarious proposition. The pool of potential winners was unlimited because operators didn't place restrictions on how often a particular number could be chosen. Thus, numbers operators without a big financial cushion in their banks could be broken by a run of bad luck. Eventually, Harlem's control of the numbers business passed to a group with deeper pockets and a keener sense of how to organize illegal enterprises: the Mob.

Although it has been popularly believed that organized crime moved into the numbers business after Prohibition was repealed in 1933, the Mob actually took control more than a decade earlier. While many mobsters, most notably Dutch Schultz, knocked heads and slit throats to take over the numbers rackets, some Harlem operators welcomed organized crime for other reasons. A U.S. Justice Department study published in 1982 noted that the Mob's influence over the New

York political machine and the police force, as well as ample bootlegging dollars that funded the numbers banks, appealed to many operators. The report noted that even "Harlem's newspapers admitted that, after the Schultz takeover, the banks were better managed and more likely to pay off winning numbers."

The Mob never exercised airtight control over the numbers business, and its strong position fragmented as time went on. But regardless of who ran the games, by the 1930s and 1940s whites, blacks, and Hispanics were all active numbers players in New York. Millions of illegal Irish Sweepstakes tickets were also smuggled into midwestern and northeastern cities starting in 1930. The "Sweeps" funded hundreds of millions of dollars worth of hospital construction in Ireland, and its enormous popularity in North America made it one of the world's largest lotteries for decades.

Though the numbers action dwindled sharply in later years, it was a lucrative business for the Mob at least until the 1960s. In 1958, *The New York Times* reported that one Harlem numbers ring investigated by the local district attorney's office had been handling $300,000 in bets per day, or $1.6 million a day in 1996 dollars. Figures like these are worthy of skepticism, because law enforcement has always had a vested interest in inflating the size of illegal gambling operations. Law enforcement officials are typically the only public sources to track illegal betting, and because the size of policing budgets reflect the perceived severity of a problem, authorities have an incentive to puff up their data. Nevertheless, by any measure the Harlem operation uncovered in 1958 was huge. Such impressive results weren't lost on states searching for new ways to raise revenue. Just six years after that Harlem numbers operation was broken up, and with the stench of the Louisiana lottery long since dissipated, New Hampshire opened the door to a new era in lottery gambling. It didn't take long for New York to follow suit.

THE STATES JOIN THE ACTION

At first glance, New Hampshire is the most unlikely of states to have legitimated gambling in the late twentieth century. Small, mountainous, and so fiercely independent that its state constitution explicitly protects the right to revolution, New Hampshire is home to a rock-ribbed conservatism that resents any intrusion of government into the lives of its residents. That antipathy toward government carries with it an aversion to taxes, and in the early 1960s New Hampshire had no state income or sales tax. The state's budget was financed strictly by property taxes and a variety of "sin taxes" on such things as liquor and horse-race betting, sources that were increasingly inadequate.

The New Hampshire legislature had tried repeatedly to legalize lotteries, first in 1937 and again in 1955. In 1963, confronted with the possibility of having to introduce a sales tax to fund much-needed educational aid, New Hampshire chose to establish a state lottery instead. The first drawing was held early the next year. To give its lottery a trustworthy glow, New Hampshire hired Ed Powers, a former FBI agent credited with solving a celebrated Brinks armored car heist, as its first lottery director.

In the beginning, the New Hampshire lottery was a far cry from the numbers games of the time or the lotteries of today. It was run much like eighteenth- and nineteenth-century lotteries. There were only two drawings per year, and tickets, which cost $3, could be purchased at racetracks and liquor stores, nowhere else. Like the numbers games, the New Hampshire lottery determined winners according to the results of a horse race. (This also permitted the state to circumvent a 10 percent federal gambling tax, because racing had been given an exemption from that tax.) Unlike the numbers game, however, the lottery didn't allow bettors to choose their own number. It was already printed on the ticket. Although federal laws passed seventy years earlier to curtail the Louisiana lottery forbade interstate lottery sales by mail, New Hampshire still managed to sell the bulk of its tickets to visitors from outside the state. It had to. The state hoped to retain $4 million on annual lottery sales of $12 million—or 4 million tickets sold, at a time when the state's population was only 630,000. Things got off to a much slower start. In its first year, the New Hampshire lottery rang up sales of only $7.5 million.

By 1964, other states were also considering lotteries. In California, a cement contractor named Robert Wilson successfully pressed the legislature to place a lottery referendum on the fall ballot in 1964. The referendum was crushed, having sparked so much opposition that another two decades passed before California legalized a lottery. (Undeterred, Wilson moved to a South Pacific island where he rolled out the "Worldwide Lottery" in 1965. It was soon shut down, after California police discovered Wilson's tickets being sold illegally in Los Angeles.) Rhode Island and Vermont considered lotteries in 1963; Massachusetts had already debated having one, more than two decades earlier. But all of these states ultimately had backed away from the proposition. New Hampshire moved forward alone.

Yet a decade later, ten states had lotteries, and New York was one of them.

When New York began considering a lottery, state finances were already complicated by a variety of budgetary subterfuges planted by the Rockefeller administration. Nelson Rockefeller, the charming, brash, and strong-willed grandson of the founder of Standard Oil, first came to Albany as governor in 1958. He would hold on to the post for the next fifteen years. Easily the most powerful Republican in the state, Rockefeller had political, business, and social connections matched only by his command of prodigious wealth and by the scale of his dreams. He possessed, in the words of the historian Robert Caro, "an appreciative imagination of a high order, an ability (rare in itself) to grasp and judge the inspirations of other men. . . . He could see—not only visualize but judge and assess the value of, and determine to bring to reality—proposed physical developments."

"Physical developments," in the Rockefeller era, meant universities, housing, prisons, highways, and high-profile projects like Empire State Plaza, all artfully financed. Hemmed in by a mandate in New York's constitution requiring the state to maintain a balanced budget, yet determined to find the money he needed to realize his ambitions, Rockefeller set up a hodgepodge of "off-budget" public agencies called authorities to finance and supervise construction. The authorities provided little public information on their inner workings. And they pursued Rockefeller's goals by independently floating bonds that weren't officially on the state's budget but were, nonetheless, backed by the state's credit. As long as authority and state revenues could meet the bond payments, gambling with the state's finances might work. But because Rockefeller's construction binge was so massive and so swift, and because few of the authorities generated enough revenue to be self-supporting, the scheme quickly overwhelmed the state's finances. By 1966, it was growing impossible for Rockefeller to meet the balanced-budget requirement. When federal housing subsidies destined for New York were later diverted to fund the Vietnam War, Rockefeller had to issue even more shaky bonds to keep his housing plans on track. Debt kept piling up, and the underpinnings of the local economy, particularly around New York City, were beginning to splinter. It was in this climate that Albany considered instituting a lottery.

Rockefeller had originally opposed a lottery because he considered it a regressive tax—that is, a tax whose burdens fell most heavily on the poor, those who could least afford to pay it. (Yet in 1964, two years before New York voters approved a lottery, Rockefeller had successfully pushed for a hike in the extremely regressive sales tax.) Regardless of his stated discomfort with the idea of a lottery, Rockefeller brought his considerable energy to bear on the enterprise once voters had approved it.

He suggested that tickets be sold in vending machines for 25 cents, and he wanted an advertising budget to promote the game. Instead, the legislature initially approved $2 tickets sold only in hotels, motels, and banks for drawings held four times a year. One high-minded bank, Franklin National, said it refused to sell tickets because lotteries undermined the public image of banking as a "symbol of stability." Stolid and conservative Franklin National collapsed seven years later, after embarking on an ill-fated bout of currency speculation.

In early 1967, several months before the first lottery tickets went on sale, Rockefeller said the lottery could earn the state $45 million annually and help balance a record budget. By April, the legislature had endorsed cheaper tickets and more frequent drawings. Tickets would now cost just $1, drawings for a $100,000 prize would be held monthly, and there would be three $250,000 drawings a year. The legislature was now projecting the state's annual lottery haul to be $48 million on sales of $180 million. Entranced by the potential windfall, the state set its goals ever higher. On the eve of the lottery's opening, Albany said it hoped to sell $360 million of tickets each year. All these projections proved to be thunderously wrong.

When the green-and-white tickets finally went on sale in June, the betting was frenzied, particularly in business districts and low-income residential neighborhoods. One bank reported selling 200 tickets in the first fifteen minutes they were available. Then betting came to a screeching halt. Only $6.5 million was wagered that month, about one-fifth of the monthly average needed to meet Albany's targets. Betting dropped the next month to $4.1 million. Sales the first year were $48.5 million, less than one-seventh of what the state had planned on.

Federal laws in the late 1960s forbade lotteries to advertise on television or in newspapers, but at Rockefeller's recommendation $1.5 million had been set aside to promote New York's lottery by other means. At first, the billboards and matchbook ads promoted the lottery with a decorous "Help Your Schools" message. In the summer of 1967, Fuller, Smith & Ross, the lottery's ad agency, changed tactics in an attempt to boost lackluster sales. The ads now carried a new message: "Get-Rich-Quick." Albany followed this up by sending a motorcade of pretty women in miniskirts through the streets of New York City to pitch the lottery's virtues. But sales continued to slump.

Taking a different tack to jack up lottery betting, Rockefeller requested that more frequent drawings be considered, and successfully petitioned the legislature in 1968 for an expansion of ticket sales to movie theaters, retailers, and newsstands. Sales at banks had been banned in late 1967 by the federal government. U.S. Representative Wright Patman of Texas offered the following observation when introducing the legislation forbidding lottery sales in banks: "If Mr. Rockefeller wishes to support his state government by trickery, slickery, shell games, gambling, and fast buckism, that is a matter that rests between him and the voters of New York. But when he attempts to slip these ingredients into the Federal banking system, then it is time for Members of Congress to teach him a basic lesson in the proper and time-honored separation of State and Federal Government."

New York's lottery tickets continued to be duds, even though they were now on sale almost everywhere except in banks. Even the weather conspired against Albany. One winter day in 1968, thousands of lottery tickets spilled from crates as they were being moved into storage at a bank in New York City. A howling wind scattered the tickets across the city's streets, and drawings were delayed for almost two weeks.

In order to balance the state budget that same year, Albany repealed the portion of the lottery's enabling legislation that required proceeds to be earmarked for education. Instead of being specifically targeted for public school funding—the carrot that had been dangled before voters when the lottery was approved—lottery funds could now be channeled into the state's general fund to be used at legislators' discretion.

THE WINNING FORMULA

The New York lottery stumbled along for almost a decade. When Hugh Carey became New York's governor in 1974, he prepared to come to terms with the titanic debt Rockefeller and New York City had amassed. "The days of wine and roses are over," he declared. He soon discovered that the lottery was as mismanaged as the state's overall finances.

Albany was barely keeping tabs on how much money the lottery was pulling in, although estimates put sales at an average of $78 million a year between 1967 and 1975. In some cases, the state wasn't sure how much money was being funnelled into jackpots. In 1975, when a computer snafu caused Albany to print hundreds of multiple tickets with identical numbers for a $1.4 million drawing, Carey dismissed all 325 of the lottery's employees and shut the game down for a year.

Clearly, Albany hadn't yet hit upon the correct formula for extracting wagers from the betting public. Rockefeller had identified two hindrances to betting—infrequent drawings and limited availability of tickets—but two more crucial barriers were still in place: bettors had no choice of wagers, and jackpots were small. New York's lottery required bettors to sign their names and write their addresses on the back of tickets, hand them over, and then wait weeks or months to find out if they'd won. It was just like an old-fashioned sweepstakes, and nobody liked it very much except for the poor; even they had a greater allegiance to the illegal numbers games. After all, the numbers operators offered bigger and more frequent payoffs, lines of credit, and cheaper tickets.

It would be up to neighboring New Jersey, the third state to legalize a lottery, to demonstrate the explosive potential of frequent action when its lottery opened for business in 1970.

New Jersey sold cheap, 50-cent tickets, held drawings once a week, and offered jackpots ranging from $25 to $1 million. The state also increased the prize pool, or "payout rate," of its lottery to 45 percent of the revenue earned on all tickets sold. New York's payout rate was only 30 percent and New Hampshire's was 35 percent. The results were amazing. In the New Jersey lottery's first eleven weeks, sales rocketed past targets set for the entire year. By the end of 1971, the lottery had grossed $73 million, returning $33 million to the state. New Jersey's first million-dollar winners were trotted out on a national television talk show, and the accompanying publicity demonstrated the benefits of glowing media coverage of lottery winners: lottery sales in New Jersey almost doubled the next year to $138 million. Large states with troubled economies, such as Massachusetts, Illinois, and Michigan, took notice and jumped on the lottery bandwagon.

But the masterstroke came in 1975, when New Jersey's lottery became the first in the country to offer computerized betting that allowed players to choose their own numbers and find out the same day if they had won. The maneuver was consciously modeled to compete with the illegal numbers game, and while it never put illegal operators out of business, as the state had claimed it would, it did drum up a lot more betting. Lottery sales had slackened to $77 million in 1975, when New Jersey first offered its computerized numbers game. Sales more than doubled the following year, to $158 million. By allowing gamblers to feel more directly involved in the betting and in control of their fate in some small way, computers were starting to do as much for the lotteries as slot machines were doing for the casino business. And then Albany reentered the lottery business with a vengeance.

After cleaning up its lottery's management problems, Albany burst on the scene again in 1976 with a major innovation: it linked computers to weekly drawings based on an old Italian lottery game it called Lotto. Players were given a choice of picking six numbers from a field of thirty-six; and if they picked the correct ones they won the jackpot. But because the odds of winning—1.9 million to 1—were so horrendous, the jackpots grew huge. For once, Albany had hit a nerve. Lottery players loved the prospect of winning $10 million, or $20 million, or $30 million, and sales in New York took off. In 1977, sales were $197 million, with the state keeping $91 million before costs; in 1982 sales were $425 million, and the state kept $165 million. In 1984, a year after the state increased Lotto drawings from once to twice a week, $890 million of tickets was sold, with the state's take $375 million; in 1987 Albany sold $1.46 billion of tickets and kept $654 million, making New York's the biggest lottery in the country.

For a time, Lotto was the state of the art in lotteries. Eventually, smaller states that didn't have enough residents to produce big jackpots for lotto games linked up with one another in multistate drawings such as PowerBall. But the big lotto games, while garnering much of the media attention and for a time proving to be the backbone of most state lotteries, weren't the key to most lotteries' survival. That distinction would belong to yet another lottery milestone: "instant" games.

In 1974, at the same time that New Jersey was computerizing the numbers business, Massachusetts introduced scratch-off tickets with preprinted prizes. In a nod to the obvious, the state called this the Instant Game; its dextrous use of such games eventually helped make Massachusetts gamblers the heaviest lottery players in the country and revolutionized how lotteries were marketed.

Thus, by the end of the 1970s the three major types of games that all lottery states would later adopt had come into existence: big jackpot "lotto" games; daily "numbers" games; and "instant" games. Regional and cultural differences accounted for differences in the popularity of games from state to state. Bigger states tended to drum up more interest in lotto games, because they could offer bigger jackpots. The numbers game was more popular in eastern states than in most midwestern and western states, because of local familiarity with the game. And some states would claim that the popularity of their instant games reflected the fact that their residents had already found paradise:

"People play lotteries to have fun and to provide or fulfill dreams," says Ed Stanek, director of Iowa's lottery. "Lotto games are played by people looking for lifestyle changes, and people in certain parts of the country want lifestyle changes because of where they are. People in Iowa are happy and aren't looking to move, so the instant games are more popular here."

Whatever form they took, most lotteries thrived, convincing almost two dozen new states to begin offering lotteries in the 1980s and 1990s. All these new entrants, which created the biggest wave of state-sponsored gambling in U.S. history, were pulled into the gambling business by an economic riptide. This economic undercurrent was called the

Reagan Revolution, and it involved budgetary machinations that made Rockefeller's dice rolls look like child's play.

During the twelve years that Ronald Reagan and George Bush occupied the White House (1981 to 1993), the federal budget deficit ballooned from $79 billion to $327 billion as massive hikes in the defense budget were matched by sweeping tax cuts and slashes in state and local aid. States, like the battered towns and cities that were welcoming casinos, scrambled to plug their budget gaps. As it had so many times before, gambling seemed to offer states the possibility of an easy and expeditious solution, especially when the speculative economy of the 1980s deflated into a recession. During the 1980s alone, seventeen states and the District of Columbia took the bait and joined the lottery movement. Six more states entered the fray in the early 1990s. Where most lotteries centuries ago were used to fund special projects and then shut down, modern lotteries had become perpetual piggy banks for legislators. By 1996, faced with cold economic realities, thirty-seven states and the District of Columbia had become deadly serious about fine-tuning their lotteries and getting gamblers to play them.

"VIDEO CRACK"—THE DRIVE FOR INSTANT ACTION

"Microwave popcorn, one-hour photo, Priority Mail, ATMs, Pay Per View, satellite news, fax modems, electronic mail, pagers—Let's face it. It's 1996, and phrases like 'right away,' 'ASAP,' and 'now' roll naturally from our tongues," observed *Public Gaming International*, a trade publication for lottery operators, in a story informing readers that computer-generated "fast draw" games played on video terminals were the lottery industry's future.

Indeed, in an era when a premium is placed on instant gratification, state lotteries have kept pace. Defending state promotion of gambling, lottery operators are quick to point out that lotteries haven't traditionally appealed to compulsive gamblers as much as casino games because, they say, the action has never been fast enough to produce real addiction. Times are changing, however, and new instant games are the reason.

Sam DePhillippo, executive director of the Massachusetts lottery, offers three reasons why instant games have been so popular in his state. "We have a much higher payout [than other states]—we give back sixty-eight percent to seventy percent to players. We also have good themes to our games, like blackjack and roulette wheels. The third thing we do is keep the player in the game until the last scratch." DePhillippo's instant games are designed so each spot that conceals a prize can be rubbed off individually rather than all at once, with the swipe of a quarter or a fingernail. This little artifice keeps the player "in the game": Involved. Focused. Hungry.

Should the ticket be a loser, it can be entered in a drawing for a guest appearance on a lottery game show sponsored by the state. "It's kind of like a regular game show with the skill factor out," DePhillippo says.

Of course, lotteries themselves are games "with the skill factor out," and this forces lottery operators to constantly repackage them to maintain their appeal to bettors. Massachusetts has led the charge in putting a wide variety of instant games with various prices and features on the street in order to attract as many different types of gamblers as possible. In fiscal 1996, Massachusetts residents gambled an average $505 each on lottery tickets. In comparison, New Yorkers bet $198, Texans $187, Illinoisans $140, and Californians just $73 on the lottery.

Massachusetts' virtuosity at peddling its lottery has drawn the attention of other states, because all are now confronting what the industry calls jackpot fatigue in their big lotto games. Where a $1 million prize was attractive to bettors two decades ago, the pot has constantly had to grow since then to keep gamblers interested. Lottery directors in PowerBall states who once drew plenty of action on $10 million lotto jackpots say $40 million is the minimum now needed to draw substantial play.

Not only do big jackpots draw gamblers, they make for good newspaper copy. "A single news story, if it's positive, is worth ten advertisements," says the Iowa lottery's Stanek. "People put much more credibility in a news story than in advertising. But you need to have much bigger winners for the media to pay attention."

Fawning media attention hasn't obviated lottery administrators' penchant for indulging in a little promotion of their trade. In fiscal 1996 lotteries nationwide spent $343 million advertising their wares. Federal advertising and mailing restrictions imposed on lotteries in the late nineteenth century were lifted in 1975 after the laws were challenged by states. Over the years, ads have been one of the lotteries' favorite ways to show bettors the fastest way to Easy Street. The messages are rarely subtle.

A 1980s television ad for the Connecticut lottery portrayed a solitary fisherman sadly admitting that he could have saved for his children's education or his own retirement, but had neglected to be so responsible. He then soberly confided to viewers that he had played the lottery instead. Then, after a slight pause, came the kicker. The fisherman shouted for all to hear that he was rich! rich! rich! It was a sales pitch with perennial appeal.

In 1996, after enduring withering public criticism, the Massachusetts lottery removed posters it had placed near ticket machines several months earlier. Titled "How to Make Millions," the poster showed two plans. On the left side of the poster, "Plan A" advised: "Start studying when you're about 7 years old, real hard. Then grow up and get a good job. From then on, get up at dawn every day. . . . Do this every day for 30 years, holidays and weekends included." The right side of the poster, "Plan B," had a picture of two lottery tickets.

It isn't only states that take advantage of the raw human need to dream and to escape. The modern lottery, like other forms of gambling, has attracted its share of earthworms that prey upon the weaknesses of gamblers. A sprawling cadre of lottery ticket "resellers" has emerged who specialize in reselling apparently genuine state and foreign lottery tickets to gamblers in the United States who wouldn't normally have the opportunity to buy them. In the summer of 1997, the U.S. attorney's office in Seattle filed forfeiture charges against a network of reselling companies in Canada and Barbados owned and operated by James Blair Down of Vancouver. According to an investigation by the U.S. Postal Inspection Service, Down used a sophisticated telemarketing operation to defraud at least 190 lottery players of about $10 million between 1989 and 1996 by purporting to resell tickets to them.

Down's companies allegedly contacted gamblers, most of them senior citizens, by telephone and convinced them to buy shares of lottery tickets purchased by the companies. Investigators said he sold far more shares, or "memberships," than the number of tickets he purchased. In 1995 alone, Down allegedly resold $70 million of lottery tickets. Ray Cogdill, an eighty-three-year-old Army veteran, says he amassed a pile of credit-card debt and lost all of his savings, for a total of more than $100,000, gambling with Blair's companies between 1995 and 1996. Like many of the elderly, Cogdill was an easy mark for telemarketers preying upon his loneliness.

"They kept telling me I'd win something, but all I ever won was about twelve hundred dollars, and that was right at the end. They told me I was their friend, and I got to trusting them," says Cogdill, who lives in a small Comfort Inn motel in Ardmore, Oklahoma. "I kept asking them, 'Are you lying to me, or am I gonna win a lot of money?' And they kept telling me that I was going to win."

While reselling has proven to be a lucrative line of business, jackpot fatigue means that the days of easy money for states proffering legal lotto games have passed. Jackpots can be boosted only so high, usually by making the odds worse. In 1988, Albany increased the field of numbers in New York's lotto game from thirty-six, where it was when the game was introduced, to fifty-four. That hiked the odds of picking the correct six numbers from 1.9 million to 1 to 26 million to 1. The odds of winning one of the huge PowerBall drawings offered in other state lotteries are 55 million to 1. Ironically, lousier odds produced fewer winners, which created bigger jackpots, which drew more action from gamblers. Of course, states such as New York don't cite these astronomical odds on their lotto tickets or advertisements. But in a nation fixated on superlatives and on having the biggest and the best, big jackpots have become humdrum. Lotto pots just can't get big enough quickly enough anymore. Gamblers want more than riches. They want "action." They want instant games.

The repetitive, immediate fix of action is the hook that keeps many gamblers in front of slot machines, at blackjack tables, on stock exchange trading floors, and in front of television sets watching sports hour after hour. Winning money is, of course, the goal, but few gamblers win regularly. Action, on the other hand, is its own reward. It keeps gamblers on the edge, in a certain solitary place where they find purpose. It keeps them involved in the world.

Henry Lesieur, a former Illinois State University professor and a leading authority on compulsive gambling, has observed that a serious gambler's life is "a continuous stringing together of action." For serious gamblers, action is a state of mind. In his book *The Chase*, Lesieur recounts another observer's view of action: " 'Action.' Supposedly the word speaks to the process of betting. I suspect it speaks more deeply to what happens within the gambler. He places the bet, juices flow, he feels really alive: action. When the bet is on, his existence is confirmed."

But action isn't the province only of serious gamblers. It also offers its embrace to amateurs, for whom its joys may register as so many emotional pinpricks. Wagers don't have to be large and the setting doesn't have to be grand for action to appear. Action's home can be found in a setting as mundane as the corner grocery store. Action can be purchased for a couple of dollars, and its energies released with every scratch of a quarter across the flimsy surface of an instant lottery ticket.

Instant games are the fastest-growing segment of the lottery business and where most states are now placing their bets. New York's lottery had sales of $3.6 billion in fiscal 1996, up from $2 billion in fiscal 1992, making it the country's biggest. Of that total, sales of instant-game tickets have rocketed from $286 million in 1992 to $1 billion in 1996. On the other hand, sales of Lotto tickets were $717 million in 1992 and rose, much more slowly, to $753 million in 1996. The Ohio lottery, enamored of its instant games, now mails promotions for the tickets directly to residents' homes.

The instant game envelope is being pushed even further by states that offer interactive video lottery terminals, or VLTs. As of 1996, nine states, including New York, have them. Cousins of slot machines, VLTs are usually placed in bars, restaurants, or stores, and allow gamblers to play video poker, blackjack, or "quick-draw" keno. Keno gamblers bet on a set of ten numbers they pick from an eighty-number field displayed on a video terminal. The computer spits out twenty numbers, and if the bettor's ten numbers are among them, the gambler wins. The computer can generate a new keno game every five minutes and with that, the frequency of lottery games has increased from quarterly, to monthly, to weekly, to daily, to a dozen times hourly.

Despite being dubbed the "crack cocaine of gambling" or "video crack" by critics troubled by their potential addictiveness, VLTs are now being considered by other states, among them New Jersey. California briefly offered VLTs before banning them. Illegal VLTs have been operating in many states for more than a decade, and the industry has long been dominated by organized crime, particularly on the East Coast. While stings have broken up some of the illegal rings, law enforcement officials say organized crime still has a strong hand in the industry. Bob Buccino, an organized-crime investigator with the New Jersey State Attorney General's office, estimates that the profit on a single VLT is about $500 to $1,500 per week; he believes the Mob controls about 30,000 machines in the metropolitan New York region—an operation that apparently brings in about $1.6 billion a year to various organized crime groups.

A 1991 report by New Jersey's State Commission of Investigation offered the following repartee between a state regulator and Joseph Fay, who had profited from Mob associations, testifying about VLTs called "Joker Poker" machines:

> Q: You spoke earlier about having 60 or so Joker Poker machines out on the street. What kind of locations were they in by that time?
> A: Candy stores, bars, gas stations, funeral parlors, car washes.
> Q: You had Joker Poker machines in funeral parlors?
> A: One funeral parlor.
> Q: Do you recall how many machines you had in that funeral parlor?
> A: Five or six, seven, it depends.
> Q: Do you know where in the funeral parlor exactly these machines were located?
> A: In like, a lounge area where you would, whatever, have coffee or, you know.

The conversation continued:

Q: Do you know about how many machines did you put into people's homes?

A: Usually two or three, depending on how much action was there, how much money you could make, how many people were waiting to play.

Q: How many of these places did you have? How many individual private homes, do you recall?

A: Not too many, maybe eight or nine.

Q: Did you make the same kind of split with the private home owner as you did with any other location—50/50 split?

A: Yes, actually, I did give them 50/50 but what would happen was the guy that had it in his house was addicted to the game so they usually ended up with nothing anyway.

BIG DADDY GTECH

Like Joseph Fay, J. David Smith also got started in the gambling business by selling illegal video poker machines. In the early 1980s, Smith sold the devices to bars and restaurants in Kentucky before being arrested on a felony charge of illegal gambling. He pleaded guilty to a misdemeanor charge in 1981, and then went to work for a small lottery company. His next employer was the big daddy of the modern lottery business: Gtech Corporation.

Gtech, based in Rhode Island, provides the computer systems that make most lotteries hum, and it has dominated the business for more than a decade. Although little known outside its industry, Gtech has become a formidable presence, thanks to products and services that state lottery officials say are peerless. For a fee ranging from 1.5 percent to 5 percent of sales, Gtech helps states design games and then sells them the software and terminals needed to turn grocery stores and restaurants into little casinos. Gtech's technology lets states process hundreds of thousands of bets per minute for games ranging from lotto to quick-draw keno. Gtech's sales jumped from $8 million when it was founded in 1981 to $744 million in fiscal 1996.

But more than peerless technology has boosted Gtech's fortunes. It has won its contracts for twenty-eight of the country's thirty-seven lotteries through fevered lobbying of public officials that has left a trail of legal problems and accusations that the company wields too much power in the industry. While Gtech certainly isn't the only lottery company that lobbies for contracts, it brings a distinct ferocity to its efforts. Maryanne Gilliard, former director of the California lottery, says that Gtech tried to "intimidate" her when it met with her in late 1996 to seek renewal of its $400 million contract with the state. Gilliard says the company threatened to release a critical report detailing how poorly California's lottery had been managed by her predecessors unless its contract was renewed. Gtech, in a written response to questions, said it never threatened to release its report to the public and said there was no connection between the report and the renewal of its contract.

"They are a very, very aggressive company," says Gilliard. She thinks Gtech's influence has cowed lottery directors elsewhere into being less frank about the company's methods. "I think, by and large, you have people in this industry that like their jobs and when you have a vendor who controls all the contracts, [directors are] afraid to buck the system."

Such allegedly direct pressure is unusual for Gtech. In state after state, it is consultants hired by the company who typically have been accused of wrongdoing. That was the case in California in 1993, when a former Gtech lobbyist named Clayton Jackson was indicted and later imprisoned on racketeering and bribery charges.

A tape recording played during his trial revealed Jackson referring to California lottery director Sharon Sharp as "our gal" at a time when he was Gtech's lobbyist. Sharp resigned, but Gtech itself was never charged with any crimes. Texas' lottery director was fired in 1997 after alleged improprieties arose involving Gtech. Similar problems have surfaced in several other states.

At the center of many of the scandals has been J. David Smith, who was convicted of fraud in New Jersey in 1996. Smith, who was Gtech's national sales manager from 1987 to 1994, was accused by federal prosecutors in New Jersey of accepting kickbacks from consultants hired by Gtech who had close ties to state officials. The consultants arranged meetings with New Jersey lottery officials to discuss adding computerized keno to the state's gambling menu. Smith had been accused of a similar crime in Kentucky in 1995, but a judge there threw out the case before it went to a jury. Nonetheless, in late 1996 federal prosecutors in New Jersey, as part of a continuing probe, subpoenaed the employment records of James Hosker, who went to work for Gtech after leaving the presidency of the Kentucky lottery, according to individuals familiar with the matter.

Gtech wasn't charged with a crime in New Jersey, and the company was portrayed as a victim of some of Smith's schemes—in fact, Gtech has never been indicted, even though it has been frequently investigated. But according to reporter Bill Bulkeley of *The Wall Street Journal*, during Smith's trial Gtech chief executive Guy Snowden, who had a close personal relationship with Smith, stated that he permitted Smith to do freelance work for Gtech's consultants because Smith was integral to the company's success. Bulkeley also quoted a federal prosecutor, who noted that Gtech had a $20 million annual budget for lobbyists and consultants: "If they're paying $20 million to buy access to public officials, there has to be something wrong with that."

Given the fact that Gtech controls about 70 percent of the lottery market, it is hard for any state to ignore it. Gtech occupies an entire floor of the New York lottery's headquarters, which were recently moved away from the monolith at Empire State Plaza in Albany to a new building in nearby Schenectady. Jeff Perlee, director of the New York lottery, represents a new generation of lottery chiefs, those schooled in both public policy and marketing. "You have to be able to push on your sales and marketing as hard as you need to reach certain goals, but not too hard to upset the political balance," says Perlee. "There are real governmental and public policy issues that lottery directors need to be concerned about. The most obvious one is, 'Is it appropriate even if it sells?' That's not an easy question to answer."

Perlee says that although the state's video keno game, Quick Draw, pulled in $342 million in fiscal 1996, its first full year in operation, there is no evidence that it caused most people to gamble beyond their budgets. Perlee says that the portion of the New York lottery pie devoted to instant games will continue to grow. He points out that "with instant games, you can participate as much as you want as often as you want, and that's what makes it compelling." Exactly. Quick Draw is compelling because it can be played continuously, much like a slot machine, and thereby increases the likelihood that far more compulsive gamblers will join the ranks of the state's lottery players. "Problem gamblers [in New York] in 1996 are significantly more likely than problem gamblers [in New York] in 1986 to have purchased lottery products," notes a study by the New York Council on Problem Gambling. The study, which reports a sharp overall rise in the prevalence of problem gambling in New York since 1986, estimates that there were at least 118,000 compulsive gamblers in the state in 1996.

While Albany has stopped advertising Quick Draw, that hasn't dampened the creativity of some of its other advertising endeavors. The state maintains an Internet site where prospective gamblers can go online with their personal computers to learn such facts as that the number 404 is the "luckiest combination" for players of the lottery's numbers game, "winning 17 times since the game was introduced in 1980." Such revelations are meaningless, since there are no predictable patterns in the randomly generated world of lottery numbers. But to speed things along, the same Internet site also connects gamblers to an on-line version of *LottoWorld* magazine.

LottoWorld is owned by a private company that has a marketing partnership with Albany. In *LottoWorld*'s pages, one can find advice from "Palm Harbor Blackie" and "Mr. Z" about the best numbers to choose for upcoming lottery drawings, and suggestions about what a gambler's horoscope portends ("Gemini: If you travel to another town, purchase red scratch-off tickets with the word Holiday on them. Or play numbers with a value of 6"). The January 1996 issue of the magazine advised gamblers to pick lottery numbers associated with the risk-loving actress Demi Moore, whose movie *Striptease* was "a chancy film for which dazzling Demi risks being stereotyped as a low-talent actress who gets paid top dollar because she'll take off her clothes." Hence, gamblers should pick the number sixteen—the age at which *LottoWorld* says Moore dropped out of high school to pursue a modeling career. This snake oil peddled by Albany competes with the as yet unvanquished illegal numbers game in New York, which still offers its bettors advice in tracts such as *Red Devil Almanac and Dream Book* and *The Wizard*, popular updates of their nineteenth-century counterparts. Indeed, in spite of law enforcement's recent crackdown on prolific and established illegal numbers operators such as José Battle and "Spanish" Raymond Marquez, the numbers racket in New York has barely been dented by Albany's gambling operation.

WHO PAYS THE PRICE?

Demi Moore, José Battle, and Spanish Raymond aside, Perlee points out that Albany, almost three decades after it changed course, is focusing its lottery ads once again on the benefits accrued to the state's public schools rather than on dreams of getting rich quick. But New York's education budget hasn't grown because of lottery proceeds. Over the years, instead of boosting school funding, Albany has merely substituted lottery dollars for the tax revenue that would normally be allocated to education in the state's budget. New York isn't the only state playing this game.

Increased educational spending is one of the most popular justifications states use for promoting their lotteries. But a 1994 study of state lotteries by Thomas Jones, an education professor at the University of Connecticut, and John Amalfitano, head of special education at a Rhode

Island high school, examined whether those claims were true. Their conclusion: "Lottery revenues do not help schools. . . . It is well settled in public finance economics that earmarking funds for particular uses has no effect. What is surprising—and to our minds unjustifiable—is that states should rationalize their gambling implementations through appeals to this discredited technique."

After George Pataki was elected governor of New York in 1994, he pledged that lottery dollars would be earmarked as additional public school funds rather than substitute for normal funding. That concept died in the legislature. In 1997, Pataki proposed using lottery proceeds to reduce property taxes that are primarily used to fund the state's public schools. But the property tax break would mainly benefit the state's homeowners, a group that typically doesn't include the poor. In another context, that might be an irrelevant public policy concern, but in the world of lottery gambling it calls for scrutiny.

Critics of lotteries regularly claim that the poor are heavier lottery players than other income groups, but extensive research has shown otherwise. The poor don't bet more on lotteries than gamblers with larger incomes. In such games as lotto, betting actually increases with income as jackpots grow larger. The reverse tends to be true of the numbers games, where betting increases as income drops.

Low-income gamblers do, however, spend a much larger *portion* of their income betting on the lottery than do wealthier bettors. A 1995 study of New York lottery players conducted by *Newsday* found that annual household lottery spending for each $10,000 increment of family income was eight times higher in the lowest income areas compared with the highest income areas. Households with annual income below $20,000 spent an average of $420 a year on the lottery.

Because lottery betting, like casino gambling, is heavily concentrated among a small percentage of bettors, averages such as this distort an important aspect of lotteries: many poor gamblers don't bet on the lottery at all. However, among those who do, many wager large chunks of their income. Economists Clotfelter and Cook cite a 1984 Maryland survey that found that the most active 20 percent of lottery players with annual incomes below $10,000 spent an average of $128 *per month* on the Maryland lottery. "What is amusement to the affluent may seem more like an investment to those less well off," the economists note.

The result is that the poor bear a larger burden than higher income groups do of the cost of programs or expenditures funded by lotteries. That makes lotteries a highly regressive form of taxation. As Albany directs lottery funds toward property tax relief, the poor, usually unable to buy property, will be footing a lopsided share of the costs of the benefit granted their more prosperous neighbors. While many state officials dispute the characterization of lotteries as a tax, since gamblers are not legally required to play, lotteries certainly represent an implicit tax, since their proceeds are earmarked for government use. Nor do lottery proceeds, for whatever use they are targeted, leave other sources of state tax revenue untouched. States that depend heavily on sales and excise taxes, rather than income taxes, to fund their operations can lose up to 24 percent of their revenue from those sources after a lottery is instituted.

Policy arguments are of little concern to the lines of lottery players who cash welfare and other checks at a Pay-O-Matic Corporation's check-cashing branch at 136th Street and Broadway in Harlem. The Pay-O-Matic check cashing chain is by far the leading vendor of instant tickets in New York State, and this particular branch is the seventh-busiest site in the state. Check cashing firms have always served as banks of last resort for poor people, and it is impossible for any of them to miss the lottery products that line one wall in front of Pay-O-Matic's blue-caged cashiers' windows.

One lottery player, a small Hispanic man in his forties wearing a blue bandana who says his name is Felix Rivera, says he cashes his welfare check twice a month and spends part of it right away on Pay-O-Matic's lottery offerings.

"I'm trying to make money, man. My percentage is not too good. I'm better at the horses. I play at the OTB on 125th Street," Rivera says. "People keep thinking they can make it. Just look at those lines. In this neighborhood, everybody plays the lottery. This is a lottery-playing neighborhood. Everybody wants to get rich. This is America. That's the dream. To get rich."

Even given the loyalty of gamblers like Rivera, states will need to pitch gambling ever more aggressively to their residents if they hope to compete with the rapid-fire, coital pleasures offered by their competitors in the casino business. They merely have to look to their local racetracks to discover the price of not keeping up with the times.

The Compulsive—II

I was really big into big gambling. Going all the time. All the time—three, four, five nights a week. I was going down to Atlantic City. Coupled with work, I was just dead, dead. And then I'd go home. And I'd lost big money. And I'd stay home for three days, use three-day sick pay. I would just lay in bed, for three days straight, not eat, not do anything, just lay in bed, three days straight.

And that would happen four or five times a year . . . just total depression, like now, I'm like really depressed now. . . . I mean, I've gained thirty pounds. I've never been this heavy. Pants don't fit me.

I want to do the deed, believe me I want to do the deed. I just—it's not the way out, especially for my kids. I couldn't do that.

I watch TV and I cry all the time when I see things that make me think about my father. I'm afraid to go out. I'm afraid to even go out. I'm really just afraid. . . . Where am I gonna get money right now? Work? How many hours can I work? How much am I gonna make? So what am I gonna do? Go out and steal, and get a couple thousand and try one more before I go. That's what I'm feeling.

So, I don't want to have the temptation to go, because if I do go and I lose, then I'm gonna really try and steal and get some money. To go back. What am I gonna do? If I steal now, what am I gonna do? Save money, buy a TV, buy a pair of shoes. I'm not gonna buy a pair of shoes! You know what I'm saying? This money's going one place.

There's a lot of times I would go down to Atlantic City I would play one or two hands until I got into a big game, where I could make big money. Unfortunately, the more you make, the more you lose. Everybody thinks, "Oh, look at all that money. Look, he's a big gambler." You see people, they come up behind and they go, "Look, look, look, those are hundreds, those are all—he's betting a hundred at a time."

It was important that people noticed. That was very important to me. Very important to me. Not only being onstage, I felt powerful. I felt like I was somebody, I really felt like people couldn't know who I was. They didn't know if I was a millionaire, or they didn't know anything about me, all they could know was what I was playing. And if I was playing hundreds of dollars or thousands of dollars or whatever, it was what they thought in their own minds. And that's always been important.

◆ ♣ ♥ ♠

You don't even think about it, you know, like a drug addict. You go get your drugs, or he steals or robs. He doesn't think, he's only thinking to get that next hit. To get that next high.

In a way I have to justify it for myself, the stealing [I did]. I never in my life ever hurt anyone physically, to get any money. Burglary, steal, sell stuff, property. Buy stolen property, sell it. I'm sure I've caused a lot of emotional pain, in the home or whatever. And that really runs across my grain. And that hurts me.

It's almost like I can't let that in. I can't allow that to deter me from getting the money to gamble. You know you always think, "Well, if I really make a big one, I really get a lot of money, maybe I'll send some money, I'll just send a check. They won't know."

When I'm gambling, or I'm trying to get the money to gamble, I can't think of anything else. It's almost like those blinders go on. The only thing I'll think about. And I'll go to Atlantic City and I'm driving. And I got to hear this one song, like Frank Sinatra. I love Frank Sinatra. If I hear a Frank Sinatra song, like, I'm gonna win.

I never played sports betting. I never did that, and I hear people saying, "Oh, if my dog's here and the guy's winning and my dog gets up and he moves, I got to grab my dog and put him back to the same spot when they were winning." And all this bullshit, and I'm saying, "What the hell is that?" But I'm thinking to myself, "If I don't hear a Frank Sinatra song when I'm on the Atlantic City Expressway going to Atlantic City . . ." I'm trying thirty stations trying to get a Frank Sinatra song. I hear Frank Sinatra, I'll win.

The bouts driving home were incredible. Sometimes I don't even know how I made it home. How many times I wanted, I mean I threw an $800 Cartier watch, leather band, right over the bridge. I'd roll the window down, right off, right off into the water. Rings into the ocean, and all kinds of shit. And I'd come home and I'd say, "How much would it hurt if I ran into that damn pillar? Or ran off the road into the water." And what am I gonna say and how am I gonna get this money? What am I gonna tell people?

This was 1988. . . . I came home, I had a bad beat. . . . I lost like $3,000 of mine, and I owed like $3,000 or $4,000. So it was a bad beat for that night. . . . So I came home. I had a little [shooting] range set up in the basement. And I had a couple of guns, I had an assault rifle, I had a lot of guns. And I took them out, it was about two or three o'clock in the morning. My kids were upstairs sleeping; Lisa was upstairs sleeping. Started shooting them [the guns] in the basement. Next morning, eight o'clock, unbeknownst to me, she had called the chief of police, said that I had just come back from Atlantic City, I'd been losing a lot of money.

She was scared for her life, I was firing my guns. She didn't know what was happening. And they came the next day and took all my guns. Handguns, rifles, and everything. And they said you got to go, we'll send you to the psychologist. Well, that night the only thing I could think of was going back to Atlantic City. As soon as [Lisa] had called that was it. [He left her and was kicked off the police force.]

I'm with Cathy and I'm borrowing money from Cathy on credit cards. Cash advances, everything. Probably $8,000. In about 1990, I'm *in a total down spiral and I decide my brother's gonna give me a job at the grocery store.*

I'm counting money every night. $60,000 to $70,000 every night. . . . Never stole money. . . . I had four girlfriends, gambling constantly, funding it by working and stealing from the neighborhoods, when people were not there. As it progressed, I couldn't go to Atlantic City with $100, $200, $500, $1,000. I couldn't think of going to Atlantic City right now, with less than $3,000 or $4,000. . . . I could not grind out a $5 blackjack table now. It would be impossible. I could not go to a $5 or $10 or $15 craps table.

Well, the way I lost that [grocery store] job, believe it or not, they had a $60,000 robbery one night. . . . There was a night crew working and alarm system, so it had to be an inside job. And I was the only one to fail the lie detector. . . . No charges were filed against me [but I quit anyway, and started dating Patty].

We're gonna move out to Las Vegas. Full-time gambler—we're in '90 here. So we moved to Vegas. Packed up everything. . . . We went out there, and then she had to come back to finish off two weeks.

Now I'm out there alone. First day, I walk into a casino, sit down at a poker game, playing $30, $60, I win $22,000 that night. At the Mirage. I'm like, I don't lose a hand. I literally don't lose a hand. . . . I had money, I win money. And I go out and I buy an $11,000 motorcycle, cash. A big mistake.

Now I've got about $25,000 left, plus the bike. I go back, I play very slow until Patty comes out. . . . From the start, I was doing good, and one day we got it up to like six figures. I had a good system where I wouldn't lose. I'd bring $10,000 to the casino every night. Never had money in the bank, never put money in the bank. And that was it, win or lose, $10,000 a night.

There were some guys who play big games. . . . I never played in that game. But I'm playing $150 hands. . . . I get beat down the river, higher straight. Next hand, full house, hand after hand, get beat all down the river. Bigger full house . . . I lost $80,000 that night.

Now I'm like total tilt, anything I do, I'm just losing everything. I can't, I don't have any patience. [Patty's] pissed off at me, you know we fight and everything. . . . Six months in Vegas. In that time we lost not only her $20,000, but six figures that I had, that I accumulated. About $140,000. . . . I bought the motorcycle for $11,000. Maybe two months later, I sold the bike for $7,500.

And you know every gambler, we know all the lines. We just know how to suck it out of you. "Oh, Patty, please, just one more thousand, just let me try, I'm telling you. Look, I lost $9,000 now, what's one more *thousand?"* . . . *At that time she was very much in love with me. She had to be, because she wouldn't have done what she did.*

Now I'm back to stealing, myself actually going out and stealing. I'm in Vegas, now. I'm stealing in Vegas. I don't even have to tell you what that means. That's a very closed society. . . . [I took] jewelry . . . all kinds of stuff like that, guns, one gun worth $10,000. And I got jewelry, but I don't got real money.

So I ask Patty, "Patty, this guy's been in Vegas a long time, does he know somebody?" Sure enough, he knows somebody. He gives me somebody. We go to a bank. We do it right in front in the bank—no problem—the guy's legit, he wanted to buy stolen property. Just like I wanted to buy, but he goes right to the bank, I go right to the casino.

Well, his friend gets robbed. They think it's me. I'm nowhere. I'm in the casino doing something. He sets me up. . . . They take me to Clark County jail. Judge gives me $5,000 bail. Patty's family is visiting. . . . I was scared. I didn't know what I was facing. Patty borrows the money from her parents. . . . Went back to New Jersey.

Now I'm a fugitive from the Feds. I left Nevada. I jumped bail. Not only do I jump bail, but Patty's mom loses the money. You jump bail, you lose the money.

I see my kids and everything and I tell them I have to leave. That was really good, you know, like a real asshole. First time I'm back in a couple of months and I give 'em this shit. So then I go to Canada.

After about two months up there, I write Patty a letter. Mistake. They've got Patty all scanned out. They know I'm in Canada now.

So I go to New York. I live at Lisa's house for like three months. . . . I'm swimming with the kids [and] about fifty guys jump out of everywhere. "Freeze. FBI." Right in front of my kids. Well, my kids start screaming and crying.

They take me to Vegas. If nothing else, that should have stopped me from ever gambling again . . . Ten months in Clark County jail . . . finally they gave me twenty-three months [in a federal prison]. . . . All through prison I've been gambling. . . . Just poker . . . You don't actually play money, we played chips.

I get out and I don't got one inkling. I go right to work. I go right into the home improvement. . . . And I'm making money. I was going to probation every day. I haven't gambled. I get a sponsor after three months. He calls me up once in a while, but he made it clear after a while, "Listen, if you need help, you got me. I can't be calling you. You got a problem, you come into a problem, you think you know, you got to call me." You got to make it work. I never worked the program.

So I stopped going. Because I wasn't gambling. I wasn't stealing, I wasn't doing anything, I was doing good. So I'm on probation, finishing my—trying to get through my probation. And I wanted to get out, I wanted to get out. I hate New York. I hate New Jersey. I hate the traffic. I hate the hustle and bustle. I just want to get out of here. I wanted to go to Vegas. I wanted to gamble.

So I started gambling a little bit, not too bad. . . . We're early '95. . . . I'm gambling at my brother's brother-in-law's house. . . . My brother says, "Are you all right?" "Yeah, it's all right, it's all right, it's not a problem."

Of course, I lose big one day. . . . I'm depressed, of course. It's like, how many times can you get hit in the head?

Now we're like '96. . . . If I have $2,000 or something I'm [going to Atlantic City]. . . . And I'm playing that radio, just when I'm over that bridge, that last bridge. I'm always playing that radio, especially if I get a good song. I'm playing that radio the loudest I can. And I'm singing, screaming. I'm ready. I'm trying to pump myself up. You know, 'cause I'm like screaming. I'm yelling. Screaming. Singing the song.

CHAPTER 7

LOUISVILLE:

FADING JEWEL OF THE SPORT OF KINGS

FOR A BRIEF MOMENT at the end of each three-beat gait, all four hooves of a galloping racehorse are suspended above the ground. In that instant, the entire thousand-pound animal is as Pegasus was dreamt to be—free of the earth, a bundled force of pure momentum. Propelled by thick slabs of rippled muscles in its hindquarters and steadied by perilously slender front legs, a winning thoroughbred can run the Kentucky Derby's mile and a quarter in just two minutes.

All of the relentless pounding produced by the horse's pumping back end is borne by the hock joints, which jut out halfway down the hind legs and give them the shape of boomerangs. Like boomerangs, the hind legs, tightly cocked, will launch the horse from the starting gate and return it home. The product of 55 million years of evolution and breeding, horses inspired cave paintings by early human beings; were used as polo mounts by Persians 2,600 years ago; had their images molded into glazed earthenware by Chinese artists during the Tang Dynasty; carried generations of European armies into war; and for ages, from chariot races in Rome to the annual Derby gala at Churchill Downs, have attracted the eager wagers of legions of gamblers.

Cavonnier, a three-year-old gelding born to an inexpensive mare and stud, was one of nineteen horses vying for the blanket of roses and $870,000 at the Kentucky Derby on May 4, 1996. Bursting out of the starting gate and running the race's first half-mile in a blistering forty-eight seconds, Cavonnier still fell behind four other horses, including the favorite, Unbridled's Song, as the field thundered down the backstretch.

Bob and Barbara Walter, Cavonnier's owners, stared intently at their horse as he began pulling ahead. "I shout and get involved in any race, whether it's a ten-thousand-dollar claimer or a graded stakes race," Barbara says. "But I was completely numb at the Derby. I've never been so quiet before."

Horses at the Derby reach speeds of forty miles per hour, and those not used to traveling so fast can panic. Although the field was crowded and the pace furious, Cavonnier, a seasoned horse with thirteen races and a triumph in the Santa Anita Derby to his credit, remained unflappable.

"Haaaaahhhh!" Cavonnier's jockey, Chris McCarron, shouted into his mount's ear, positioning him for the lead as the field turned for home. "Unbridled's Song was ducking in and out then and I knew I had a shot at it," McCarron recalls. "He veered to the right sharply and I moved my horse inward."

There was a quarter-mile left in the race. "Stay focused on the task at hand—ride Cavonnier to the wire," McCarron, a two-time Derby winner, said to himself. Just then, the jockey on a nearby horse accidentally lashed Cavonnier across the face with his whip. Lesser horses might have pulled up completely, but Cavonnier only flinched. Then he blew past Unbridled's Song.

In the home stretch, Cavonnier took a one-length lead. There was only an eighth of a mile left between him and the wire. "My God, he's gonna win it," Cavonnier's trainer, Bob Baffert, thought as he stood with the Walters, transfixed by the race's climax. Barbara Walter, silent until the home stretch, felt chills run up and down her spine as Cavonnier raced to Churchill Downs' finish line. She began screaming wildly. McCarron kept Cavonnier charging straight ahead, and when he hit the wire he felt the rush of victory—for a moment.

It is almost impossible to predict the Kentucky Derby's outcome. The Derby is the first time any of the three-year-olds in it have raced a mile and a quarter; track conditions vary, and the pressure of a major race takes its toll on jockeys and horses alike. But some respond to pressure in extraordinary ways.

As Cavonnier reached the finish line, he was passed by Grindstone, a horse that had run in only five races before the Derby and had never won a highly graded contest. Yet with Cavonnier five lengths ahead of him, Grindstone burned up the last quarter-mile in slightly less than twenty-five seconds, the fastest Derby quarter in sixteen years. As Grindstone, masterfully ridden by jockey Jerry Bailey, flashed past the wire, he beat Cavonnier literally by a nose. The margin of victory, a photo finish requiring five minutes of anxious consideration by track judges, was a few inches. It was the closest Derby finish in almost four decades.

Waiting for the photo to be developed, Baffert still believed Cavonnier had won. Then the results were posted on the track's tote board. "Will we ever get back here again?" Baffert thought. "I'll never suffer a beat like this again in my life." A year later, another Baffert horse, Silver Charm, would win the Derby and the Preakness, and enter the Belmont with the chance to be the first horse in almost twenty years to win the Triple Crown. But Silver Charm was overtaken in the last hundred yards of the Belmont, losing by less than a length.

Sustained by pageantry and spectacle, the Kentucky Derby remains a singular event in American horse racing. But what Baffert calls "the mother of all races" is the brightest star in an industry that is fading. Only twenty-five years ago, racing was the most popular form of legal gambling in the country and one of the nation's top spectator sports.

But track attendance has been sliding, the sport's image has been tarnished by repeated evidence of race fixing, and the volume of on-track betting has plummeted. Horse racing's savior has been off-track betting, which has made up for the plunge in wagering at the track. Nonetheless, the total "handle," or gross wager, on horse racing has been thoroughly eclipsed by the amount gamblers now spend on lotteries and at casinos. Between 1982 and 1996, the on- and off-track racing handle grew only about 28 percent, from $11.7 billion to $15 billion. Over the same period, lottery wagering grew about 950 percent, to $42.9 billion; wagering at casinos grew 395 percent, to $501.6 billion. Horse racing today is just a minor appendage of the nation's gambling behemoth.

There was a time when horse racing was the only high-profile, legal game in town, and local tracks had a monopoly on gamblers. Those days are long gone, however, and part of the reason for horse racing's decline is that it is an anachronism. Horse racing thrived in an era when gambling was an unhurried, ritualistic social event rather than—as modern casinos and their slot machines so amply demonstrate—a commercial enterprise mass-marketed and reduced to its lowest common denominator.

Racing has also been poorly served by the shortsightedness of tracks and owners and by a rapacious attitude toward the magnificent animals that have given the sport its charm. Running in place, some tracks are now trying to link up with casino companies or offer slot machines in a last-ditch effort to save their franchises from extinction. Yet horse racing appears to be stuck in a downward spiral; and, as the racing world shrinks, the Runyonesque culture that surrounded it—a culture of bookies, handicappers, wiseguys, horse farms, and cigar-chomping gamblers—is also fading.

"SECURING PLEASURE FOR THE RICHER CLASSES"

"It has seemed very strange to many visitors that a city as populous and prosperous as Louisville has no drive, and no place of resort where the owners of horseflesh could reap so much pleasurable enjoyment and at the same time promote various interests of the city," *The Daily Louisville Commercial* opined in June 1874, promoting the construction of a fancy new racetrack. "The cost of such a park must not be underrated . . . if the scope of thought in Louisville has a boundary sufficiently wide to discern the wisdom of securing pleasure for the richer classes, with an ultimate view of benefiting their fellow-citizens who toil from morn til eve without hope of obtaining naught but moderate enjoyment. Here is a field for philanthropy at little cost."

By the time Louisville's elite had espoused the novel idea that separating working stiffs from their money at the racetrack constituted philanthropy, the city was almost one hundred years old. It had been founded in 1778 by several dozen settlers led to the edge of the Ohio River by George Clark, a colonial military officer on his way to attack British troops in the region. Named in honor of the French monarch Louis XVI, Louisville was smaller and less important than other Kentucky cities, such as Lexington and Frankfort, in the period before the territory achieved statehood. After Kentucky became a state in 1792, Louisville remained a typical American frontier town. Diseases such as smallpox and malaria were common, earning Louisville the moniker Graveyard of the West, and gambling, drinking, and billiards were popular pastimes. And by 1815, there was a small racetrack.

Although Louisville was well situated along the Ohio River, blessed with an excellent port, and surrounded by fertile farmland, river traffic was slow in the city's early years because the Ohio was laced with dangerous rapids that were hard to navigate. Most cargos had to be taken off the river, hauled overland to get around "the Falls" near Louisville, and refloated on calmer waters. Louisville's fortunes shifted in 1830, however, with the construction of the Louisville and Portland Canal. The canal opened a clear route along the Ohio from Pittsburgh to the Mississippi River, and Louisville began to prosper, eventually becoming Kentucky's largest city.

The city competed with Cincinnati for dominance of a number of commercial ventures, including cargo hauling and meatpacking. But it was the Civil War that gave Louisville a leg up. Kentucky, a slaveholding state with residents fighting for both the Union and the Confederacy, was neutral at the beginning of the Civil War. It then quickly sided with the Union, only to flip-flop to the Confederacy once hostilities ended.

This dainty about-face was driven in part by the city's own distinctly southern character, but also by a very calculated run for the money. The grain belt lay to the north and tobacco and cotton to the south: Louisville's business community recognized that by flying the colors of the beaten-down South the city could set itself up as an entry point for rebuilding the region after the Civil War.

Christening itself the Gateway to the South, Louisville grew robustly in the post–Civil War period. It blossomed as a diversified manufacturing center, found its voice as a progressive leader of the New South, and, despite Kentucky's large Baptist contingent, shaped up to be one of the country's most able purveyors of the vices. Distilling and tobacco founded some of Louisville's largest fortunes. But liquor and cigarettes wouldn't bring the city its greatest reknown. That distinction would fall to horse racing, which, for more than a century, was America's dominant form of legalized gambling.

Horse races were part of the ancient Olympics, and in the Iliad Homer offers a lengthy description of a chariot race. But the modern horse-racing industry, built on the backs of Thoroughbreds and supported by regular meets, was born in England some 300 years ago. During the seventeenth century, two of England's Stuart monarchs, James I and Charles II, were enthusiastic patrons of horse racing, and the involvement of the royal court spurred the breeding of ever faster horses to enliven the "Sport of Kings."

The horse races of the seventeenth century were very different from those run centuries later. One race, attended by Charles II and his entourage in 1680, involved only two horses in a head-to-head match on an exhausting course, six miles long; wagering was limited to large sums placed by the small group of aristocrats invited to attend.

Prior to the Stuart kings' involvement, European horse breeding had focused on producing heavy workhorses suitable for both the farm and the battlefield. But as weighty armor gave way to light artillery, speedier warhorses were needed. And once horse racing's popularity began growing in England, an even greater premium was placed on speed. The best horses, however, couldn't be found in England. Three centuries ago, English horses that were good sprinters lacked endurance. Mounts with the wherewithal to run longer distances usually lacked speed. In their search for horses that combined speed and endurance, the English turned to the Middle East. The Arabs were careful breeders, and only the finest Arabian stallions, sprinters that were also capable of traveling dozens of miles a day across the desert, were allowed to mate. Arab Bedouins so treasured their small, swift mounts that a valued mare or stallion usually shared a tent with its owner. These extraordinary animals, superior to any others available to Europeans in the late seventeenth century, provided the male stock from which the modern Thoroughbred sprang.

All Thoroughbreds racing in America today are descended from three Arabian stallions that were mated with English mares in the late seventeenth and early eighteenth centuries. The first Arabian acquired by the English was the Byerly Turk, captured in battle by Captain Richard Byerly from Ottoman Turks in 1688. The Darley Arabian was the second to reach England, purchased in Syria in 1704 by a merchant named Thomas Darley. The last stallion, the Godolphin Barb, followed a more circuitous path to England before Lord Godolphin purchased him in the late 1720s.

These three stallions helped spawn horses that were several inches taller and had shorter bodies and longer, more slender legs than their ancestors. But Thoroughbreds retained the unusual combination of bunched sprinting muscles and longer muscles for endurance that they had inherited from the Arabian stallions. Over the following centuries, these animals would be carefully bred for nothing other than the ability to withstand a brief, punishing test of speed against other Thoroughbreds of proper lineage.

English racing gradually became more structured. Wealthy English horse owners formed the first Jockey Club in 1750; the Derby at Epsom Downs began running Thoroughbred races in 1780; and, with the publication of the first *General Stud Book* in 1793, horses' bloodlines began to be tracked more astutely. The refined, restricted world of English racing took its grandest form in the social whirl at Ascot, which saw its first race in 1807. Once horse racing was imported into the United States from England, that rarefied world would change dramatically. Over time, it was transformed from being exclusively a gentlemen's sport into a sprawling industry built on the stud fees that a winning racehorse could generate and on the wagering of gamblers from every walk of life.

Before the breeding of Thoroughbreds in the United States, races had been run informally in colonial settlements. Many of the town streets where the two- or three-horse competitions were run still bear the name "Race" today. But public pressure to hold races away from the center of town led to the establishments of formal tracks elsewhere.

The first track to offer frequent stakes races was opened in Hempstead Plain, Long Island, in 1665. The two-mile track was named Newmarket in honor of Charles II's English track, and was founded by the king's friend Colonel Richard Nicolls, who had led the English army that wrested control of New York from the Dutch. Nicolls was an avid breeder who made Long Island the center of horse breeding in the northern colonies. But it was the Virginians who became the premier breeders of the colonial period; thanks to them, the South produced the country's greatest Thoroughbreds ever and became the cradle of American horse racing.

Virginians had shown an early enthusiasm for horse racing, and Virginia towns would frequently match their best horse against one from a neighboring hamlet. Wealthy plantation owners, including George Washington and Thomas Jefferson, gambled on the events and raised horses of their own. A stallion named Bulle Rock, whose sire was the Darley Arabian, was imported into Virginia from England in 1730; his arrival represented the beginning of Thoroughbred breeding in the colonies. The onset of the Revolutionary War in 1776 temporarily halted breeding and racing throughout the colonies, but afterward more Thoroughbreds were imported from England and the stallion Messenger, another descendant of the great Arabians, was put to stud in Philadelphia.

As a wave of religious fundamentalism swept the country in the late eighteenth century, some northern states, including New York, outlawed horse racing, even though betting was still largely confined to the upper classes. But racing continued throughout the South, and in Kentucky the foundations of racing dynasties were already being laid. Kentucky had originally been part of Virginia; the state's first settlers were from North Carolina and Virginia, and the Virginians brought with them their affinity for Thoroughbreds. Lexingtonians, as interested in the bloodlines of their fellow residents as in those of their horses, also grafted the clubby, class-conscious ways of the English horse set onto the social rites that enveloped Kentucky racing. Virginians who settled in Lexington, people such as future presidential candidate and secretary of state Henry Clay, permitted racing on Main Street, and the city was the site of Kentucky's first racetrack, built in 1780.

The Virginians also stumbled onto some of the richest grazing land in the world. Miles upon miles of undulating hills around Lexington were carpeted with Kentucky's unique long-stemmed bluegrass—"blue" mainly in the eyes of Daniel Boone, whose tall tales of the region's beauty convinced settlers to follow him there. Because of the rich limestone deposits permeating central Kentucky's soil, and the temperate climate, the bluegrass proved a marvelous conduit for transfusing bone-building minerals into the bodies of strong, championship racehorses. Lexington, a great Thoroughbred named in honor of his hometown, sired offspring that captured 50 percent of all of the country's horse-racing winnings between 1865 and 1880.

Ultimately, the area around the city of Lexington became home to some of the most famous horse farms in the world, with names like

Calumet, Claiborne, Elmendorf, Gainesway, Greentree, Spendthrift, and Whitney. But large horse farms are built and maintained by large fortunes, and to attract investors to Kentucky, the Lexington stables needed a showplace for their prized horseflesh. And for that they needed promotion. For that, they needed Louisville.

INVENTING THE DERBY

Churchill Downs isn't the oldest major Thoroughbred track in the country, nor the most beautiful. Saratoga Race Track, in Saratoga Springs, New York, opened in 1864, eleven years before the Kentucky Derby started running. And Santa Anita Race Track, at the base of the San Gabriel Mountains northeast of Los Angeles, is more beautifully situated. But Churchill Downs has distinguished itself through the years by offering the greatest horses running in an event that Louisville's promoters successfully invested with the greatest cachet.

Horse racing was already enormously popular by the early nineteenth century. During the 1840s, when the population of New York City was under 500,000, races at Long Island's Union Course reportedly drew tens of thousands of fans. When Saratoga Race Track opened in 1863, the Civil War was raging, but Northerners were still able to scare up enough decent mounts to help make Saratoga Springs, already famous for its mineral springs, a summer resort favored by the moneyed classes.

Saratoga Springs' celebrated casino, the Club House, and its racetrack got up and running under the watchful eye of John Morrissey, a former boxer, Tammany Hall insider, and U.S. congressman, who was one of the country's first modern gambling entrepreneurs. Like the casino tycoons who followed in his footsteps, Morrissey, who already owned more than a dozen casinos in New York, won acceptance for the Club House by spending lavishly on its facilities, catering to wealthy gamblers, paying off politicians, and donating generously to local churches and charities that were otherwise opposed to gambling. The Club House faded briefly, but Richard Canfield revived it, and by the late nineteenth century its patrons included such men as banker J. P. Morgan and "Diamond Jim" Brady.

Saratoga Race Track's reputation was enhanced by the involvement of three millionaires who brought their horses there: William Travers, John Hunter, and Winston Churchill's grandfather Leonard Jerome. But it was Morrissey who oversaw the gambling and the races, which were run twice a day, two days a week. The impact of the Civil War, the millionaires with their fine horses, and the showmanship of Morrissey and his successors guaranteed that until World War II, Saratoga would be the premier auction block for the country's most promising yearlings.

Unlike the North, the South had no horses to spare during the Civil War; racing virtually shut down throughout the region. Horse farms in central Kentucky were looted, and after the war ended, Woodlawn, Louisville's grandest track, fell into disrepair. The land beneath it was eventually sold. Moreover, defeat left Southerners unable to compete with the burgeoning wealth of northern industrialists in paying the exorbitant prices Thoroughbreds brought at auction.

Despite these setbacks, Lexington's breeders were still able to produce fine horses, and by 1874 they were anxious to find a new place to display their wares. Meriwether Lewis Clark, Jr., the grandson of the explorer William Clark, was inspired by visits to England's Epsom Downs to recreate that noted track in Louisville. Gathering public opinion and financial support behind his effort, Clark convened a group of 320 Louisville businessmen in July 1874, to form the Louisville Jockey Club. With $20,000 in hand, the group leased land from the Churchill family and built a racetrack on it. (The track wasn't commonly referred to as Churchill Downs until the late 1880s, after a sportswriter popularized the name.) The first Kentucky Derby, run in 1875 at a mile and a half, not today's mile and a quarter, and held on a Monday, not the first Saturday in May, drew enthusiastic crowds. But the race was still a very local event, overshadowed by better races in the Northeast. It quickly degenerated; the early Derbies often matched questionable nags, and most people suspected the races were fixed. They had good reason to be suspicious.

A race is a way to test a horse's mettle in public and thereby put a price on the animal. Most horses are traded in low-level "claiming races" in which any entrant can be bought for a few thousand dollars or tens of thousands of dollars, depending on the quality of the race. On the opposite end of the spectrum are the highest-tier Thoroughbreds, many of which are auctioned as yearlings. They can go on to earn big stud fees if they win major stake races. But all the buying and selling of horseflesh that the track supports primarily benefits breeders. Racetrack owners have to draw a much less posh crowd to earn the money that keeps the track humming. For this, the tracks rely on gambling.

Of course, gambling on horses, and on other animals such as dogs and fighting cocks, has a long history that predates Saratoga and the Kentucky Derby. But after the Civil War, American racetracks popularized horse racing in an unprecedented manner, making it the most ubiquitous form of legal gambling until the 1970s.

The growth in leisure time and disposable income that accompanied industrialization after the Civil War helped lead the masses to the ponies. And when the Kentucky Derby first got under way, bookies controlled betting at every track in the country. Track owners got their cut by charging bookies a fee for the privilege of taking bets on their premises. Some racetrack wagering in the 1880s and 1890s still revolved around "auction pools," in which each horse was figuratively "sold" to the gambler who bet the most on it. If the gambler was lucky enough to "own" the winning horse, he collected all the money in that particular pool.

But auction pools were holdovers from the era of private wagering among the landed gentry. As racing proliferated after the Civil War, bookies began to broker the thousands of small bets placed by the common gambler. Bookies of this era weren't rumpled sorts who eked out a living in a small room in a local tavern. They made profits of as much as 20 percent a day on the money they handled. At East Coast tracks, bookies did business at the "betting ring," a wooden gazebo made up of several stalls with blackboards above them listing each horse and citing the current odds. It cost serious money to become a member of the elite group of bookies who had a stall in the ring. One New York ring, the Metropolitan Turf Association, operated at several tracks in the late 1880s and was open only to bookies who had paid a $7,000 membership fee (about $120,000 in 1996 dollars)—not quite the $19,750 it cost, on average, to buy a seat on the New York Stock Exchange in 1890, but still a hefty sum.

Many of the bookies, deft rogues such as Caesar Jordan, who was shot to death in a hansom cab while in the company of a showgirl from the Floradora Sextette, used part of their wealth to buy horses and to fix the outcome of races. They would bribe jockeys to hold horses back in a race, or pay off trainers to work a particular horse so hard that it was exhausted on race day. Bookies also employed "touts" who, proffering "expert advice," roamed the track selling bogus tips to unwary gamblers searching for a winner. The bookies themselves had genuine inside information from the stables that wasn't made available to the betting public. For a time, the bookies' hold on the tracks was so tight that they were able to stamp out any threats to their hegemony—including the introduction of pari-mutuel betting.

Pari-mutuel betting systems were first used in Paris in 1865. Invented by a Parisian perfume-shop owner and gambler named Pierre Oller, pari-mutuel machines used primitive tabulating machines, not bookies, to take bets and dispense tickets. This allowed odds at the track to be determined by the gamblers themselves rather than bookies.

(Oller called his system "betting among ourselves," or *pari mutuel*.) The track merely earned a service fee on each wager and so had no interest in the outcome of the betting. By using the pari-mutuel machines, bettors simply wagered their money against one another, with the odds changing according to the level of betting on each horse. And the bookies were cut out of the action.

Oller's system eventually evolved into the electronic tote boards most tracks now use. Originally, gambling at the track meant picking the horse that finished the race in one of three positions: first ("win"), second ("place"), or third ("show"). As time went on, riskier bets were popularized, such as the daily double (the bettor picked the winning horse in two successive races); the exacta (the bettor picked the horses that won and placed in the same race—a wager the tracks copied from the sport of jai alai); and the trifecta (the bettor picked the horses that won, placed, and showed in the same race). The more exotic the bet, the worse the odds of winning. Gamblers, convinced they could beat the odds, came up with various betting strategies. Today, "wheeling" a wager involves picking a horse to win in one race and matching it up with every horse in a following race, to try to hit the daily double. Other gamblers like to "box" two or three of their favorites in one race by betting on every combination of those horses to try to win the exacta or trifecta.

But before the days of widespread pari-mutuel betting, the bookies ruled the track. When the Kentucky Derby first ran in 1875, Meriwether Clark installed a few pari-mutuel machines at Churchill Downs. Still, despite widespread concern about the integrity of racing in Kentucky, the bookies successfully battled the hapless Clark to keep their position. "The time has gone when it can be said that running races in Kentucky are not hedged about with fraud," *The Louisville Commercial* observed in 1883. "It used not to be so, but within the past two years there has been a most disgraceful change. The world is full of rascals and far too many of them are professional turfmen."

In 1890, the bookies used their leverage at Churchill Downs to get all the pari-mutuel machines there mothballed, following similar coups by bookies at New York tracks a couple of years earlier. And in 1894, a group of cash-heavy bookies, including William Applegate, Billy Boardman, Emile Bourlier, and William Schulte, bought Churchill Downs from Clark. Races inevitably continued to deteriorate; in 1899, his health slipping, Clark put a bullet through his head in a Memphis hotel room.

Heightened public distaste concerning the shady nature of horse racing combined with one of the country's periodic outbursts of moral cleansing to force the banning or reduction of racing in most states at the turn of the century. By 1900, only Kentucky, New York, and Maryland still allowed full-scale racing. In Kentucky, horse racing survived and became preeminent due to the intervention of a crafty and gifted Louisville huckster named Matt Winn.

Winn, a forty-one-year-old haberdasher with a flair for promotion—or what the locals liked to call windage—took over Churchill Downs in 1902, after Louisville's elders asked him to rescue the dying track. Winn, backed by a group of investors that included his close friend Billy Boardman, paid $40,000 for an operation that, on paper, had never been profitable in any of its previous twenty-eight years.

Yet, despite his links to bookies such as Boardman, Winn reinstalled pari-mutuel machines at the track in 1908 and made sure they never were removed again. Shenanigans didn't entirely disappear. For about the next seventy years, the race run immediately after the Kentucky Derby was known around Churchill Downs as a fuzzy. Fuzzies were races featuring a strong horse, or "ringer," that had been held back in previous races to make its record appear poorer. A poor track record results in higher odds against a horse's winning, so every gambler privy to the identity of the ringer in the fuzzy was able to make a killing on Derby day. Those familiar with the fuzzies say the practice ended around 1980. Churchill Downs officials dispute that races on Derby day were ever fixed on a regular basis. "You line up twenty people, and ten will say it happened and ten will say it didn't. You hear a lot of stories around racetracks," says Karl Schmitt, a Churchill Downs spokesman. "Was a race at Churchill Downs ever fixed or manipulated to the benefit of other individuals? Not to my knowledge."

Nonetheless, by shooing the bookies aside in 1908, Winn was able to restore credibility to Churchill Downs. He also upgraded the clubhouse, convinced bandleaders such as John Philip Sousa to stage concerts on the track's infield, and organized dinner parties at the track to attract fashionable folk. Winn also inflated his attendance figures to make the Derby appear more popular than it was, and he bribed sportswriters from out-of-town newspapers to put a glowing spin on the race. As the Derby snared more and more national attention, Winn scored his greatest triumph: in 1914, he convinced some of the Northeast's toniest breeders to enter their horses in the Derby. The following year, multimillionaire Harry Payne Whitney's filly, Regret, won the Derby, prompting Whitney to crow that his horse had won "the greatest race in America."

The Kentucky Derby had arrived.

After Sir Barton won the Derby in 1919 and unexpectedly went on to win the two other feature races for three-year-olds—the Preakness in Baltimore and the Belmont in Long Island—the racing industry invented the Triple Crown. The Triple Crown was more than just a standard of excellence in racing. It was a publicity dynamo, and thereafter much of the media's attention always focused on the first Triple Crown race, the Kentucky Derby. Starting in the 1920s, more wagering and better horses led to increasingly large purses and renown for the Derby. The Derby's best years would follow; from the 1930s to the 1970s, the race saw such champions as Gallant Fox, Twenty Grand, Omaha, War Admiral, Whirlaway, Count Fleet, Assault, Citation, Northern Dancer, Seattle Slew, Affirmed, and (arguably the greatest racehorse of all time) Secretariat.

Even though racing wasn't permitted in most states by the 1920s, gamblers still wanted to play the horses. Illegal tracks were opened in some states; Florida, for instance, had its Hialeah. But if people couldn't get to a track, well, then, the track would have to be brought to them. So the wire rooms were born, and organized crime moved in.

ANNENBERG'S WIRE EMPIRE

Moe Annenberg, a Prussian immigrant who had worked as a bartender and as a messenger boy for Western Union, first made a name for himself in the vicious Chicago "newspaper war" of 1910. At a time when newspapers won circulation by hiring goons to tear down the competition's newsstands on desirable corners and break their vendors' legs, Moe and his burly brother, Max, led the bloody street battle in Chicago as "circulation managers" for William Randolph Hearst. Annenberg later started his own circulation company in Milwaukee and then was tapped to oversee circulation in New York for the entire Hearst publishing empire.

In 1922, with horse racing fast becoming a national passion, Annenberg bought *The Daily Racing Form*, the bible of bookies and bettors, which had been languishing under a previous owner. Four years later, Annenberg left Hearst to strike out on his own. He used the cash that poured in from *The Daily Racing Form* to assemble a publishing business that eventually included *The Philadelphia Inquirer* and—after his son Walter took the reins in 1942—*TV Guide* and *Seventeen*. But for more than a decade, another pillar of Annenberg's fortune was the national network of horse-racing wires that he assembled with his buddies in the Mob.

Using telegraph wires, and later phone lines, to broadcast racing results nationally, a hodgepodge of "wire rooms" or "pool rooms" began springing up around the country in 1890. Western Union transmitted race results, until reformers forced it to drop the service in 1905. Others filled the gap and by 1920, several wire rooms could be found in every big city. Equipped with large chalkboards and loudspeakers, the wire rooms gave hundreds of gamblers and bookies who frequented them the ability to bet on horses regardless of where they lived. And through Annenberg's efforts, the wire rooms eventually gave organized crime a tidy little piggy bank, a tight grip on the nation's bookies, and the ability to fix race results.

Starting in 1927, Annenberg consolidated the fragmented industry into one wire company, Nationwide News Service, known in organized crime circles as the Trust. Annenberg got help building his network from mobsters Al Capone and Meyer Lansky. Stakes in the Trust were doled out to various Mafia factions, and soldiers like future Mob chieftain Johnny Rosselli went to work for Annenberg. The Trust's expansion coincided with a resurgence in horse racing during the Depression, when twenty-one states legalized betting at the track—up from just six in 1911. By 1940, Annenberg was AT&T's fifth-largest customer, and Nationwide had annual revenue of $50 million.

Annenberg also had the Internal Revenue Service scrutinizing his books. In a federal indictment filed in 1939, the IRS accused him of reporting annual income of only $1 million for several years when he was actually earning about six times as much. After initially fighting the charges, Annenberg pleaded guilty in 1940 and was fined and sentenced to three years in prison. He died of a brain tumor in 1942. But organized crime had started maneuvering for greater control of the wire business three years earlier, after Annenberg shut down Nationwide because of his legal problems.

Nationwide's successor was Continental Press, a Chicago company owned by James Ragen and Mickey McBride. McBride, a Mob bookmaker who had worked for Max Annenberg in the 1910 newspaper war, later founded the Cleveland Browns football team. Shortly after he sold most of his interest in Continental to Ragen, Chicago mobsters tried to force Ragen to sell Continental to them.

When Ragen refused, the Chicago Mob started a rival company, Trans-America Wire Service, to compete with him. Bugsy Siegel's first taste of Las Vegas came on a visit there to convince the casinos to use Trans-America rather than Continental. But Ragen continued to ignore challenges to his service, and in 1946 he was gunned down on the street and later poisoned to death in the hospital room where he was recovering. After Ragen died, the Mafia took over Continental, which eventually drew the attention of Mob-buster Senator Estes Kefauver in 1951.

Kefauver labeled Continental Public Enemy Number One and cited it as organized crime's "source of enormous profits and power over bookmaking." In one report, the Kefauver Committee said that "The wire service is as essential to a bookmaker as a stock ticker is to a stockbroker." So the federal government outlawed all racing wires in the early 1950s. But by then, many other states, including California, had already legalized pari-mutuel betting at horse tracks, making the wires less important. Moreover, organized crime had earlier established outright ownership or control of tracks such as Sportsman's Park in Illinois, Suffolk Downs in Massachusetts, and Tropical Park in Florida.

CORRUPTION AND DECLINE

Organized crime would remain a presence around racetracks for the rest of the twentieth century, although its influence would be tempered by the splintering of once-powerful Mob families and the conversion of some major tracks into publicly traded companies. Race-fixing scandals in the mid-1970s at midwestern and northeastern tracks, including Aqueduct and Saratoga, led to the convictions of dozens of gamblers, jockeys, owners, and trainers between 1978 and 1982. The man behind those scandals was Tony Ciulla, a New Englander tied to the Mob who used bribes to fix hundreds of races. More recently, harness races, typically the most scandal-plagued events in horse racing, were fixed at Yonkers Raceway in New York in 1995. Local law enforcement officials said that the bookmaking ring that bribed jockeys to hold horses back in the Yonkers races was linked to organized crime.

On other occasions at other tracks, jockeys have used stun guns or cattle prods to force a horse to gallop faster. But the fact that races are fixed isn't lost on gamblers at the track, and never has been. With a wink and a knowing smile, they'll all say they know that some races will be fixed from time to time, but that won't keep them from betting. They love the action. And through the 1950s, when Kefauver cracked down on the racing wires, the action at the tracks was still fast and furious. Gerry Murphy, a sixty-six-year-old retired New York firefighter, remembers the days almost fifty years ago when Aqueduct was packed to the rafters.

"When I was young, everybody used to come to the track, and so did the older guys. You'd see everybody here. Guys like Minny Wallen. Minny was a compulsive gambler who owned two soda trucks, and I drove one when I was eighteen. He'd say, 'Look, Gerry, unload all the bottles and meet me at the track at one [o'clock].' He'd bet a hundred bucks, which was a lot of money then, and he had no system. Then he'd leave after the sixth race and go bet with a bookie on basketball.

"Minny ended up losing the business, and his wife, because he owed a shylock twenty-five thousand dollars. Last time I saw him, he was driving a cab from Aqueduct to Roosevelt Raceway. But he was the exception. Most people were like me. They came on their day off and just bet a few bucks."

Aqueduct's glory days are long gone. The track, like many around the country, is a grubby husk. One afternoon, as Murphy surveys the grizzled and disheveled old loyalists clutching their tickets, he shakes his head. "The guy who gambles on a horse participates in what's happening. It's not like slot machines. You use your brain. Not that any of it comes true. Horse players like to think they have a system, but everybody who bets on horses loses."

Horse racing enjoyed its last hurrah between the 1950s and the 1970s; it was fitting that during those years Lexington recaptured its hold on the imaginations and wallets of horse owners worldwide. Unable to ship their horses north to Saratoga during World War II because the war effort had sucked up all available transportation, Kentucky's breeders decided in 1943 to set up their own auction block at Lexington's Keeneland Race Course. They quickly discovered they wouldn't need to ship horses north anymore. Buyers flocked to Lexington. While Saratoga remains one of the more important auction sites in the world, Keeneland, with yearling sales held each July and September, now dominates the market.

Lexington's resurgence coincided with a boom in the market for Thoroughbred yearlings, as the growth of commercial racing and the tremendous wealth created in the United States after World War II led to escalating bidding frenzies for horses. American breeders used their riches to buy the best European stock, which until then had been unmatched in the world, and began mating the European mounts with their own.

Between 1940 and 1949, 68,115 Thoroughbred foals were registered in the United States and Canada. Between 1950 and 1959, 99,125 foals were registered; between 1960 and 1969, 182,533; between 1970 and 1979, 280,315; and between 1980 and 1989, 463,827. Although the foal "crop" posted its largest increases in the 1970s and 1980s, decades when U.S. racing had already gone into a decline, the reason for this was simple enough: Gambling on the breeding potential of Thoroughbreds had become much more interesting than gambling on the races themselves.

A championship horse is more than just a reflection of the sporting aspirations of its owner. It is a snorting, hay-chomping annuity that earns lofty stud fees when its racing days are over. A stallion typically mates with fifty or sixty mares a season. The right to mate a brood mare with a famous racer such as Northern Dancer cost $800,000 in 1985, when the market was at its frothiest. But for all the attention paid to pedigrees and physique, breeding is still guesswork and luck. The great Secretariat turned out to be a dry well at stud, producing few winners, even though several hundred mares were trotted through his stall.

Over the years the breeding gamble has drawn not only syndicates of lesser investors who combine their money to buy a choice yearling, but also a select clique of high rollers that has included British financier Charles Engelhard, Greek shipping tycoon Stavros Niarchos, British gambling mogul Robert Sangster, Texas oilman Nelson Bunker Hunt, the Yoshida family of Japan, and the Maktoum brothers of oil-rich Dubai. The wagering grew so heated in the 1980s that the prices paid for the best yearlings became astronomical. While the price for ordinary yearlings jumped from $29,683 in 1980 to $41,396 in 1984, the price of top yearlings soared from about $53,500 in 1974 to $544,681 in 1984.

At Keeneland, the Monte Carlo of horse auctions, one yearling was snapped up by Sangster in 1982 for $4.25 million. That record price was shattered in 1983 when one of the Maktoums ponied up $10.2 million for a yearling that turned out to be a slow, infertile colt that never won a race. In 1985, a new record was set when a Keeneland colt went for $13.1 million. Then the bubble burst.

As yearlings flooded the market, and tax reforms in 1986 closed loopholes that had lightened the financial burden of horse ownership, the price of yearlings plummeted. The average price at the July 1995 Keeneland auction was $247,074, down from $537,383 in 1985. From 1987 to 1994, the North American foal crop declined for an unprecedented seven straight years; the total number of foals in the 1990s probably won't reach 380,000—a potential drop of about 18 percent from the previous decade.

The game is still being played, however. In 1996, the price of yearlings at Keeneland's July sale rebounded smartly, to an average of $349,880. But Japanese and Arab buyers are driving the market, and that leads some breeders to worry that the United States will lose its bloodstock advantage much as Europeans lost theirs to the United States fifty years ago. Others fret that the thrill of speculation has overtaken the industry's fundamentals.

"Right now, my biggest worry is that some people disregard the animal and are more interested in making money," says Dell Hancock, whose family owns Claiborne Farm, a leading horse farm outside Lexington. "While people have to be in this for the business, I hope they don't forget about the horse and the sport."

Indeed, the trading of horseflesh has overtaken the industry to such an extent that the most recognizable name in horse racing no longer belongs to a horse. The biggest star in the sport is a trainer named D. Wayne Lukas.

POUNDING THE HORSEFLESH

A sixty-year-old former high school basketball coach and quarter-horse trainer, Lukas is a tireless self-promoter with a gift for spotting great racehorses. His talent, dedication, performance, and relentless courting of wealthy buyers have made him a dominant figure since he began training Thoroughbreds eighteen years ago. When Grindstone, a horse he trained, won the 1996 Kentucky Derby, it marked a record sixth consecutive win for Lukas in one of the Triple Crown events.

Yet Grindstone was just one of five Lukas horses in the Derby's nineteen-horse field, a field so large that the Derby was more like a stampede than a race. That Lukas could prepare so many horses for the Derby was a measure of his discipline and his ability to start each racing season with more well-bred horses than other trainers. But Lukas has also been criticized for driving his horses into the ground in order to rack up victories in high-profile races that appeal to the vanity of prospective owners. After the Derby, for example, Grindstone was unable to run in the Preakness or Belmont because of a bone chip in his leg. He was subsequently retired.

True, Thoroughbreds are delicate, finicky animals, easily injured and as finely tuned as F-14s. Training them involves patience and luck, and any trainer has his or her share of injuries. However, it is also true that the premium the industry places on racing young horses, soon enough for owners to try to recoup their investments but often before an animal's bones have fully matured, endangers the horses. And it is also true that Grindstone wasn't the first Lukas horse to end its racing career early.

Most memorably, Lukas entered Union City in the 1993 Preakness even though the horse had already been badly beaten up in the Derby two weeks earlier. Many thought the stallion needed some rest. In the backstretch at the Preakness, Union City broke his leg and had to be destroyed. Tabasco Cat, the 1994 Preakness champ, eventually was too lame to continue racing, even though he was only four years old. Flanders, the 1994 Breeders' Cup champion, fractured a bone in that race, which ended her career. Both Thunder Gulch, the 1995 Derby winner, and Timber Country, winner of the 1995 Preakness, suffered career-ending injuries shortly after their victories.

Lukas pooh-poohs this litany of broken bones, saying the proof of his prowess is in how many purses he has won. "Do they want me to sit here and chew Red Man and whittle or something?" he asks, mocking media critiques of his sartorial indulgences and lucrative speaking fees. "The record speaks for itself. We've won more races than anybody else. More than Charlie. More than anybody."

"Charlie" is Charlie Whittingham, a legendary trainer whose horses, by late 1996, had won $90 million during the previous five decades, according to *The Daily Racing Form*. But by late 1996, Lukas' horses had won $176.7 million since 1974, easily the largest sum attributable to any trainer in the country. Lukas has also paid his personal dues. In the early 1990s, he didn't win a major stakes race for more than two years, a period during which he almost lost his son in a freak stable accident and endured financial hardships after Calumet Farm collapsed while still owing him millions of dollars.

Lukas retained the sponsorship of enough owners to stage a furious comeback. In 1994, he purchased thirty-one yearlings for $6.8 million, though it's worth noting that none of those high-priced picks were among the five he entered in the 1996 Derby. Since 1980, he has raced thirty-one Thoroughbreds in sixteen Derbies and finished first three times.

While the scores of authentic horse lovers still in the racing industry wince at the pounding Lukas gives his animals, gamblers bemoan another problem afflicting horses: drugs, especially drugs that keep injured horses racing.

Joe Takach, a leading handicapper, is one of those characters unique to the racing world. In 1978, his wife told him to choose between betting on the ponies and his marriage. Takach walked out the door. "I looked her right in the eye, and told her it was the horses," he recalls. "What was I gonna do, become a brain surgeon?" Ever since he left his wife he has dressed entirely in black as a reminder of his lost marriage. He ultimately found his way to San Clemente, California, where he has easy access to the racing circuit in the southern part of the state.

Takach specializes in handicapping horses on the basis of their physical appearance before, during, and after a race. He focuses on such things as their alertness, muscle tone, coloring, and stride. Takach says the pervasiveness of drugging only makes his job harder, a sentiment that has been echoed by Andrew Beyer, one of the canniest students of racing and the first handicapper to use speed statistics in a methodical and sophisticated way.

"Every trainer and racetrack will admit that drugging happens in isolated cases, but they will never admit that tons of drugs are running through their horses' veins," Takach says. "If they ever tried to institute the kind of drug tests that are administered to Olympic athletes, they'd find more drugs in the horses' bodies than in large pharmaceutical companies. They just don't want to find the drugs. Why would they want to catch eighty-nine percent of their revenue base cheating? So they deny that the problem exists."

Before 1968, it was illegal to run a horse on any type of drug. But drugs had been part of the racing scene for decades. Heroin got its street nickname, "horse," during the 1930s, when it was first widely used to juice up racehorses. But in 1968, Dancer's Image had its Derby title revoked after testing positive for a painkiller called Butazolidin, or "Bute." Many in the industry thought the ruling was overly harsh, given that Bute was looked upon as a medicinal drug, so Dancer's Image's disqualification led to a liberalization of drug laws. Eventually Bute and other "medicinal" drugs, such as Lasix, were widely administered. Thoroughbreds have delicate lungs that bleed easily during races and Lasix may help control that bleeding. It is such a potent diuretic that jockeys, who often force themselves to vomit to keep their weight low, will sometimes chug down a bit of Lasix to enlist the bathroom in their weight-loss efforts.

Medicinal value notwithstanding, horses running on Lasix show a marked improvement from previous races. This may be due to the Lasix, or to other performance-enhancing drugs that Lasix masks, but Lasix's uses are clearly more than medicinal. A controversial study commissioned by the Jockey Club in 1990 said that Lasix does give horses a speed boost, and in most cases actually failed to stop pulmonary bleeding. Critics note that the drug tests used by tracks to detect illegal use have always been several steps behind new designer drugs that find their way into horses' veins.

Still, the industry asserts the problem is not out of control. "There are always people who want to take advantage by using drugs, but I think they're a minority," says Cliff Goodrich, president of Santa Anita Race Track and head of the Thoroughbred Racing Association. Goodrich says that he is more troubled by the overall decline in the caliber of racing.

"The quality of the product is what keeps any business alive, and the product we are putting on the track, our horses, just isn't good enough," he says. "If you have a good two-year-old, you can make a lot of money, and it forces owners to run them young to recoup their investment. I think, though, that we'd be better off running them later."

A case in point is Cigar, a stallion that won sixteen consecutive races between 1994 and 1996, tying a decades-old record first established by Citation. Cigar won those races when he was between four and six years old, a geezer by modern track standards. Cigar also amassed almost $10 million in career earnings before retiring—more than any horse in history. Cigar also captivated crowds, boosting track attendance wherever he ran.

A LOSING GAMBLE

But the racing industry has never been adept at marketing attractions such as Cigar. In one of the industry's biggest blunders, it decided against regularly televising races in the 1950s and 1960s because tracks feared television would reduce their attendance. By the 1970s and 1980s, other sports, particularly basketball and football, had developed entirely new audiences through television. In Japan, where jockeys are marketed like rock stars, horse racing has become the rage among teenage girls. Here, interest in racing is ebbing away.

While the industry never embraced television as a marketing tool, it did accept broadcasting as a gambling device. Most tracks have been temporarily saved by the introduction of closed-circuit simulcasting of their races to other tracks, to Las Vegas, and to off-track betting parlors. During the last twenty years, simulcasting revenue has steadily grown and now accounts for 60 percent to 70 percent of all the money gamblers lose betting on horses. Churchill Downs, which by the mid-1980s had fallen well behind New York and California in the quality of its racing, was rejuvenated by simulcasting. Between 1993 and 1995, the track's annual revenue jumped 66 percent, from $55.8 million to $92.4 million, a change due almost entirely to the growth of its simulcasting business and the larger purses it was able to offer as a result. But for most tracks, simulcasting revenue has just replaced on-site wagering as the underlying business continues to stagnate, the gambling dollar going elsewhere. Simulcasting has also helped cause a drop in track attendance. Fewer than 35 million people nationwide went to the track in 1995 compared with 74 million in 1972, when horse racing was America's top spectator sport. This drop has hit the marginal tracks the hardest, because their races usually aren't attractive enough to simulcast, and their on-site revenue has plummeted. There are about one hundred tracks in the country, but most observers don't expect more than the top dozen to survive.

And horse races remain a tough way for a gambler to make a buck. Even if a gambler wades through racing statistics, knows the jockeys and trainers, and appraises a horse's physical condition before betting, he or she still has to contend with the "takeout." Most tracks lop off at least 20 cents of each dollar wagered to pay for the track's commission, the purses, and state taxes; that's a substantial hurdle for any gambler to overcome.

Satisfied with the lock it once had on legal gambling, racing never had to work hard to draw bettors. Most tracks still treat gamblers as nuisances and do very little to accommodate them. That is merely a reflection of the overall denial in the horse-racing business about the indispensable role gambling has always played in the "Sport of Kings." Gambling brings people to the track, and the track brings attention to the horses, which benefits the owners. But the prospect of linking up with casinos raises the hackles of many in the racing industry. When Hollywood Park decided to open a card club at its Los Angeles track, it sought support from the southern California racing establishment but was rebuffed. Hollywood Park opened up the card rooms anyway, in 1995.

Despite a growing awareness that it needs to act, the industry's own shortsightedness and the casino gambling explosion have weakened racing's foundations. Casinos are far more effective marketers than race tracks and they offer forms of gambling that are shorn of the nuances and intellectual engagement of horse racing. Anywhere a casino has opened, nearby racetracks have seen their revenue plunge. A similar fate is befalling other pari-mutuel sports such as dog racing and jai alai.

Noting the preference gamblers now have for quick fixes and better odds, some tracks have decided to join, rather than fight, the competition. Prairie Meadows Race Track in Iowa, once a slumping relic, turned itself around by adding 1,100 slot machines to the track in 1995. But slot action now dwarfs horse racing at Prairie Meadows, and racing enthusiasts worry that horses ultimately will be eclipsed at tracks that offer casino-style gambling. Hollywood Park's card club already generates more revenue than horse racing there.

Churchill Downs, itself threatened by the encroachment of riverboat casinos near Louisville, is pushing the state to allow video gambling at the venerable track. "We've lost a generation in trying to develop new racing fans," says Churchill Downs' chief executive, Tom Meeker. "We have to offer more."

Race tracks have an uphill battle when it comes to competing with casinos, and only a handful will survive the onslaught. Casinos, however, aren't the only things keeping younger bettors away from the track. The tightest grip on the gambling imaginations and budgets of younger Americans belongs to the sports world.

The Poker Player—III

First, what I try to do is visualize. How can this game develop? I'm there to play. And I'm there to make a lot of money. So I know the personali-

ties of those involved in the game. I know who the guys are that are gonna win quickly and run away from the game. Who the guys are that are gonna be staying and playing the game. I know what people I'd rather see get ahead, and what people I'd rather see get behind.

It's like a football game. The game's gonna start out, we're gonna run the ball on the ground. The good of the game being the longevity of the game. Because longevity creates situations. Longevity makes people get tired. It makes the faces be the same but the players change. It's like if you took the same eight guys and put 'em in a poker game every day, the top eight players in the world, and videotaped the game, and how the hands were played, you'd see the most different kind of poker games you ever saw in your life. Depending on who was ahead, and who was behind. And it's like character, it's a character thing.

So what I try to do, I've even done it intentionally, like if I'm in a hand in a game early in a game, and say if I got the second-best hand in a game. And somebody's betting with the best hand, and somebody's in there with the worst hand, and I think that I really shouldn't raise the pot. But my chances of winning are much better than the guy I want to see get stuck. If I have to catch a card, I'm gonna win a big pot. I'm liable to put extra money early in a game, knowing it's mathematically the incorrect thing to do, just to punish this guy, to help him get stuck, 'cause it's gonna make a better game in the long run.

I know that if he wins a little bit, he's gonna quit. The game might break up. But if he happens to get stuck (we call it getting the nose open) this game could be a hell of a poker game. So I'm liable to dump off $5,000 or $10,000 even—not really dump it off, 'cause I have a chance to win the pot too, but maybe put extra money into a hand that I wouldn't normally do, except that this face is in the game. And I'll try to create a situation. Nobody else does that. Doyle, Bobby [Baldwin], maybe. Nobody else. It's just something they don't even think about. It's marketing.

It's one of the hardest things I've had to do over the years, is to market myself with these guys. . . . You know, most of the guys that play poker today have not had to create their own action. They play in tournaments. People like Doyle and myself and Bobby, we start all the games, we call all the players, we cultivate the CEOs. Most of the people that play with us, come to play with us, not with these guys that sit there like stiffs in the game. They play with us because we're personalities, too.

I was fortunate that I got to cut my teeth with old-timers. There was much less disparity between the limits that you played. The big games *back then were like $400, $800. So you really could come up through the ranks and take a rise, take a shot, take a rise to the top. Now, we're so priced out of the market it's like they don't even try anymore. They just say, "Well, there's the big game." And it's almost like that ladder got a few spikes cut off and you can't make the jump anymore.*

I think the romance of poker as you know it is eventually just gonna die out. It's just gonna be nuts and bolts, how-to books. . . . See, back in those days, might have been in the '70s, there was a code of ethics, okay? You didn't come to a poker game to win a few pots, and run away and quit. It was more like you were going into battle and you went into battle and you stayed in the battle. We used to play poker, we'd meet every day, we'd play poker a minimum of ten, fifteen hours a day. Sometimes the games would go for multiple days. We never quit. Once I played for five days. Doyle played the whole five days, Bobby played the whole five days.

In 1978, Bobby won the World Series of Poker. And he was goin' on—we were playing at the Dunes, we were playing seven card stud. It was a great game, it lasted a week without breaking up. Bobby had a seat in the game. And I was running the poker room for the Dunes at that time. And Bobby had to go with Benny Binion to the Merv Griffin Show. He'd been up forty-eight hours. I made an executive order because he had to go do the show, he didn't lose his seat. There was a waiting list a mile long to get into this game. It was a fabulous game. First, his wife brought him down his coat and his tie. The limo picked him up. He went over to L.A., did the show with Benny, came right back, got right back in the poker game, and played for three more days.

Now that mentality was what we all had. We were warriors . . . Doyle and Bobby and I and Johnny Moss . . . I'd wake up and I'd go to the poker room. I went there to fight to win, and I played until the last guy quit. . . . We knew that if we started the game among ourselves, people would come.

You know, we all thought we had somethin' going for us, anyway. I mean, that's one of the marks of a champion: you look around the table, you see eight suckers, no matter who the faces are. . . . I've never walked up to a game and said, "What are you playing?" I don't care what the game is. I walk up to a game and say, "How big is it?" Deal me in, I don't care who's playing.

These guys today . . . they don't have any heart, just nothin'. And they're all guys that are like trying to grind out a living. They're personalities that you just detest. You can't stand to play with them.

♦ ♣ ♥ ♠

Probably one of the biggest things that people have a tough time with is losing streaks. What happens in a losing streak is you get to question your own ability. Then you change your play or you just lose it. Getting desperate, like you have to get the money back. I maybe experienced that the first few years of playing, where I didn't wanna quit. I'd go completely broke in the games.

It wasn't the money. It was [that] I didn't want to lose. And you just have to learn that. If you're gambling for a living you've only got a certain percentage going for you, which means you're gonna lose. Probably if I go to a poker game I'm gonna lose three or four out of every ten times I play. That's part of the deal. Eventually you've just got to realize that you're just gonna keep throwing it up against the wall every day. And before it's gonna stick, it's gonna fall down.

That's what happens to a lot of guys. You see all the cycles in probability. . . . The probability of an unusual terrible streak at some time in your career is going to happen. You have to deal with it when it happens. And the guys that can't deal with it are the guys that just go bust.

A lot of times what's happened to guys is that they're specialists at games. There's a couple of guys that just play lowball draw, that's all they play. Well, that's okay as long as there's good lowball draw games. But what's happened over the years, the way it's evolved is, everybody has a game that they like. So, when you get to the big money, you don't have that many players. So you have to negotiate. "I'll play this, I'll play this, let's just play them all." We'll change the dealers every thirty minutes and play 'em all.

And I'm fortunate. I might not be the best player in every game, but I play them all pretty well. So, I don't give away anything in any game.

There was a time in my career where I would bet it all. Like I wanted to get to another level. I don't think I'd bet it all on anything now. Maybe something. I mean, Why? The pleasure of winning would not even come close to the pain of losing.

I might bet it all if I didn't have a family. . . . If you were single and by yourself, and say you had a $100,000 bankroll. And believe in it so strongly, you say, "This is gonna change my life. This is gonna take me over the top. So what if I get broke? I can start over for that amount of money." But what if you had $8 million? Would you bet it all?

♦ ♣ ♥ ♠

It's the personal that it's all about. It's like, here we are. Look at me. Okay, don't stop looking at me. If you stop looking at me, you lose. Here we are. There's just two of us in this room. One of us is gonna be the man, one of us is gonna be the little girl in the room. It's that mentality. Some people like it. I thrive on it.

You know, I love it. I mean I love to sit down with somebody. I've never turned anybody down in my life to play cards.

CHAPTER 8

SAN FRANCISCO:
ALL THAT GLITTERS

BILL HENRY SITS IN A DARK, smoky bar just outside of San Francisco. His gaze is fixed on one of three television screens displaying the Green Bay Packers and New England Patriots as they butt heads in Super Bowl XXXI. Henry, who uses the alias "Heraclitus" when placing bets with his bookie, is one of 138 million people in the United States tuned in to the Super Bowl, a large but unknown portion of whom have wagered money on the game. This Sunday afternoon in January 1997 will be the single biggest sports betting day of the year and Henry, a Budweiser in one hand and a cigar in the other, has $3,300 riding on professional football's championship game.

The Packers have entered the game as the 14-point favorite, but Henry has avoided betting on who will win. Instead, he has wagered that the Super Bowl's point total will be more than 49, the "over/under" figure his local bookie and others across the nation have chosen to attract gamblers to this particular "prop," or proposition bet. A former star quarterback in high school, Henry says that winning the local football championship thirty-two years earlier was the best night of his life. Now, at fifty, a successful real estate dealer who doesn't need to work for a living, Henry enjoys the buzz he gets from gambling. When Ben Coates catches a four-yard pass from Patriots quarterback Drew Bledsoe to put New England ahead 13–10 in the first quarter, Henry erupts from his seat clapping.

"People need outlets. If I couldn't drink or smoke or gamble, I'd go nuts," he says. "I couldn't enjoy this if I was just betting a hundred dollars. I guess it's all relative. But I absolutely wouldn't be as interested in this game if I didn't have some money on it."

By the end of the second quarter, the Packers are beating New England 27–14. Near the end of the third quarter, the Patriots close the gap by mounting a crisp, seven-play, fifty-three-yard drive, ending in a touchdown and extra point that makes the score 27–21. Henry needs only two points to win his bet as the Patriots line up to kick off after their scoring drive. The kickoff arcs high into the air, then drops into the arms of Green Bay's Desmond Howard, who is poised to receive it on the Packers' one-yard line.

Five years earlier, Howard had won college football's Heisman Trophy, only to end up being cut from the first two professional squads for which he played. A hip injury nearly ended his career with the Packers, but Howard persevered, carving out a niche on Green Bay's specialty teams. Now, his legs pumping and the football in hand, he sprints forward from the one-yard line. Howard shoots straight up the middle, evading a gaggle of Patriots and then cutting left around a blocker to explode past New England's kicker, Adam Vinatieri, near the thirty-five-yard line. The rest of the field is wide open, a stage that Howard streaks across on his way to a touchdown, the longest kickoff return in Super Bowl history, and an award as the game's most valuable player.

Henry, rising slightly off his chair as Howard begins his touchdown run, slaps both of his palms against his forehead, and then rocks back into his seat when Howard glides into the end zone. Henry accepts high fives from the men sitting around him and then orders a round of drinks for the sixty or so people in the bar. Although it's only the third quarter, the game is over for him.

"It's just such a rush. It's a rush to win money, but I also get a rush from the fear of losing money," Henry confides, as Green Bay completes a 2-point conversion to take a 14-point lead. "It feels good. But winning does not feel as good as losing feels bad."

A few moments later, after lighting up a fresh cigar, Henry basks in his victory. "This is nirvana. I'm not worried about a long bomb with five seconds left that gets tipped in the air and ruins everything."

For everyone else in the bar, however, the game is not over, even though the Packers have a Super Bowl victory sewn up. The score, 35–21, means that the Packers haven't beaten the point spread. Bettors backing the Patriots can only hope that the Packers don't score again so the gamblers can salvage a tie with the 14 points they've taken. When the Packers set up for a field goal with three minutes left in the game, the bar is silent. "There's a hundred trillion bucks riding on this snap," someone mutters under his breath. Chris Jacke, the Packers' kicker, boots the ball to the right of the goal posts—no good. For the first time since the Super Bowl debuted in 1967, the game ends exactly on the bookies' point spread. Refunds will be given to everyone who bet on either team to win. It is a disappointing finish all the way around.

Still, gambling has served part of its purpose. It has kept people riveted to the Super Bowl long after the winner was determined, allowing television networks to use even the late stages of the game as bait to charge advertisers more than $1 million for 30 seconds of broadcast space. It has kept fans' eyes glued to the flickering screen as Packers quarterback Brett Favre spreads a line of milk across his upper lip after the game and transforms himself into a walking billboard for the dairy industry. It is directly responsible for making football one of the most popular sports in the country, a hot topic of friendly conversation for gamblers in office pools, homes, college dormitories, high schools, stock exchanges, restaurants, bars, country clubs, apartment buildings, and street corners. It has also induced generations of gamblers to attempt to fix contests in a variety of sports, fed the coffers of organized crime, and helped introduce children and teenagers to the commercial wonderland of modern sports.

Some estimate that $88 billion is gambled illegally on sports each year, with $4 billion to $5 billion bet illegally on the Super Bowl alone. All such claims are, at best, guesswork. Bookies don't publish annual reports. Bookmakers in Las Vegas, where the craft is legal, handled $2.46 billion in wagers in the year that ended in June 1996, keeping only about 4.28 percent, or $105 million. It is certain that the illegal sports-gambling market dwarfs the Las Vegas "sports books." It is also more than likely that sports gambling is at least as big as the lottery business and may run second, though a very distant second, to casino gambling, which totaled $501.6 billion in 1996.

Whatever its size, sports gambling in its earliest days made boxing and baseball two of the country's favorite pastimes and later, when coupled with television, propelled football and basketball to the forefront of the nation's fantasies. Today, in spite of the often tawdry commercialization of sports and the fact that few sports bettors come out on top, the games continue to draw the allegiance of millions.

"I'm definitely minus overall on my betting," Henry admits a few days after the Super Bowl. "I've probably lost $150,000 since 1981. But this is San Francisco, and I like to get my thrills."

VICE ON GOLD MOUNTAIN

Everyone who came had visions of gold. The Chinese who immigrated to California in the 1840s and 1850s called it Gam Saan, "Gold Mountain." For Catherine Haun, who moved to California with her husband in 1849 to seek a fortune in the Sacramento Valley, the state promised "castles of shining gold."

"[We,] being financially involved in our business interests near Clinton, Iowa, longed to go to the new El Dorado and 'pick up' enough with which to pay off our debts," Haun later recalled. "At the time the gold fever was contagious and few, old or young, escaped the malady. On the streets, in the fields, in the workshops and by the fireside, golden California was the chief topic of conversation."

Famously inspired by the discovery of gold near Sutter's Mill, hundreds of thousands of prospectors poured into the Sacramento Valley and the Sierra Nevada foothills in 1849 in a furious bid to lay claim to their dreams. They came on wagons from the Midwest and the East Coast, on ships around the tip of South America, and on barges across the Pacific Ocean from China. They were speculators one and all, gamblers to the core. Most thought they would strike it rich and return home. So the place where most of the new arrivals hunkered down was nothing more than a glorified base camp made up of thousands of canvas tents pitched near Yerba Buena, a tiny settlement that developed after the Spanish discovered the magnificent bay in 1775.

The Spanish had first landed in California near present-day San Diego in 1542, searching for the realm of a fabled king who covered his body in gold dust and was called El Dorado, "The Gilded Man." Conquistadores christened the new territory California after a magical island in a sixteenth-century Spanish novel. The region had long been inhabited by several tribes of Native Americans, who, as elsewhere in North America, would gradually and brutally be forced aside. Those Indians who were Christianized helped the Spanish build a string of missions northward along the coast beginning in 1769. Villages sprouted around the missions as control of the region eventually passed to Mexico and in 1848, after the Mexican War, to the United States.

A three-century quest by the Spanish to find gold to prop up what was then the most far-reaching empire in the world had been unimaginably successful in Latin America, but proved fruitless in California. And then, on a January day in 1848, a lone mill worker named James Marshall stumbled on gold along the American River near Coloma. When word spread the following year, the gold rush was on. Seismic shifts in people, money, and history were set in motion. Over the following decades, billions of dollars in gold would be found in California. Marshall would die broke.

Only about 800 people lived around Yerba Buena before Marshall got lucky. Two years later, California was a state, Yerba Buena had been renamed San Francisco, and 25,000 people were living in the town. Tents gave way to shacks, which gave way to clapboard houses, stores, bordellos, and gambling halls. "No man, young or old, should go to Cal-

ifornia unless he has firmness of principle enough to resist, and forever
hold at bay, all the vices of the country, in whatever disguise they may
present themselves and in however fascinating shapes they may appear,"
a preacher named Daniel Woods warned would-be settlers in 1849.
There was much in San Francisco to provoke the preacher's indignation.

San Francisco was swarming with people in the early gold rush days.
Estimates put the ratio of men to women at ten to one, and many of the
female residents were prostitutes. In the area that became the Barbary
Coast, topless hookers sat in street-level windows offering "texture
checks" of their breasts—one squeeze cost a dime, two cost 15 cents. If sex
was desired, patrons could walk upstairs to one of hundreds of tiny rooms
called cribs and indulge themselves. On at least one occasion in an arena
at Mission Dolores, then part of a small village outside the city, bulls and
bears were chained together in fights to the death. Interested San Franciscans were invited to attend what the contest's promoters termed "the raci-
est sport of the season." Tickets for the performance cost $3.

San Francisco was a cauldron of treasure hunters, seamen, merchants, migrants, immigrants, scamsters, and thugs, and it was utterly
lawless. Justice was dispensed by large vigilante groups, which were
formed whenever things were deemed a bit too out of control. The most
famous of these was the Committee on Vigilance, which lynched several
rowdies in 1851 and thereafter would occasionally be resurrected to
hang an undesirable or even, as in 1856, be used by one political faction
to do away with members of another. Even after "law and order" were introduced, politicians and police remained hopelessly and dangerously
corrupt. Amid the swirl were the casinos.

Most of the streets around what is now Jackson Square were littered
with gambling joints. Acknowledging the forces that drew everyone to
this place where the continent spilled off into the sea, one of the casinos
was named El Dorado. It stood near Denison's Exchange, Parker House,
the Veranda, Aguila de Oro, St. Charles, and Bella Union. Dozens of
lesser gambling joints were scattered about. Female dealers were an attraction, and several casinos had them. Gold nuggets and sacks of gold
dust could be laid on the tables for a wager. "The greatest crowd is about
the El Dorado; we find it difficult to effect an entrance," observed
Bayard Taylor, a journalist visiting San Francisco in 1849.

There are about eight tables in the room, all of which are thronged;
copper-hued Kanakas, Mexicans rolled in their sarapes and Peru-
vians thrust through their ponchos, stand shoulder to shoulder
with the brown and bearded American miners. . . . Along the end
of the room is a spacious bar supplied with all kinds of bad liquors,

and in a sort of gallery, suspended under the ceiling, a female violinist tasks her talent and strength of muscle to minister to the excitement of play. . . . The atmosphere of these places is rank with tobacco smoke and filled with a feverish, stifling heat, which communicates an unhealthy glow to the faces of the players. . . . They have no power to resist the fascination of the game. Now counting their winnings by the thousands, now dependent on the kindness of a friend for a few dollars to commence anew, they pass hour after hour in those hot, unwholesome dens. . . . There are other places, where gaming is carried on privately and to a more ruinous extent—rooms in the rear of the Parker House, in the City Hotel and other places, frequented only by the initiated. Here the stakes are almost unlimited, the players being men of wealth and apparent respectability. . . . Here are lost, in a few turns of a card or rolls of a ball, the product of fortunate ventures by sea or months of racking labor on land.

Abutting Jackson Square was Chinatown. The Chinese who came to San Francisco were almost all young, uneducated men fleeing war-torn southern China, where jobs were scarce. They sought work in the gold mines and took on grueling, perilous, and indispensable jobs building legs of the transcontinental railroad. Wages were meager. The Chinese were confined to an area off Portsmouth Square and most lived in squalid tenement buildings along DuPont Street. Respected self-governing bodies like the Six Companies brought order and resolved disputes within the Chinese community; they co-existed with stores, restaurants, opium dens, whorehouses, and gambling halls. Descriptions by outsiders of Chinatown at the time were clouded by "yellow peril" anxieties, so the ubiquity of illicit activities may have been overstated. But there is no question that vice and gambling were as widespread in Chinatown as in the Barbary Coast and that Chinese casino owners secured their survival with the same bribes used so effectively by their European and American rivals a few blocks away.

Separated by language, dress, and racism, the Chinese and European-American immigrants in San Francisco were linked by the most slender of threads: their love of gambling. Great fortunes were as revered in China as they were in the United States, but the Chinese had been on the hunt for thousands of years. The games that gave Chinese gamblers a taste of that chase were just as old, as were the superstitions that ruled them. Mah-jongg, a tile game whose rules were similar to gin rummy, was played for low stakes in most homes in China and was a centerpiece of family life there. Outside the home, mah-jongg bets could climb much higher. But the most popular games in Chinatown's casinos were fan-tan and pai gow. Fan-tan was played using a pile of coins, buttons, or other tokens, which were spilled onto a table by a dealer who immediately covered them with a metal dish. Bettors tried to guess how many tokens would be left over after the pile under the cover was divided by four. Pai gow was a tile game similar to dominos, but played at a much faster clip. Gamblers were dealt four tiles; the objective was to arrange the tiles into two pairs that offered the best combinations according to rankings on a chart. Chinatown also ran a lottery that was wildly popular with Chinese and non-Chinese alike. Tickets were sold at hundreds of spots around Chinatown and drawings were held twice a day. The lottery was called pak kop piu, or "white pigeon ticket," because the white slips of paper used in the drawings had originally been transported by carrier pigeons in China so the lottery's operators could avoid arrest. Gamblers selected ten numbers from a field of eighty and tried to match those against twenty numbers that were selected in the drawings. Later generations of casino and lottery gamblers in the United States would call the game keno.

Meanwhile, San Francisco kept growing. By 1860, 56,000 people were living there. A decade later, the population had shot up to 150,000, and by 1880 it had doubled again. As the city took shape, corruption and vice became institutionalized. In 1860, rather than fight a losing battle, the city ruled that gambling and prostitution had to be confined to the Barbary Coast district. While railroad magnates and gold and silver tycoons bought off local politicians, squashed business competitors, and divvied up Nob Hill in the 1870s, the Barbary Coast sprawled beneath them—bawdy, available, and unshakable. After the great earthquake and fire of 1906 devastated most of the city, the Barbary Coast remained, rolling on until vice squads formally shut much of it down in 1917. But the action just continued illegally until World War II, when the military insisted that the carnival move further underground. Prior to the war, seemingly innocuous stores were fronts for illegal floating card and dice games, like the cigar shop in the Tenderloin known as the Padre Club where a young boy and future governor named Edmund "Pat" Brown worked for his father, a former bookie.

Chinatown was never given as much leeway. Whites' grudging acceptance of the Chinese waned as San Francisco's early boom slowed down. When gold mining got soft, silver from the Comstock Lode of 1859 and railroad construction kept the local economy vibrant. But by 1869, the Comstock Lode was depleted and the transcontinental railroad was built. Thousands of unemployed Chinese railroad workers began competing with European immigrants for jobs, even as still more

Chinese immigrated to San Francisco. Anti-Chinese hysteria built up in the city, and businessmen gladly exploited the animosity by using the Chinese as strikebreakers. After a national depression in 1873, Chinese all over the West began to be arbitrarily beaten and murdered by angry white mobs. In San Francisco, the charge was led primarily by the Irish. Then, in 1882, Congress countenanced the hatred by passing the Chinese Exclusion Act, which barred entry to new Chinese immigrants, restricted those who had already arrived from holding certain jobs, and denied all of them citizenship.

Shut off and unprotected, the Chinese sought refuge in any form Chinatown could provide. Increasingly, that meant tongs, or "meeting halls." Tongs started out as civic organizations similar to the Six Companies, and were made up of people in similar occupations, such as merchants or laborers. But they also had ties to secretive "triads" in southern China and soon developed into criminal gangs. As the Six Companies' attempts to cooperate with San Francisco's white power brokers collapsed in the face of racial backlash, the tongs gained a greater following in Chinatown. The tongs, like their Jewish, Italian, and Irish counterparts in cities such as New York, helped the Chinese find work and shelter, lent money to merchants, and took control of vice and gambling operations. They also engaged in bloody, lethal confrontations with one another as each tong sought to expand its turf.

All this turmoil was papered over as the city's residents set out to prove that a civilized San Francisco was a white San Francisco. Although high-priced bordellos and wood-paneled gambling rooms could still be found in the finer part of town, the city built a new boulevard, Broadway, to allow its more refined citizens to bypass the Barbary Coast. And as San Francisco came of age, its residents worked hard to adopt the mainstream fashions, tastes, and interests of late-nineteenth-century America.

Among the various passions that began sweeping across the country at the time was organized sports. Gambling would be inextricably linked to the proliferation of organized sports in America, and San Francisco provided one of the first stars of modern athletics: a local boxer and bank teller named Jim Corbett.

BARE KNUCKLES, BIG BUCKS

When Jim Corbett defeated John L. Sullivan in 1892 to win the nation's heavyweight boxing title, he was so moved by the fallen champion's humble concession speech that he offered the following compliment:

"Sullivan is a man. Who could have said anything more square and more manly than that?" Corbett spoke for his times. He belonged to an age when America first began defining and verifying masculinity through organized sports. Boxing rings were one of the initial proving grounds. Corbett's era also witnessed the emergence of mass spectator sports, and the spectators, who at first were predominantly male, kept their own testosterone flowing by cheering for their favorite athletes and by demonstrating that they had the guts to bet money on them. Sports and sports gambling also were boosted by new communications technologies, such as the telephone, telegraph, high-speed printing press, and photoengraving machine, all of which came into widespread use during this period. Indeed, from now on, advances in communications played a key role not only in the growth of sports but also in the growth of sports betting.

From the early eighteenth century to the 1890s, boxing in the United States had consisted of brutal, bare-knuckle matches where wrestling, eye gouging, biting, head butting, and disfiguring injuries ruled the day. San Francisco became a premier training ground for bare-knuckle boxers, because the Barbary Coast offered them plenty of work. Saloons regularly staged some bouts between just two fighters, and others in which several fighters would crowd into a ring and beat one another silly until one man was left standing to claim the prize money. Boxers were also hired as "crimps" who helped beat up and kidnap, or "shanghai," unwary sailors from boardinghouses for involuntary service on outgoing ships. Shanghaiing remained a steady-paying sideline for San Francisco's boxers until about 1910.

Boxing might have remained an underground sport had not a few states, such as California, condoned it, and were it not for the arrival of John L. Sullivan, America's first great celebrity-athlete. Sullivan, a Boston stonemason and a master of bare-knuckle slugfests, had become famous and sought-after at home and abroad after touring the country in the 1880s and taking on all challengers; his autobiography was titled *I Can Lick Any Sonofabitch in the House!* In the last championship fought with bare knuckles, an 1889 bout between Sullivan and Jake Kilrain featuring an enormous $20,000 purse, fans wagered on who would be the first to bleed; the referee himself bet $700 on Sullivan; and the fight was promoted by two New Orleans gamblers, Bud Renaud and Pat Duffy.

But purses in most fights were far smaller than this, and most of the money floating around a prizefight was gambling money. Sportswriter and boxing aficionado Bert Sugar tells how bets on each fighter were placed on two handkerchiefs at the edge of the ring and watched over by a "grubstake holder" charged with doling out the winnings. (Rough-and-tumble Western mining states were fertile territory for spawning boxers; the word "grubstake" originally referred to money lent to gold or silver prospectors in return for a share of their discoveries.) Fighters frequently bet on themselves and were well aware of the other money riding on their performance. It was common for fighters, if they were losing badly enough, to punch an opponent in the groin to draw a foul. They would lose the bout, but because of the foul all bets would be off. Bets would also be called off if fans interfered with the fight, a rule that caused some anxious gamblers to go to extremes to upset a bout. The most notorious example of fans fixing a fight was an 1860 bout near London that boxing historians consider the first international heavyweight championship. During the fight, a group of heavy-betting English aristocrats stormed the ring to create a "riot" when their favorite, a local named Tom Sayers, began to take a beating from John Heenan, a fighter from a small town north of San Francisco. Police interrupted the fight, canceling all bets.

A show was made of staging the 1889 Sullivan-Kilrain fight covertly on a Mississippi farm, but the event was an open secret all over the South. After Sullivan won the seventy-five-round marathon, both fighters were arrested, and soon released, by local militia who suddenly appeared on the scene. But the fight that brought down the curtain on the bare-knuckle era was just a prologue to Sullivan's great bout with Corbett three years later. Sullivan, more than any boxer, pushed for the use of boxing gloves and for stricter ground rules in bouts. Still, the distinctions between Sullivan and his challenger were glaring. Whereas the "Great John L." was a hard-drinking working-class brawler, "Gentleman Jim" Corbett was a member of the ascendant middle class, who sparred at San Francisco's exclusive Olympic Club and weight-trained at an Oakland gym under the tutelage of a renowned bodybuilder named Tom Carroll. (Other fighters who trained at Carroll's gym included Jim Jeffries, Corbett's sparring partner and a future heavyweight champ.) And while the venues for illegal fights were riverboat barges, remote fields, and Barbary Coast saloons, the Sullivan-Corbett prizefight was held in a New Orleans sports club that seated thousands of people.

At the time, Louisiana was one of the few states where boxing was legal, and New Orleans' Olympic Club (unconnected to the club in San Francisco) was the only establishment able to provide the $25,000 purse demanded by Sullivan. Sullivan also required challengers to match his own $10,000 side bet on the outcome of the fight—a requirement he published in newspapers across the country. Corbett, who had gone four rounds with Sullivan in San Francisco a year earlier, anted up, put on the gloves, went in as the 4–1 underdog, and knocked Sullivan out in the twenty-first round.

The fight generated enormous publicity and was the first sporting event to snare truly national attention. Fans and gamblers crowded around telegraph stations in cities across the country to hear each round's result. In San Francisco, Western Union ran a telegraph wire directly to the Orpheum Theater, where two boxers reenacted the fight as news of it flowed in from New Orleans. Corbett's brother, Harry, one of San Francisco's biggest bookies, received "betting privileges" that allowed him to set up several wagering booths inside the Orpheum. With such luminaries as famed lawman Bat Masterson serving as timekeeper in Corbett's corner, the fight also flashed a bit of glamour that captivated the New Orleans audience. "The streets were thronged with visitors of all classes, from the millionaire to the baker to the fakir," the *New Orleans Democrat* reported the day after the fight. "Politicians, lawyers, merchants and gamblers elbowed each other in all public places on comparatively equal terms."

The attention lavished on the Sullivan-Corbett prizefight launched boxing into the realm of big-time entertainment. It also signaled the growing public acceptance of the sport, even though boxing remained just a cut above the bull-and-bear brawls staged at Mission Dolores. Protestant ministers busy promoting "muscular Christianity" extolled sports such as boxing as the best preparation for the hardships of carrying out one's moral duties in life. Clerics also saw sports as a solid alternative to the lures of vice. Eventually, Theodore Roosevelt, a sickly teenager who was transformed by his own pursuit of the athletic life, would put the prestige of the White House behind organized sports. He advocated sports, and boxing in particular, as a tonic for a nation of sissies. And in 1912, the University of California at Berkeley would become the first college in the country to field a boxing team. The ranks of boxing swelled with successive generations of Irish, Jewish, Italian, African-American, and Hispanic fighters drawn by the illusion that here was a way out of the gutter, and the apparatus that kept the whole enterprise moving was money and gambling. New Orleans' Olympic Club made a profit of $50,000 on the Sullivan-Corbett bout, and that haul drew the attention of every sharpie in the country.

Promoters started pushing title fights into any state that would accept them, though these were still few. Popular and bloody professional slugfests were viewed much less favorably by local authorities than amateur boxers' pursuits of physical fitness. Religious groups opposed to professional boxing's violence also contributed to the sport's containment. Louisiana outlawed boxing after the Sullivan-Corbett fight. New

York had some title fights, but betting scandals and fixed fights shut down legal boxing there by the turn of the century (although illegal bouts continued). Soon, boxing had been run out of every part of the country except the West, with Nevada and California the favored show-grounds. San Franciscans staged private fights in upper-class establishments such as the California Athletic Club and the Olympic Club. Public bouts were held at Mechanic's Pavilion near City Hall and Woodward's Pavilion on Valencia Street, and several fights in the city were refereed by gambler and legendary gunman Wyatt Earp. Jim Jeffries fought five title defenses in San Francisco, Oakland became an important center of the fight scene, and California began proclaiming itself "Boxing Capital of the World."

But it was a fight that San Francisco refused to touch, promoted by a gambler and friend of Earp, that began the career of Tex Rickard, the father of modern prizefighting.

Tex Rickard had made and gambled away a fortune as a gold prospector in the Klondike before opening a casino and saloon, the Northern, in Goldfield, Nevada, in the early 1900s. Earp, who had prospected with Rickard in Alaska, briefly worked as a pit boss at the Northern. Rickard hit upon the idea of staging prizefights in Goldfield to help fill his casino, and in 1906 he even let women and children into a fight that reportedly drew more than 7,000 fans. But he really put himself on the map in 1910, when he brought Jeffries out of retirement to challenge Jack Johnson, the first black heavyweight champion. Johnson was outspoken, dated and married white women, and drew the wrath of racists, such as San Francisco writer Jack London, who couldn't stomach the idea of a black champion. San Francisco having passed on the fight, it was held nearby in Reno, Nevada, and Rickard shamelessly played up the racial paranoia surrounding the bout. He offered the refereeing to President Taft and to writer Arthur Conan Doyle, both of whom declined. So Rickard made himself the referee. Johnson, who trained in Oakland gyms and had amassed a series of victories in the Bay Area, won handily. But his victory sparked race riots across the country, and he was later hounded out of boxing.

Rickard went on to become the leading showman of the sport, largely through his re-creation of Madison Square Garden in New York and through the fights he arranged for a young thug and drifter from the Western mining camps named Jack Dempsey. Dempsey had boxed in Goldfield and the Bay Area under the guidance of a gambler named Jack Kearns. When Rickard and Kearns linked up to promote Dempsey, boxing began its slow crawl back East and into the cradling arms of gambling's high priesthood, organized crime. But on the way, legalized boxing would face competition from other sports that were starting to pull in big crowds, the most popular of which was baseball.

BETTING AT THE BALLPARK

In 1897, four and a half years after he knocked out Sullivan, Jim Corbett lost his heavyweight crown to Bob Fitzsimmons. That same year, Jim's twenty-year-old brother Joe won twenty-four games and lost eight as a pitcher for the Baltimore Orioles.

Joe Corbett had left San Francisco because the Midwest and East had more active baseball leagues, which offered better pay than he could get locally. The previous year, the Orioles had won the National League championship and played the league's second-place team, the Cleveland Spiders, in a post-season series for a trophy called the Temple Cup (a predecessor of the modern World Series). The 1896 season had been a memorable one for the Orioles. On their way home from spring training, they had stopped to play exhibition games to put some extra cash in the players' pockets. Hometown fans beat up visiting Orioles they found wandering alone, and local umpires openly favored the home team. Not that the Orioles were above similar behavior. Young toughs such as John McGraw didn't hesitate to trip opposing base runners or dig a spike into a passing shin. When the Orioles confronted the Spiders in post season play, the Orioles faced a team that boasted a powerful pitcher named Cy Young and harbored a reputation for viciousness that equaled their own. The Spiders were known to punch umpires for bad calls and to trash a locker room with their bats if they lost a game. But what goes around comes around: after one Temple Cup game in Baltimore, Orioles fans threw rocks at the Spiders as they departed for their hotel. Such was the state of the national pastime at the turn of the century.

Joe Corbett's pitching played a key role in defeating the Spiders for the 1896 Temple Cup, so after winning two dozen games the following season he asked the Orioles' owners for a $1,000 raise. His request was nixed. Corbett quit the team and returned to San Francisco to find a different profession, certain that he would never get rich playing baseball. Of course, few baseball players ever made much money in the early days; that was why the lads gambled on their own games so much.

Legend has it that baseball got started in 1839 near Cooperstown, N.Y., the invention of a West Point cadet named Abner Doubleday. Like many sports tales, the story is hooey. But a version of the game was being played in Manhattan in 1845 by an amateur club, and by the 1850s baseball was something of a mania in the Northeast. Gambling was involved from the get-go.

Wagering was common even when baseball was an upper-class club sport, and owners added better players to their teams in order to win bets. Even the language of the early game was that of the gambler: runs were called aces, and a turn at bat was called a hand. As the sport took off, gamblers and bookies were in ready supply at most baseball fields. As ballparks and then stadiums were built in the following decades, it was common knowledge that bookies could be found plying their trade in the right-field bleachers. Much of the betting was just good-natured socializing with casual wagers placed on favorite teams. In other cases, players were bribed by gamblers to help their teams lose a game or two, and fans helped steer the action: "An outfielder, settling under a crucial fly ball, would find himself stoned by a nearby spectator, who might win a few hundred dollars if the ball was dropped," baseball writer Eliot Asinof says of the era. "On one occasion, a gambler actually ran out on the field and tackled a ballplayer. On another, a marksman prevented a fielder from chasing a long hit by peppering the ground around his feet with bullets." In 1865, two players for the New York Mutuals, owned by Tammany Hall's corrupt chieftain, William Marcy "Boss" Tweed, were evicted from baseball and then reinstated after they tried to bribe a teammate to help throw a game.

But baseball's unique public appeal helped it ride out early betting scandals. Before long, its supporters were touting it as the "national game," and in 1871 players organized the first salaried league. But investors lost money on the teams because of poor attendance and because many players were hooligans and gamblers. Players and professional gamblers were widely seen as conspirators who, in the jargon of the time, were "hippodroming," or fixing games. When the early league fell apart in 1876, it was replaced by the National League. Control of baseball shifted from the players to the owners, who, among other things, made sure that players' salaries were slashed and that gambling was formally prohibited. Owners also inserted the infamous "reserve clause" in the contracts of their top players, requiring great athletes to stay with the same team for their entire career—an issue that would be at the center of struggles between owners and players over the next century. In the short run, the antagonism helped worsen the quality of play. And despite rules against it, gambling was rampant.

In 1877, four players for the Louisville Grays, including the league's best pitcher, were bribed by a gambling ring to throw several late-season games that cost their team the pennant. The players said they accepted the bribes because the Grays' owner hadn't bothered to cough up their salaries. They were kicked out of the league, and the Louisville franchise was disbanded. But gambling and fixes continued, and the players weren't always the ones at fault. Richard Higham, an umpire, was kicked out of baseball in 1882 for letting professional gamblers in on a little secret: how he planned to call the games he was officiating. Not missing a beat, Higham became a bookie after his expulsion. During the 1880s and 1890s, Chicago White Stockings manager Cap Anson was busy purging baseball of black players and regularly betting on his own team's games. Anson, who was later elected to the Hall of Fame, asserted that it was standard procedure at the time for a team with championship prospects to bribe other teams to play harder against contenders for the league's crown.

At the turn of the century, the American League was formed, boasting that it would offer a cleaner brand of baseball. Increased competition, and requirements that owners police their ballparks more effectively, resulted in a dramatic improvement in the quality of the games. Much of the buffoonery and flagrant cheating that had permeated baseball for the previous two decades abated. With these changes came greater social acceptance of the sport, which now started to be praised for some of the same healing virtues as boxing. Clergymen saw baseball as a bulwark against the corrupting vices of cities, and Theodore Roosevelt added it to a list of "the true sports for a manly race." In 1913, a best-selling manual called *Training the Boy* pointed out that "No boy can grow to a perfectly normal manhood today without the benefits of at least a small amount of baseball experience and practice." It was also, apparently, hard to grow to a perfectly normal manhood without indulging in a bit of gambling.

Gambling was tolerated in baseball to some extent because betting on one's own team to win was seen as a way for underpaid players to supplement their salaries. And, with African-Americans locked out of the game, professional baseball in its early years was dominated by immigrants and the children of immigrants, who didn't share the Protestant establishment's aversion to gambling. Often, gambling was just part of the fun. But by the early twentieth century, it had clearly become more than a by-product of the game. It stood right in the middle of the action.

Attempts were made to fix the first World Series in 1903 and the second in 1905 (no World Series was played in 1904). There were unproven rumors that the 1912 World Series was fixed. After the seemingly unbeatable Athletics were trounced in the 1914 World Series by the upstart Boston Braves, the As' frustrated owner, Connie Mack, openly speculated that his players had colluded with gamblers to throw the championship. From the time he entered the majors in 1905 to play for the New York Highlanders (later the Yankees) until he was banned from baseball in 1920, first baseman and slugger Hal Chase openly cheated and conspired with gamblers to fix games. Although everyone in the game knew that Chase was trying to fix games with a devotion that inspired others to do the same, it took more than a decade for baseball to get rid of him. Perhaps the league was slow to act because a close look at Chase might also have meant scrutinizing baseball's owners, such as Chase's first bosses. The Yankees were founded by a corrupt former police chief, "Big Bill" Devery, and a leading bookmaker and casino operator, Frank Farrell, both of whom were at the center of illegal gambling in Manhattan. Farrell's gambling riches allowed him to commission the noted architect Stanford White to design his most opulent casino, at 33 West Thirty-third Street. So every time Chase dropped a ball or ran a tad too slowly, he may have been playing exactly the way his bosses wanted him to play.

Baseball officials were also hesitant to crack down on gambling too severely because it was so popular. For fans reluctant to bet with bookies, illegal baseball "pools" were widely available that offered cheap, lottery-style tickets for each game. In addition to wagers on winning teams, bets were accepted on run totals, the number of victories in a week, and many other propositions. The pools bribed the police to keep quiet, and baseball's owners tolerated them at ballparks because they believed that betting kept fans, especially children, interested in games.

THE BLACK SOX AND THE MAN UPTOWN

Nineteen-nineteen was a landmark year for sports and gambling. In that year, Jack Dempsey thrashed Jess Willard to win the heavyweight boxing championship. The fight was held in Toledo, a town friendly to gamblers and hoodlums, despite opposition from the Ohio legislature and Tex Rickard's inability to bribe the governor. The Eighteenth Amendment prohibiting the sale of liquor was passed in 1919; this business opportunity would transform street crime into organized crime and provide the financing that helped solidify the Mob's control of illegal sports betting. And in that same year, an event occurred that forced baseball, the biggest entertainment industry in the country, to finally make a grand display of trying to rid itself of gambling: the 1919 World Series was fixed.

As the drama unfolded, baseball's potentates tried to brush off the most notorious scandal in American sports history as the last act of a bygone era.

Christy Mathewson, a former pitching star and manager with a spotless reputation and the well-deserved nickname "The Christian Gentleman," had seen to it that Hal Chase was briefly suspended in 1918, two years before the first baseman was permanently barred from the sport. And Mathewson was among the first to suspect that the 1919 championship contest between the White Sox and the Reds was fixed. A year later that suspicion had erupted into a widely publicized fact. Bookmakers had made the White Sox a 5–1 favorite going into the Series: the team was loaded with some of the greatest ballplayers in history, including "Shoeless Joe" Jackson. But the White Sox also played for one of baseball's biggest skinflints, Charlie Comiskey, who got their services at a rock-bottom cost thanks to the onerous reserve clause. As soon as one of the White Sox players, Chick Gandil, let it be known to gamblers that he wanted to throw the Series, the sharks moved in. Orchestrating the "Black Sox" fix was Arnold Rothstein.

Modern illegal gambling and racketeering begin with Arnold Rothstein. He was "the Man Uptown," "the Brain," "the Big Fellow." He started life as the son of a successful New York cotton merchant, an Orthodox Jew, but then chose a very different career path. Although he neither smoked nor drank, Rothstein had a passion for gambling that led him at an early age to learn the trade from such luminaries as Saratoga's Richard Canfield. By 1910, Rothstein owned his own casino in Manhattan, and he later became deeply involved in bootlegging, horse racing, sports betting, narcotics, loan-sharking, real estate, and the securities industry. He mingled with the upper crust who frequented his establishments and counted among his patrons journalists such as *New York World* editor Herbert Bayard Swope, Broadway star Fanny Brice, and many famous athletes, including New York Giants manager John McGraw, with whom Rothstein owned a pool hall. Rothstein also co-owned a racetrack with McGraw's boss, Giants owner Charles Stoneham, who got his start as a miner in California. McGraw, Joe Corbett's old teammate and one of the ablest managers in baseball, frequently gambled on games and was accused of conspiring with umpires to fix the 1912 pennant race in favor of the Giants. McGraw was never formally charged with any wrongdoing in the incident.

Rothstein's clout was obvious enough to have F. Scott Fitzgerald use him as a model for Meyer Wolfsheim, the gangster in *The Great Gatsby*, while sportswriter and compulsive gambler Damon Runyon was more direct, barely disguising Rothstein as "Armand Rosenthal." In the real world, two of Rothstein's disciples were young gangsters named Meyer Lansky and Charles "Lucky" Luciano, who learned from the master the benefits of bringing a corporate sensibility to criminal undertakings.

Bookmaking had grown up alongside horse racing in the nineteenth century; as sports betting increased, individual bookies brokered ever more sizable bets, which threatened to put them out of business if they were on the wrong side of the wagers. Rothstein came up with a solution that simultaneously limited the risk to individual bookies and expanded and coordinated the bookmaking network nationally. It was called the layoff system. Bookies made money by balancing their books—that is, by making sure they had equal amounts of betting on both teams in a baseball game so they could simply collect the "vigorish," or "vig," a 10 percent handling fee absorbed by the losing bettors. (The word "vigorish," from the Russian *vyigrysh*, "winnings," was first used by immigrants to describe the usurious interest rates loan sharks charged them.)

Ideally, the odds posted on a game would be balanced enough to attract equal amounts of betting on each team, essentially causing the bettors, rather than the bookie, to pay one another after the game. But oddsmaking was a subjective endeavor, and bookmakers could make a poor appraisal of a team's weakness or strength. Baseball, like all sports, could also be affected by random, unpredictable events, like player substitutions, errors, or great plays. Such situations could force the odds to be out of whack and expose bookies to backbreaking losses. Bookies would classify some games as "off the board" if they suspected a game was fixed or felt it was too difficult to handicap accurately. Other games might be "in the circle"—acceptable, but dangerous to set odds on and usually requiring betting limits. But both of those choices forced bookies to turn away potentially lucrative business from gamblers.

Rothstein convinced bookies in separate cities that they could overcome these problems by spreading the risk around, by hedging their bets. If a bookie in New York had too much money riding on the Yankees in a match-up with the White Sox, he could "lay off" the excess by placing it with a bookie in Chicago who had too much money wagered on the White Sox. Now both gentlemen had balanced their books and could accept more wagers. This made interstate communication and a national "line," or odds, on a game all the more important to bookies and to those who bankrolled them. The system was elegant for its time, spurred the growth of the still immature gambling industry, and produced tidy profits for the Man Uptown. The profits were even fatter if gangsters charged bookies lofty interest rates to borrow money, or if the outcome of a game could be fixed without the average bettor in the stands knowing about it.

"The majority of the human race are dubs and dumbbells," Rothstein once observed. "They have rotten judgment and no brains, and when you have learned how to do things and how to size people up and dope out methods for yourself they jump to the conclusion that you are crooked."

The extraordinary breadth of Rothstein's influence would not come to light until after he was murdered in 1928. Because he used intermediaries to bribe or attempt to bribe players in 1919, he was never brought to justice for his role in the "Black Sox" scandal. Among those used by Rothstein to dangle $80,000 in front of the eight White Sox who initially showed interest in throwing the Series was Abe Attell, a former boxing champion from San Francisco whose bouts had been promoted by Tex Rickard and whose career had ended amid accusations that he was throwing his fights. Once the Series began, Rothstein deployed a hitman to warn ace White Sox pitcher Lefty Williams of the consequences to him and his family if he failed to play miserably. The White Sox lost the World Series, and the fix was hushed up until the middle of the next baseball season. When an investigation was launched after the scandal broke, Rothstein was questioned before a grand jury. He claimed innocence, blamed Attell, and walked away unscathed. None of the players or gamblers involved in the scandal were sent to jail, but the league subsequently banned the eight White Sox from baseball for life. Fans began cheering "Play bail!" instead of "Play ball!" at the nation's baseball stadiums.

FROM THE BABE TO CHARLIE HUSTLE

In the decade that followed the Black Sox scandal, the stock market skyrocketed and then fell to earth. And baseball's reputation was restored as Babe Ruth burst onto the scene. Already a phenomenon when the Black Sox scandal occurred, Ruth dominated the game in the 1920s. His swagger and towering home runs helped make baseball one of the biggest draws in the country. An average of 9.3 million fans attended games each year in the 1920s, far more than the 5.6 million fans who watched baseball each year of the preceding decade and well above the average of 8.1 million a year during the 1930s. The only other sports drawing as much interest were boxing and horse racing.

Boxing in the 1920s had its own Babe Ruth in the person of Jack Dempsey, but Dempsey didn't have Ruth's athletic gifts, and he competed in a sport that never even tried to clean itself up. Baseball players and their game were often capable of rising above the seediness that surrounded them to offer heart-stopping theatrics. Boxing had rare moments of poignancy, but the entire sport rolled over to the gamblers who controlled it.

This is not to say that gambling didn't continue to hover over baseball. Baseball historian Bill James counts at least thirty-eight players who were involved in betting scandals between 1917 and 1927. Legends Ty Cobb and Tris Speaker, among the first players to be inducted into the Hall of Fame, were forced to briefly resign from baseball seven years after the Black Sox scandal. They were accused of having fixed a game in 1919 so Cobb's Tigers could claim third-place prize money that year. Fearful of another damaging scandal, American League president Ban Johnson tried to sweep the matter under the rug when it leaked out in 1926. Johnson made the stars quit, but then mentioned the incident to the baseball commissioner, Kenesaw Mountain Landis, who called for a probe. After hearings during which both players proclaimed their innocence, they were reinstated, but both left baseball after the following season. Other stars who were big gamblers but didn't try to fix games were handled with kid gloves. Rogers Hornsby, one of the greatest hitters and hardest players of all time, had bookies all over the country, and his heavy betting in 1927 drew Landis' attention. Hornsby, also a later Hall of Famer, pointed out to the commissioner that gambling was no worse than investing in the stock market. Landis let the matter slide, but Hornsby's career ended after he was fired from his job as Cardinals manager in 1937 because of his constant betting.

With racism locking African Americans out of white baseball, the Negro League blossomed briefly in the 1930s. All of the teams were owned or controlled by gamblers. Gus Greenlee, for one, parlayed a rich numbers business in Pennsylvania into ownership of the Pittsburgh Crawfords, one of the best baseball teams ever, black or white. Greenlee's expertise in liquor hijacking and gambling funded the careers of black baseball legends such as James "Cool Papa" Bell, Josh Gibson, and Satchel Paige. Greenlee's résumé wasn't unique among the black league's owners, because numbers was one of the few businesses lucrative enough to keep the African-American teams afloat during the Depression. So even a team such as the New York Black Yankees, ostensibly owned by dancer Bill "Bojangles" Robinson, was really controlled by a numbers kingpin, Eddy Semler.

Gambling clung to ballparks and locker rooms for the next six decades. "I associated with a lot of hoodlums in Cleveland myself," said Bill Veeck, Jr., the candid owner of three major league franchises. "I've always found the so-called hoodlums to be colorful people. And good customers of a ball club." Veeck had grown up around baseball. His father was president of the Chicago Cubs in 1919, when a grand jury investigation of charges that the team threw a three-game series to the Phillies led to the unveiling of the Black Sox scandal. Young Bill, as likable (and outlandish) a personality as any in baseball, got the money to buy his first team, the Indians, in 1946 from Sam Haas, a Cleveland attorney who represented the local Mob. The loan passed through several banks in an attempt to disguise its origins. Louis Jacobs, who introduced Veeck to Haas, dominated the food and beverage business at the nation's sports stadiums and was closely tied to organized crime. Veeck himself was never accused of being involved in any betting scams, but he welcomed professional gamblers into his ballparks as long as they kept the action under the table. Phillies owner Bill Cox, on the other hand, was expelled from baseball for betting on his team in 1943.

In the late 1940s, bookies freely roamed the Brooklyn Dodgers' clubhouse, where cards and craps were regularly played. The Dodgers' manager, Leo Durocher, a compulsive gambler and a consummate hustler, socialized with gangsters such as Bugsy Siegel throughout his career. He was suspended from baseball for a year in 1947 for a variety of murky allegations including associating with gamblers and bookies. As late as 1969, Durocher was managing the Chicago Cubs when they blew a commanding lead over the Mets late in the season and lost the pennant race. Speculation that Durocher bet against the Cubs and made managerial blunders to ensure their demise led to an investigation by the commissioner's office, but it didn't result in any charges.

Denny McLain, a gifted hurler who won the Cy Young Award twice while pitching for the Detroit Tigers, invested in a bookmaking operation during the 1967 season. "Ballplayers gamble," said McLain's wife, Sharyn, the daughter of Hall of Famer Lou Boudreau. "You go to the dog track, you see ballplayers. They play cards. What else do you do with all that free time?" In 1970, Sports Illustrated reported that Mob enforcer Tony Giacalone had dislocated two of McLain's toes in 1967 to persuade him to make good on a horse-racing bet placed at Denny's own bookie joint. McLain, while acknowledging his stake in the bookmaking business, came up with three different explanations for his injury, none of which included Giacalone beating him up. Whatever its cause, it prevented McLain from pitching from the middle of September until he reappeared on the mound in October—on the last day of the season. He lost the second game of a doubleheader, and the Tigers lost the pennant race by one game. Giacalone reportedly bet heavily against the Tigers in that game.

McLain was suspended in 1970, but never expelled from the game. He washed out of baseball two years later, when he was just twenty-eight years old, and wound up making a living gambling on golf courses until he landed in jail for racketeering and cocaine possession in 1985. He sold his Cy Young trophies so he could pay a lawyer.

And on it went. Seventy years after the Black Sox scandal, Pete Rose was kicked out of baseball for betting on games. The player who had shattered Ty Cobb's record for most career hits and seemed destined for the Hall of Fame reportedly bet hundreds of thousands of dollars a year on his own team. Rose apparently never wagered against the Reds, but his betting during his tenure as their manager tipped off bookies to what he thought of the team's prospects, and especially those of the pitcher he was fielding, on any given day. Charlie Hustle was ultimately convicted of tax fraud. (He served a short prison sentence.) During his trial, he admitted that to feed his gambling habit he had sold the bat he used to break Cobb's record. The league had investigated Rose's betting as early as 1970, but took no action until 1989. Philadelphia Phillies president Bill Giles, who was once warned by the league to stop his own gambling, was one of Rose's former bosses. When asked by Rose's biographer Michael Sokolove why he never turned Rose in for a gambling problem everyone knew had existed for years, Giles reduced the game's economics to this blunt distillation: "Well, he was our bread and butter. He was putting fannies in the seats."

Kevin Hallinan, professional baseball's security director since 1986, investigated Rose and said he found no evidence that Rose tried to throw games. "On my watch, to my knowledge, there has not been a player compromised," Hallinan said in 1996. "Bookies will wrap these athletes up so quickly. They record phone calls of athletes placing a bet and then use that to their full advantage to compromise the athlete."

While the volume of illegal betting on baseball games by the 1960s was most likely much greater than on any other sport, including boxing or horse racing, no evidence has emerged to indicate that any pennant playoffs or World Series games were fixed after 1919. If and when the fixes were in, it apparently happened during the thousands of regular-season games. Boxing was a very different matter.

THE FRIDAY NIGHT FIXES

Among the suspects in Arnold Rothstein's 1928 murder was Nate Raymond, a West Coast gambler and baseball fixer who had visited Rothstein the evening he was shot. When Raymond was married on an airplane over Mexico, one of two witnesses he invited to travel with him was Jack Dempsey. Dempsey, one of the elite millionaire-athletes of the 1920s, was the Mob's boy.

After Dempsey won the heavyweight crown in Toledo in 1919, Tex Rickard decided to ride his star right into New York. Rickard selected challengers who posed no real threat to Dempsey, and, with a few drinks and a few dollars dumped on obliging newspaper reporters, used the media to inflate his fighter's reputation. In 1921, he staged a bout between Dempsey and French boxer Georges Carpentier in New Jersey, where boxing was still illegal. Dempsey hammered his much smaller opponent in front of 80,000 people. The fight got loads of press and took in $1.8 million from attendance alone, the first time a boxing "gate" had passed $1 million. (Before this fight, the biggest gate had been $271,000 for the Johnson-Jeffries bout, more than a decade earlier.) However questionable his opponents and his abilities, Dempsey, spun by Rickard and Kearns' publicity machine, was a phenomenon. Boxing was making real money now; the stage was set for its return to New York, where the sport had been legalized in 1921.

No major prizefights were fought there, however, until Dempsey beat up Luis Firpo in the confines of Charles Stoneham's Polo Grounds in 1923. Dempsey then spent the next three years refusing to fight Harry Wills, a talented black heavyweight, before losing to Gene Tunney twice, in 1926 and 1927. The first fight with Tunney, in Philadelphia, attracted 121,000, still the largest live audience ever for a boxing match. Not quite as many people attended the follow-up fight in Chicago, but the gate was much bigger, topping $2.6 million. Seated at ringside for the Chicago fight were various Vanderbilts and Astors, Charlie Chaplin, and, in the company of Damon Runyon, Al Capone.

Capone's presence underscored the sway organized crime held in the boxing world. Jack McGurn and other Capone gunmen were former boxers, and Capone's gang controlled boxing in Chicago, deciding who fought whom and when to stage a "barney"—their term for a fixed fight. Capone had backed Dempsey for years and, as Dempsey later recalled, "the word was out that [Capone] had enough dough and influence spread around to make sure I would win" the Tunney rematch. Rumors circulated that Capone had tried to bribe the fight's officials, so the referee was changed just before the bout began. Dempsey lost, after Tunney survived the famous "Long Count." After retiring, he went to work for the Capone gang, helping them to fix fights. Later still, Dempsey became a front man for a Miami casino owned by Meyer Lansky.

Not satisfied with having the best meal ticket in boxing, Tex Rickard also decided to build the best forums in the sport. He decided the first would be in New York, and he saw it as the linchpin in a nationwide chain of boxing arenas stretching back to San Francisco.

The location Rickard set his sights on was originally a large railroad warehouse built in 1836 in a lower Manhattan park near Madison Square and later used by P. T. Barnum for circus shows. William Vanderbilt had bought the building in the late 1870s, naming it Madison Square Garden. Investors razed the warehouse and built Manhattan's most fashionable sports center, topped by a thirty-two-story tower, on the site in 1887. But the enterprise lost money until Rickard came along. He leased the facility twice before the owner knocked it down in 1924. Rickard then built a new arena uptown, on Eighth Avenue between Forty-ninth and Fiftieth Streets. Like its predecessor, it was called Madison Square Garden. It had three levels, could seat 18,500 people, and staged its first prizefight in 1925. But state boxing regulators wouldn't let Rickard book the first Dempsey-Tunney match in New York because Dempsey had been ducking Wills. When Rickard died a few years later, no heavyweight championships had been fought in the arena. But the Garden, which would later be rebuilt and relocated one more time, to Thirty-third Street and Eighth Avenue, was destined to become the Mecca of Mayhem, the Palace of Pugilism, the center of boxing in the country. As such, it was also organized crime's little breadbasket.

There is no way of gauging how much money the Mob earned from fixed fights. For gamblers, however, Mob involvement meant that the outcome of any bet on a fight had more to do with the whims of the ring's puppeteers than with the abilities of the boxers. Bootlegger Owney Madden controlled New York boxing after Dempsey and Rickard passed from the scene, and fixed fights were fought by circus acts such as Primo Carnera, who was controlled by Madden. Max Baer and Jim Braddock's 1935 heavyweight title bout was believed to have been fixed. Attendance at fights fell off in the 1930s, until Joe Louis started punching his way to the top in 1935 as the first black fighter accepted by the boxing establishment. Although Louis also was backed by mobsters, his abilities were indisputable, and attendance shot up; 70,000 people watched him beat Max Schmeling at the Garden in 1938, and the gate was more than $1 million. Friday Night Fights became a hit at the Garden, big money was back, and the Mob tightened its grip on the sport even further.

From the mid-1940s until 1964, boxing was controlled by one man, known to most people in the sport as Mr. Gray. His real name was Frankie Carbo. A "made" member of the Mob, formerly a murderer in the employ of Bugsy Siegel, and a bookie, Carbo gave orders to managers and, through them, to their fighters. He also controlled the head of Madison Square Garden, Mike Jacobs, and the head of the International Boxing Club, Jim Norris, who had made a fortune speculating in grain on the Chicago Board of Trade. Jake LaMotta, Rocky Graziano, and

Sugar Ray Robinson were all caught in Carbo's web, either directly or indirectly. Carbo, working with his enforcer, Blinky Palermo, staged some memorable gambling coups. And they bumbled others. When Billy Fox and Jake LaMotta were on the card at the Garden in 1947, Carbo ordered LaMotta to take a dive. As word of the fix leaked out, the odds on the day of the fight had Fox a 2–1 favorite, then 3–1, then 4–1, until finally bookies took it off the board. LaMotta, dragging his heels and his fists, lost the fight in the fourth round. While everyone knew a fix was in, it would be more than a decade before Carbo's role came to light.

Carbo also had his hooks into Sonny Liston, who cracked heads to break up labor strikes as a Mob goon when he wasn't boxing. When Liston defended his heavyweight title against a young fighter named Cassius Clay in 1964, the odds favoring Liston ranged from 7–1 to 10–1. When the bell for the seventh round rang, Liston didn't get up off his stool. He wasn't knocked out, mind you; he just didn't get off his stool. Money gambled on Clay won big. When the two fighters met in a rematch a year later, Clay had become Muhammad Ali, and Liston mysteriously crumpled in the first round from what appeared to be a glancing blow. A fix was suspected in both fights, although it was never proven in either case. In any event, Ali would have risen to the top of the boxing world without fixes. Although Chris Dundee, brother of Ali's manager, Angelo Dundee, worked closely with Carbo, the Mob never stuffed Ali into its pocket, and Ali subsequently made the boxing world his own.

Ali's gifts would keep prizefighting in the public eye, but by the 1960s boxing and baseball were already being eclipsed in the hearts of sports fans and the bankrolls of gamblers. Football and basketball now began to dominate sports and sports gambling. Two things were responsible for the change: television and the invention of the point spread.

ENTER THE POINT SPREAD

Before football, and later basketball, won over sports fans, television's first meal ticket was boxing. In 1952, televised boxing reached an average of 5 million households a night, and three years later 8.5 million households were tuned in. But once the novelty of the medium wore off and other programming became available, boxing's ratings plunged. Whereas 31 percent of the television audience watched boxing in 1952, only 11 percent was watching by 1959. In time, the epicenter of boxing moved away from Madison Square Garden and toward the Las Vegas casinos. By the 1980s and 1990s, the price of hiring world-class fighters to pound one another's brains into jelly had become too high for any arena to make money on the bouts. But some casinos felt they didn't need to: high rollers loved to fly into town for big fights, allowing a few of Las Vegas' (and to a lesser extent Atlantic City's) largest casinos to absorb a losing boxing gate because the action at the gambling tables more than made up for the loss. Using boxing as a lure for high rollers, even when the math sometimes didn't add up, became so attractive to some casinos that they went out of their way to secure the allegiance of modern boxing's answer to Tex Rickard, a ubiquitous huckster named Don King.

In early 1995, according to Securities & Exchange Commission filings, Las Vegas' MGM Grand gave Don King Productions an interest free $15 million loan to buy more than 618,000 shares of the casino's stock. King, who manages heavyweight Mike Tyson, agreed to provide the casino with six "Tyson events" before September 1997, one of which had to be a title fight. King was allowed to repay the loan out of gate receipts for the fights, and the MGM Grand guaranteed him that the value of his shares wouldn't fall below $30 million by the time the deal concluded, regardless of the stock's market price.

But despite King's ministrations, major boxing matches today only exist as handmaidens to the casino business. Football and basketball, on the other hand, are industries unto themselves. And, like the progress of boxing and baseball, the growth of football and basketball has been intimately tied up with gambling and gamblers.

Before television intervened, football and basketball were more popular as college sports than as professional sports. Football descended from English rugby; Princeton and Rutgers played the first college game in 1869, though how many of the players were actually students, or academically eligible, is debatable. The game was played more like a mixture of rugby and soccer than like what we know as football until Yale coach Walter Camp developed rules in the 1880s and 1890s that came to define the modern sport.

As with all sports, gamblers swarmed around the playing fields as football's popularity spread to other campuses. Although San Francisco was still a young city in 1892, Stanford University and the University of California at Berkeley then began an annual tradition known locally as the Big Game. Originally played on the Haight Street ballfield, the game drew quite a crowd. "It had long been talked of and eagerly looked forward to, and never has there been aroused such enthusiasm as that manifested in both institutions when the eventful day dawned," *The San Francisco Chronicle* reported in 1892.

Football games were often bloody mud fights, and for many fans that was part of the attraction. Academically ineligible players were hired by colleges to fill out rosters, and crippling injuries and deaths were common, brought on by such formations as the flying wedge, in which blockers would lock arms to mow down tacklers. In 1904, several college presidents wanted to banish football because of problems with cheating and violence, but Theodore Roosevelt convened a White House summit to discuss reforming the game rather than eliminating it. The following year, after eighteen players were killed playing football, several schools formed a body that later became the National Collegiate Athletic Association, or NCAA, to monitor the sport.

Some weren't convinced anything would change. "It is childish to suppose that the athletic authorities who have permitted football to become such a brutal, cheating, demoralizing game could be trusted to reform it," Harvard president Charles Eliot said at the time.

Nonetheless, college football provided all of the sport's early heroes, some of whom were plucked out of school early to play for the small professional teams struggling to gain a foothold. College athletes had been paid to join professional teams as "ringers" for one or two games as early as 1892, but the only pro teams that were able to regularly draw fans were those in towns that had a fierce rivalry with another community. So it was that tough mining and mill towns in Ohio and Pennsylvania gave birth to many of the first pro teams. In Ohio, the Canton Bulldogs and Massillon Tigers played each other in frenzied contests for almost two decades beginning in 1903. Coaches, players, and fans all bet heavily on the games, and in 1906, the same year college football first allowed the forward pass, Canton's coach was accused of throwing a game. Canton locals, incensed over the bets they lost, rioted and then banned football until 1911.

After Olympic hero Jim Thorpe started playing for the Bulldogs in 1915, the team enjoyed lots of attention—enough, by 1920, to convince about a dozen men to convene in an automobile showroom in Canton and found the American Professional Football Association. It was soon renamed the National Football League; each charter member ponied up $100 to join. Thorpe was the league's first star, followed by Red Grange for a couple of years in the 1920s, but football remained a ragtag affair that many disdained because it was seen as a playground for gamblers—as, in fact, it was.

As the league developed in the 1920s, entrepreneurs like Chicago Bears owner George Halas, who received some financial backing from Capone crony and Hawthorne Race Track owner Charlie Bidwill, proved that large crowds would come to see players like Grange. But it was apparent that as long as teams were mainly located in small midwestern towns, pro football would never flourish. High school and college football were much more popular, while many of the early pro teams teetered on the edge of bankruptcy. But some of the owners were able to tap other sources of income.

Under the direction of league president Joe Carr, the NFL started to corral owners in major cities. Its first big catch was Tim Mara in New York. Carr had initially offered a place in the league to a New York boxing promoter named Billy Gibson, who declined and referred him to Mara. Mara, who ran a large, and legal, bookmaking franchise at local racetracks, jumped at the opportunity and bought the New York Giants football team for $500 in gambling winnings in 1925. "It was said that before the autumn of 1925 Mr. Mara had never seen a football game," *The New York Times* observed in Mara's 1959 obituary. "But the promoters of the National League of Professional Football Clubs knew that bookmakers were of a type extremely susceptible to new forms of investment."

In 1933, a close friend of Mara's named Art Rooney bought the Pittsburgh Pirates (later the Steelers) with money he had earned as a bookie. A fixture in Pittsburgh gambling circles, Rooney regularly used his gambling winnings, including what he described as a two-day racetrack haul of $250,000, to keep his sagging football team afloat. Rooney, a former boxer, spoke openly about placing his bets through Frank Erickson. Erickson, who headed the Mob's East Coast bookmaking syndicate, was notorious for fixing horse races.

Other early owners with gambling ties were the Chicago Cardinals' Bidwill and the Cleveland Browns' Mickey McBride. Later generations of owners would be cut from similar cloth. Oil heir Clint Murchison, Jr., founder of the Dallas Cowboys, was an avid gambler; his family co-owned Del Mar Race Track near San Diego. Some of the Murchisons' real estate holdings were financed with Teamsters pension funds, and the family had other alleged ties to organized crime. Carroll Rosenbloom, a heavy gambler who wagered in the company of Meyer Lansky associate Louis Chesler and had a stake in a Havana casino, owned the Baltimore Colts and later the Los Angeles Rams.

The San Francisco 49ers were originally part of a West Coast expansion league and were owned by Tony Morabito, a Bay Area businessman with lumber and trucking interests. When the Morabito family sold the 49ers in 1977, the buyers were Edward DeBartolo, Sr., and his son. DeBartolo made his money building shopping malls and owned racetracks in the Midwest and Louisiana. Throughout his life, the senior DeBartolo, an avid gambler and frequent visitor to Las Vegas, was dogged by allegations of organized-crime ties, which he and his family repeatedly denied.

The man who brought the Morabitos and the DeBartolos together was pro football's perennial badboy, Al Davis. Davis, owner of the Oakland (later Los Angeles) Raiders, had come up through football's ranks as a scout and coach and at one time was a partner with Stardust Casino owner Allen Glick in real estate developments that were funded with Teamsters money. At the time, the Stardust was being looted by organized crime, and it housed the leading sports bookmaking operation in Las Vegas. Davis was never charged with any wrongdoing involving the Stardust.

All of these men, from Halas through Davis, were, in the gentle parlance of earlier times, "sportsmen." And without them football would have foundered, for they understood exactly what made the sport tick. Many of them were willing to risk their money in a still-unproven business or on lackluster teams. Like those who built Las Vegas' casinos, they understood the magnetic power of spectacle, especially if the spectacle involved competition, speed, and operatic, unvarnished violence. Most of all, they knew that if the show was good enough, gamblers would throw their money at it.

The problem with getting people to bet on football in the sport's early days was that the games were so lopsided that few bookies cared to risk taking wagers on them. Enter the point spread.

Bookies and sportswriters argue endlessly about the origins of the point spread, agreeing only that it wasn't widely used until after World War II. Charles McNeil, a University of Chicago mathematician who worked as a stock market analyst in the morning and a sports gambler in the afternoon, is usually credited with inventing the point spread in the 1930s. But two bookies prominent from the 1930s to the 1950s, Ed Curd of Lexington, Kentucky, and Bill Hecht of Minnesota, are also cited as the authors of the point spread. Whoever the inventor, once the point spread was adopted it expanded the gambling universe exponentially. While Rothstein's layoff system had helped bookies balance their books, it did nothing to reduce their exposure to games that were poorly handicapped. If the Bears were expected to be easy winners over the Browns, bookies had to set odds that would draw betting on both teams in a game people might otherwise ignore. But if odds of 7–1 against the Browns were too generous, a Browns victory could crush a bookie. If the odds on the Bears were too restrictive, nobody would bet on them. And setting odds was so subjective that savvy gamblers could easily exploit weak bookies and handicappers.

The point spread did away with much of the subjectivity and risk that made a bookie's existence so tenuous. If, instead of setting odds, handicappers gave a poor football team imaginary points and added those points to the underdog's score, the bet might just become attractive. Was the underdog good enough to win with the points tossed in? Was the favorite so good that it could "make the spread"—that is, run up a score large enough to win not only on the field but in the gambling world as well? Gamblers loved trying to answer both of those questions. For bookies, the beauty of the point spread was that it provided a sliding scale, which could be adjusted so that any game would draw wagers, and thus made every contest interesting to fans. Gamblers wagered $11 to win $10 (or $110 to win $100, or $1,100 to win $1,000, and so on), with the extra 10 percent representing the bookies' vig. If gamblers didn't want to take the Browns plus 19 points, bookies could tweak the spread to 19½, 20, or 20½ points, whatever it took to get people to bet on the Browns. The first "line" on the game was based on a handicapper's instincts and judgment, but all adjustments after that were responses to how gamblers perceived each team's chances. The line wasn't an attempt to forecast a final score. It represented handicappers' attempts to split the betting evenly on both teams so that the bookies' risk was minimized.

RIGGING ROUNDBALL

Basketball, also often played by unevenly matched teams, was another sport that blossomed because of the point spread. The sport had been concocted in 1891 in Springfield, Massachusetts, by Dr. James Naismith as a winter regimen for local football players. Seven years later a short-lived professional league was formed, but until the late 1960s, the pros took a backseat to the college game. Although the University of Kentucky started a basketball program in 1903, it wasn't until the 1930s that the popularity of college basketball took off. The launchpad was Madison Square Garden.

The Garden was in a slump in the 1930s because of the Depression and a lack of interest in the steady diet of fixed fights being offered by boxing's whiz kids. Ned Irish, a New York sportswriter and publicist, took note of the enthusiastic crowd at a college basketball game in a small Manhattan gymnasium and decided that, if the sport was properly promoted, it might be able to fill the Garden's empty seats. In 1934, Irish put on the first of what became a string of hugely successful basketball doubleheaders, pitting local teams St. John's and NYU against Westminster and Notre Dame. Among the great teams of the era that later traveled to the Garden to play the New York teams were Kentucky and Stanford. A Stanford player, Angelo "Hank" Luisetti, introduced the one-handed set shot in 1936, while Kentucky's extraordinary players, led by legendary coach Adolph Rupp, would give basketball something entirely different: one of its first major gambling scandals.

While gambling undoubtedly always was a part of the mix at basketball games, not until basketball's commercial appeal was apparent did the wiseguys try to move in on the sport. There was no better place for fixers to work their magic than the Garden, since it was already familiar turf to bettors who wagered on fights there. Much like baseball, basketball had generated plenty of interest on its own merits, but gambling clearly focused extra attention on the games. In 1938, Irish held the first National Invitational Tournament, with six teams, at the Garden. A year later the National Collegiate Athletic Association began offering a college championship sponsored by coaches bridling under Irish's heavy hand. City College of New York was the only team ever to win the NIT and NCAA championships in the same season, and it dominated college basketball in the late 1940s. Indeed, City College was so adept that it could win championships even while selling out to gamblers.

In 1951, seven City College players fessed up to having "shaved" points in games during the previous two seasons. Shaving was entirely a point-spread phenomenon. Point spreads allowed players to win a game but "shave" their margin of victory close enough so that they didn't beat the spread, thus allowing gamblers to cash in their bets. An investigation into shaving by Manhattan College players had uncovered the City College scam, and the City College investigation led in turn to the revelation of shaving by Long Island University players. So well connected was the network of gamblers behind the shaving scandals that their uncovering led to the ouster of dozens of police officers and the resignation of New York's mayor, Bill O'Dwyer. When the dust had settled, thirty-three players from seven colleges, including the University of Kentucky, had been implicated. Investigators claimed that eighty-six basketball games had been fixed between 1947 and 1950, and Adolf Rupp himself admitted to a relationship with bookie Ed Curd.

NCAA teams refused to continue playing at the Garden because of the lock gamblers had on the arena, and the blow left college basketball suspect for decades. "The gambling craze has swept the country with the avariciousness of a prairie fire," hyperventilated *The New York Times* in the wake of the shaving scandal. "The flames are out of control. Nothing can extinguish them now. And the faggot that fed the blaze is the satanic gimmick of the point spread. It made gambling irresistible to those hitherto uninterested in a wager."

Shaving would never fully disappear as an issue in college basketball. In 1961, Jack Molinas, who played for Columbia University during the 1951 scandal before being kicked out of professional basketball for gambling, orchestrated a shaving scheme that snared players at several colleges. In 1981, Rick Kuhn of Boston College admitted taking a $15,000 bribe to shave points in six games three years earlier. Four years later, a Tulane basketball player shaved points for cocaine. When Richard Perry, a fixer convicted for his role in the Kuhn affair, resurfaced in the company of members of the University of Nevada at Las Vegas' basketball team, the ensuing publicity led to the resignation of UNLV's head coach, Jerry Tarkanian, in 1992. In 1997, *Fresno Bee* reporters Stevan Rosenlind, Andy Boogard, and Tom Kertscher broke the news that law enforcement officials were investigating allegations that a player on Tarkanian's new team in California, Fresno State, was shaving points, allegations that the player and Tarkanian denied. The Fresno State investigation was matched by an ongoing FBI probe into possible point shaving in two 1994 basketball games involving Arizona State.

At about the same time that the early shaving scandals were undermining the integrity of college basketball, professional football also started to have its share of gambling problems. Redskins quarterback Sammy Baugh came under surveillance for allegedly associating with bookmakers in 1943, and in tape recordings unearthed by reporter Dan Moldea almost fifty years later was heard discussing spreads and bookies with his teammates at the time. On the morning of the 1946 NFL championship, fixer Alvin Parris tried to bribe New York Giants players Frank Filchock and Merle Hapes to shave points in their game against the Bears. Both players refused the money but were suspended for failing to report that they had been approached. Filchock later returned as head coach of the Denver Broncos. In 1963, the Detroit Lions' Alex Karras and Green Bay Packers star Paul Hornung were suspended for betting on their own teams. Shortly after the Jets won the 1969 Super Bowl, their quarterback Joe Namath was forced to sell his stake in a New York nightclub, Bachelors III, that was frequented by bookies and gamblers with ties to organized crime. According to bookies and gamblers in Las Vegas, several games involving the Kansas City Chiefs in the late 1960s were taken off the boards because of concerns that the Chiefs were shaving points.

Art Schlicter, a gifted Colts quarterback and a compulsive gambler, was suspended by the NFL in 1983 for gambling. Schlicter, like baseball's Denny McLain and Pete Rose, had a severe problem that wasn't addressed by the league until it had spun out of control. "It was a tragic situation that wasn't known to the NFL until after it surfaced with the FBI," says Jay Moyer, who monitored gambling issues for the NFL between 1972 and 1996 and now is a consultant to the league. "Schlicter was never really cured. We must have had half a dozen encounters with him."

Professional basketball had far fewer gambling scandals than the college game, but was also far less popular until the late 1970s, so its problems didn't draw as much scrutiny. A professional league had briefly appeared in 1937, only to be supplanted when stadium owners, including Ned Irish, formed the Basketball Association of America in 1946. Four years later, it was renamed the National Basketball Association. The only reason for the league's existence was the desperation of stadium owners anxious to fill their playbills with anything they could get their hands on, from ice skating to hockey to basketball. But professional basketball was a slow game hampered by stalling defenses and racial segregation. It didn't deliver the action that fans or gamblers wanted. The instruments of professional basketball's deliverance would be racial integration and television.

Television had already raised football to commercial heights that would have stunned most of that sport's early founders. The television era in sports began during the 1958 NFL championship, when the Colts squeezed by the Giants in overtime on a burst into the end zone by Alan Ameche. That game was broadcast to millions of fans on national television, and it was a sensation. Although the 1947 baseball World Series had also been broadcast to a sizable audience, baseball proved too slow and too cerebral to compete on television with the more kinetic pleasures of the gridiron. And in 1947 there were only about 1 million television receivers in use. By 1958 there were almost 50 million, and the rollicking response to the NFL championship that year marked the beginning of football's march past baseball for the allegiance of fans and gamblers. The march would be sustained by the stewardship of a San Francisco public relations executive named Pete Rozelle. More than anyone else in sports at the time, Rozelle, football's commissioner from 1960 to 1989, understood the commercial power of television. By 1962, he had convinced CBS to cough up $4.65 million for broadcasting rights, and by 1970 he had introduced Monday Night Football on ABC.

Basketball grew fitfully until 1979, when Indiana State's Larry Bird and Michigan State's "Magic" Johnson squared off in the most watched NCAA championship to date. ESPN, an all-sports cable television network, debuted that year and expanded on the strength of its college basketball coverage. ESPN, offering nonstop, detailed sports coverage that didn't require fans to leave their couches to find a game, was a gambler's dream come true. Wagering on college basketball boomed, and the NCAA tournament would ultimately rank just behind the Super Bowl in terms of dollars wagered on a sports event. When Johnson and Bird joined the NBA in the 1980s, they revived the slumbering professional league and paved a runway for Michael Jordan's eventual ascent to the jet stream. All of these athletes would be packaged and promoted by NBA commissioner David Stern, who followed Rozelle's playbook and unleashed basketball's commercial potential on the airwaves.

The media, scooping up the lucrative bounty spilling from the corporate sports machine, continued to help stoke the gambling fever. By the mid-1980s, *USA Today* was publishing a daily crush of sports statistics that was a feast for gamblers. And point spreads entered the popular lexicon courtesy of the NFL, CBS, and a chubby Las Vegas bookie named Demetrios Synodinos, better known as Jimmy the Greek. The Greek, who was pardoned by President Gerald Ford in 1974 for a gambling conviction, offered point spreads each Sunday on CBS' pregame show from 1976 to 1988 in a tacit acknowledgment by the NFL and CBS of exactly why their core audience was watching. It wasn't until 1990, after Pete Rozelle had already stepped down as commissioner, that the NFL officially banned television chatter about point spreads.

"Pete, as strong as he felt about gambling and point spread talk, felt that there wasn't a lot he could do about it. Eventually the league and TV saw eye-to-eye and they put an end to it," says the NFL's Moyer of his late boss. "Gambling is the biggest single danger pro sports face. It goes to the integrity of the game."

KIDS AND SPORTS GAMBLING

While some of the gambling banter on TV only supported innocent and harmless adult wagering such as office pools and fantasy sports leagues, it was also clear that young television viewers were getting the message. Gambling had been part of children's relationship to sports long before television came along, but TV, laden with game shows and programming that glamorized instant gratification, wove the bond ever tighter.

Howard Shaffer, a clinical psychologist at Harvard University Medical School and a leading authority on gambling addiction, says that sports betting is the leading form of gambling among children in grades seven through twelve. Shaffer estimates that 14 percent to 20 percent of children in that age group experience psychological or social problems related to their gambling, with sports betting and card playing acting as "gateways" to other forms of gambling and to substance abuse.

Other researchers of adolescent gambling have drawn similar conclusions. "Between 4 percent and 8 percent of adolescents across North America have a very serious gambling problem," says Jeffrey Derevensky, a professor of child psychology at McGill University in Montreal. "The reason problem gambling has gone on undetected among kids is because they don't have houses, wives, or savings to lose. But they lose their friends, do poorly in school, and become preoccupied with one thing: gambling.

"We've had teenagers tell us that they have images of roulette wheels flashing in their heads at night or they dream about the click-click-click sound of the roulette wheel. They see money as something you gamble with, not something you get from working.

"Parent awareness of this problem is extremely low. You wouldn't find the same low level of awareness about drugs and alcohol, which must be because gambling is seen as more acceptable. Where do most kids learn to gamble, anyway? From their parents."

But even when parents aren't leading the way, society offers kids plenty of other opportunities to pick up the gambling bug. Sega International, which makes popular children's video games such as Sonic the Hedgehog, has a U.S. subsidiary that manufactures slot machines. That subsidiary, Sega Gaming Technology, also provides "virtual reality" computerized gambling units to casinos.

The market for sports trading cards has also been accused of fostering gambling among children. Once an innocent hobby, sports card collecting became more serious in the early 1990s with the introduction of rare "insert cards" of famous athletes. Competition for the prized cards turned the sports card market into a floating bazaar. Adolescent collectors now carry voluminous price guides and studiously track the odds (printed on card packages) of finding rare inserts. As reported by *The Wall Street Journal*'s Stefan Fatsis, lawsuits filed against card companies in 1996 allege that trading sports cards amounts to illegal gambling because it involves payment, chance, and a prize. For their part, the card companies scoff at the suits, contending that insert cards aren't prizes because they have "no guaranteed resale value."

A little further up the ladder, the stakes in sports gambling among high school students were getting more serious. In 1992, a San Francisco high school student was arrested for running a bookmaking operation that accepted $30,000 worth of bets a week on football and basketball games from dozens of students at three local high schools. Students who had run up losses totaling thousands of dollars had become too scared to attend classes. Three years later, across the country in Nutley, New Jersey, two teenagers were arrested as part of a high school betting ring that involved more than two dozen student gamblers, raked in $7,500 per week, was tied to organized crime, and led the two teenagers to briefly kidnap one student who fell behind on a $500 debt he owed them.

Sports betting among college students was even more deeply entrenched. By the 1990s, bookies on college campuses were as ubiquitous as the parlay cards they distributed. Much of the college betting was casual and for low stakes. According to a 1991 University of Illinois study of more than 1,700 students at six colleges, 85 percent of the students surveyed had gambled, but most had wagered less than $100. Sports betting was popular, although not nearly as popular as slot machines and other casino games. Of greater concern than the size of the wagers was their impact on the students. The survey revealed that 20.5 percent of the students surveyed said they were compulsive or problem gamblers.

Perhaps the most vulnerable segment of the student population was college athletes. In 1996, another betting scandal erupted at Boston College, where thirteen members of the school's football team were charged with gambling on their team's games. The local district attorney alleged that two of the football players had bet against their own team and that bookies involved in the scandal had ties to organized crime. As the investigation of the betting widened, eight student-bookies were arrested, and it was revealed that one student had been hospitalized earlier in the year after a New York bookie beat him with a two-by-four for not paying a debt promptly.

Of course, no one could blame the students for being a little confused about the lessons they were learning. Like Claude Rains in *Casablanca*, the Boston newspapers were shocked, *shocked* to discover gambling going on at Boston College, even though the papers themselves have always carried point spreads and betting advice from their writers. The gambling franchise was something few newspapers were willing to give up. When the NCAA threatened in 1997 to revoke press credentials for *USA Today* and other newspapers that carried ads for "tout services" offering (usually poor) sports betting advice, the papers slapped back by invoking the First Amendment.

"It is our prerogative what we want to run in the newspaper, not the NCAA's," said *USA Today*'s editor, David Mazzarella, adding that the paper has no intention of stopping ads for tout services. "It puts us in a judgmental position about what people do with their time and money, and that's a position I'd rather not be in. You're not going to stop people from gambling simply by not having information and advertising about it."

The NCAA backed down from its threat in 1997, just as it had two years earlier when it tried to take a similar stand against papers that carried point spreads. But the association had some cause for concern. A study of 648 college athletes conducted by the University of Cincinnati for the NCAA in 1995 indicated that 25 percent of the players gambled, with about 4 percent betting on games in which they played. Moreover, three of the athletes surveyed said they had accepted bribes from gamblers to play badly in a game.

payoffs; and "banks" such as Mission Jewelry were the clearinghouses for all of the action, bundling sums as large as $500,000 at a time and handing them off to Information Unlimited's "couriers," who transported the loot between the United States and the Dominican Republic. Sacco's operation also helped scores of smaller bookies in several U.S. cities lay off bets. Information Unlimited, according to law enforcement officials, also had ties to organized-crime families on the East Coast, who picked off about two-thirds of the profits. But a wiretap planted by federal agents at Mission Jewelry brought the whole enterprise crashing down, and Sacco pleaded guilty to illegal bookmaking charges in 1994.

A few miles from the Mission District, Chinatown remains a centerpiece of Asian-American gambling, its tongs still the dominant participants in gambling operations found in Chinese neighborhoods. Asian Americans' propensity to gamble has fueled the rapid growth of California's legal card clubs, some of which have been fingered by federal authorities as fronts for Asian organized crime. In less formal settings, such as basements, restaurants, and ceremonial halls run by tongs, friendly and high-stakes games of mah-jongg and pai gow still flourish, particularly on weekends and during spring and autumn celebrations. As it does in other communities, gambling occasionally ruins individuals and tears Chinese families apart, but that does little to diminish its popularity among the Chinese. Indeed, modern tongs have added sports betting to more traditional Chinese gambling fare, and Chinese bookmaking has expanded beyond Chinatown into other San Francisco neighborhoods such as the Richmond. And a few blocks from Chinatown, on streets where the Barbary Coast's casinos once thrived, San Francisco's Financial District now stands. Riches from a new gold rush kicked off by technology companies in nearby Silicon Valley have helped make the Financial District one of the most active outposts of a casino that throws opens its doors early every business day: the stock market.

The Veteran—III

I've been a gambler all my life, really. I love to take chances. My husband is not a gambler. He doesn't like to take chances. Actually, money means nothing to him. That's probably because I take care of the money. But he hasn't a care in the world about money. . . . And so he's not interested in gambling. And I can never figure out why.

He was in the Navy, too. In fact, he was in seven years before the war, and he was aboard ship almost all that time. . . . I always had the feeling that he gambled so much and won a lot, but at one point he must have lost a lot, and he probably said, "I'll never gamble."

He's gone to Atlantic City a couple of times with me. Because of different circumstances, he had to go down. . . . So we go into Harrah's and I went right to the roulette table. I said to my husband, "What're you gonna do?" "Oh, just stand around and watch people." And I said, "Here's fifty dollars, play these machines here."

And I went over to the table and I lost and I came back, because I thought he'd be bored. My brother [Frank] and him are both standing there, and I said, "What'd you do? Lose the fifty?" And he said, "No." And Frank said, "Don't tell her." He won two jackpots for $500 on a $10 roll of quarters. So then I thought, "We'll be going to Atlantic City." He put it in his pocket. It was maybe the end of September. He used it for his Christmas money.

And he never went back to Atlantic City after that. I'd say, "You want to go to Atlantic City?" "Uh-uh, you go, Paul." So that's how I started going on the bus.

I do not like gambling for young people. Because we're at the point in life if we lose $200, we still have a lot to lose if we go crazy with it, but there's no way we're gonna be out on the street. But young people, when you stop to think, yes, it's a moral issue. Because you can get hooked on gambling, and for young people who have young children and a home and mortgages and the car and tuition . . . I would hate to see my daughters and my granddaughters spend time in a casino when they have so much ahead. Or even my unmarried granddaughter. Let's face it: there's too much for young people to think of.

You know what gambling's really about? There's no guarantee that you're going to win. For people our age—you know, sixty-four, and seventy-five, eighty-five—what have they got to lose? Not too much. They may as well go down and look at some of these people and say, "Thank God," that they're able to get out of the house with their crutches, and their wheelchairs.

I read somewhere that the casinos are using some kind of scented oxygen to get people to play. And I think I've smelled that. This one night I kept smelling this sweet, citrus smell.

There's a girl at Harrah's, Betsy, and I called for a room and she said, "Oh, I see your birthday is Thursday." And I said, "Yes." And she said, "When you get down here have me paged and I'll have a birthday gift for you." So when I went down, I had her paged but she wasn't there so we went up to the Boardwalk. We got back late and the phone was blinking, and it was Betsy and she said, "I have to leave the casino but I left your birthday gift at the front desk." So I went down and it was a Lennox [china] dolphin and it was in the factory box and it had the price underneath. I guess she didn't know. It was $69. It was beautiful.

♦ ♣ ♥ ♠

[In the 1950s] the Elks Club always had gambling. They had the horse races. You could spend a lot of money at one of those things. They had films of authentic races from different tracks. But you never knew the horse's name or what track. You bet on them. They were fund-raisers, really.

Before I had done any gambling in Atlantic City, one of the things [I did for fund-raising] was Las Vegas Night. I had it at Pines Restaurant up here and it was fantastic. I think we made $7,000 that night. . . . We only charged $5 a ticket, but when you came in you bought whatever amount of play money, you couldn't use real money. You bought play money, and you couldn't give out money, you gave out prizes. And I used to get the prizes on consignment.

I'll tell you, I had them three years in a row and they all made over $5,000. . . . I checked with [state regulators] to see if I could have a Las Vegas Night, and they said yes, as long as real money wasn't involved in the prizes. And there was no problem. But then I got a letter from the state saying gambling was illegal no matter where you have it or what you do with it. And if I insisted on having it, they would not themselves do anything unless they had a complaint. And if they had a complaint, they could walk in the midst of this and confiscate everything—the money that we collected, the prizes, the equipment that we rented. So then I was afraid to have any more.

One person that came in was an attorney. You could spend as much money as you want. You could buy $500 worth of chips for roulette. . . . He came up to me crying, actually crying. He lost $6,000. He won $6,000, but he actually lost $6,000 because all he could get was $6,000 worth of prizes, and he didn't know that. I said, "I'm sorry. The rules were posted at the door. And you're an attorney and you don't know that gambling is illegal?" And so it was actually his business money. He was in with another fella and $6,000 then was a lot of money.

So I was glad in a way we couldn't have any more [Las Vegas Nights] because there were so many complications. But they were really big moneymakers, and that's why I knew Atlantic City was going to be a big hit, because there were all these people who wanted to gamble and had no place to gamble. We were sold out of tickets the second one we had. We had exceeded the seating limit. . . . We had hat shows, fashion shows, and [gambling] was by far [more popular]. It was over-whelming. I didn't even have to look for people to buy tickets. They were calling for tickets. And this was way before Atlantic City.

So I knew when Atlantic City opened up they would have no trouble finding gamblers, because almost everybody is a gambler at heart, one way or another.

CHAPTER 9

NEW YORK:
RISKY BUSINESS

ED THORP IS A SOFT-SPOKEN, slender money manager. At one moment amused and the next intensely serious, he can talk about mentally visualizing "whole regions of card-counting space" while slyly uttering a few jokes that bring a thin, elfin smile to his face. Thorp is responsible for refining two of the most influential approaches to late-twentieth-century gambling: card-counting in blackjack, and stock market hedge funds.

Able at age three to count to a million, at four to do basic arithmetic, and at five to impress customers in the corner grocery store by totaling their bills in his head faster than the owner's adding machine, Thorp was a mathematical prodigy as a child and an accidental gambler as an adult. It all began in 1958, when, on a trip to Las Vegas with his wife and armed with an academic study of blackjack strategies by four statisticians, the twenty-six-year-old college math professor discovered the pleasures of trying to beat the house.

Thorp was only the latest in a long line of mathematicians to become obsessed with gambling. More than 300 years before Thorp first set foot in a casino, the French mathematicians Blaise Pascal and Pierre de Fermat developed probability theory after observing repeated tumblings of dice in Parisian casinos. But Thorp was able to play the game using a computer.

After discovering that his blackjack strategy was imperfect, he set out to improve it with the aid of a then-rare mainframe computer housed on the campus of his employer, MIT. Thorp taught himself how to program the computer and then fed it information to analyze myriad variations of blackjack hands, a task that would have been impossible to complete using paper and pencil. From Thorp's research came the basic principles of card counting, a gambling strategy that calls in part for rigorous tracking of the 10s, picture cards, and aces in a blackjack deck. And it worked.

Initially bankrolled by two millionaires, Thorp says he was winning as much as $1,000 a day at blackjack in the early 1960s before casinos started drugging him, threatening to beat him up, and inserting card cheats into games to bilk him. He took revenge in 1962 by publishing a best-seller, *Beat the Dealer,* that instructed other gamblers how to count cards. Then the mathematician began looking for a new challenge. By the late 1960s, he had found it.

"I thought, 'What is the most interesting gambling game in the world?' " Thorp recalls. "It was the securities market."

The vehicle Thorp designed to start gambling on the financial markets was a high-octane version of the practice of hedging, already in use by some money managers and speculators. Hedging is an attempt to make a profit while limiting exposure to market risk by buying offsetting financial instruments. When Thorp got started, a typical hedge involved identifying stocks linked to overpriced or underpriced convertible securities, such as warrants or options. If a warrant looked overpriced, hedgers would "sell it short" (that is, borrow shares, betting that they could be replaced more cheaply later if the price dropped), then buy the common stock. If the warrant appeared underpriced, hedgers would buy it and short the underlying stock. In either case, hedgers could make a tiny profit from the price differential between the two securities while greatly limiting their downside if prices swung in an unanticipated direction.

Thorp entered the game with the same discipline he had brought to card counting, and in the late 1960s he developed a computer-based hedging strategy that was state-of-the-art. Although hedgers were already active in the markets, many of them relied on economic forecasts, hunches, and gut instincts that Thorp dismissed as "astrology." As he had with blackjack, Thorp developed a computer program loaded with proprietary data—stock prices, volatility, and conversion terms—and then used the program to direct him toward the best hedging opportunities.

Again, the strategy paid off. In 1969, Thorp opened a money management firm with a stockbroker named Jay Regan. Thorp was living in Newport, California, and Regan in Princeton; and their firm, Princeton Newport Partners, made both men rich. The partnership earned its investors an average of 15 percent a year after fees and expenses, a stellar performance that included not a single money-losing quarter. Then Regan's side of the business got ensnared in 1988 in the federal investigations of Ivan Boesky and Michael Milken and went out of business. Thorp was never accused by regulators of any wrongdoing.

"Gambling reallocates wealth with no social benefit," he offers. "I think speculation makes the market more efficient for investors. If mispricing is discovered, then people will exploit it until the pricing becomes more accurate."

But establishing fair prices is only one role the financial markets play. They also help to shape private and public investment priorities and have become indispensable yardsticks for measuring quality. They help to decide which businesses get cash in the real economy—the economy of workers, owners, and products that exists apart from the action on Wall Street and yet can be so brutalized when intelligent investing on Wall Street gives way to heated betting. And since Thorp started using computers to wager on the markets, swarms of imitators, most of them large institutions, have crowded into the field, creating a blinding swirl of trading in stocks, bonds, currencies, commodities, and derivatives that reflects all the strengths and weaknesses of the American financial system.

It is a financial system primarily devised not to preserve capital but to reward risk; a financial system that evolved on the principle that the economic and social dangers of heavy losses were more than offset by the payoffs earned by prescient gambles; a financial system built upon an increasingly innovative and elegant framework of mathematical models and predictive constructs that often trembles beneath the weight of ever speedier, immense, and random movements of money that are spurred along by the vagaries of imagination, greed, and the inexact intuition of gamblers.

The system emerged in this country at the southern tip of an island called Manhattan, on a block whose name—Wall Street—became synonymous with both high finance and high rolling.

BUBBLES AND BUCKET SHOPS

They lie together in the graveyard of Trinity Church in lower Manhattan: Alexander Hamilton, the patron saint of early American public finance and the public-private partnership known as mercantilism, and Robert Fulton, inventor of the commercial steamboat and one of the country's first great entrepreneurs. The creditors and speculators enriched by Hamilton's policies would eventually lay claim to the corporations started by entrepreneurs who dared to follow in Fulton's footsteps, and the forum for this uneasy coexistence would be housed along the thoroughfare running eastward from Trinity Church's gates.

Wall Street takes its name from a wooden bulwark the Dutch built there in 1653 to protect the residents of New Amsterdam. The harbor beyond the stockade was one of the New World's best, and ships laden with goods from Europe and the West Indies regularly unloaded their cargoes in the city the English renamed New York. Trade, in dry goods and human flesh, was New York's reason for being. By 1725, commodities such as wheat and tobacco were being exchanged on Wall Street. Slaves were bought and sold there until 1788. When Hamilton, a New Yorker and the country's first treasury secretary, recommended in 1790 that the federal government assume responsibility for Revolutionary War bonds issued by the former colonies and the Continental Congress, Thomas Jefferson, a Virginian and secretary of state, balked, fearing a concentration of fiscal power in the North. So the two men cut a deal. Hamilton won the right to assume the former colonies' debts in exchange for eventually moving the new country's capital from New York to a Southern city. The deal opened the door to the country's first, brief flirtation with the joys and sorrows of financial speculation, and helped ensure that Wall Street would eventually become the center of the action.

Speculators began trading Hamilton's bonds furiously, and he pumped up the action further by selling the public stock in the First Bank of the United States, which he chartered in 1791 to regulate the national money supply. It was a small clique of insiders who traded in these securities, mainly in Boston, Philadelphia, and New York. To trade their shares, leading New York merchants scheduled daily outdoor auctions on Wall Street, and interested parties left their securities with auctioneers who took a commission for each stock or bond sold. To limit access to the game and to ensure that they could charge outsiders a tidy fee for their services, two dozen brokers convened in 1792, as the story goes, beneath a buttonwood tree on Wall Street and there founded the Stock Exchange Office. Quick to take advantage of naive investors and soon reviled by the general public and respectable folk as parasites, these traders sometimes met on the curb, at other times inside the Tontine Coffee House, a hotbed of gossip, news, commerce, and gambling.

By setting up shop in a coffeehouse these early traders forged a symbolic link to a gambling tradition that predated them by more than a century. English coffeehouses, centers of local gossip and information before newspapers came along, had served a similar purpose in late-seventeenth-century London. Edward Lloyd inaugurated his insurance company in his coffeehouse, where news, gossip, and hard information about shipping could be obtained. In a maritime nation that increasingly depended on the unpredictable course of overseas shipping, insurance policies underwritten by men like Lloyd flourished. Though first used primitively in the Middle East around 1790 B.C., and later by the Romans, insurance in its modern, commercial form was an English invention created for limiting risk, for quantifying the unknown. It is no surprise, then, that the two great European maritime powers of the seventeenth century, the Netherlands and England, outward-looking nations tied to shipping and trade, broadened the roles of banking and credit and also experienced some of the most frenzied financial gambling of that era. In Holland, speculation manifested itself famously between 1636 and 1637 as the price of tulip bulbs, subject of a short-lived craze, skyrocketed and then crashed, leaving the shattered fortunes of merchants and shopkeepers in its wake. In England, speculation took on more formal attire.

Indeed, the English term "to speculate," which until the middle of the eighteenth century had meant "to contemplate an issue deeply," now took on a new meaning: "to gamble in financial markets." "Speculator" also became a handy euphemism for gamblers who didn't like to think of themselves as gamblers. Stockbrokers—or, as the English called them, "jobbers"—first appeared shortly after Lloyd's went into business in 1687, as did a variety of new corporations willing to sell their shares to the public. Both commercially and socially, England was "a society swept up by the gambling craze" between 1690 and the mid-eighteenth century as trade and overseas exploration enriched the tiny country. Insurance could be purchased against almost anything, including adultery and lying. And shares could be bought in almost anything, including ventures located thousands of miles away in regions promising untold riches.

For nine riotous years starting in 1711, England's South Sea Company, which had assumed a large part of the country's war debt in exchange for a monopoly on south Atlantic trade, issued stock that fueled one of the great commercial "bubbles" of the century. When first issued, the stock took off, and remained strong for several years. But at its heart, the South Sea Company was a swindle: its income from trade routes didn't begin to cover the costs of the war debt. Dividends dried up, and when investors rushed to sell their stock, its price collapsed. "I can calculate the motions of heavenly bodies, but not the madness of people," lamented one shareholder who lost £20,000, physicist and mathematician Sir Isaac Newton.

A similar bubble emerged at the same time in France. John Law, a Scottish gambler whose success at the card tables had brought him to the attention of the French court, sold the French nobility on the radical idea that credit and paper currency could be useful substitutes for gold as the standard of wealth. Law convinced the French to create a much-needed national bank in 1716. The bank then funded the Mississippi Company two years later to explore North America, and offered shares in the company to the public. While Law's banking ideas were ahead of their time, the Mississippi Company was a tinderbox. Law's bank loaned money to investors to purchase, and prop up, the company's stock. When the vast gold fields expected in the Louisiana Territory didn't materialize, the bubble burst, and the French rushed in vain to redeem their worthless shares. Although shares in the South Sea and Mississippi companies deflated in the same year, 1720, the South Sea Company survived. The Mississippi Company collapsed because England and France responded to the crises in very different ways.

France dissolved its central bank and developed a cultural aversion to banks and stocks that lasted for the rest of the century. The English, however, simply forced the South Sea's directors to fork over their own estates and pay a liquidating dividend to the company's shareholders. The government, having already limited the formation of new joint-stock companies before South Sea's stock swooned, then stabilized the Bank of England and clamped down on speculation. England passed a series of laws in the eighteenth century that outlawed trade in speculative insurance policies and forbade such practices as "difference transactions" by stockjobbers. Difference transactions were wagers that didn't involve actually purchasing a stock. A gambler wagered on which direction a stock's price would move between two specified dates, and a jobber agreed to pay the bettor the amount by which the stock rose or fell, without any stock actually changing hands. The difference transaction had nothing to do with greasing the wheels of commerce, supporting capital formation to build industry, or providing a mechanism that helped determine prices. It was gambling—no more, no less. Although England cracked down on it, it didn't disappear. Difference transactions were commonplace in the U.S. stock market until the early twentieth century as England's progeny in the colonies came to embrace financial gambling with a fervor, a decadence, and ultimately a precarious sophistication that are still unmatched in the world.

"The prospect of getting rich is highly motivating, and few people get rich without taking a gamble," observes veteran money manager and financial historian Peter Bernstein. "As the growth of trade transformed the principles of gambling into the creation of wealth, the inevitable result was capitalism, the epitome of risk-taking."

And as trading societies matured and then industrialized, financial markets reflected each country's confidence in its ability to tempt chance, to anticipate the future. For, as Bernstein so gracefully puts it, "Time is the dominant factor in gambling. Risk and time are opposite sides of the same coin, for if there were no tomorrow there would be no risk, and the nature of risk is shaped by the time horizon: the future is the playing field."

In theory, the industrial nations that fully embraced financial markets developed instruments such as stocks and futures so as to fund new companies, to grapple successfully with the unknown, and to help their economies to prosper. In practice, and until very recently, the markets were really playpens for those inside the game. And much of the game, even though it seeks to free its players from the constraints of the clock, is still played minute to minute, and even second to second, rather than year to year. Speculators and traders, theoretically liberated from time, have instead become slaves to it. Little of this, however, was apparent when Wall Street's founders began meeting in the Tontine Coffee House.

The stock and bond markets almost evaporated in the United States after the first wave of euphoria in 1792. By 1815, only about two dozen stocks were traded on Wall Street, and the market was just an anemic sideshow to the real commercial activity taking place in small businesses and on farms and plantations. While the market's usefulness to the commercial sector remained dubious, it began to grow considerably starting in 1825. In that year, the Erie Canal was completed and New York's harbor was linked to the Great Lakes, transforming a second-tier city into the world's busiest port (a distinction New York would maintain until 1960) as the American heartland was opened up to industry, heavy farming, and manufactured goods. Frantic land speculation in the 1830s, followed by the gold mania of the 1850s, helped foster an environment hospitable to gamblers eager to play the stock market.

All the market needed now was someone to peddle its paper. Few banks and even fewer brokerage firms existed, but one industry had already gained a peculiar financial expertise through decades of operating the most elaborate gambling network of its time: the lottery.

Just as the stock market began perking up again, a wave of scandals had forced many state lottery operators to shut their doors. Most towns of 1,000 people or more had a lottery concession, and the owners had learned how to exchange various state currencies in order to sell their lottery tickets. After repeated lottery frauds resulted in crackdowns, many of the operators, including a young man named John Thompson, decided to become bankers. Thompson founded two of New York's largest banks, National City Bank (later Citibank) and Chase Manhattan Bank.

Lottery operators were also accomplished shills—P. T. Barnum began his career as a lottery man—and they were adept at playing to, and taking advantage of, the average citizen's dreams of riches. This talent proved handy in the world of stock sales. One lottery company, S. & M. Allen of New York and Philadelphia, became one of the nineteenth century's most prestigious brokerage firms. A sister firm, E. W. Clark & Company, was founded in Philadelphia by a relative of the Allens who had learned the lottery business from them before branching out into currency exchange and stock sales. Clark eventually spawned Jay Cooke & Company, one of the most active, and notorious, Wall Street investment banks and one of the first firms to sell bonds to small investors.

By 1863, Wall Street's little clique of stock operators had already renamed the Stock Exchange Office the New York Stock and Exchange Board and were busy offering shares in new railroad and canal companies that fearless speculators could snatch up like so many chips on a poker table. Banks added fuel to the fire by offering generous loans to speculators. After depositing as little as $1,500 in cash at a bank, speculators in the 1850s were able to borrow as much as $300,000 to finance a Wall Street shopping spree "on margin." Predictably, stock prices gyrated wildly year to year, and financial panics were common.

"A speculator in the nineteenth century was someone who bought stock on margin, and they were considered gamblers and racy people," says Hofstra University business historian Robert Sobel. "They weren't the kind of people you'd want your daughter to marry."

The Civil War introduced the most frantic period of financial gambling Wall Street had witnessed to date. In this frenzy, stocks took a backseat to gold. Usually it had been wealthy men who bought stocks and gold, but their ranks now included women, clerics, and members of the new professional classes, such as merchants and lawyers. These brave souls could choose among some twenty exchanges that had sprung up on Wall Street to handle their business, including the newly renamed New York Stock Exchange. Many stayed open late into the night, with the real action taking place on the Gold Exchange. Few of the exchanges offered anyone actual title to stocks or commodities. Most were "bucket shops" that allowed visitors to bet on the direction in which the price of a stock or commodity might move on a given day—exactly the sort of difference transaction that had been outlawed in England.

While New Yorkers were swept up by Wall Street's bucket-shop casinos, Chicagoans put financial gambling to a socially and economically useful purpose. They linked the harvests of lush midwestern farmlands to the pricing pits of the country's first futures mart, the Chicago Board of Trade. Opened in 1848 by semiliterate grain merchants who enticed others to trade by offering free cheese and beer, the Board of Trade allowed farmers to sell deliveries of their wheat and corn for a specified price at a future date, enabling them to lock in a price for their crops months before the harvest. This reduced the risks of such unpredictables as the weather and let farmers plan ahead, assured that they could find a buyer.

Still, it was always hard to predict where prices might go. The future prices of commodities were decidedly random, beholden—then and now—to such uncontrollable influences as inflation, exchange rates, political turmoil, natural disasters, and the weather. Nobody knew what price the ball would land on when the market stopped spinning. So speculators fixed the game. Those with deep pockets and iron wills attempted to "corner" certain commodities, buying so much corn or wheat (and a cornucopia of other products that later traded on the Board) that they were able to determine the direction of prices in the short run. Thus, while futures trading helped wheat prices to fluctuate much less than they did before trading existed, it also provided a forum in which ruthless speculators could reap a quick fortune, as Ben Hutchinson did by cornering the wheat market in 1866. Corners soon became monthly occurrences on the Board; Hutchinson, for one, maintained his hammerlock on wheat well into the 1890s. As on Wall Street, bucket shops sprang up all over Chicago's LaSalle Street and were "so popular that gambling in grain came to be viewed as a national pastime at the turn of the century."

The fun and games disgusted many onlookers. Some states banned futures trading as illegal gambling, even though it was manipulation rather than the futures markets themselves that caused prices to seesaw. By the 1890s, farmers, their world in eclipse as industrialization took hold, had also grown weary of seeing the prices for their crops manipulated, and they pushed for federal legislation to ban futures trading.

"The property of the wheat grower and the cotton grower is treated as though it were a stake put on the gambling table at Monte Carlo," said U.S. Senator William Washburn, a Minnesota Republican, in 1892. "The producer of wheat is compelled to see the stocks in his barn dealt with like the peas of a thimblerigger, or the cards of a three-card-monte man. Between the grain-producer and the loaf eater, there has stepped a parasite . . . robbing them both."

Although Congress considered legislation banning futures trading on several occasions at the turn of the century, none passed. The Board of Trade, recognizing that gambling in bucket shops made for bad public relations, squeezed many of these competitors out of business by cutting off their access to market quotes. In 1905, the Supreme Court upheld the board's right to stamp out bucket shops, while also affirming the legality of futures trading on large exchanges. "People will endeavor to forecast the future and to make arrangements according to their prophecy," Justice Oliver Wendell Holmes, Jr., wrote for the Court. "Speculation of this kind is the self-adjustment of society to the probable. Its value is well known as a means of avoiding or mitigating catastrophes, equalizing prices and providing for periods of want."

Holmes understood how central the gambling instinct was to the nation's financial markets. But what seemed practical from the lofty aerie of the Supreme Court became a different matter in the rough-and-tumble world of the trading floor. Manipulation in the commodities markets continued unabated for the next several decades. And manipulation assumed even greater proportions back on Wall Street, where the arrival of industrialization caused the stock market—and the gambling attendant to it—to take off like, well, a locomotive.

"AN INTEREST IN EVERY JACKPOT"

Wall Street folklore has it that the term "watered stock" came into existence prior to the Civil War through the wiles of a young cowherd named Daniel Drew. Drew supposedly fed his cows salt so the thirsty bovines would suck down extra gallons of water, thus tipping the scales in his favor when they were weighed for sale in New York. Drew later brought his know-how to Manhattan's financial district, selling worthless "watered" stock certificates that had been churned out on a printing press in the headquarters of his company, the Erie Railroad.

Railroads created modern Wall Street, not the other way around. Railroads required far more money than any previous commercial enterprise. Between 1840 and 1870, 70,000 miles of track were laid in the United States. Between 1870 and 1900, another 130,000 miles of track were added to the web. The series of regional canals built between 1815 and 1860 had been financed for about $118 million, much of it raised through state and municipal bonds. Railroads, in comparison, had inhaled $1.1 billion by 1859, and most of that money was from private funds raised in just the previous ten years. Railroads were also the first businesses to raise capital from outside the region where they operated; investments came from as far away as Europe in many cases. All of these unique financial circumstances made Wall Street's exchange houses and brokerage firms intermediaries between the moneymen and the railroads.

There's no question that Wall Street, in conjunction with the federal government's land grants, allowed railroads to expand rapidly. Owners of the Pennsylvania Railroad raised $87 million between 1869 and 1873, about half in stock and half in bonds. No other business in the United

States had been able to raise that much money that quickly before. Wall Street helped make large-scale, sprawling, risky ventures possible.

But only a few of those who risked their money financing railroads were interested in the long-term health of the businesses. Most of them were gamblers content to make a short-term killing and then walk away from any mess they had created—a situation that would repeat itself a century later when traders feasted during the "merger mania" of the 1980s. Speculators like Drew, Jim Fisk, and Jay Gould regularly staged stock raids on railroads, depleting the companies of valuable financial resources. Other speculators promised much more than they could deliver. Jay Cooke's Northern Pacific Railroad company, profitable on paper and a sure thing according to the publicity Cooke whipped up for investors, never generated enough business to support a railway that stretched from Wisconsin to Puget Sound. The Northern collapsed spectacularly in 1873, setting off a national financial panic. That was only one of the era's many such panics, each of which rocked the economy to its foundations.

"The buccaneer style of the railroad financiers was not without its advantages, for by getting the roads built in a hurry, they expeditiously unlocked the riches of a continent," write Thomas Doerflinger and Jack Rivkin in their history of venture capital. "But the excesses of railroad finance were so outlandish that its social and economic costs were prodigious. Redundant railroads, squandered capital, widespread bankruptcy, frequent mismanagement, and dissatisfied customers riddled the industry."

As another depression arrived in 1893, a quarter of the nation's railroads were in bankruptcy, with great lines such as the Union Pacific and the Reading among them. Established financiers regarded Wall Street with scorn. Why didn't J. P. Morgan, the most formidable financier of the early twentieth century and a large shareholder in most of the huge industrial and financial combinations of his time, trade more actively on the New York Stock Exchange? "I never gamble," he sniffed.

The stock markets, entirely given over to speculation, whipsawed wildly around the turn of the century. Sober-minded investors put their money in bonds; stocks were strictly for gamblers, and only those who believed they had inside information dared to enter Wall Street's casinos. The Northern Pacific, again the quarry of speculators, saw its stock shoot up to $1,000 from $63 a share in just five days in May 1901. On May 9 the shares plunged to $600 from $1,000 *on a single trade.* The risks gamblers tried to corral on Wall Street were still largely distinct from the risks entrepreneurs embraced in the real world. Indeed, the two most successful corporations of the late nineteenth and early twentieth centuries, Carnegie Steel and Ford Motor, remained successful for as long as they did largely because they were closely held by their founders and were thus spared the predations of the stock market.

Although legions of speculators lost their shirts playing the markets, the action was just too delicious for some to avoid. By 1912, the biggest brokerage firm in the country was a bucket shop, Jones & Baker. Yet all this was just a prelude to the trading frenzy that arrived in the 1920s.

Post–World War I prosperity, borne on the wings of big oil, the automobile and electronics businesses, and new industries such as radio and aviation, created the kind of wealth and betting opportunities that fostered speculation on a grand scale. In 1914, 511 stocks were listed on the New York Stock Exchange. By 1929, 6,417 stocks were listed. Easy money and easy credit made it simple to buy a seat at the table. Annual trading volume on the "Big Board" soared from 171 million shares in 1921 to 1.1 billion shares in 1929; most of the sales had little to do with the real-world value of any of the companies that the shares represented. Still, only about 10 percent of American households owned stock at the end of the decade. Wall Street remained the domain of high rollers.

"Speculation is very similar to playing a game of cards, whether it be poker, bridge, or any similar game," said Jesse Livermore, who frequented Boston's bucket shops before hitting the big time as a Wall Street speculator in the 1920s. "Each of us is possessed with the common weakness of wanting to have an interest in every jackpot."

Wall Street gamblers were also possessed with the common weakness of forgetting how quickly the good times could end. But while it lasted, the show during the 1920s, starring the likes of Billy Durant, a quintessential American entrepreneur, and Joseph Kennedy, a quintessential stock manipulator, was really something.

Although the automobile industry's tremendous growth between 1900 and 1920 had been financed without help from Wall Street, market mavens like Durant still saw the Street as a useful venue for empire building. Durant was, according to an associate, "one hell of a gambler." He parlayed his horse-drawn-carriage company into ownership of Buick Motor in 1904, which became General Motors in 1908. Without missing a beat, he then used GM's stock to fund an acquisition spree that created a wobbly pyramid of auto companies so unstable that Durant lost control of the jumble in 1910. Never at rest, he went on to cofound Chevrolet in 1911 and then regained control of GM in 1915. After losing tens of millions of dollars in a fierce and failed trading effort to prop up GM's stock, Durant lost control of the company again to the DuPont family in 1920. A subsequent start-up failed, and Durant re-created his fortune by speculating on Wall Street in the 1920s. He was ruined when the market crashed in 1929.

Joe Kennedy, on the other hand, got out of the market with a titanic fortune intact because he understood that trading was just a game and that a speculator succeeded by making his own rules. In a decade when insider trading and a host of other dubious tactics were perfectly legal, Kennedy made enough money to fund a political dynasty. Operating from a Waldorf-Astoria Hotel suite loaded with telephones and a stock ticker, Kennedy ran "pools" made up of brokers, bankers, and traders who openly colluded to rig stock prices. The pool would plant a favorable newspaper story about a company, furiously buy blocks of its stock to drive the price up, and then sell at the top to unwitting traders who weren't in on the game. One Kennedy pool, which included GM vice president John Raskob and officials of M. J. Meehan & Co., a brokerage firm, made $5 million in one week in 1929 by rigging RCA's stock price.

Wall Street's antics were initially followed with glee in the popular press and didn't raise anyone's dander until people realized that banks—supposed guardians of financial security—were also playing poker with the big boys. Not only did banks have large margin loans out to speculators, but also some prominent bank executives profited nicely from the pell-mell. Chase president Albert Wiggins made a windfall, later investigations revealed, by shorting his own bank's stock—with an $8 million loan from Chase. Meanwhile, National City president Charles Mitchell was repackaging his bank's bad loans as bonds and directing his massive sales force to dump them on unwitting investors.

Of course, most of the madness abated after the stock market crashed in 1929. But for all of the attention paid to the crash, it had, at most, a tangential relationship to the Great Depression which followed. Wall Street was still only loosely connected to the real economy. Well before the crash, the U.S. economy had already slowed down, bank loans unrelated to Wall Street were souring, wage inequality was growing, and monetary policy was inconsistent. All these factors played a much larger role in causing the Depression than the crash did. The crash's direct effect on industrial activity was minimal, its impact more psychological than tangible. But by symbolizing the consequences of the gambling euphoria of the 1920s, the crash intensified the public reaction to the Depression. As the Dow Jones Industrial Average, a barometer of overall market sentiment, sank almost 90 percent between 1929 and 1933, speculators ceased being the subjects of amused cocktail chatter. Now they were seen as villains whose wagering needed to be regulated.

In 1933, bucket shops were outlawed, investment banking and commercial banking were legally separated, and, a year later, the Securities &

Exchange Commission was established to police the Street. Options trading was banned in the 1930s, and, to curb easy credit that nurtured gambling on stock exchanges, the Federal Reserve required speculators to put up at least 50 percent of the purchase price of any stock. (The Chicago Mercantile Exchange found a way around this requirement almost fifty years later when it allowed speculators to wager on the Standard & Poor's 500 Index of stocks for a down payment of just 5 percent to 10 percent—the ramifications of which became clear when the market crashed again in 1987.)

The great crash and the reforms of the 1930s kept the action relatively quiet on Wall Street during the next three decades. Speculation, of course, continued, as did the more primary stock market function of raising money for businesses. But, save for a brief revival during the "go-go years" of the 1960s, the financial markets did not accommodate a comparable burst of gambling until the 1980s. By that time, a host of innovations had radically remade the financial markets. Not only would these innovations provide businesses with unique tools for hedging risk and surviving in an unpredictable world—the same goal pursued by Europe's merchants centuries earlier—they also would allow gamblers to make outsized financial bets on a scale speculators of the 1920s never would have thought possible. And when some of these bets failed, they ripped through the surface of financial markets like the long, burning plumes of solar eruptions.

NEW GAME ON LASALLE

Professional traders are the market's combat pilots, buying and selling stocks, bonds, currencies, and commodities in a dizzying daily whirl of instant decisions and bruising competition. Many of them are former high school or college jocks, familiar with the rivalries and demands of sports long before they arrive on the trading floor. Theirs is a world of dicey gambits fueled by hormones, sometimes by drug abuse, and always by a love of betting. Traders will, in fact, bet on almost anything—the color of dress worn by the next woman to enter the room, the Super Bowl, tomorrow's weather, or the closing price of a stock. Traders are the heart of the market.

"I think traders gamble a lot more than the general population. You're used to the fever, the stress level, and it's a very macho environment. Traders like to compete and take risks, and it's an easy step from there to craps or blackjack," says one senior currency trader for a major Wall Street bank. "If you're going to buy something and hold on to it for twenty years, then yeah, maybe that's not gambling. That's not trading, though. That's investing. In our business, there's so much information and technology at your fingertips that you never hold on to anything for very long. Things are just changing so fast and you'd be stupid to hold on."

Whereas foreign currencies, and a host of other financial instruments, were at one time either thinly traded or not traded at all, today they are swapped regularly in a new form of financial free-for-all. In part, financial markets have been shaken up by the 1980s movement toward deregulation and by the increasing globalization of trade. More influential, however, have been revolutionary trading innovations introduced in the 1970s, which were later coupled with the information-processing might of computers. The combination has helped trading grow exponentially. In 1945, 507 million shares of stock traded on the New York Stock Exchange; the total rose to 3.5 billion shares by 1970. By 1980, trading volume on the Big Board had leaped to 12.5 billion shares. In 1987, 53.2 billion shares changed hands, and by 1995 the figure had soared to 90.5 billion. On October 28, 1997, the busiest trading day in New York Stock Exchange history, almost 1.2 billion shares were traded on the Big Board—slightly more than were traded throughout *all* of 1929—as the stock market rose 337 points after falling 554 points the day before. The U.S. stock market had put on a bravura performance, managing massive numbers of trades with an efficiency no other stock market in the world could have matched and avoiding a financial meltdown like the one that occurred in 1987. Technology was catching up to people's seemingly limitless trading habits.

But these mammoth trading numbers represent more than financial innovation or the increased market involvement of individual investors through vehicles such as mutual funds. The trading volume on those record days in 1997 was sharply boosted by options that ramped up selling pressure once price declines set in. Fears about weakening Southeast Asian economies had sent tremors through the U.S. stock market, and traders were scrambling to bet correctly on the impact of events that weren't going to be clearly understood for months. The year's trading milestones spoke to the desire of people with unprecedented wealth and technology at their command to get rich quick rather than to invest. They spoke to the tremendous impatience that distinguishes many participants in contemporary financial markets—and many gamblers.

It is tempting to allow Texas' Hunt family to raise the curtain on the modern era of financial gambling. They seem perfectly suited for the part. The family patriarch, H. L. Hunt, used poker winnings to fund an oil empire built on the risky drilling gambits of a wildcatter. His three sons later spread the riches around, founding the American Football

League and taking big positions in the stock and commodities markets. When Bunker, Herbert, and Lamar Hunt (the latter nicknamed "Games" as a child) rolled into the precious-metals market in 1979, they gobbled up more than 60 million ounces of silver. At the same time, they also bought futures contracts for the metal, which helped drive up the price of their own silver holdings. By 1980, just four months after the Hunt boys went to work, the price of silver had spiked up to $50 an ounce from less than $11 an ounce. Two months later, silver had plummeted back below $11 an ounce. In the process, the Hunts lost about $1 billion; they stood accused of engineering a classic "corner," and had shown that markets sometimes create just as much volatility and irrational pricing as they are credited with dispelling.

But the Hunts weren't gambling. They were engaging in the age-old art of manipulation, and their plan was akin to the insider trading schemes that ensnared Ivan Boesky and Michael Milken several years later. The real dawn of modern financial gambling occurred in the sober environs of MIT. There, three professors were perfecting a tool that speculators like Ed Thorp, fresh from his stint counting cards in casinos, had already been deploying in primitive ways and with buoyantly lucrative results.

The professors, Fischer Black, Myron Scholes, and Robert Merton, created the first formula for pricing stock options. Their invention, announced in 1973 just a month after the Chicago Board of Trade opened its options exchange, shook up the entire financial world. Options, first used in ancient Greece, give investors and speculators the right to buy or sell an asset at a later date but, unlike futures, don't *require* their owners to exercise that right. There's no firm commitment. The valuing of stock options, however, had always been a fly-by-night undertaking, and options trading occupied a disreputable backwater reserved for the market's most aggressive gamblers. The Black-Scholes model changed all that. By correlating interest rates, prices, volatility, and time, Black-Scholes gave users the most sophisticated tool in history for assessing when an option was fairly priced. Like an insurance policy, Black-Scholes attempted to put a price tag on uncertainty.

At the same time, the Chicago Mercantile Exchange had introduced currency futures, which allowed users to reduce their exposure to foreign-exchange risk—and gave speculators a whole new way to gamble. Trading in financial options and futures on the Board of Trade and the Merc quickly surpassed the trading in agricultural futures for which the exchanges were originally created. This transition represented American finance at its most lithe and creative. Between 1976 and 1996, trading volume in exchange-based futures in the United States grew tenfold, as hedging became standard practice for large corporations, investment firms, and even the financial managers of union pension funds and the endowments of elite universities.

The new products permitted users to hedge their bets against unforeseen market swings and plan much further into the future. "It was the financial equivalent of breaking the sound barrier," says Garrett Glass, head of risk management for banking giant First Chicago/NBD. "People now think that thirty years is no different than five days."

Yet, since all financial products straddle that very fine line separating temperate, calculated gambles from irrational, impassioned betting, it was only a matter of time before some market players put options and futures to very dubious uses. The first hint of what might be afoot came shortly after the Chicago Mercantile Exchange introduced the first futures contract that was not pegged to the price of a single stock or bond, but linked to the direction of the entire stock market.

Before the Merc could offer stock market index futures, it needed a special legal dispensation. Until the early 1980s, Illinois gambling laws (and similar laws in other states) had been invoked to forbid traders to pay off futures with cash instead of delivering the actual commodity the futures contract represented. Cash settlement was deemed a form of illegal gambling, precisely the stuff of old-fashioned bucket-shop wagers. After the Merc successfully lobbied to get those rules waived on one of its futures products in 1981, it teed up its Standard & Poor's 500 Index for a waiver, too. In 1982, the U.S. Congress paved the way for the options boom by ruling that state gambling statutes were nullified by federal securities regulations. In other words, Congress ruled, as long as it was happening in the financial markets it wasn't gambling. Shortly after that, the Merc and the Board of Trade introduced index options, just as the heady bull market of the 1980s got under way. And then the fun really began.

Index futures had a reasonable enough purpose when they were introduced. The S&P 500 Index represented an imaginary basket of hundreds of widely held stocks, and index futures were said to provide "portfolio insurance" for investors who worried that their holdings might get pummeled in a market downturn. If you wanted to protect the value of your stock portfolio, you sold the futures as stock prices fell, using gains from the sales to offset stock losses.

But embedded in portfolio insurance was a simple flaw: it presumed there would always be a buyer for every seller. That fallacy became terribly apparent when the market crashed in October 1987. As common sense would suggest, if a market panic is nasty enough there will be very few people willing to gamble on a stock or an index representing a group of stocks—no matter how attractive the price—until everyone's blood pressure settles down. And, of course, index plays attracted swarms of people who had no interest in hedging. They just wanted to make some money. Quickly.

"In my judgment, a very high percentage—probably at least 95 percent and more likely much higher—of the activity generated by these [stock index futures] will be strictly gambling in nature," warned legendary investor Warren Buffett in a letter to Congress written in 1982, as regulation of the new products was being debated. "In the long run, gambling-dominated activities that are identified with traditional capital markets, and that leave a very high percentage of those exposed to the activity burned, are not going to be good for the capital markets."

Buffett, rather than trading ferociously, had made a fortune buying stocks carefully and patiently holding on to them, and his concerns about index futures were prescient. Index plays proved irresistible to speculators. For a $5,000 to $10,000 down payment, a buyer could control an index future or option worth about $100,000. Even some casinos balked at credit lines that generous. But speculators, ignoring ample evidence that very few of them actually made money wagering on the direction of markets, kept anteing up.

"I became more and more fascinated with the options market, and the mathematician in me began charting prices," says Chris Anderson, a former stockbroker who went broke trading index options and their kindred between 1983 and 1987. "I fell in love with charts. Every gambler has a system that they use to govern their behavior. Handicapping [horse races], for example. My system was charting.

"I would estimate that five percent to ten percent of the people who worked with me were compulsive options traders. And you gravitate toward clients who are compulsive traders," adds Anderson, who now works for an Illinois group that helps treat compulsive gamblers. "I was under such stress that I would leave my house each morning, and I would cry for the entire drive to work. I didn't want to go in, because I knew I was going to lose money.

"The problem is that some people fall in love with the action and forget about their systems. The disciplined trader and the disciplined gambler stick with their system—they know when to hold 'em and when to fold 'em. Problems start when you love the action more than the system."

Ah, but what wasn't there to love? The tarot of charting prices seemed infallible when the market was rising so briskly. Between 1982 and 1987, the Dow Jones Industrial Average tripled. And as the action picked up, the Chicago exchanges, which once aimed to create price stability for farmers, brought an unprecedented and massive dose of volatility into the stock market. Traders programmed their computers to exploit small price discrepancies between index futures and the stocks they represented, a practice known as index arbitrage that frequently caused the market to whipsaw violently on days when contracts expired. Almost $3 billion worth of S&P futures contracts traded on the Merc in 1982, the year they were introduced. By 1987, $315 billion of S&P futures trades flooded through the Merc. It was once rare for stock orders of any size to move the market, but by the mid-1980s it was as common for market prices to yo-yo sharply as it was for the Sunday football line to shift after a big bet was placed.

Then the bubble burst.

On October 19, 1987, the market crashed. In less than seven hours, $600 billion in paper wealth was wiped out as the Dow Jones Industrial Average plummeted 508 points, or almost 23 percent—well in excess of the 13 percent market crash on October 28, 1929. Although computerized trading related to portfolio insurance and index arbitrage would be blamed for the crash, the market had risen stratospherically only in tandem with similar speculative vaults in the real estate market and the banking industry during the 1980s.

Everybody, it seemed, had the gambling bug. Greed and impatience had temporarily driven market prices to unsustainable levels, and when speculators thought the game was up, computerized trading only exacerbated the collapse. More than half of the market drop occurred in the last seventy-five minutes of trading, as the Dow fell 1 point every seventeen seconds. As *Wall Street Journal* reporters Jim Stewart and Dan Hertzberg would later report, financial markets averted a near meltdown the next day only through an extraordinary regulatory intervention that apparently included rigging one of the major futures indexes so further damage could be avoided.

"LIKE RUSSIAN ROULETTE"

The real-world potential of the companies represented in the stock market didn't change after the 1987 crash. The valuations the market had placed on them were, simply, incredibly askew, both before and after the crash. As the crash showed, stock prices during short segments of time don't reflect a company's intrinsic value. Stock prices are often merely an indication of the relative prosperity of market participants and the willingness of speculators to gamble.

While the stock market has proved to be an excellent tool for helping companies raise operating capital, after the company has its cash its stock is beholden to traders. And the money gleaned from trading accrues only to the gamblers who whack stocks back and forth to one another like Ping-Pong balls. Yes, trading provides liquidity—stock is easier to buy and sell if there are lots of buyers and sellers—but as trading volume has surged, it has also become difficult to discern how much of the back-and-forth serves an economic purpose and how much of it is pure, recreational wagering.

Such is the primacy of trading that the market is now subject to a numbing welter of daily economic "data" (much of it remarkably similar to the content of tout sheets sold to sports bettors), that washes across computer stock screens and on-line services in a steady downpour. What is Fed chairman Alan Greenspan thinking? What will next week's labor report reveal? Where is consumer confidence headed these days? Much of this is the kind of random, transitory dross that long-term investors label noise. It gets in the way of clear thinking.

Yet the 1987 crash, despite some of the bitter lessons it provided, proved to be nothing more than a lull in what became, over the next decade, the longest bull market in U.S. history. Many companies that had much to gain from long-term planning began obeying a market discipline that focused on the short-term goals adored by speculators, such as a single-minded emphasis on boosting profits quarter to quarter. Earnings, especially quarterly earnings momentum, were the market's new mantra. If massive employee layoffs boosted immediate profitability, yet potentially left companies short-handed when it came to meeting long-term goals (such as better serving customers), then so be it.

Nor did the futures and options markets fade away after 1987. The financial community developed other financial models and products that are the children of Black-Scholes. Options and futures, derived from the value of an underlying asset such as a stock, bond, or commodity, gave birth to other financial "derivatives" that by the 1990s had become infinitely more complex in their makeup.

The recent boom in derivatives use still carries with it all the baggage that accompanied the arrival of financial futures in the early 1970s. How much is hedging? How much is simple gambling? Derivatives, an expression of the creativity and innovation that give American financial markets a competitive advantage globally, do have their place. For companies or investors that use them wisely, perhaps even sparingly, derivatives certainly help users limit their risk. Any company operating abroad, and therefore exposed to sudden changes in the value of foreign currencies, is grateful for the protection derivatives provide from such unexpected swings. But other derivatives have a speculative life of their own.

"Derivative mortgage-backed securities have not increased access to mortgage credit or lowered its cost relative to other benchmarks," observes economic policy guru Robert Kuttner. "Mainly, these securities have provided an outlet for one more form of gambling—and enriched the casino."

The new crop of derivatives is designed by the young computer wizards Wall Street affectionately refers to as "rocket scientists." Rocket scientists regularly whip up gourmet investment treats, sure that a dash of currency futures, mixed gently with a few tablespoons of stock options or commodity hedges and then simmered inside their personal computers will be the derivative recipe a customer needs. But, like Victor Frankenstein, Wall Street's youngsters tempt the fates by believing they can control them. Or perhaps they don't really believe they're controlling anything. Maybe, because they observe firsthand the daily irrationality of the market, they know they're wagering.

When Bankers Trust, one of Wall Street's most innovative and aggressive financial laboratories, became embroiled in a series of customer complaints about derivatives that went haywire in the early 1990s, telephone transcripts surfaced that revealed what some of the bank's employees and customers thought of the products. In 1993, a Bankers Trust salesman named Kevin Hudson offered a P&G treasury analyst named Dane Parker a derivative that was essentially a bet that interest rates wouldn't rise for two months. "I like this, and I like the bet," Parker responded. Later, Hudson told Parker that if another derivative worked out it would be like "P&G hit the lottery." Shortly after this, Hudson told a co-worker that a derivatives contract sold to P&G was "like Russian roulette, and I keep putting another bullet in the revolver . . . every time I do one of these." Unfortunately, the gambits ultimately soured and Bankers Trust and P&G subsequently had to hash out in court who was responsible for the failed wagers.

THE GAME GOES ON

For all the data-processing power computers have given Wall Street, the products the Street peddles still have very subjective guesses built into them, such as wagers on the direction of interest rates—or of entire economies. Witness one Nick Leeson, a young trader in Singapore for Barings Bank, the 233-year-old British institution that financed the Napoleonic Wars and managed the Queen of England's personal fortune. In 1995, the twenty-eight-year-old Leeson, routinely given immense trading leeway by his superiors at Barings, deployed index futures as part of a huge bet that the Japanese stock market would stop sliding downward. Oops. The market kept falling, and Leeson's $1.3 billion loss caused one of Britain's most venerable firms to go belly-up almost overnight.

Closer to home, Orange County, California, declared bankruptcy in 1994 after the county's treasurer, Robert Citron, racked up trading losses of $1.7 billion investing in exotic derivatives and other risky securities peddled by Merrill Lynch and other Wall Street brokerage firms.

The great fear among securities regulators is that the fallout from bad derivatives wagers could multiply rapidly, putting the entire financial system at risk. In early 1997 the SEC estimated the notional, or underlying, value of all outstanding derivatives to be $70 *trillion*. But the derivatives market is largely made up of privately negotiated transactions that are recorded off the books and traded away from exchanges. This makes the little devils hard to assess, regulate, or track, unless one of them bursts into daylight when it detonates.

It's all enough to spook even one of Wall Street's biggest high rollers, George Soros. Derivatives had enabled Soros to assemble a tidy fortune by making massive currency wagers against several central banks around the world. In 1992, Soros made $1 billion, and helped derail European attempts to establish a common currency, by betting—correctly—that the Bank of England would devalue the British pound. His bets weren't always correct, however. Two years later, Soros lost about $1 billion to $1.2 billion betting that the dollar would rise against the Japanese yen. Yet shortly thereafter, his own riches safely in pocket, Soros began campaigning *against* the increasingly exotic currency derivatives. He likened the currency derivatives known as knockouts to crack cocaine and, managing to keep a straight face, cited them as a source of destabilization in financial markets. By 1997, his conversion apparently complete, Soros wrote in *The Atlantic Monthly* of the threat of "the untrammeled intensification of laissez-faire capitalism and the spread of market values into all areas of life."

It isn't only high rollers such as Soros who have been swept up in the bull markets of the 1980s and 1990s. Some individual investors, the market's low rollers, also have the fever. Mutual funds, stoked with the savings of the average Joe and Jane, have made the middle class an influential force in the stock market for the first time. And many mutual funds take the same hardcore trading approach as every other major player in the market, sharply bidding up some stocks and quickly flipping out of others in a relentless, computer-assisted search for earnings "momentum."

This self-induced need for speed, the same thirst for action that fuels gamblers' betting spurts in casinos and with bookies, has created some interesting fireworks. In the spring of 1996, Comparator Systems, a company purporting to have a revolutionary fingerprint identification technology, set three consecutive trading records on the Nasdaq composite index as its stock streaked to almost $2 from 3 cents a share. In the blink of an eye, the market had valued Comparator in excess of $1 billion. Then the stock dropped like a stone after the SEC sued the company for allegedly inflating the value of most of its assets.

Yet even with Comparator splattered on their windshields, aggressive mutual funds and low-rolling individual investors hot-rodding through the market still adored risky small stocks. Until a sharp correction in mid-1996 cooled things off, initial public offerings of new stocks had been soaring. Between 1980 and 1995, the total annual value of IPOs leaped from $1.4 billion to $30.2 billion (with offerings in 1993 soaring to $58 billion). In many instances real value was created. Among those IPOs were stocks of companies, such as Microsoft, that couldn't have lined up a lot of money from any other source and then went on to add enormously to the economy. The later stages of this IPO and "small-cap" boom included companies with extremely bright prospects and no track record (Netscape, an Internet company that had never turned a profit, went public in 1995 at $28, was trading at $171 three months later, and fell to about $57 by the end of 1996) as well as companies with scant prospects and shaky finances, like Audre Recognition, a software company that climbed aboard the American Stock Exchange at about $5 a share in 1992 and was in bankruptcy proceedings by 1996. The lure of the game tends to blind some people to its downside, particularly since most IPOs are priced high and have bad long-term odds. Of all new companies that went public between 1985 and 1995, only 50 percent were still trading in 1995. Of those that went public between 1990 and 1995, only 66 percent were still trading in 1995.

In the meantime, the English, key progenitors of the modern stock market, have started to take a much more straightforward approach to the whole affair.

A few large bookies in England now feature a popular offering called spread betting, which is supervised and approved by the country's securities regulators. Each day English bookies set a price range, or "spread," in which they expect the country's stock exchange, currency, or a host of other financial products, to trade. Customers bet whether the closing price will be lower or higher than the spread. As in the bucket shops of yore, no securities are ever swapped, and the bookies conduct their business apart from the local exchanges. It's all pure gambling, relying on the financial markets for the sort of random, unpredictable events that make for a nice day at the races. But in the United States, financial betting has yet to come out of the closet; it remains safely disguised amid all of the rituals and trappings that Wall Street can muster.

After all, many Americans chase the dollar with religious zeal, and Wall Street's elaborate rites help dignify the hunt. Yet with the market offering such spiritual relief, it's getting harder for the country's other houses of worship to compete. Churches and synagogues, long dependent on charity gambling events to help make ends meet, are losing their patrons to more appealing, commercial forms of betting.

CHAPTER 10

CHICAGO:
CHURCHES, CHARITIES, AND CHANCE

IT IS A COOL FALL EVENING in 1996, and Father Mark Sorvillo, pastor of St. Margaret Mary's Church on Chicago's North Side, has just returned from a brief gambling trip. Father Sorvillo enjoys these occasional visits to Las Vegas, where, in the company of as many as ten fellow priests, he likes to try his luck at the $2 blackjack tables.

Tonight, however, Father Sorvillo is overseeing the first of St. Margaret Mary's two annual Las Vegas Nights. Scattered around the parish's small gymnasium are several low-stakes roulette, craps, and blackjack tables. The church has hired a charity-gambling company to run the event; several dealers and supervisors in tuxedos roam the floor. But most of the 200 or so people who sit down to gamble on this Friday night are dressed casually, greeting friends from the neighborhood with a smile and chatting excitedly in the darkened gym where God and Mammon comfortably rub shoulders.

"This is something that's just an evening of entertainment," says Father Sorvillo, who, bald, plump, and good-natured, could easily play the part of a poker dealer in an old-time Hollywood film. "It's not hardcore gambling, where people get hurt."

St. Margaret Mary's, founded in 1921 in a neighborhood filled with the children and grandchildren of immigrants from Ireland and Luxembourg, now is also home to younger generations of Hispanic and Filipino immigrants. Yet like so many other Catholic parishes in Chicago and around the United States, St. Margaret Mary's congregation is growing smaller, and its finances are growing tighter. Gambling used to help plug a bigger part of the church's budget, but St. Margaret Mary's will gross only about $6,000 for the two nights of gambling it offers this year. And as the parish continues to lose out to the newer, more appealing forms of commercial gambling now located nearby (Bingo City on Western Avenue, the riverboats plying the Mississippi, the state lottery) its gambling haul gets leaner every year.

"There are only so many gambling dollars out there," says Father Sorvillo. "This used to be special for folks in our community, and it's not special anymore."

Members of Father Sorvillo's parish agree. "It used to be, years ago, you had to go to Las Vegas to gamble, and that's why these [church] events were so popular," says Jim Brockhagen, who has been a St. Margaret Mary's parishioner for thirty of his fifty-four years. "People don't come over to play cards anymore. Being an Irish Catholic, anytime we got together with our aunts and uncles, we played poker. And it was usually my grandmother who got the game going. Those days are gone."

The passage of informal, social gambling events from neighborhood churches such as St. Margaret Mary's into the hands of more market-savvy operators tells more than just the story of commercial gambling's, particularly casino gambling's, triumph over most other forms of wagering in America. It illuminates a largely immigrant nation's struggle with shifting moral standards. And gambling's arrival in mainstream American culture also reflects how the moral strictures of the country's earliest immigrants have been overshadowed by the values of later newcomers. It is a tale that has unfolded in cities such as Chicago, a brawny metropolis built from a patchwork of different nationalities and faiths, where the urgent need to tend to one's soul has always coexisted with an equally passionate love of the dice.

DOES GOD THROW DICE?

Chicago burst forth in the prairie because, as with almost every other American city, commerce demanded it. But in its prime, Chicago was a commercial hub unlike any the country had yet seen. Home first to Native Americans, and later explored and settled by French and Canadian fur trappers, Chicago quickly became the fastest-growing city in U.S. history after the Illinois and Michigan Canal opened in 1848. Fixed astride one of the world's most bountiful agricultural regions, Chicago secured its economic primacy in the Midwest by loading tons of traffic onto railroad lines as fast as they were built. When the Civil War began, the "Big Junction" already had 3,000 miles of railroad lines crisscrossing it, making it the busiest railroad nucleus in the world. Chicago was growing so quickly during the middle and late nineteenth century that many observers thought it might even surpass New York. Its inhabitants, full of enough self-confident bluster to earn their town the sobriquet "Windy City," firmly agreed. "Sir," opined a railroad brakeman of the era, "Chicago is the boss city of the universe."

Although the city's first power brokers were Protestant transplants from the East Coast, most of whom disparaged the motley collection of immigrants who followed them, Chicago was a town where bloodlines and social connections mattered far less than in places like Boston and Philadelphia. Indeed, some of the most influential Chicagoans, such as former New York politician and real estate mogul Bill Ogden, married Catholics and reached out to immigrants to consolidate their political power. Chicago was a freewheeling frontier outpost until late in the nineteenth century, and, as long as you weren't an African American, you were basically welcome to cast your lot there. And millions did just that, making Chicago one of the country's great immigrant cities.

They all came for the seemingly endless stream of jobs thrown off by the stockyards, the railroads, the farms, and the factories. In one Chicago neighborhood mapped by Hull House's social workers in 1893, at least eighteen different ethnic groups were identified within thirteen short blocks. Among others, the mix included Arabs, Italians, Scandinavians, Irish, Chinese, Eastern European Jews, African Americans, Turks, Germans, and Greeks. When the U.S. census was taken seven years later, roughly 77 percent of Chicago's 1.7 million inhabitants had at least one foreign-born parent. By 1930, Chicago had 3.4 million residents. Only Dublin had more Irish inhabitants; only Warsaw had more Poles.

As distinct ethnic neighborhoods, many of them slums, took shape in Chicago during the late nineteenth and early twentieth centuries, immigrants could find newspapers written in their native tongue, bakeries and restaurants offering traditional foods, beer gardens and saloons, and other welcome reminders of the life they had left behind in Europe. And almost every one of these neighborhoods was anchored by a church or a synagogue. Chicagoans, particularly Irish Catholics, were just as likely to identify where they lived by naming the churches they attended as they were by using their street addresses.

Gambling also was part of the cultural baggage European immigrants brought with them to Chicago. Although former riverboat gamblers had helped make Randolph Street, between Clark and State Streets, "Gambler's Row" after the Civil War, it was the immigrants who made gambling a mainstay of Chicago life. The neighborhoods where gambling halls thrived most openly were gritty, dangerous "patches" along the Chicago River offering cockfights and dogfights among the betting attractions. Gambling and prostitution in the Levee, a vicious district in the South Side's notorious First Ward, were controlled by two corrupt aldermen, "Bathhouse John" Coughlin and Michael "Hinky Dink" Kenna. But gambling dens could be found in finer neighborhoods as well.

While legend has it that the great Chicago Fire of 1871 was started when Mrs. O'Leary's cow kicked over a lantern in her West Side barn, others whispered that the lady's son and his friends had been playing dice secretly in the barn and knocked over the lantern themselves. Whatever truth resides in either tale, it is true that "Big Jim" O'Leary grew up to be one of Chicago's gambling kingpins during the 1890s. Big Jim's club, located on Halsted Street, was one of the city's grand gambling dens. It featured secret passageways designed for easy escapes, although Chicago's perpetually corrupt police force rarely enforced the city's antigambling laws. Big Jim also indulged his patrons with steam baths, a bowling alley, and a barber shop.

At about the same time, local politico Michael Cassius McDonald controlled one of the city's biggest bookmaking operations and bankrolled the boxing career of John L. Sullivan. After the fire, McDonald, who also founded Chicago's first organized crime syndicate (stocked entirely with fellow Irishmen) opened his casino, the Store, in a luxurious four-story building on the corner of Clark and Monroe Streets. McDonald provided protection to other gambling dens, used his wealth and influence to take control of the local Democratic party, and was instrumental in getting Carter Harrison elected mayor in 1879. In return, Harrison, ever the political realist, resisted calls from Protestant civic groups pushing to close Chicago's saloons and gambling halls.

"A Republican is a man who wants you to go t' church every Sunday," said Bathhouse John, of the First Ward. "A Democrat says if a man wants to have a glass of beer he can have it."

Churches took a similar view. Religion and ethnicity determined political affinities in Chicago at least as much as economic and class interests did. Few of Chicago's immigrants shared the religious views or social values of their Protestant predecessors, especially when it came to gambling.

Gambling originated as part of ancient mythic and religious rituals that "involved primitive efforts to compel the changing of fate." Greek mythology has it that Zeus' daughter Tyche, the goddess of luck, juggled a ball in her hand as a reminder of the vagaries of chance; one's fortunes could always go up or down. The mortal who failed to offer generous sacrifices to Tyche faced certain humiliation and loss.

Ancient Israelites declared war, selected kings, and distributed land by rolling dice. Gambling was socially acceptable among Jews as long as it wasn't excessive, although Jews looked down on professional gamblers and forbade them to testify in court. Other religious groups were less accommodating. Although Arabs drew lots to determine guilt in disputes, the Koran forbade gambling for entertainment, calling it the work of Satan. Muslims weren't the only ones who rejected the notion that human destiny might be guided by fate rather than the will of a supreme being. The early Christian church threatened to excommunicate any of its members, clergy or laity, who gambled, seeing it as a sign of preoccupation with the material world at the expense of the afterlife.

During the Middle Ages, however, this view began to soften. Europeans drew fewer distinctions between magic, superstition, and religion as they gradually accepted an unpredictable world. As David Newmark points out in his essay "Covert Religious Aspects of Gambling," dice were thrown during early divination ceremonies for priests, and the early Catholic church used lots to determine promotions within its hierarchy. Newmark also notes that medieval Catholics commonly bet on the election of a new pope in an exuberant rite that bore similarities to modern betting on horse racing. Chance was embraced more openly after Thomas Aquinas, in thirteenth-century writings that would establish him as one of the church's great theologians, emphasized that divine providence didn't necessarily exclude the workings of fortune. But by the 1500s, with the church's hegemony beginning to splinter, acknowledging the existence of chance was again attacked, particularly in England. Magicians were executed along with alleged witches and sorcerers, as any supernatural force other than God was roundly condemned. The world was not beholden to the luck of the draw, for, as John Calvin, torchbearer of the Protestant Reformation, believed, "God, who enlightens all, is not blind."

Calvin's views informed the thinking of French Huguenots, Dutch and Scottish Protestants, and, most importantly for the way gambling was introduced into the New World, English Puritans. Puritans pressed the Church of England to "purify" itself of any vestiges of Roman Catholic rituals and to accept only those teachings that Puritans believed were found in the Bible. But unable to safeguard themselves or their beliefs in England, they set sail for the New World, bringing with them their dour view of the flesh and of the vices. Though gambling is not expressly banned in the Bible, Puritans in Massachusetts outlawed the ownership of dice, cards, and gambling tables. By 1737, Massachusetts legislators had softened their opposition to gambling: "All lawful games and exercises should not be otherwise used than as innocent and moderate recreations, and not as trades or callings, to gain a living or make unlawful advantages thereby." But Puritans still considered gambling the work of the devil. Hardly a unanimous view in the New World, this collided with the predilections of other colonists who enjoyed wagering, and the disagreement reached fever pitch when immigrants began pouring into cities such as Chicago more than a century later.

It wasn't that Protestants entirely resisted the urge to gamble, nor that they didn't, when pursuing a wager, sometimes go to odd lengths to resolve the moral quandary in which they found themselves. Henry Flagler, who cofounded Standard Oil with John D. Rockefeller and was the son of a Presbyterian minister who had led Ohio's temperance movement, built several of the grandest resorts and hotels in Florida in the late nineteenth century. At each hotel, Flagler built a casino, but, as if to hedge his moral bets, he also erected a chapel on the same grounds. So the Ponce de Leon Hotel in St. Augustine, for example, featured both the Bacchus Club and the Memorial Presbyterian Church. But Protestants never embraced gambling with the unabashed gusto of the immigrant masses who were recasting the country's moral and cultural preferences in a decidedly un-WASPy mold.

"There is considerable truth to the stereotypes about certain cultures being more prone to prefer gambling. It is a demographic fact that the largest religious blocs among those who prefer to gamble are Catholics and Jews, with WASPs coming in way down the line," says James Smith, an American studies professor at Pennsylvania State University at Abington-Ogontz. "It might have to do with people's relationship with God. In some religions, it is wrong to tempt fate, because God is always an angry God and never merciful. You don't trivialize your fate in some cultures by leaving it to chance. But that's not a problem in most non-Protestant religions."

It certainly wasn't a problem in Chicago. After reformers were finally able to shut down the Levee's more prominent gambling halls at the turn of the century, gambling remained largely underground in the city until Italian crime syndicates led by Jim Colosimo, Johnny Torrio, and a young entrepreneur named Al Capone revived the festivities in the 1920s and 1930s. As blacks migrated to Chicago from the South, the illegal policy racket also blossomed. Gambling also continued in informal, out-of-the-way places. Jean Haddock, a seventy-year-old New Jersey resident who spent her childhood in Chicago, remembers her father and mother going off to wager together during the late 1930s at a little gambling den hidden behind a newsstand on the 6800 block of Stony Island Avenue on Chicago's South Side.

"I've got ten dollars. Should I pay the rent or go back to the joint and build on it?" Haddock remembers her father asking her and her older sister.

"Pay the rent!" her ten-year-old sister would respond.

"No, go back to the joint and build on it!" her mother countered. So off Haddock's parents went, once or twice a week, leaving their children behind.

"This was how they dreamt of making a million," Haddock recalls. "But gambling was not respected at all. It was something you hid, like the brown relief bags from the social services."

FINGERS IN THE CHARITY TILL

Amid the action resurrected by Capone and his cohorts, churches and synagogues began offering a bit of gambling themselves. In 1929, eight years after St. Margaret Mary's was founded, a new game called beano debuted at a carnival near Atlanta. Modeled on a sixteenth-century Italian lottery game, beano was retooled by a toy salesman named Edwin Lowe, who introduced it to his friends in New York as "bingo." An early, simple version of the game began to spread. After a priest in Pennsylvania complained to Lowe that there were too many duplicate winners at his parish bingo games, Lowe enlisted a Columbia University math professor named Carl Leffler to devise 6,000 different bingo cards. Armed with these, Lowe began marketing bingo in 1930. It was so popular that by 1934 an estimated 10,000 games were being played weekly, primarily in churches, synagogues, and charitable organizations.

During the 1930s, bingo was the first form of gambling to be decriminalized in many states. Rightly so, said Father Francis Talbot, writing at the time in the Catholic journal *America:* "I cannot grow frenzied with the puritanical precisionists who rate the bourgeois pastime of bingo as a major sin . . . the worst harm that bingo causes is a sore throat. Church bingo parties are a healthy substitute for gossip teas, lovesick movies and liberal-minded lectures."

Church and synagogue bingo was also a healthy supplement for donations from the congregations. The Depression had eaten into the treasuries of all but the most well-heeled houses of worship at the time. Bingo nights kept many churches, parochial schools, and synagogues across the country afloat during those years, and for decades to follow: the games hit their peak during the 1950s and 1960s.

So distressed were some Jews by the popularity of bingo that the Union of American Hebrew Congregations passed a resolution in 1959 discouraging bingo and other forms of gambling at synagogues. Although no one tracks how much bingo is currently played at synagogues, Rabbi Ira Youdovin of the Chicago Board of Rabbis says the issue still splits a "substantial number" of congregations. "Judaism's position on gambling is somewhat ambiguous, in that it is neither condemned nor condoned," says Rabbi Youdovin. "One is not supposed to make gambling one's primary occupation, but it is permitted as long as it isn't destructive.

"Synagogues never have enough money, and bingo looms as the most attractive way of doing it. It's a way of getting revenue from nonmembers, but people worry about whether people lose their lunch money or whether organized crime is going to get involved."

While Rabbi Youdovin and Chicago law enforcement officials say there haven't been any recent instances of organized-crime involvement at synagogues in Chicago, financially strapped synagogues in New York have recently held illegal, high-stakes casino nights run, New York law enforcement officials say, by organized-crime associates who keep most of the winnings for themselves. Kissena Jewish Center, in the New York borough of Queens, is one of the synagogues that the Queens district attorney's office has cited as allegedly being involved in illegal gambling. New York law enforcement officials say raids of some of the illegal synagogue games between 1994 and 1996 have done little to stop the gambling. The fines are minimal, and local police are hesitant to make arrests because of the political fallout that ensues when they arrest elderly gamblers.

Christian churches are equally vulnerable to such problems. Although Catholic doctrine has traditionally accepted gambling as long as it doesn't harm individuals or a community, and as long as gamblers didn't put superstition before faith in the Lord, some parishes' dependence on gambling led the late Chicago cardinal Joseph Bernardin to repeatedly call for local churches to wean themselves from it. The church's goal, says Father Michael Place, the research theologian of the Catholic Archdiocese of Chicago, is for parishes to sustain themselves on the contributions of their members, not on gambling.

When three large casino companies, Circus Circus, Hilton, and Caesars World (now owned by ITT) joined forces to propose a large land-based casino in downtown Chicago in the early 1990s, the Catholic church, as well as leaders from other religious denominations including Jews and Methodists, came out strongly against the proposal. The casinos said they were bringing new jobs to Chicago, and city hall said taxes on the casinos could fund schools. But the church and its allies said that the casinos would bring misery to gamblers and that educational funding shouldn't be linked to such unpredictable sources as gambling revenue. The proposal was defeated. Father Place says the church's stance wasn't hypocritical, because parish bingo and Las Vegas Nights are recreational, noncommercial activities that don't cause the same social disruptions as casinos. "We never said gambling was immoral per se, we just said that the consequences of casino gambling weren't commensurate with the goals it hoped to achieve," says Father Place.

Besides, says the archdiocese, bingo and casino nights aren't as important as they once were to the finances of most churches, except for those in poorer neighborhoods: Bingo and casino nights contributed only $2.1 million to its 378 parishes in 1996, less than .5 percent of the total budget.

That's not to say, however, that charity gambling is small potatoes. About $7.6 billion was gambled at events sponsored by some 64,000 charities nationwide in 1995, generating about $780 million for groups in thirty-two jurisdictions tracked by the National Association of Fundraising Ticket Manufacturers in Minneapolis. Bingo and pull-tab games accounted for most of the loot, with raffles, casino nights, and other events kicking in less than 20 percent of the total. Most of that $7.6 billion was distributed as prizes or taxed, but roughly $1 billion was funneled to the innumerable private companies that run gambling events for the charities. Two states in particular, Minnesota and Alaska, have large charitable-gambling industries because nonprofits in those states are permitted to sell pull-tab games in bars. North Dakota's charity gambling interests have proved formidable enough to quash the introduction of a lottery in that state.

In the mid-1980s, the charity gambling business in Illinois was swamped with allegations that loose regulatory standards had led to skimming, money laundering, and organized-crime involvement in the industry. The Illinois Department of Revenue, which regulates charity gambling in the state, says it has stepped up its oversight since then and that most of the abuses that plagued the industry have been stamped out. Nonetheless, problems have continued to crop up.

In 1994, *Chicago Sun-Times* reporter Deborah Nelson revealed that Rockford Casino Players, a large local supplier for charity gambling events, used a related consulting company to routinely violate state regulations and turn charity casino nights into windfalls for professional gamblers who frequented the charity circuit. Nelson's story showed that Illinois charities' take from professionally run casino nights was shrinking even as the professional operators' share was growing, and it helped cause a revision in Illinois' charitable gambling law. The law now forbids consultants, as well as suppliers, from directly promoting or operating charitable-gambling events.

Rockford, which continues to do business in the state, disputes the idea that its events were set up to favor professional gamblers at the expense of the charities sponsoring them. "Before we came along, the churches weren't making any money," says Rockford's president, James

Kasputis. "We made it more like Vegas rules so the player had a chance. That benefited the players and the charities. . . . Everybody won more, including the charities, because there was a lot more play."

Bingo has had its share of worries as well. According to a 1992 report by the Pennsylvania Crime Commission, organized-crime figures in that state skimmed bingo revenue meant for charities, typically keeping about 95 percent of the loot at bingo halls there and in other states, including Maryland, Florida, and Ohio. Florida law enforcement officials filed racketeering charges against ten companies and temporarily shut down nine bingo halls in late 1995, alleging that the operators were siphoning about $4 million a year from charities (the charges are pending). A grand jury report in the Florida matter found that operators typically earned $365,000 to $730,000 a year from one bingo hall, with charities getting about a tenth of that amount. "A high degree of commercialization exists in the seven-day-per-week bingo halls, and they operate, in effect, as mini-casinos," the report noted. "The commercial operators routinely deducted extremely high rental rates and charged the charities inflated or nonexistent expenses, cheating them out of money belonging to them."

None of the scandals keep bingo fans away from their game, of course.

BINGO CITY

Not too far from St. Margaret Mary's, on Western Avenue, sits Bingo City, one of the largest bingo halls in Illinois. City of Hope, a nonprofit medical and research center based in Duarte, California, which once ran an entire network of bingo halls to help support itself, opened Bingo City in 1971. While all the other bingo halls owned by City of Hope have closed, Bingo City, with 12,000 square feet of bingo space, keeps 'em coming.

"Bingo is such a midwestern thing," observes Bingo City's manager, Richard Triffler. "Maybe it's because this is such an immigrant, ethnic area. A lot of these people are superstitious and into numerology, and they love playing bingo because of the numbers."

Bingo City has games every day of the week and is open from eight A.M. to ten P.M. on most days. On a typical day, 200 to 300 people try their luck there. As in most bingo halls, the players are mainly women, and mainly senior citizens. While winning money matters to them, most come for the camaraderie. Bingo gives them a sense of belonging.

"There's certain people that I like to see when I come. I also like how nervous I get seeing about my luck," says Leah Elmalech, who, at forty-nine years old, is a youngster among Bingo City's patrons. "Everybody comes here for company—and maybe to make a little money."

Gambling times may be flush for Bingo City compared with the slim pickings at churches like St. Margaret Mary's, but even Bingo City says that the spread of riverboat gambling and state lotteries has taken a big bite out of its business. Illinois regulations require that Bingo City, and all other bingo halls in the state, award prizes totaling only $2,250 daily and no more than $500 per game. Except for little old ladies who first learned bingo in their local church or synagogue, most gamblers today aren't attracted to such relatively small jackpots. The modern gambler is accustomed to a world in which casinos and lotteries dangle the glimmer of far larger, instantaneous riches before their eyes. Bingo has been a lucrative venture for some Native American tribes, but only because their sovereign-nation status allows them to offer high-stakes games. Once a reservation opens a casino, the casino's gambling handle usually shoots past the bingo hall's take.

Anyway, times have changed in Chicago.

Many of the European immigrants who once crowded into the city's neighborhoods have moved, and much of the gambling that they did followed them into the suburbs. The high-stakes craps game that floated through Chicago gambling joints such as the Nightingale Social and Athletic Club on West Twenty-sixth Street, the Tomahawks Athletic Club off Twenty-fourth Street, and Wentworth Avenue, and the Viaduct Lounge in Cicero during the 1950s and 1960s eventually found a new home in little towns outside the city.

More recent immigrants to Chicago have brought a taste for gambling with them, but bingo, especially church bingo, is not an important part of their repertoire. Chicago's Chinese immigrants prefer mahjongg, and cockfighting has grown apace with the expansion of the city's Hispanic population. And as the number of Chicago's neighborhood churches and synagogues dwindles, along with the informal gambling traditions that surrounded them, commercial gambling continues its steady march forward.

Traditional religious institutions' weakened hold on the spiritual allegiances of Americans highlights commercial gambling's emergence as one of capitalism's most popular secular religions, complete with its own rituals and epiphanies. The rituals are easy enough to see—in casinos, at sports bars, behind the trading desk of any brokerage firm. Whether they involve stacking a pile of chips a certain way, adopting various strategies for winning at the track or blackjack, or charting securities prices the way ancient mystics once plotted the stars, gambling's rituals are often imbued with as much bombast as any sermon broadcast from the Crystal Cathedral. Bettors have replaced praying with playing, and their religion is the religion of money.

This may not be true for all gamblers. Passion is often its own reward, and for many bettors gambling is first and foremost a passionate act. There are also gamblers who thrive on the competitive juices that betting uncorks. But for most others, caught in lives circumscribed by an overwhelming insecurity about money, gambling promises a fast break, a way out. We're a nation of coupon clippers and bargain hunters, yet we are ready to toss away those strange disciplines once we stroll up to a gambling table or a slot machine. A visit to a casino holds out the faintest hope that we can win enough money to, oddly enough, forget about money. Gambling gives us the chance to bow down before money at the very same moment that we pretend to rebel against it.

The Compulsive—III

About five months ago, around June, I started working for a limousine service . . . I get my CDL license, my commercial driver's license. Now I'm working eighty to ninety hours a week. I find out that there's no way I can do home improvement. I have to only do the driving. But now I say to myself, well, I try to say this to Patty. I got to try. She's gotta see a turnaround for me to get back, for us to start getting—you know. And we have a fight.

So I was taking a lot of shit from her in the last year. I deserve it. It's not a relationship I want to be in. It really's [not] serving me and serving her.

So I'm thinking if I drink a couple of shots or something, I would get real drunk coupled with the sleeping pills. I just fall asleep. I'll never wake up. And it always comes back to my kids. Every time I think about suicide, it always comes back to my kids.

Well, what happened is this: I'm doin' good. I'm doing very few rides to Atlantic City. . . . It's about three months, I get my first ride [to Atlantic City]. I go down to the casino, I go into the casino. . . . I'm only making about $700 a week. . . . I went to the Sands. . . . I lose. I don't play any poker. I only play blackjack.

Immediately, I lose $1,400. Immediately. I'm feeling like this is impossible. . . . I violated parole because I was gambling. That was a stipulation. I had to go to Gamblers Anonymous meetings, and not gamble. So I was doing that, and how could they check? How would they know?

So I'm, like, really psyched, because every time I've been off of gambling for a while and I went back I always, usually, had a good win. I sit down in the Sands. And I've had some bad losses, blackjack losses at the Sands dating way back. And I just sit down and I lose everything. I mean, I can't get a break. . . . Every time I win a hand I double down, then I lose. Every time I get a split I lose. I lose my money. So now I'm really pissed. . . . I got no money.

So I drive this one guy, and I know he's going to California for a week. He's got a Jeep Cherokee. Now I know a lot of people. I think I can get rid of this Jeep. Just gonna take the Jeep. I'll take the Jeep, I'll sell it, I'll get money. I'll at least have my money back. . . . And Patty won't find out. At least I can recoup the money.

I don't check about the Jeep first. In other words, I don't go to x, y, or z, and say how much can you get for this Jeep. I just go get the Jeep. I do the burglary. Just the keys. I get the keys. Take the Jeep out, drive the Jeep away.

I have the Jeep for a week and half. I can't get rid of it. The Jeep's outside my frickin' apartment, it's half a block away. Nobody will buy it off me. . . . The police check . . . come to my place. What am I gonna say? I gave them the keys. . . . So, they get the Jeep back, perfect. . . . And I get bail, $500. This is October [1996].

I get out. I have some money, like $1,000. So I go down to Atlantic City. . . . Every time I go to Atlantic City and I play poker, it's just like inevitably in the first two hours I win. Because I'm very patient. . . . If I don't have a solid hand to go to the river, I don't play. Three, four times, I go down. I got like $600,000, makin' money. . . . Then, I go down, I fuckin' lose it. . . . Unbelievable, right?

♦ ♣ ♥ ♠

Lisa gave me some money. She wanted me to pick up a book, an SAT book for [one of the kids]. So, I want to go to Barnes and Noble to get the book. . . . I want to go into a store to buy some stuff to take it home. So I see all these cars coming out of this one street. I mean, it's just a lot of cars. I figured, people coming out of the street, that means people are leaving their houses.

I'm dressed in regular clothes, my regular blue jacket. I have a pair of gloves in the car, a flashlight. So I go to my trunk and I take like a screwdriver, like a chisel. So I go over there . . . I just walk down the street, and I saw this house. I go into the house. I could tell it was empty. I checked there about twenty minutes, ringing the back door, *ringing the front door. Makin' sure nobody was home. I finally get into a front window. I'm in the house not even a minute. The lady comes home.*

She opens the front door. Now, I'm thinkin' if she shuts the front door, I'm gonna be in the house by myself, with her, by myself. So I'm there. There's no way I can get out the window, it took me long enough to get in the window. Well, the back door is between me and her. So I have to pass her. So, what do I do?

She's saying good-bye to whoever dropped her off. And so what am I gonna do? I'm behind a couch. I have to stand up. Person drives away, so she's at the door, the screen shuts, she's gonna shut it. I stand up. I stand up, she sees me, she screams, she runs out. Police.

I go out the back door and I go away. And they got me. The cops catch me walking. I don't have anything on me but they bring me back and say she could identify me. Which she probably could, because I looked her right in the face. I was more scared than she was.

The state is looking at it, they want to give me five years and another five years, consecutive. They're saying since I had this gun charge and I had this previous breaking and entering. . . . I don't have a professional person to support my claim that I'm a gambler.

At this time, sitting right here, this just doesn't even seem possible. . . . All this time, all these years, I never hurt anybody trying to make it right for myself. But, does that really matter, that I didn't hurt anybody? . . . Trying to make it right. Trying to say I deserve this.

Gambling leads to something else, it leads to me trying to get money the fast way, stealing. God knows I made enough money doing the right thing, and you know, making that money grow and getting the things I want again, stuff like that. It just hasn't worked out.

And no matter how much time I put with the kids, or teaching the kids—I love teaching the kids basketball—no matter how much time I put in it, it's just almost nothing. It doesn't help. It doesn't stop me from doing it. It doesn't stop me from gambling. And that doesn't stop me from stealing and getting money.

They're really looking to hammer me. And like Patty says, "Well, yeah, but you're not a murderer, you're not an armed robber." You know, "Listen Patty, I'm a three-time loser, so to speak." It's not criminal, I'm not dangerous, it's not violent crimes, it's in felonies. They're still a felony. It's a lower class of felony, it's a Class Three felony. Class One being the most serious, Class Four being the least. But still, it's a felony.

I'm thinkin' I was a cop, that could really help me here, then I was in the Marines. . . . So where I am today is in this apartment. Scared to *even go to work, scared to even go out. Just getting $5 an hour. I've got $46 in my pocket. My car doesn't work.*

I must've went through this scenario a million times when I was in prison, just laying there in some of the dungeons on the way to Oklahoma—to lockup in Oklahoma. It's just a state that you step in, the draw of the action, the chance of turning that card over and it's the right card. You know what that feeling is like? Whew, I thought about it awhile and that's better than any sex I ever had.

EPILOGUE:
ENDGAME

IN 1997, DETROIT BECAME the latest American city to seriously consider legalizing casino gambling. Detroit is a perfect candidate for the ministrations of commercial gambling's soothsayers, and it is being prodded to consider gambling for familiar reasons. The Motor City's economy has long since sputtered, and just across the Detroit River a Canadian casino is hauling in more than $500 million a year—about 80 percent of which comes from Michigan residents. Why let the other guys get the loot when such an easy solution is at hand?

Steve Wynn and Kirk Kerkorian are among the casino moguls pitching their wares in Detroit, with Donald Trump and former mayor Coleman Young left on the sidelines after the city rejected their bids. Detroit, boasting unemployment of 9 percent, almost twice the national rate, projects a windfall of some 15,000 jobs from three potential casinos. Expected revenue from the casinos is pegged as high as $1.2 billion, with the city getting some $200 million of that in taxes. But these are all projections, and the experiences of New Orleans and Atlantic City show how unlikely it is that casinos will solve Detroit's gritty, urban economic problems. Harrah's Entertainment, still ensnared in its casino debacle in New Orleans, took a look at Detroit and dropped out of the bidding. Detroit has never been a must-see for tourists, it has fewer residents than Phoenix, and it lacks adequate roads and sewers to support whatever influx casinos might bring. Still, Motown presses on, ready in its desperation to become another link in the national gambling chain.

Meanwhile, for the first time in two decades, a federal commission has convened to examine gambling's social and economic impact. The National Gambling Impact Study Commission was created in 1996 with a slim $4 million budget and a two-year mandate to carry out its task. The commission has been a political football since its inception and has been heavily stocked with appointees who have clear biases about gambling—biases that threaten to keep the group from accomplishing substantive work before it has to shut down.

Appointments to the commission's nine-member panel were split among Senate Majority Leader Trent Lott, House Speaker Newt Gingrich, both Republicans, and President Bill Clinton, a Democrat. In the inevitable horse trading that followed, appointments were subjected to the financial and political influences of the gambling industry's opponents and proponents.

Lott picked James Dobson, president of a conservative Christian group, and Paul Moore, a radiologist whose apparent qualification is nothing more than the fact that he is Lott's neighbor back home in Mississippi. Senator Tom Daschle, a South Dakota Republican given a vote by Lott, appointed Leo McCarthy, a former lieutenant governor of California. Gingrich chose Kay James, a dean at evangelist Pat Robertson's Regent University who was also named head of the commission, and Terrence Lanni, chairman of MGM Grand, one of the largest casino companies. Richard Gephardt, a Missouri Democrat given a vote by Gingrich, named John Wilhelm, head of the Hotel Employees and Restaurant Employees International Union, which represents thousands of casino workers. For his part, Clinton chose Bill Bible, chairman of the Nevada Gaming Control Board; Richard Leone, head of a New York public policy think tank, the Twentieth Century Fund; and Robert Loescher, a Native American who is a member of Alaska's Tlingit tribe. The commission's members will also name their own executive director at some point.

The views of the commission members may change over time, but some of their perspectives are fairly clear. Lanni is a gambling stalwart. Wilhelm and Loescher are also likely to be strong supporters of commercial gambling. Dobson and James are morally opposed to gambling. McCarthy, who opposed the legalization of the California lottery, and Leone, who opposed the legalization of casino gambling and the state lottery in New Jersey, are nonetheless considered to be neutral. Likewise, Bible, even though he comes from a gambling state, is considered neutral. Moore's views are also considered neutral. The commission has been beset by disagreements over policy and tactics, disagreements that threaten its ability to make the most of its limited resources and powers.

As it carries out its task, the commission can subpoena documents but not individuals. People can be requested to elaborate on information in documents, but have the option of appearing before the panel in person or responding by letter. All information collected by the commission that already isn't in the public record must remain confidential. The House version of the bill authorizing the commission originally allowed for the subpoena of witnesses and had no confidentiality clauses, but those aspects were watered down before the Senate let the bill pass. Whatever recommendations come out of the commission's inquiry won't be enforceable, so states won't have to adopt or even pay any attention to them.

However toothless the commission may be, it has the ability to shed light on aspects of commercial gambling that have thus far eluded careful examination. Chief among these may be the extent to which the industry relies on compulsive and problem gamblers for its livelihood. Compulsive gambling could emerge as the industry's albatross, in much the same way as nicotine addiction gave the public a clearer understanding of how the tobacco industry operates. But some members of the commission are skeptical that the group will produce any bold statements.

"I anticipate there will be no unanimous report by this commission," says Leo McCarthy. "There will be unanimity on bland issues, but not on controversial issues."

McCarthy declines to say what he believes are the most "controversial issues" facing the commission, but compulsive gambling is certain to be among them.

Wherever the commission's work leads, its very existence underlines the national anxiety that has accompanied commercial gambling's emergence as one of the country's fastest-growing industries. On a broad scale, commercial gambling ignites the same fears that arise when any industry begins to dominate the communities in which it operates. Local and national political processes can be warped or corrupted by the industry's influence, and unforeseen or unfamiliar social problems can surface. The very real hope that new jobs and fresh tax revenues bring to any community is tempered by nagging doubts about what else happens after the gambling genie is let out of the bottle. Of course, gambling has been tightly woven into the fabric of so many aspects of American life since the country was founded that it can hardly be considered a newcomer in most places.

What is new, however, is how this once largely informal activity is being institutionalized and marketed with the same vigor and innocence as breakfast cereal. Commercial gambling's modern maestros like to point out how long gambling has been with us, without acknowledging how very different their product is from its predecessors. Lotteries have come and gone in the past, but they have never been as ubiquitous, frequent, and permanent as they are now. Sports and sports betting have always been twins, but television and the personal computer have ramped up the action and the stakes. And cyberspace has freed gambling from the constraints of borders and time. Horse racing, perhaps the most venerable form of gambling in America, is simply too slow and too involved to compete with these merchants of speed.

Lording it above all others in this new universe of fast-paced, commercial gambling are casinos. Roughly 86 percent of the $586.5 billion wagered in 1996 was wagered in casinos, and about 50 percent of the $47.6 billion lost by gamblers that year was lost in casinos. Casino gambling is the most enticing and most cleverly marketed form of gambling in the country. Casinos, deft veterans in the art of extraction, for the most part have found homes in communities that only a generation ago had no need or no desire for their presence. At once enthralled by the prospect of riches and despondent about economic woes, these communities, like gamblers themselves, are putting their chips on the table. Some communities have won their bets, but all of them are experimenting with an industry that inflicts social and human costs not yet fully understood.

Although most people gamble for recreation, commercial gambling is not just another form of recreation. It reduces human desire and imagination to a thirst for action and a relentless quest for one narcotic— money. Gambling is an ancient activity, but in America, land of the slot machine and the instant lottery ticket, it is part of a new tale. It is a tale of immediate gratification and packaged, spiritless amusement, brought out of exile in the desert and into your backyard with all the icing and enchantment of a bakery confection. It is a tale of a country absorbed in the most dangerous of games, and that tale is just beginning to unfold.

NOTES

All book citations are noted by the book's author; full citations can be found in the bibliography. Court documents, manuscripts, journal articles, and studies are noted individually below, as are citations from newspapers and magazines. Of particular help were the *New York Times, Wall Street Journal, International Gaming & Wagering Business, Las Vegas Review-Journal,* and *New Orleans Times-Picayune.*

Introduction
Going for Broke

4 In 1976, we bet $17.3 billion: 1996 United States Gross Annual Wager, *International Gaming & Wagering Business,* August 1997, p. 8.; Commission on the Review of the National Policy Toward Gambling, October 15, 1976, p. 63.

4 Judged by dollars spent: 1996 United States Gross Annual Wager, *International Gaming & Wagering Business,* August 1997, p. 42.

Chapter 1
Cyberspace: Borderless Betting

7 "We all can't just hop in a jet and fly to Las Vegas": interview with the author, October 12, 1997.

8 While the exact size of the nambling market: 1996 United States Gross Annual Wager, *International Gaming & Wagering Business,* August 1997, p. 60.

10 Information on Internet nodes is from the National Science Foundation.

11 "I believe this is going to be a huge, huge market": interview with the author, June 11, 1996.

12 "Those philosophies are about living for the moment and embracing change": interview with the author, June 30, 1997.

12 There are currently about thirty Internet: interview with the author, June 16, 1997.

14 The FBI executed a search warrant: The FBI search is mentioned in the company's 1997 SEC filings. The Missouri indictment is from *State of Missouri v. Interactive Gaming & Communications Corp. and Michael F. Simone,* 197CF0014, Circuit Court of Greene County, Missouri, 6/26/97.

Mr. Simone declined to comment for this book. His statements were made on July 31, 1997, before a trade group representing the on-line gambling industry. A release summarizing that statement was faxed by Interactive Gaming to the author.

15 A key figure behind Interactive is Louis M. Mayo: Securities & Exchange Commission Litigation Release No. 3768, June 28, 1967; *U.S. v. Louis M. Mayo, Jr., et al.* CV95-0082, U.S. District Court for the Eastern District of Pennsylvania. Mayo and Moscariello could not be reached for comment. Mayo's attorney, Robert E. Welsh, did not return phone calls.

15 "The great concern is": interview with the author, June 27, 1997.

Chapter 2
Las Vegas: Let the Games Begin

22 For thirty-six years, Benny, a former bootlegger and a convicted murderer: Reid and Demaris, p. 155.

22 Variously described as the caretaker "of underworld investments in Las Vegas" and "one of the architects of the skimming process": Barlett and Steele, p. 323.

22 Dalitz had gotten his professional start: *Investigation of Organized Crime in Interstate Commerce*, 81st Congress, 2d Session, Part 2, pp. 174–75.

24 "For those whose interests lay": Fabian, pp. 3, 42.

24 "The gambling propensity": Veblen, pp. 276–77.

25 "rowdy little community like Tijuana": Findlay, p. 121.

26 He had operated clubs in Los Angeles: Reid and Demaris, pp. 62–64.

27 In 1945, Siegel, Meyer Lansky, and several other mobsters bought the El Cortez: Lacey, p. 477.

27 After its initial and unsuccessful flirtation: James Smith, "Ben Siegel: Father of Las Vegas and the Modern Casino-Hotel," *Journal of Popular Culture*, spring 1992.

28 "There were mountains and palm trees": interview with the author, December 16, 1995.

28 Las Vegas' population had tripled to about 64,000: U.S. Dept. of Commerce, Census of Population, 1960.

28 "These innovations are expensive": Best and Hillyer, "Fanciful Press Agentry," cited in Tronnes, p. 123.

30 But when Clark, who began building the Desert Inn in 1947: Moehring, pp. 74–75, 89.

31 While a *Wall Street Journal* writer estimated: *The Wall Street Journal*, August 2, 1955.

31 "the individual who oversees the operations": Neff, p. 219.

31 Hoover was an avid gambler: Summers, pp. 234–41.

32 Dalitz began pressuring the commission: Farrell and Case, pp. 49–52. Laxalt declined to be interviewed for this book, instead providing a written response to questions.

33 Hughes had been looking around: Barlett and Steele, p. 289.

33 Together, the two resorts' combined profits: ibid., p. 367.

33 Hughes would ultimately invest: *The Wall Street Journal*, July 31, 1973.

33 As late as 1979: *The Wall Street Journal,* August 6, 1979.
34 "Roman Empire Reborn in L[as] V[egas]": *Las Vegas Review-Journal,* August 5, 1966.
35 "Over the years that I have been creating hotels": *Las Vegas Sun Magazine,* October 14, 1979.
35 Such touches contributed to construction: ibid.
35 In 1958, his Atlanta motel: Brill, p. 209.
35 Federal Bureau of Investigation memos: ibid., p. 210.
35 Jimmy Hoffa was in attendance: *Las Vegas Review-Journal,* August 6, 1966.
36 "The pit was the game": interview with the author, December 12, 1995.
37 "a teddy bear or a photo of you": *The Wall Street Journal,* February 24, 1969.
37 In 1971, the fund purchased: Brill, p. 216.
38 "He [Dorfman] told me": *Chicago Tribune,* December 4, 1985.
38 Between 1969 and 1974, he had lost almost $4 million: *The Wall Street Journal,* March 18, 1975.
38 "They decided you didn't need high rollers": interview with the author, December 14, 1995.
40 "Slot machines aren't intimidating": interview with the author, December 15, 1995.
41 "He was a manufacturer": interview with the author, April 2, 1996.
41 There were 90,612 slot machines in Nevada's casinos: W. Bruce Turner, *Gaming Equipment Supply Outlook,* Salomon Brothers, Inc., January 17, 1995.
42 Las Vegas' clientele "skews old": interview with the author, December 16, 1995.
43 Ralph Engelstad owns the Imperial Palace: Engelstad declined to be interviewed for this book.
43 "I've always tried to give them a theme": Associated Press, October 7, 1988.
44 "I only play video poker because you can pretend": interview with the author, December 17, 1995.
44 "I'm a reformed woman": interview with the author, July 4, 1997.
45 "I tell you that there are no suckers": interview with the author, December 12, 1995.
45 Conventional wisdom has it that compulsive gamblers: *International Gaming & Wagering Business,* July 1996; author's interview with William Eadington, October 27, 1997.
45 A Harvard Medical School: *Estimating the Prevalence of Disordered Gambling,* Harvard Medical School Division on Addictions, December 10, 1997.
45 Jeffrey Lowenhar: interview with the author, August 20, 1996.
46 In Atlantic City and the newer riverboat casinos: author's interviews with officials of Harrah's Entertainment, Inc., and Casino America, Inc., August 20 and 23, 1996.
46 Casinos "don't target compulsives": interview with the author, October 18, 1997.
46 "My concern is that this is not a minor issue": interview with the author, October 17, 1997.

46 "Are we suggesting that our love affair": interview with the author, December 12, 1995.

47 But Wynn's mentor: author's interview with Parry Thomas, December 15, 1997; author's interview with Alan Feldman, January 12, 1998.

47 Friedman was a ubiquitous: *U.S.* v. *Jack William Tocco, et al.*, CR-96-80201, U.S. District Court for Eastern District of Michigan.

48 "I've got to see that this community stays healthy": *Las Vegas Review-Journal*, December 31, 1964.

48 Continental had a checkered history: *The Wall Street Journal*, May 23, 1969; February 23, 1976.

48 Shortly after Continental agreed: *The Wall Street Journal*, December 19, 1969.

49 Wynn now says the $439 million package: interview with the author, December 12, 1995.

49 In 1983, New Jersey regulators censured: State of New Jersey Commission of Investigation, *Abuse and Misuse of Credit Controls at Atlantic City Casinos*, June 1983.

49 The Atlantic City Nugget's second-largest shareholder, Edward Doumani: *The Wall Street Journal*, December 13, 1984.

49 And Mel Harris, marketing chief: *Las Vegas Review-Journal*, March 8, 1992.

50 "I have never met or had any contact with a hoodlum": interview with the author, December 12, 1995.

50 "I think it's premature to pronounce the Mob dead": interview with the author, March 15, 1996.

53 Although retirees have been a key component: *American Banker*, March 15, 1996.

53 local police say Las Vegas is home to some one hundred street gangs: *The Washington Post*, December 26, 1995.

53 Another 1997 study, which showed: *The Personal Bankruptcy Crisis, 1997*, SMR Research Corp.

53–54 While one local health care official estimates that 12 percent: *Las Vegas Review-Journal*, January 14, 1996.

54 "There's a lot of wealthy people": interview with the author, November 15, 1995.

55 Casino executives say that Australian media kingpin: MGM declined to talk about Packer.

56 simply a "better mousetrap": interview with the author, December 12, 1995.

56 "Gaming didn't become a big business": interview with the author, December 12, 1995.

Chapter 3
Atlantic City: Resort of Broken Promises

63 "Aliases and deception": Quotations are from Claridge dossier, obtained by the author.

63 "When I started out": interview with the author, June 28, 1996.

63   "sold its wares cash-on-delivery": Funnell, p. 47.
64   "I unrolled a great and well-finished map": Levi and Eisenberg, p. 4.
66   "A remarkable myth about the city": Funnell, pp. 143–45.
66   "What are we going to do with our colored people?": *Philadelphia In-quirer,* July 23, 1893.
67   "No public road or building could be let": *Reader's Digest,* May 1942.
68   "It was like the scene in *2001: A Space Odyssey*": interview with the author, April 15, 1996.
69   In 1984, Crosby's losing trades: *The Wall Street Journal,* November 14, 1985.
69   In 1967, Resorts appointed Eddie Cellini: Demaris, pp. 99–101.
70   Resorts had been pushing for legalization in Atlantic City since 1970: Mahon, p. 121.
70   A well-oiled lobbying and public relations: Sternlieb and Hughes, p. 52.
70   "Look, it's no big honor": *The Wall Street Journal,* October 29, 1976.
71   "a lesson in civics": Mahon, p. 132.
71   The CCC's first chief, Joseph Lordi: Sternlieb and Hughes, pp. 58, 149–51.
71   Similar circumstances surrounded: *The Wall Street Journal,* November 14, 1985.
72   "I think we have committed ourselves": Levi and Eisenberg, p. 208.
73   More than 173,000 teenagers: *The Wall Street Journal,* February 27, 1989.
74   "You're all alone": interview with the author, May 1, 1996.
75   According to a state investigation in 1983: State of New Jersey Commission of Investigation, *Abuse and Misuse of Credit Controls at Atlantic City Casinos,* June 1983.
76   Several European countries assert parentage: Scarne, p. 350.
77   A security guard at Binion's told authorities: *Houston Chronicle,* March 14, 1989.
78   "We're the casino": interview with the author, June 28, 1996.
79   "The [card] players are the front line": interview with the author, April 13, 1996.
81   In 1989, one casino had to ask: *The Wall Street Journal,* March 19, 1991.
81   "When we started going here": interview with the author, April 12, 1996.
82   "The thing people don't know about me": interview with the author, April 22, 1996. All other quotations of Trump are from the same interview, unless otherwise noted.
82   "broke quickly, like the weak puppies": *The New York Times Magazine,* November 19, 1995.
83   "It's very important for [Trump]": interview with the author, August 21, 1996.
83   a "colossal new force": Barrett, p. 210.
83   a fortune once estimated: *New York Newsday,* March 22, 1987.
85   "I don't think Donald has the patience": interview with the author, April 12, 1996.
87   Moreover, as reported by: *The Wall Street Journal,* June 18, 1990.
87   In 1996, Trump said: interview with the author, August 23, 1996.
88   Financial columnist Allan Sloan: *The Washington Post,* February 4, 1997.

89 "We can now transport the entertainment megaresort": interview with the author, April 17, 1996.

90 a 1997 study found: *The Personal Bankruptcy Crisis, 1997*, SMR Research Corp.

91 "There has been some good": interview with the author, April 15, 1996.

Chapter 4
New Orleans: Mischief in the Big Easy

101 In Vicksburg, Mississippi, in 1835: Chafetz, pp. 55–63; Findlay, pp. 63–69; Fabian, pp. 31–38.

101 "Our streets everywhere": Fabian, p. 36.

102 By 1849, there were 600 packets: Keating, p. 14.

102 "Beau Brummell in all his glory": Chafetz, p. 74.

103 At the height of the steamboat era: Longstreet, p. 44.

103 "Some men are born rascals": Devol, pp. 150–51.

103 "It's very pretty to read about": *Baton Rouge Sunday Advocate*, September 4, 1994.

104 "You press against a small lever": Maskelyne, p. 294.

104 "Few people doubted": Findlay, p. 74.

106 Charles Howard, a fast-talking: Ezell, p. 243.

106 "The man who buys a ticket": Davis, pp. 284–85.

107 By 1890, the Louisiana lottery: Ezell, p. 254.

107 Although most other lottery companies: ibid, p. 247.

107 According to one estimate: Dufour, p. 219.

107 And "priests were kept so busy": *Smithsonian Magazine*, January 1980.

108 According to recently declassified Federal Bureau of Investigation files: *Christian Science Monitor*, June 14, 1993.

112 "These guys were real mom-and-pop operators": The former regulator requested anonymity.

112 The Schillings: The Schillings could not be reached for comment.

113 "These people are Bible Belt": interview with the author, July 12, 1996.

113 "I think there would be a mad rush": interview with the author, July 12, 1996.

114 Gus' place served black-market: *Mississippi Coast Magazine*, summer 1994.

114 Local officials openly admitted: Humes, p. 113.

115 "There was an awful lot of bitterness": interview with the author, July 10, 1996.

116 "It's a high, high degree": interview with the author, July 10, 1996.

117 "These guys should have stayed": interview with the author, November 21, 1995. Other quotations from the same interview.

119 "We still have a lot to learn": interview with the author, December 15, 1995.

119 Limited studies of casino employees: *International Gaming & Wagering Business*, July 1996.

119 "I worry about compulsive gamblers": interview with the author, April 12, 1996.

120 The gambling industry dished out: *Mother Jones*, July/August 1997, p. 35.

120 but the consultants were quite happy: *Chicago Tribune*, March 28, 1995.

120 Former Illinois governor James Thompson: Neither Cellini nor Thompson responded to repeated interview requests. Argosy says it is not a target of the Indiana investigation and says it is company policy not to comment on the activities of major shareholders.

121 "I'll go to what Marc Antony": *Baton Rouge State Times*, February 15, 1986.

122 Yet the subsequent public outcry: *Baton Rouge Advocate*, January 4, 1996.

122 "a place where public officials": *New Orleans Times-Picayune*, December 9, 1994.

122 According to a 1991 FBI debriefing: From FBI debriefing obtained by author.

122 And according to a confidential report: August 24, 1995, New Jersey Division of Gaming Enforcement report obtained by author. See also: U.S. District Court for the Eastern District of Louisiana, Miscl. No. 92-2344, Section E, In the Matter of the Application of the United States of America for an Order Authorizing the Interception of Oral Communications; Demaris, pp. 196–97.

123 But Bally later resumed doing business with the distributor: ibid.

125 "We still think that, had the casino opened": interview with the author, August 29, 1996.

125 "The demand for gaming": *Standard & Poor's Creditweek Municipal*, March 18, 1996.

Chapter 5
Mashantucket: The Rainmaker

130 Native Americans interviewed for this book said it is acceptable to refer to them as either Native Americans or Indians. The author switches freely between the terms.

130 Nationally, revenue from Native American gambling climbed to $5.3 billion: 1996 United States Gross Annual Wager, *International Gaming & Wagering Business*, August 1997, p. 13.

131 "We attempted to empower": interview with the author, August 7, 1996.

132 "We live in fear": interview with the author, August 12, 1996.

133 At one time, the Pequots: Hauptman and Wherry, p. 46.

133 "blotted out": ibid., p. 76.

135 The Yakima Indians were heavy bettors: Information on Yakimas, Mohave, Mandan, et al., from Henry Lesieur, "Pathological Gambling, Work, and Employee Assistance," *Journal of Employee Assistance Research*, vol. 1, no. 1, summer 1992.

137 In 1991, *San Francisco Chronicle*: *San Francisco Chronicle*, September 4, 1991.

141 "The first years were a little tough": interview with the author, August 7, 1996.

142   "When we arrived here eleven years ago": interview with the author, August 7, 1996.

143   "If you look at some of the Indians": *Barron's,* October 18, 1993; *Buffalo News,* October 6, 1993.

143   Trump's accusation is exaggerated: interview with the author, June 3, 1996.

143–144   "We do in excess of $3.6 million a day": interview with the author, August 27, 1996.

145   "Indian gambling grew so quickly": interview with the author, September 17,1996.

146   By the end of 1996, 184 tribes: U.S. General Accounting Office, *A Profile of the Indian Gaming Industry,* May 1997, p. 3.

148   "They were the lily-fingered": Bennett, p. 139.

149   "You'd think people wouldn't come": interview with the author, August 10, 1996.

150   But Tommy Tibbitts: interview with the author, August 9, 1996. The tribe forced Turnkey out in late 1996, and it now runs the casino. The tribe said it now audits the casino regularly.

150   "Everybody saw what happened in Connecticut": interview with the author, August 9, 1996.

Chapter 6
Albany: Dollars and Dreams

156   Gamblers lost $16.2 billion: 1996 United States Gross Annual Wager, *International Gaming & Wagering Business,* August 1997, pp. 59–60.

158   Before the Revolutionary War: Scarne, p. 150.

158   "You could scarcely imagine": Ezell, pp. 177–78.

158   "[Nineteenth-century] lotteries appear to have": Clotfelter and Cook, p. 35.

158   "not regarded at all": ibid.

159   With the assistance of these operators: Brenner, p. 231.

159   "In no place have I seen": Ezell, p. 215.

160   "I want to see our State evangelized": Henretta, et al., p. 300.

160   In 1850, the city had about 6,000 gambling halls: Commission on the Review of the National Policy Toward Gambling, October 15, 1976, p. 169.

161   "African-American city dwellers": Fabian, p. 107.

161   Store owners welcomed the action: *Illegal Gambling in New York,* U.S. Department of Justice, April 1982, p. 81.

161   Within the black community: Fabian, pp. 142–49.

163   "Harlem's newspapers admitted": *Illegal Gambling in New York,* U.S. Department of Justice, April 1982, p. 82.

163   In 1958, *The New York Times: The New York Times,* March 25, 1958.

164   The state hoped to retain $4 million: *The Wall Street Journal,* March 27, 1964.

165   "an appreciative imagination of a high order": Caro, p. 1068.

166 One high-minded bank: *The New York Times*, June 17, 1967.

166 When the green-and-white tickets: *The Wall Street Journal*, June 2, 1967.

167 "If Mr. Rockefeller wishes to support": National Institute of Law Enforcement, p. 614.

169 "People play lotteries": interview with the author, November 21, 1996.

170 "Microwave popcorn, one-hour photo": *Public Gaming International*, March 1996.

170 "We have a much higher payout": interview with the author, December 20, 1996.

171 In fiscal 1996, Massachusetts residents: *LaFleur's Fiscal 1996 Lottery Interim Report*, p. 11.

171 "A single news story": interview with the author, November 21, 1996.

172 In the summer of 1997, the U.S. Attorney's Office: U.S. District Court, Western District of Washington, C97-0931, June 5, 1997. Down couldn't be reached for comment, and one of his attorneys declined to respond to the allegations.

172 "They kept telling me I'd win": interview with the author, July 1, 1997.

173 "a continuous stringing together": Lesieur, p. 23.

173 " 'Action.' Supposedly the word speaks": ibid., p. 44.

174 Bob Buccino, an organized crime investigator: interview with the author, December 9, 1996.

174 A 1991 report: State of New Jersey Commission of Investigation, *Video Gambling*, September 1991, pp. 28–29.

175 He pleaded guilty: *Chicago Sun-Times*, June 16, 1988. Gtech officials declined repeated requests to be interviewed for this book; it responded to questions in a letter written shortly before publication.

176 Maryanne Gilliard: All quotations of Gilliard are taken from an interview with the author, January 22, 1997.

176 That was the case in California in 1993: *The Wall Street Journal*, April 14, 1993.

176 A tape recording: *Sacramento Bee*, November 21, 1993.

177 But according to reporter Bill Bulkeley: *The Wall Street Journal*, October 7, 1996.

177 "You have to be able to push": interview with author, November 20, 1996.

177 "Problem gamblers [in New York]": Report to the New York Council on Problem Gambling, *Gambling and Problem Gambling in New York*, July 1996, pp. vii, 52.

179 "Lottery revenues do not help schools": Eadington and Cornelius, *Gambling: Public Policies and the Social Sciences*, p. 568.

179 Critics of lotteries regularly claim: Eadington and Cornelius, *Gambling and Commercial Gaming*, pp. 309–311; Clotfelter and Cook, pp. 91–104.

179 A 1995 study of New York: *Newsday*, December 4, 1995.

179 Economists Clotfelter and Cook cite: Clotfelter and Cook, p. 80.

180 States that depend heavily: Eadington and Cornelius, *Gambling and Commercial Gaming*, p. 270.

180 "I'm trying to make money, man": interview with the author, March 7, 1997.

Chapter 7
Louisville: Faded Jewel of the Sport of Kings

187   "I shout and get involved": interview with the author, September 30, 1996.

187   "Haaaaahhhh!": interview with the author, October 1, 1996.

187   "My God, he's gonna win it": interview with the author, May 5, 1996.

188   "Will we ever get back here again?": interview with the author, September 30, 1996.

188   Between 1982 and 1996: 1996 United States Gross Annual Wager, *International Gaming & Wagering Business*, August 1997, p. 14.

189   "It has seemed very strange": Cited in Thomas, p. 37.

190   One race, attended by Charles II: Sasuly, p. 8.

192   Lexington, a great Thoroughbred: Auerbach, p. 32.

195   One New York ring: Chafetz, p. 267.

196   "The time has gone": Cited in Thomas, p. 72.

197   "You line up twenty people": interview with the author, June 4, 1997.

199   got help building his network from mobsters Al Capone and Meyer Lansky: *San Diego Union Tribune*, January 23, 1994.

199   By 1940, Annenberg was AT&T's: Fox, p. 103.

199   Kefauver labeled Continental: Moldea, p. 71.

199   "The wire service is as essential": Sasuly, p. 178.

200   Local law enforcement officials said: interview with Westchester County district attorney's office, New York, May 21, 1997.

201   "The guy who gambles on a horse": interview with the author, October 25, 1996.

201   Between 1940 and 1949, 68,115 thoroughbred foals: All data on foals from the Jockey Club's *1996 Fact Book*, p. 7.

201   The right to mate a brood mare: *The Wall Street Journal*, November 21, 1985.

202   While the price for ordinary yearlings: Jockey Club, *1996 Fact Book*, p. 25.

202   the price of top yearlings: *The Wall Street Journal*, October 25, 1989.

202   "Right now, my biggest worry": interview with the author, October 1, 1996.

203   "Do they want me to sit here": interview with the author, May 5, 1996.

204   "Every trainer and race track": interview with the author, June 12, 1996.

205   "The quality of the product": interview with the author, June 13, 1996.

206   Fewer than 35 million people: Thoroughbred Racing Association; Scarne, p. 34.

207   "We've lost a generation": interview with the author, November 13, 1996.

Chapter 8
San Francisco: All That Glitters

212   Bill Henry sits: Bill Henry is not the gambler's real name. He requested anonymity.

212   "People need outlets": interview with the author, January 26, 1997.

214   Some estimate that $88 billion: *International Gaming & Wagering Business,* April 1, 1996, *Newark Star-Ledger,* January 24, 1997.
215   "[We,] being financially involved": Henretta, et al., p. 433.
215–216   "No man, young or old": Quaife, p. 293.
216   In the area that became the Barbary Coast: *San Francisco Examiner,* April 8, 1991.
216   On at least one occasion: Quaife, p. 297.
216   "The greatest crowd is about": ibid., pp. 139–42.
218   Tickets were sold at hundreds of spots: Dillon, pp. 85–96.
218   Prior to the war: Flamm, pp. 33, 134–35.
220   "Sullivan is a man": *Boston Globe,* November 7, 1993.
220   Boxers were also hired as "crimps": Pickelhaupt, p. 44–57.
220   In the last championship fought: *Los Angeles Times,* July 8, 1989.
220–221   Sportswriter and boxing aficionado: interview with the author, December 9, 1996.
221   Other fighters who trained: *Oakland Tribune,* August 2, 1992.
222   In San Francisco, Western Union: Flamm, p. 73.
222   "Politicians, lawyers, merchants": *St. Louis Post-Dispatch,* September 13, 1992.
222   Protestant ministers busy promoting: Sammons, p. 4.
222   And in 1912, the University of California: *Sacramento Bee,* August 11, 1991.
223   Jim Jeffries fought five title: Sammons, p. 24.
223   Rickard hit upon the idea: *Los Angeles Times,* June 12, 1988.
224   after one Temple Cup game: *Baltimore Sun,* July 9, 1996.
225   Even the language: Asinof, p. 10.
225   "An outfielder, settling under": ibid., p. 11.
225   Players and professional gamblers: Gutman, p. 170.
226   Anson, who was later elected to the Hall of Fame: Voigt, p. 6.
226   "the true sports": Kimmel, p. 140.
226   "No boy can grow": ibid.
226–227   After the seemingly unbeatable Athletics: Ward and Burns, p. 61.
227   The Yankees were founded: Chafetz, p. 314.
227   The pools bribed the police: Asinof, p. 13.
228   He mingled with the upper crust: Chafetz, pp. 422–24.
228   Rothstein also co-owned: Kowet, p. 51.
228–229   In the real world, two of Rothstein's disciples: Fox, pp. 43–44, 58.
229   Rothstein came up with a solution: Commission on the Review of the National Policy Toward Gambling, October 15, 1976, p. 170.
230   "The majority of the human race": Chafetz, p. 424.
230   An average of 9.3 million fans: James, p. 129.
231   Baseball historian Bill James: ibid., p. 134.
231   Hornsby's career ended: Gutman, p. 223.
231   So even a team such as: Ward and Burns, p. 201.
231   "I associated with a lot of hoodlums": Fox, p. 353.
232   Veeck himself was never accused: ibid.
232   Speculation that Durocher bet: Eskenazi, pp. 22, 300.
232   "Ballplayers gamble": *Time,* April 1, 1985.
232   In 1970, *Sports Illustrated: Sports Illustrated,* February 23, 1970.

233   "Well, he was our bread and butter": *Ottawa Citizen*, November 1, 1990.

233   "On my watch": interview with the author, December 6, 1996.

234   Jack McGurn and other Capone: Bergreen, pp. 232, 375.

234   "the word was out": Dempsey, p. 217.

234   After retiring, he went to work: Bergreen, p. 236.

235   Bootlegger Owney Madden: Sammons, p. 95.

235   He also controlled: ibid., p. 146.

236   Whereas 31 percent of the television: ibid., pp. 145, 174.

237   a ubiquitous huckster: Newfield, pp. 1–19.

237   In early 1995, according to Securities & Exchange Commission: MGM declined to comment on the arrangement with King, saying the SEC filing "has to speak for itself." Interview with the author, May 16, 1996.

237   "It had long been talked of": Hogan and German, p. 18.

238   "It is childish to suppose": *USA Today*, July 10, 1991.

238   who received some financial backing: Moldea, p. 40.

239   Carr had initially offered: *Atlanta Journal and Constitution*, August 23, 1987.

239   "It was said that before the autumn": *The New York Times*, February 17, 1959.

239   In 1933, a close friend: Harris, p. 155.

239   A fixture in Pittsburgh gambling: Kowet, pp. 34–35.

239   Erickson, who headed the Mob's: Moldea, pp. 39, 48.

239   Some of the Murchisons' real estate: ibid., pp. 103–105.

239   Carroll Rosenbloom, a heavy gambler: Harris, p. 45.

239   The San Francisco 49ers were originally: interview with former San Francisco 49ers president Al Ruffo, February 12, 1997.

239   DeBartolo made his money building shopping malls: *The Wall Street Journal*, October 9, 1986; *Barron's*, June 12, 1989. The DeBartolos declined to be interviewed for this book.

240   Davis, owner of the Oakland: *Oakland Tribune*, June 1, 1975; Harris, pp. 203–204. Davis declined to be interviewed for this book.

242   "The gambling craze has swept": Sasuly, p. 190.

243   In 1997, *Fresno Bee* reporters: *Fresno Bee*, March 7, 1997. Fresno State declined to comment and declined to make Tarkanian or his players available for comment.

243   Redskins quarterback Sammy Baugh: Moldea, p. 54.

243   Shortly after the Jets won: *The Wall Street Journal*, July 30, 1969.

243   According to bookies and gamblers: interviews with the author, May 13–17, 1996.

243   "It was a tragic situation": interview with the author, May 2, 1997.

245   "Pete, as strong as he felt": interview with the author, May 2, 1997.

245   Gambling had been part of children's: Eadington and Cornelius, *Gambling Behavior and Problem Gambling*, pp. 143, 396–97.

245   Howard Shaffer, a clinical psychologist: interview with the author, November 3, 1997.

245   Other researchers of adolescent: interview with the author, October 16, 1997.

246   As reported by *The Wall Street Journal*: *The Wall Street Journal*, October 25, 1996.

246 In 1992, a San Francisco high school: *San Francisco Chronicle,* December 5, 1992.
247 According to a 1991 University of Illinois study: Eadington and Cornelius, *Gambling Behavior and Problem Gambling,* pp. 477, 482.
247 "It is our prerogative": interview with the author, March 11, 1997.
248 "The whole issue of sports wagering": interview with the author, December 4, 1996.
248 "I'm not recommending that people bet": interview with the author, May 15, 1996.
250 "At the height of its powers": *The National,* June 6, 1990.
250 "We used to say you could write": interview with the author, May 11, 1996.
252 "Unc" Mahony, a Las Vegas sports bettor: "Unc Mahony" is a pseudonym. The bettor requested anonymity. Interview with author, May 12, 1996.
253 According to a lawsuit filed against Sacco: *United States* v. *Ronald Sacco,* U.S. District Court for the Northern District of California, CR-92-0048.

Chapter 9
New York: Risky Business

259 "I thought, 'What is the most interesting gambling' ": interview with the author, June 12, 1996.
259 "Gambling reallocates wealth": ibid.
261 By setting up shop in a coffeehouse: The moorings of this brief history of the coffee houses and the insurance industry are found in Peter L. Bernstein's book *Against the Gods.*
262 "a society swept up by the gambling craze": Brenner and Brenner, p. 105.
262 "I can calculate the motions": Kindleberger, p. 28.
263 England passed a series of laws: National Institute of Law Enforcement, p. 29; Brenner and Brenner, p. 105.
263 "The prospect of getting rich": Bernstein, *Against the Gods,* p. 21.
263 "Time is the dominant factor in gambling": ibid., pp. 14–15.
264 By 1815, only about two dozen: Leffler, p. 83.
264 Most towns of 1,000 people: Ezell, p. 82.
264 Thompson founded two of New York's largest banks: Weinstein and Deitch, p. 9; Commission on the Review of the National Policy Toward Gambling, October 15, 1976, p. 145; *American Banker,* April 29, 1986.
264 One lottery company, S. & M. Allen: Ezell, pp. 82–83.
265 Clark eventually spawned Jay Cooke & Company: ibid., p. 84.
265 After depositing as little as $1,500: Leffler, p. 87.
265 "A speculator in the nineteenth century": interview with the author, April 6, 1997.
266 Thus, while futures trading: *American Journal of Agricultural Economics,* February 1, 1995, p. 182.
266 "so popular that gambling": Markham, pp. 5, 9.
266 "The property of the wheat grower": Teweles, p. 12.
266 "People will endeavor to forecast": *Board of Trade* v. *Christie Grain and Stock Co.,* 198 U.S. 236 (1905).

267   Between 1840 and 1870, 70,000 miles: Information on amount and cost of railroad and canal building is from Chandler, pp. 88–90.

267–268   No other business in the United States: ibid., p. 155.

268   "The buccaneer style": Doerflinger and Rivkin, p. 58.

268   As another depression arrived in 1893: Leffler, p. 94.

268   "I never gamble": Chernow, p. 305.

268   The Northern Pacific, again the quarry: ibid., p. 92.

269   By 1929, 6,417 stocks: Leffler, p. 97.

269   "Speculation is very similar": Livermore, p. 20.

269   "one hell of a gambler": Doerflinger and Rivkin, p. 168.

270   One Kennedy pool: *Financial World*, September 16, 1986.

270   Chase president Albert Wiggins: Chernow, p. 356.

270   Meanwhile, National City president: Kindleberger, p. 73.

271   "I think traders gamble a lot more": interview with the author, March 25, 1997.

272   In 1945, 507 million shares: Trading data are from Securities & Exchange Commission Form R-31.

274   "It was the financial equivalent": interview with the author, October 7, 1996.

274   The first hint of what might be afoot: Board of Trade and Merc representatives declined interview requests for this book. "We really don't see a reasonable connection between gambling and our markets," Board of Trade spokeswoman Kiki Melonides told the author on October 4, 1996.

275   "In my judgment, a very high percentage": *Fortune*, December 7, 1987.

275   "I became more and more fascinated": interview with the author, October 8, 1996.

276   Almost $3 billion worth of S&P futures: Trading data from Chicago Mercantile Exchange.

276   As *Wall Street Journal* reporters: *The Wall Street Journal*, November 20, 1987.

278   "Derivative mortgage-backed securities": Kuttner, p. 167.

278   When Bankers Trust: *The Procter & Gamble Company* v. *Bankers Trust Company*, U.S. District Court, Southern District of Ohio, C-1-94-735.

279   Two years later, Soros: *The Wall Street Journal*, November 10, 1994.

279   "the untrammeled intensification of laissez-faire": *Atlantic Monthly*, February 1997. Soros did not respond to interview requests.

280   Then the stock dropped like a stone: *Securities and Exchange Commission* v. *Comparator Systems Corp.*, U.S. District Court, Central District of California, CV-96-3856.

280   Between 1980 and 1995, the total annual value of IPOs: Data from Securities Data Company.

280   Of all new companies that went public: ibid.

Chapter 10
Chicago: Churches, Charities, and Chance

282   "This is something": interview with the author, October 11, 1996.

283   "It used to be": interview with the author, October 11, 1996.

283   When the Civil War began: Miller, p. 96.
284   "Chicago is the boss": National Geographic Society, p. 246.
284   In one Chicago neighborhood: Census and ethnic data from ibid., pp. 248–49, 250.
284   Although former riverboat gamblers: Chafetz, p. 254.
285   Big Jim's club: *Chicago Tribune*, March 22, 1987.
285   At about the same time, local politico: Dedmon, p. 140.
285   "A Republican is a man": Miller, p. 445.
285   "involved primitive efforts": Eadington and Cornelius, *Gambling and Commercial Gaming*, p. 450.
285   Gambling was socially acceptable: McGowan, p. 3.
286   As David Newmark points out: cited in Eadington and Cornelius, *Gambling and Commercial Gaming*, p. 451.
286   "All lawful games": Brenner and Brenner, p. 78.
287   At each hotel, Flagler: Chafetz, p. 410.
287   "There is considerable truth": interview with author, April 17, 1996.
287   "I've got ten dollars": interview with the author, December 21, 1996.
288   Modeled on a sixteenth-century: National Association of Fundraising Ticket Manufacturers, *Charity Gaming in North America, 1995 Report*, pp. 12–13.
288   "I cannot grow frenzied": Brenner and Brenner, p. 83.
289   "Synagogues never have enough": interview with the author, May 29, 1997.
289   financially strapped synagogues in New York: The author interviewed law enforcement officials on June 11, 1997. Kissena officials declined to be interviewed for this book.
289   The church's goal, says Father Michael Place: interview with the author, May 30, 1997.
290   Bingo and casino nights contributed: spokesman's interview with the author, June 4, 1997.
290   The Illinois Department of Revenue: interview with the author, June 10, 1997.
290   In 1994, *Chicago Sun-Times*: *Chicago Sun-Times*, February 27, 1994.
290   "Before we came along": interview with the author, June 16, 1997.
291   According to a 1992 report: Pennsylvania Crime Commission, 1992 Report, p. 5.
291   "A high degree of commercialization": Report of the Twelfth Statewide Grand Jury Regarding the Operation of Commercial Bingo Halls in the State of Florida, Florida State Supreme Court, Case #83,964, October 25, 1995, pp. 3–4.
291   "Bingo is such a midwestern thing": interview with the author, June 10, 1997.
291   "There's certain people": interview with the author, June 10, 1997.

Epilogue
Endgame

299   "I anticipate there will be": interview with the author, October 16, 1997.

BIBLIOGRAPHY

Abt, Vicki, James F. Smith, and Eugene Martin Christiansen. *The Business of Risk: Commercial Gambling in Mainstream America.* Lawerence, Kan.: University Press of Kansas, 1985.

Alvarez, A. *The Biggest Game in Town.* Boston: Houghton Mifflin Company, 1983.

Ainslie, Tom. *Ainslie's Complete Guide to Thoroughbred Racing.* New York: Simon & Schuster, 1979.

Asinof, Eliot. *Eight Men Out: The Black Sox and the 1919 World Series.* New York: Pocket Books, 1963.

Auerbach, Ann Hagedorn. *Wild Ride: The Rise and Tragic Fall of Calumet Farm, Inc., America's Premier Racing Dynasty.* New York: Henry Holt & Company, 1994.

Barlett, Donald L., and James B. Steele. *Empire: The Life, Legend, and Madness of Howard Hughes.* New York: W. W. Norton & Company, 1979.

Barrett, Wayne. *Trump: The Deals and the Downfall.* New York: Harper-Collins, 1992.

Bear Stearns. *Global Gaming Almanac.* New York: Bear Stearns & Company, 1997.

Bennett, Estelline. *Old Deadwood Days.* New York: J. H. Sears, c1928. Reprint, Lincoln, Neb.: University of Nebraska Press, 1982.

Bergreen, Laurence. *Capone: The Man and the Era.* New York: Simon & Schuster, 1994.

Bernstein, Peter L. *Against the Gods: The Remarkable Story of Risk.* New York: John Wiley & Sons, 1996.

———. *Capital Ideas.* New York: The Free Press, 1992.

Beyer, Andrew. *Beyer on Speed: New Strategies for Racetrack Betting.* Boston: Houghton Mifflin Company, 1993.

Brady, Matthew. *The Old Town: Real Life in Early Frisco.* San Francisco: Independent Books, 1992.

Brenner, Reuven, with Gabrielle A. Brenner. *Gambling and Speculation: A Theory, a History, and a Future of Some Human Decisions.* Cambridge: Cambridge University Press, 1990.

Brill, Steven. *The Teamsters.* New York: Simon & Schuster, 1978.

Brown, Dee. *Bury My Heart at Wounded Knee: An Indian History of the American West.* New York: Henry Holt & Company, 1970.

Caro, Robert A. *The Power Broker: Robert Moses and the Fall of New York.* New York: Vintage Books, 1975.

Chafetz, Henry. *Play the Devil: A History of Gambling in the United States from 1492 to 1955.* New York: Bonanza Books, 1960.

Chandler, Alfred D., Jr. *The Visible Hand: The Managerial Revolution in American Business.* Cambridge, Mass.: Belknap Press, 1977.

Chernow, Ron. *The House of Morgan: An American Banking Dynasty and the Rise of Modern Finance.* New York: Atlantic Monthly Press, 1990.

Clotfelter, Charles T., and Philip J. Cook. *Selling Hope: State Lotteries in America.* Cambridge, Mass.: Harvard University Press, 1989.

Commission on the Review of the National Policy Toward Gambling. *Gambling in America.* Washington, D.C.: U.S. Government Printing Office, 1976.

Davis, Edwin Adams. *Louisiana: A Narrative History.* Baton Rouge: Claitor's Book Store, 1961.

Dedmon, Emmett. *Fabulous Chicago.* New York: Atheneum, 1981.

Demaris, Ovid. *The Boardwalk Jungle.* New York: Bantam Doubleday Dell, 1986.

Dempsey, Jack. *Dempsey.* New York: Harper & Row, 1977.

Devol, George H. *Forty Years a Gambler on the Mississippi: The Best Gambling Book Ever Published in America.* Cincinnati: Devol & Haines, 1887. Reprint, Bedford, Mass.: Applewood Books.

Dillon, Richard H. *The Hatchet Men: The Story of the Tong Wars in San Francisco's Chinatown.* New York: Ballantine Books, 1962.

Doerflinger, Thomas M., and Jack L. Rivkin. *Risk and Reward: Venture Capital and the Making of Americas's Great Industries.* New York: Random House, 1987.

Dombrink, John, and William N. Thompson. *The Last Resort: Success and Failure in Campaigns for Casinos.* Reno: University of Nevada Press, 1990.

Dostoyevsky, Fyodor. *The Gambler.* Harmondsworth, Eng.: Penguin Classics, 1966.

Dufour, Charles L. *Ten Flags in the Wind: The Story of Louisiana.* New York: Harper & Row, 1967.

Eadington, William R., and Judy A. Cornelius, eds. *Gambling and Commercial Gaming: Essays in Business, Economics, Philosophy, and Science.* Reno: Institute for the Study of Gambling and Commercial Gaming, 1977.

———. *Gambling Behavior and Problem Gambling.* Reno: Institute for the Study of Gambling and Commercial Gaming, 1977.

———. *Gambling Public Policies and the Social Sciences.* Reno: Institute for the Study of Gambling and Commercial Gaming, 1993.

Eskenazi, Gerald. *The Lip: A Biography of Leo Durocher.* New York: William Morrow & Company, 1993.

Ezell, John Samuel. *Fortune's Merry Wheel: The Lottery in America.* Cambridge, Mass.: Harvard University Press, 1960.

Fabian, Ann. *Card Sharps, Dream Books, and Bucket Shops: Gambling in Nineteenth-Century America.* Ithaca, N.Y.: Cornell University Press, 1990.

Farrell, Ronald A., and Carole Case. *The Black Book and the Mob: The Untold Story of the Control of Nevada's Casinos.* Madison: University of Wisconsin Press, 1995.

Findlay, John M. *People of Chance: Gambling in American Society from Jamestown to Las Vegas.* New York: Oxford University Press, 1986.

Flake, Carol. *Tarnished Crown: The Quest for a Racetrack Champion.* New York: Doubleday & Company, 1987.

Flamm, Jerry. *Hometown San Francisco: Sunny Jim, Phat Willie, and Dave.* San Francisco: Scottwall Associates, 1994.

Fox, Stephen. *Blood and Power: Organized Crime in Twentieth-Century America.* New York: Penguin Books, 1990.

Funnell, Charles E. *By the Beautiful Sea: The Rise and High Times of That Great American Resort, Atlantic City.* New York: Alfred A. Knopf, 1975.

Goodman, Robert. *The Luck Business: The Devastating Consequences and Broken Promises of America's Gambling Explosion.* New York: The Free Press, 1995.

Graves, Robert. *The Greek Myths.* London: The Folio Society, 1996.

Gutman, Dan. *Baseball Babylon: From the Black Sox to Pete Rose, the Real Stories Behind the Scandals That Rocked the Game.* New York: Penguin Books, 1992.

Harris, David. *The League: The Rise and Decline of the NFL.* New York: Bantam Books, 1986.

Hauptman, Laurence M., and James D. Wherry, eds. *The Pequots in Southern New England: The Fall and Rise of an American Indian Nation.* Norman, Okla.: University of Oklahoma Press, 1993.

Helm, Mike. *A Breed Apart: The Horses and the Players.* New York: Henry Holt & Company, 1991.

Henretta, James A., W. Elliot Brownlee, David Brody, and Susan Ware. *America's History.* Chicago: Dorsey Press, 1987.

Henwood, Doug. *Wall Street: How It Works and for Whom.* London: Verso, 1997.

Hogan, William, and William German, eds. *The San Francisco Chronicle Reader.* New York: McGraw-Hill Company, 1962.

Humes, Edward. *Mississippi Mud: A True Story from a Corner of the Deep South.* New York: Pocket Star Books, 1995.

James, Bill. *The Bill James Historical Baseball Abstract.* New York: Villard Books, 1986.

Johnston, David. *Temples of Chance: How America Inc. Bought Out Murder Inc. to Win Control of the Casino Business.* New York: Doubleday, 1992.

Keating, Bern. *The Mighty Mississippi.* National Geographic Society, 1971.

Kimmel, Michael. *Manhood in America: A Cultural History.* New York: The Free Press, 1996.

Kindleberger, Charles P. *Manias, Panics, and Crashes: A History of Financial Crises.* New York: John Wiley & Sons, 1996.

Kinkead, Gwen. *Chinatown: A Portrait of a Closed Society.* New York: HarperCollins, 1992.

King, R. T. *Always Bet on the Butcher: Warren Nelson and Casino Gaming, 1930–1980s.* Reno: University of Nevada Oral History Program, 1994.

Kleinknecht, William. *The New Ethnic Mobs: The Changing Face of Organized Crime in America.* New York: The Free Press, 1996.

Kowet, Don. *The Rich Who Own Sports.* New York: Random House, 1977.

Kuttner, Robert. *Everything for Sale: The Virtues and Limits of Markets.* New York: Alfred A. Knopf, 1997.

Lacey, Robert. *Little Man: Meyer Lansky and the Gangster Life.* Boston: Little, Brown & Co., 1991.

La Fleur, Teresa, and Bruce La Fleur, eds. *La Fleur's 1996 World Gambling Abstract.* 4th ed. Maryland: TLF Publications, 1996.

————. *La Fleur's 1996 World Lottery Almanac.* 4th ed. Maryland: TLF Publications, 1996.

Le Bon, Gustave. *The Crowd: A Study of the Popular Mind.* 1897. Reprint, Greenville, S.C.: Traders Press, 1994.

Leffler, George L. Revised by Loring C. Farwell. *The Stock Market.* New York: The Ronald Press Company, 1963.

Lesieur, Henry R. *The Chase: Career of the Compulsive Gambler.* Cambridge, Mass.: Schenkman Publishing Company, 1984.

Levi, Vicki Gold, and Lee Eisenberg. *Atlantic City: 125 Years of Ocean Madness.* New York: Clarkson N. Potter, 1979.

Livermore, Jesse L. *How to Trade in Stocks: The Livermore Formula for Combining Time Element and Price.* Greenville, S.C.: Traders Press, 1991.

Long, Patrick, Jo Clark, and Derek Liston. *Win, Lose, or Draw: Gambling with America's Small Towns.* Washington, D.C.: The Aspen Institute, 1994.

Longstreet, Stephen. *Win or Lose: A Social History of Gambling in America.* Indianapolis: The Bobbs-Merrill Company, 1977.

MacKay, Charles. *Extraordinary Popular Delusions.* 1841. Reprint, Greenville, S.C.: Traders Press, 1994.

Mahon, Gigi. *The Company That Bought the Boardwalk: A Reporter's Story of How Resorts International Came to Atlantic City.* New York: Random House, 1980.

Mandel, Leon. *William Fisk Harrah: The Life and Times of a Gambling Magnate.* New York: Doubleday, 1981.

Manteris, Art, with Rick Talley. *Super Bookie: Inside Las Vegas Sports Gambling.* Chicago: Contemporary Books, 1991.

Markham, Jerry W. *The History of Commodity Futures Trading and Its Regulation*. New York: Praeger, 1987.

Maskelyne, John Nevil. *Sharps and Flats: A Complete Revelation of the Secrets of Cheating at Games of Chance and Skill*. New York: Longmans, Green and Co., 1894. Reprint, Las Vegas: Gambler's Book Press.

McGowan, Richard. *State Lotteries and Legalized Gambling: Painless Revenue or Painful Mirage*. Westport, Conn.: Quorum Books, 1994.

Miller, Donald L. *City of the Century: The Epic of Chicago and the Making of America*. New York: Simon & Schuster, 1996.

Millman, Gregory J. *The Vandals' Crown: How Rebel Currency Traders Overthrew the World's Central Banks*. New York: The Free Press, 1995.

Moehring, Eugene P. *Resort City in the Sunbelt: Las Vegas 1930–1970*. Reno: University of Nevada Press, 1989.

Moldea, Dan E. *Interference: How Organized Crime Influences Professional Football*. New York: William Morrow & Company, 1989.

Newfield, Jack. *Only in America: The Life and Crimes of Don King*. New York: William Morrow & Company, 1995.

Niederhoffer, Victor. *The Education of a Speculator*. New York: John Wiley & Sons, 1997.

National Geographic Society. *Historical Atlas of the United States*. Centennial Edition. Washington, D.C.: National Geographic, 1988.

National Institute of Law Enforcement and Criminal Justice Law Enforcement Assistance Administration, United States Department of Justice. *The Development of the Law of Gambling: 1776–1976*. Washington, D.C.: 1977.

Neff, James. *Mobbed Up: Jackie Presser's High-wire Life in the Teamsters, the Mafia, and the FBI*. New York: Dell, 1989.

O'Donnell, John R. *Trumped!: The Inside Story of the Real Donald Trump—His Cunning Rise and Spectacular Fall*. New York: Simon & Schuster, 1995.

Pickelhaupt, Bill. *Shanghaied in San Francisco*. San Francisco: Flyblister Press, 1996.

Pileggi, Nicholas. *Casino: Love and Honor in Las Vegas*. New York: Simon & Schuster, 1995.

Quaife, Milo Milton. *Pictures of Gold Rush California*. New York: The Citadel Press, 1967.

Reid, Ed, and Ovid Demaris. *The Green Felt Jungle*. Cutchogue, N. Y.: Buccaneer Books, 1963.

Salomon Broithers. *Salomon Brothers 1995 State of the Industry Report: Gaming*. New York: Salomon Brothers Inc., 1995.

Sammons, Jeffrey T. *Beyond the Ring: The Role of Boxing in American Society*. Urbana, Ill.: University of Illinois Press, 1990.

Sasuly, Richard. *Bookies and Bettors: Two Hundred Years of Gambling*. New York: Holt, Rinehart & Winston, 1982.

Scarne, John. *Scarne's New Complete Guide to Gambling*. New York: Simon & Schuster, 1961. Reprint. Fireside Edition, 1986.

Skolnick, Jerome H. *House of Cards: The Legalization and Control of Casino Gambling*. Boston, Little, Brown & Company, 1978.

Slater, Robert. *Soros: The Life, Times, & Trading Secrets of The World's Greatest Investor*. New York: Irwin Professional Publishing, 1996.

Smith, John L. *Running Scared: The Life and Treacherous Times of Las Vegas Casino King Steve Wynn*. New York: Barricade Books, 1995.

Spanier, David. *Welcome to the Pleasuredome: Inside Las Vegas*. Reno: University of Nevada Press, 1992.

Stedman, Edmund Clarence, ed. *The New York Stock Exchange: Its History, Its Contribution to National Prosperity, and Its Relation to American Finance at the Outset of the Twentieth Century*. New York: Greenwood Press, 1969.

Sternlieb, George, and James W. Hughes. *The Atlantic City Gamble*. Cambridge, Mass.: Harvard University Press, 1983.

Sugar, Bert Randolph. *The Caesars Palace Sports Book of Betting*. New York: St. Martin's Press, 1992.

Summers, Anthony. *Official and Confidential: The Secret Life of J. Edgar Hoover*. New York: G. P. Putnam's Sons, 1993.

Taylor, Joe Gray. *Louisiana: A Bicentennial History*. New York: W. W. Norton & Company, 1976.

Teweles, Richard J., Charles V. Harlow, and Herbert L. Stone. *The Commodity Futures Game: Who Wins? Who Loses? Why?* New York: McGraw-Hill, 1974.

Thomas, Samuel W. *Churchill Downs: A Documentary History of America's Most Legendary Race Track.* Louisville: Kentucky Derby Museum, 1995.

Thorp, Edward O. *Beat the Dealer: A Winning Strategy for the Game of Twenty One.* New York: Vintage Books, 1966.

————. *The Mathematics of Gambling.* Hollywood: Gambling Times, 1984.

Tronnes, Mike, ed. *Literary Las Vegas: The Best Writing About America's Most Fabulous City.* New York: Henry Holt and Company, 1995.

Veblen, Thorstein. *The Theory of the Leisure Class: An Economic Study of Institutions.* New York: The Viking Press, 1931.

Vogel, Harold L. *Entertainment Industry Economics: A Guide for Financial Analysis.* Cambridge, England: Cambridge University Press, 1994.

Ward, Geoffrey C., and Ken Burns. *Baseball: An Illustrated History.* New York: Alfred A. Knopf, 1994.

Weinstein, David, and Lillian Deitch. *The Impact of Legalized Gambling: The Socioeconomic Consequences of Lotteries and Off-track Betting.* New York: Praeger Publishers, 1974.

Wolff, Rick, ed. *The Baseball Encyclopedia: The Complete and Definitive Record of Major League Baseball.* Ninth Edition. New York: Macmillan Publishing Company, 1993.

INDEX

ABOUT THE AUTHOR

TIMOTHY L. O'BRIEN is a reporter with *The New York Times*. He previously was a reporter for *The Wall Street Journal*. He is a graduate of Georgetown University, and has master's degrees in U.S. History, Journalism, and Business, all from Columbia University. He lives with his wife and two children in Montclair, New Jersey. This is his first book.